ॐ ॐ

WOMEN AND THE VISUAL ARTS IN
ITALY c. 1400–1650

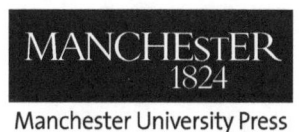

Manchester University Press

Women and the visual arts in Italy c. 1400–1650

LUXURY AND LEISURE, DUTY AND DEVOTION

A *sourcebook*

ಶಿ ಇಥಿ

**Selected, translated and introduced by
Paola Tinagli and Mary Rogers**

Manchester University Press

Published by Manchester University Press
Altrincham Street, Manchester M1 7JA, UK
www.manchesteruniversitypress.co.uk

British Library Cataloguing-in-Publication Data is available

Library of Congress Cataloging-in-Publication Data is available

ISBN 978 0 7190 8099 9 *paperback*

First published by Manchester University Press 2012

This edition first published 2016

Printed by Lightning Source

CONTENTS

ACKNOWLEDGEMENTS

We are grateful to those friends and colleagues with whom we have discussed issues related to this book and to women's history in general, and who have encouraged us over the years. We would like to thank especially Lucy Davis, who read the manuscript in the final stages and made useful suggestions. The anonymous reader of an earlier version of the manuscript made several suggestions for improvements. Sally Hickson generously allowed us to read an article before publication, while Ian Campbell helped with the translation of some architectural terms. Thanks also to Suzy Knight for supplying one of the documents.

The staff of the Warburg Institute Library and the British Library in London, and of the Kunsthistorisches Institut and Biblioteca Nazionale in Florence, were most helpful. Many thanks also to the staff of Manchester University Press, who have been most patient.

Our most heartfelt gratitude to Stuart Wallace and John Dunstan, who have given us their support and help during these years.

∻ ∾

ILLUSTRATIONS

Cover image: Lorenzo Lotto, *A Lady with a Drawing of Lucretia*, c. 1530–33, (London, National Gallery).

꙳ ꙳

INTRODUCTION

This book, an anthology of translated sources relating to Italian women in connection with their material environments, is intended as a companion volume to our earlier *Women in Italy, 1350–1650* (Manchester, 2005), though one that may be read independently of it. Whereas the earlier volume was written with students and scholars from a variety of disciplines in mind, the present one is geared primarily to the needs of a narrower group, those concerned with the history of art or of material culture. The readers we envisage will almost certainly have had some grounding in the history of art during the Italian Renaissance, the study of which today usually takes more account of female cultural participation than used to be the case. From monographs and exhibitions, it has been possible to gain a fuller idea of female artists of the period and on their critical reception. Pioneering books on women's patronage in general have been followed by specialised studies of groups or individuals within their particular historical and ideological settings. And Renaissance art history in general has become much broader than it was a generation ago.

One prominent and fruitful tendency, which has very much affected the selection of textual sources in this book, has been the growth of interest in types of object traditionally considered as 'decorative art'. The fifteenth and sixteenth centuries (quattrocento and cinquecento) in Italy saw changes not only in the styles, formats and subjects of what we think of as 'fine art', but in the reorganisation of urban environments and of ecclesiastical and secular buildings. Many such buildings were on a very large scale, and by the later sixteenth century they came to be filled with a huge number of furnishings and other artefacts, as stressed most

influentially by Richard Goldthwaite.[1] This change is clearly registered in painting, if one compares many sixteenth-century biblical
images of subjects like the *Marriage at Cana* or *Christ in the House
of Mary and Martha* with the sparsely furnished interiors of early
fifteenth-century saintly *Birth* scenes. The bedchambers in the
latter show simply equipped beds surrounded by plain benches,
made softer only by the odd cushion. In late cinquecento birth
scenes, however, beds may acquire more sumptuous canopies
and other drapery, and in rooms for feasting and entertainment
we often see imposing sideboards (*credenze*) laden with vessels,
or dining tables bedecked with damask tablecloths, sometimes set
on top of oriental carpets, and finely wrought cutlery and delicate
glassware. Whether these objects were imported (Turkish carpets,
Franco-Flemish tapestries, Spanish tooled leather wall-hangings,
Greek icons), made by foreign craftspeople in Italy (Flemish weavers, German woodcarvers, Greek embroiders), or produced in the
many centres for textile, ceramic and glass production that developed in the peninsula itself, objects both for everyday use and for
luxury display had attained a marvellous variety and refinement.

Scholars in recent decades have explored both the particularities
and the generalities of this phenomenon, in studies of individual
types of object, of the processes through which they were made,
sold, bought and used, and of the wider patterns of international
trade and economic change of which they form part.[2] Chinese
porcelain was acquired by aristocratic families and painted by
Giovanna Garzoni; Persian or Turkish carpets were found in the
dwellings of Neapolitan nuns or Venetian merchant families like
those portrayed by Lotto and Licinio.[3] More relevantly for this
book, historians have probed the many implications of this intoxi-
cating material abundance. Specialised vocabularies developed
to distinguish and evaluate novel artefacts, their techniques and
their component parts, vocabulary found in many of the texts we
have included. Social life became not only extremely lavish at the
pinnacles of society but more comfortable and elegant for those
of moderate means. Urban dwellings or country villas became
sites for genteel entertainments, and their rooms and furnishings
consequently became more specialised.[4] Though research is still
continuing on the layout and functions of rooms in houses in the
different centres of Italy, there seems to be some consensus that

the basic divisions were the *sale* or reception rooms, which could accommodate large numbers of guests, and the *camere*, not only for sleeping but at times used for small-scale gatherings. Depending on means and on space available, a married woman might share the matrimonial *camera* or have her own room or even suite of rooms. To this might be added, as well as rooms for cooking, bathing, and accommodating servants, anterooms, halls or galleries where larger-scale paintings came to be hung, and *studioli*, not only for intellectual activities or the conduct of business but for the assembly of precious or unusual goods. In country villas, ladies and gentlemen might converse, sing and make music in gardens with elaborate statuary or fountains, as depicted in an illustration in the 1499 *Hypnerotomachia Poliphili* (**figure 1**) or in many literary sources. Sixteenth-century treatises consider the lady of the house not merely, as in Alberti's *Della famiglia* and other earlier works, as a dutiful custodian of her husband's possessions, and one barred from the inner sanctum of his study, but as a judicious arranger and overseer of the household goods.

The appropriate acquisition and use of artefacts generally came to be perceived as marking the individual as a civilised and moral being. The burgeoning literature of manners in the sixteenth century would recommend graceful dress and table manners in public, or, especially with clerical writers, prayer before a suitably decorated religious painting or sculpture in private. On an official level, the sumptuary laws of many cities attempted, probably largely unsuccessfully, to regulate not only public dress but the furnishings in private dwellings. Both treatises and legislation, of course, imply that people's behaviour needed guidance, lest the new profusion of goods corrupt the foolish or the presumptuous and disturb the social hierarchy. This fear of social disruption is heard most stridently in Renaissance moralising literature against the acquisitiveness of courtesans, though more light-heartedly in Pietro Aretino's creation of Pippa, who dreams that when she becomes successful in the game she will dwell in a large, beautiful room lined with rich hangings and with a bed covered in sumptuous brocade.[5] Pippa was thinking of existing interiors, but some scholars have toyed with the idea of other more intelligent courtesans as leaders of fashions in clothing or furnishings.[6] However this might be, for the Renaissance individual, as well as for the modern scholar, not only

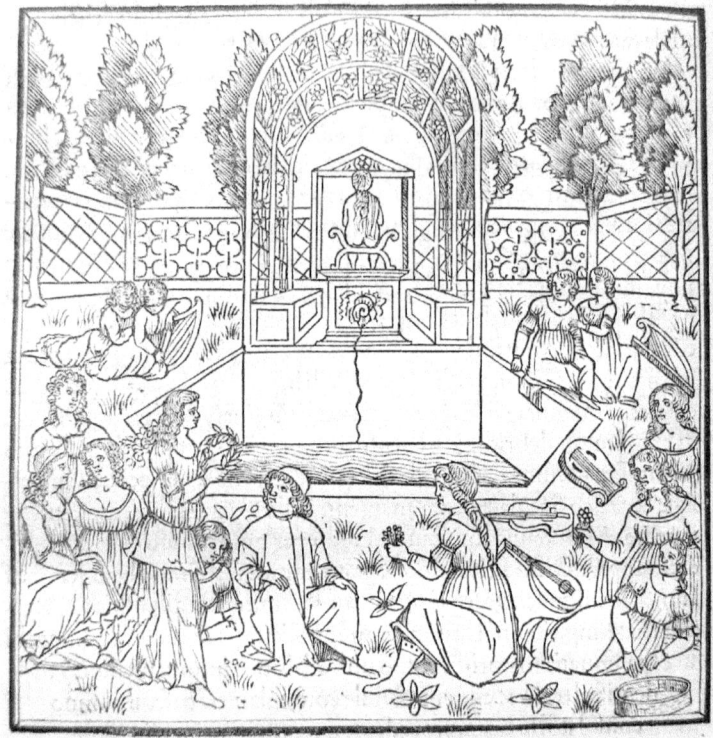

1. Anon., Scene in villa garden, woodcut illustration from Francesco Colonna, *Hypnerotomachia Poliphili* (Venice, 1499).

'art' but clothing, domestic furnishings and the accessories of religious devotion were not frivolous matters but ones on which much effort, thought and money were often expended. Over time, and particularly for women, they might acquire sentimental overtones and become freighted with diverse meanings, as both letters and wills reveal.[7]

These general issues must be kept in mind by the reader of this book. Our prime task, however, is to make texts available in English that document the ways in which different women inhabited, interacted with and helped shape their material environments. Although we have abandoned the 'ideals and realities' structure which dominated our earlier book, we have included many theoretical texts

concerned with women's dwellings, dress and decorous comport-
ment, whether from treatises on architecture or from those on social
behaviour, whether written by civic or by ecclesiastical authorities.
In some cases, these clearly reveal the gendered nature of female
experience: women's rooms would be less accessible in palaces, for
example, and when moving in public places, something they did less
frequently than did men, their dress and demeanour would be likely
to be censured as frivolous or unchaste. As is now well known, legal
constraints prevented women other than widows or members of
ruling houses from commissioning works of art or architecture in
their own names, and notions of feminine modesty often inhibited
women from taking credit for artistic projects or having themselves
portrayed prominently in public. Private devotion and the visual and
material aids which accompanied it were relatively more important
for women, whose roles in religious confraternities tended to be
more limited than were men's. Yet in other respects both men and
women were subject to similar contemporary notions of social rank,
civility, decorum and much else, which affected the ways in which
they presented themselves or organised their surroundings, and in
how they made use of material things to these ends.

Part I of the book broadly deals with the material dimensions
of the various worlds in which women existed, generally shared
with and largely shaped by men, with women participating in ways
which are usually not clear. How much, we might speculate, did
material surroundings contribute to making new wives feel like
the 'passing guests' in their husbands' houses that they have been
characterised as, how much, on the contrary, like queens of their
domains?[8] The latter is implied in the engraving c. 1610 by Giacomo
Franco (**figure 2**), where an extravagantly costumed Venetian lady
sits, as if enthroned, on an upholstered armchair against a hanging of brocade, while a richly dressed page boy proffers fruit on a
platter. How much psychological support might women gain from
the comparative privacy of having 'a room of one's own', whether
a chamber or a cell, and from choosing and arranging the objects
in it, whether of aesthetic or of sentimental value? Such questions
arise in relation to the first two chapters, where we consider the
buildings and their contents which formed women's everyday surroundings and shaped their lives. Since objects of especial relevance
to women such as wedding chests or birth salvers have been much

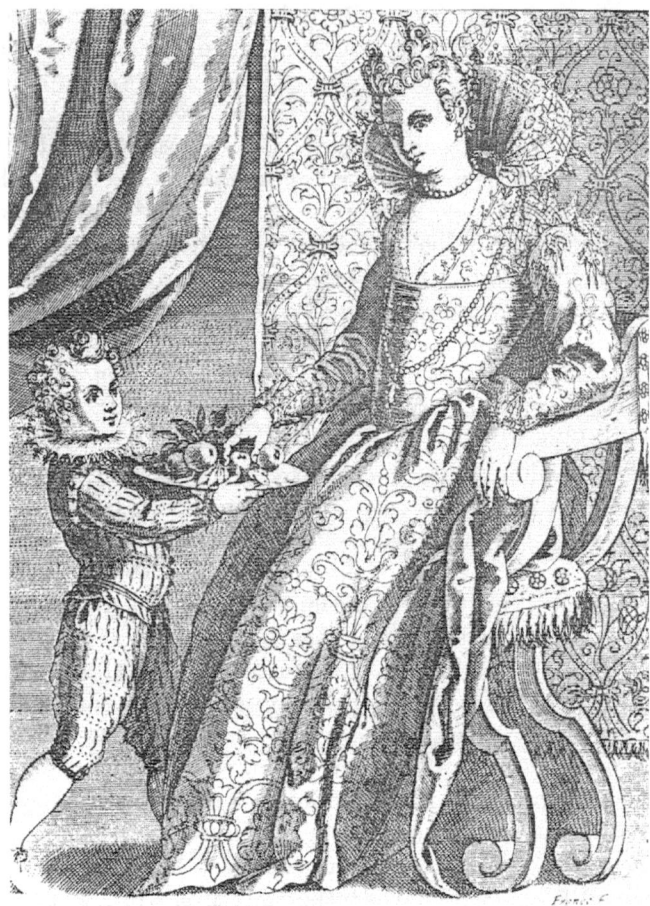

2. Giacomo Franco, seated Venetian gentlewoman with page offering fruit, engraving from *Habiti d'huomini e donne venetiane* (Venice, 1610).

studied in recent years, we have devoted relatively little attention to these as opposed to other articles of furniture or tableware.[9] The next two chapters show women outside the home, as evoked in legislation or letters, or in printed works which testify to their readers' lively interest in the costume and behaviour of women as observed in the streets of different cities. Women are also spectacles in chapter 4, participants but also observers at the lavish processions and

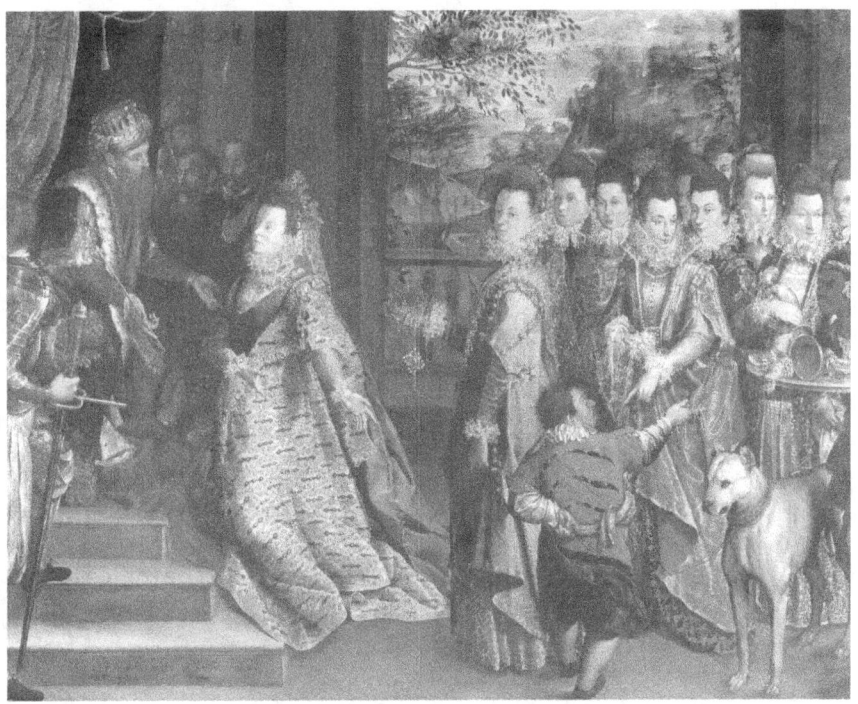

3. Lavinia Fontana, *The Visit of the Queen of Sheba*, c. 1600
(Dublin, National Gallery of Ireland).

receptions that accompanied aristocratic weddings, births or ceremonies of welcome, where their gowns and jewellery would speak
of the honour of their families or their cities. In her painting from
c. 1600 of the reception by Solomon of the Queen of Sheba and
her ladies (**figure 3**), a female painter, Lavinia Fontana, adapts her
knowledge of such ceremonial display to the Old Testament theme.
The chapter also includes letters written by women which observe
the buildings, townscapes or scenery in other cities, testifying to
a broadening of horizons of a kind which might aid other women
when they considered their own future projects of patronage.

This patronage will be the subject of the first two chapters in Part
II, which document women building or embellishing palaces and
villas and amassing art collections through various means. Portraits
of themselves or of their family members and friends formed an

important part of these, so that this subject has been given its own chapter. The last chapter in this section establishes how relationships between influential women and artists were not confined to particular projects: though they might at times irritate the more touchy or temperamental of their craftspeople, ladies at court might lend their protection to artists they had used or introduce them to new clients. Many recent studies of women's patronage in the Renaissance have tried to move away from the 'great ladies', notably Isabella d'Este, to which attention has traditionally been devoted, examining either lesser-known aristocrats or women of more modest status. Much valuable archival work on such figures continues to be done. However, we make no apologies for featuring prominently such women as Isabella, her mother, Eleonora of Aragon, and her sister, Beatrice d'Este, and, later, several Medici princesses. Not only are they abundantly documented, but their letters are often exceptionally eloquent, demonstrating both the growth of the specialised vocabulary that accompanied the explosion of material goods and the diffusion of an understanding of architectural principles or classical mythology and allegory among women of the elite. Many of the texts we publish give a sense of the evolution of their taste with increased age and experience, and of their relationships with networks of female family members and friends. Such examples may reinforce the current reaction against older characterisations of Isabella as an interfering pedant, constraining the imaginative freedom of a Giovanni Bellini, or, alternatively, as an avaricious and uncontrolled shopper, and may show that both her patronage and collecting and her attempts to set fashions in dress were purposeful and well-informed.[10]

In Part III we turn to women's experience of art in the service of religion. This is for convenience, rather than to imply that religion was set apart from everyday life rather than integrated with it. Public ceremonies had their religious components, and the sacred pervaded the secular house, as almost every dwelling, however lowly, in early modern Italy would have contained some sort of religious image, usually in the bedroom, exerting its protective power while the occupant slept.[11] Inventories testify to the widespread possession of artefacts such as crucifixes, rosaries, Agnusdei and books of devotion, objects often luxuriously crafted, like the seventeenth-century rosary of gold, crystal and pearls reproduced here (**figure 4**). The connection between the increasingly personal and empa-

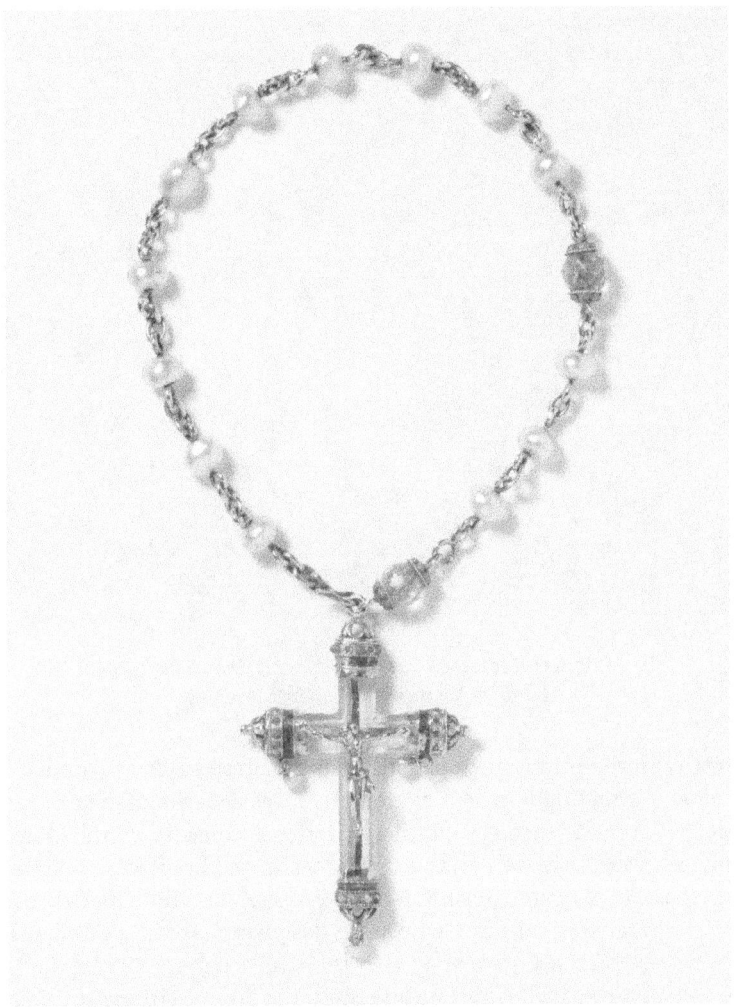

4. Italian, seventeenth century. Rosary with crucifix in crystal, enamelled gold and pearls (London, Victoria and Albert Museum).

thetic devotion that developed from the later Middle Ages onwards and the piety of women has become well established. The monitory texts by churchmen and moralists, the witness accounts of the experiences of the pious, and the drier evidence of inventories all

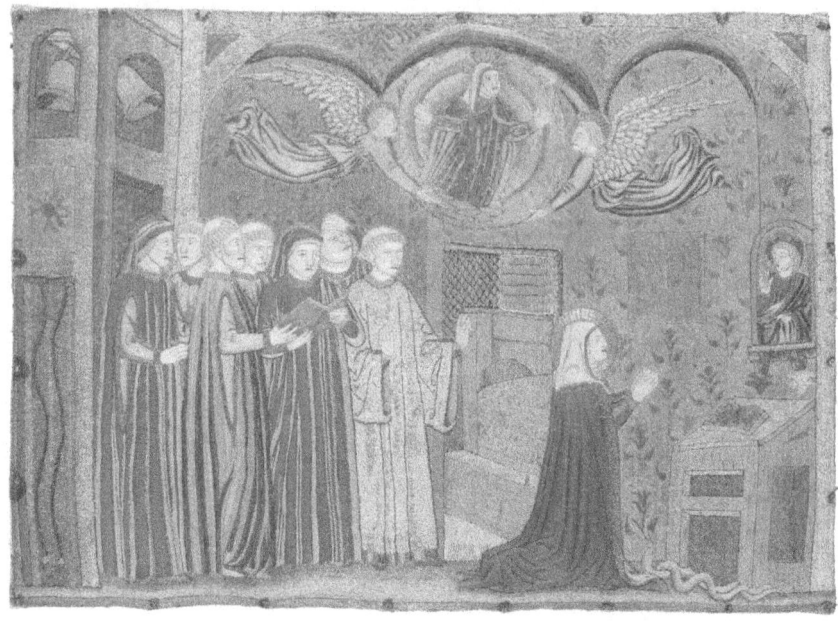

5. Anon. embroiderer, *S. Verdiana at her Devotions* c. 1440
(London, Victoria and Albert Museum).

testify to the importance of artistic and material aids in stimulating and directing female devotion. This was also the case in more
public arenas. Throughout the period we consider, miraculous
images were discovered, or extant ones in public places thought
to speak or to come alive. Often it was women who experienced
these miracles, and nuns who were designated as the custodians
of these objects. Other images in their turn commemorate such
events. Our next illustration, an embroidery of c.1440 that may or
may not have been worked by women, and that might have been
used as part of an altar frontal (**figure 5**), shows Christ appearing
to speak to St Verdiana through an image in what seems to be her
private room, with reverent male onlookers watching. Whether or
not owned by a convent of Vallombrosan nuns, as has been specu-
lated, such representations would perhaps have served to encourage other women towards their own mystical experiences.[12] More
closely directed by ecclesiastical or civic authorities, however,

would have been the public processions and mystery plays, accompanied by painted banners or more elaborate visual 'special effects', which were staged in public places, some with female participants, and were certainly viewed by women of all ranks. Pilgrimages, too, offered pious females an opportunity not just to give thanks or to atone for sin, but to gain sight of holy relics and holy places along the route and to donate their own offerings, such as statuettes, reliquaries, chalices or textiles to the pilgrimage site according to their means. Some of these might be 'works of art' in a modern sense, but to the pilgrim the sacred significance would have been paramount.

With the last chapter in this section we enter the more familiar territory of women as the patrons of altarpieces and related church furnishings, often for burial chapels. Here we see women sometimes acting alone, often aided by male intermediaries, and sometimes in groups. We must also remember that, though they are often not recorded in documents, many wives would have played important roles in joint commissions with their husbands, and that widows would have supervised the execution of their deceased husbands' artistic projects, a famous example being Mantegna's frescoed Ovetari chapel in Padua. How restricted access was to works in private chapels within church settings is not always clear, and similar degrees of visibility would also affect images within a convent setting. Art commissioned by and for nuns has been a rich field for research in recent years. While altarpieces for convent churches used by the laity would have been readily visible to the lay public, other devotional images within communal areas in the convent such as nuns' choirs, refectories or corridors, were accessible only to the sisters. Some might have been used in their group rituals, while others would be intimate private works for individual cells, providing food for meditation for the zealous, and solace or sentimental appeal for the less devout. Works for nuns were commissioned in different ways, by the whole convent body or by individual nuns. Affluent or prominent nuns might donate works for communal use, as with the elaborate group of altarpieces from 1443–45 in the former chancel of the nuns' church of S. Zaccaria, Venice.[13] These bear the names of the abbess and other convent officials on their frames and incorporate images of their name-saints, in the case of **figure 6** showing St Margaret in the upper left panel, commemorating the chamberlain Margherita Donato. Convents would frequently be bequeathed

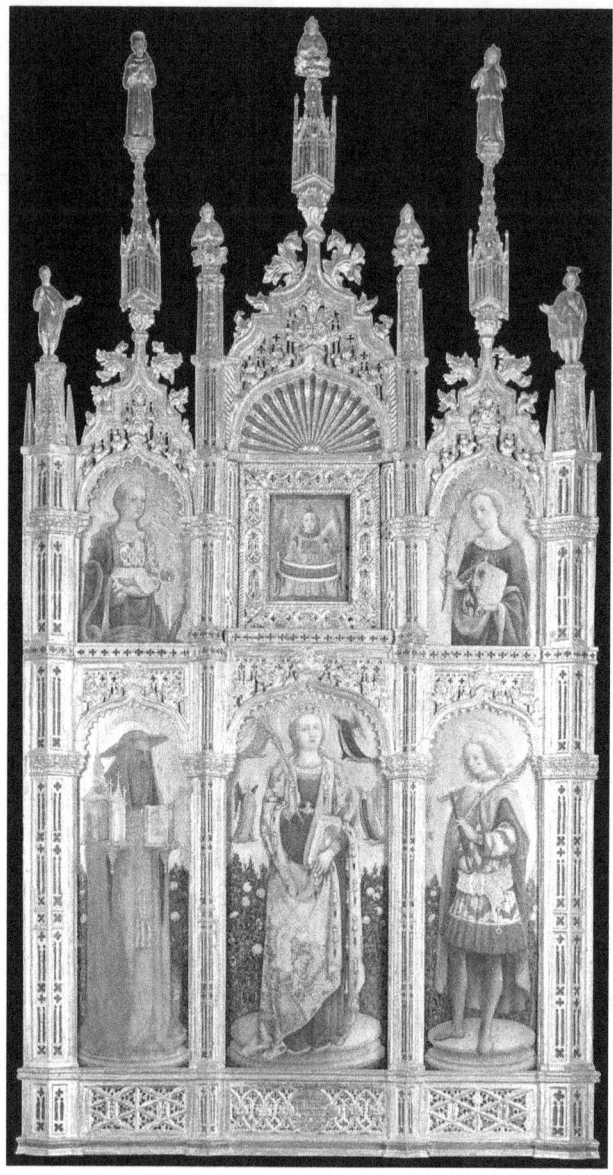

6. Antonio Vivarini, *S. Sabina Altarpiece*, 1443–45
(Venice, S. Zaccaria).

images which originally had a secular setting. One famous example was Giovanni Bellini's *Madonna with the Doge Agostino Barbarigo*, once in the Doge's private palace but donated after his death to the Muranese convent where his daughters were nuns and where he asked prayers to be said for his soul. (The move from secular to sacred setting was reversed, however, when this same convent rejected a high altar-piece they had commissioned from Titian as excessively costly, and the painting ended up with the Holy Roman Empress.) And once again, we need to remember the importance not only of paintings and statues but of metalwork, textiles and other 'decorative art' objects in the gifts of women to churches and convents.

The last part of the book deals with women creators in more obvious senses. Despite the increased knowledge of the female artists of the period, there still seems merit in giving the student closer access to the particularities of their careers and their working conditions. We hear not only of comparatively famous artists like Sofonisba Anguissola and Artemisia Gentileschi, but of less well-known figures like the still-life painter Giovanna Garzoni and the nun Orsola Caccia. We also learn of the fame of skilled female embroiderers, working either in the secular world, sometimes within trade guilds, but perhaps more commonly within convents, and of women's involvement with the novel art of lacemaking. We note that, in both embroidery and lace, amateur or professional craftswomen could produce not only ornamental but figurative work.

The final chapter shows how crafted objects, together with buildings and paintings, could serve as sources of inspiration for the women writers of the day. Poets like Lucrezia Tornabuoni, Veronica Franco or Chiara Matraini convey delight at the new luxury in tableware, bed-hangings or lace. Devotional verses show responses both to ancient icons and to modern works, and suggest the continuing inspiration of female saints, the pilgrim Helena or the penitent Magdalene. Other women authors display their *ingegno*, showing their awareness of contemporary debates on art and art theory, and inventing works of art they had never seen and were not able to create in actuality, such as the allegorical fountain in the garden where Moderata Fonte's female friends socialise, which conveys the philosophy of life of a defiantly single woman. In these and other works, Renaissance women writers show their capacity for responding to the manifold aspects of the material culture of their day and inventing their own fictional artefacts, resulting in fresh and personal creations.

In selecting the sources for this book from the many possible candidates, we have tried to steer away from texts which are very familiar or readily available in English. Space limitations have forced us to be highly selective in bibliographical citations, at the risk of offending excellent scholars from whose research we have benefited. The entries in our earlier volume may supplement the reading list in several areas. In translating and making available the texts, we have encountered particularly taxing problems, especially in relation to terminology concerning fabrics, clothes and colours, problems which have often baffled even specialist scholars. We would refer the reader to the very helpful glossaries in the book by Lisa Monnas cited, in n.2 which clarify many of these terms, and also give measurements and pricing systems, which varied widely between the regions of Italy.[14]

Finally, we would like to express our gratitude to those institutions who show consideration for the needs of scholars and students by making their rich resources available for publication at little or no cost. The acknowledgements in our list of illustrations should speak for themselves.

Paola Tinagli, Florence
Mary Rogers, London

Notes

1 R. A. Goldthwaite, *Wealth and the Demand for Art in Italy, 1300–1600* (Baltimore, 1993).

2 P. Thornton, *The Italian Renaissance Interior 1400–1600* (London, 1991); P. Hills, *Venetian Colour. Marble, Mosaic, Painting and Glass 1250–1550* (New Haven and London, 1999); L. Syson and D. Thornton, *Objects of Virtue. Art in Renaissance Italy* (London, 2001); P. Fortini Brown, *Private Lives in Renaissance Venice. Art, Architecture and the Family* (New Haven and London, 2004); E. Welch, *Shopping in the Renaissance: Consumer Cultures in Italy 1400–1600* (New Haven and London, 2005); M. Ajmar-Wollheim and F. Dennis (eds), *At Home in Renaissance Italy* (London, 2006); A. Bayer, ed., *Art and Love in Renaissance Italy* (New Haven and London, 2008); L. Monnas, *Merchants, Princes and Painters. Silk Fabrics in Italian and Northern Paintings 1300–1550* (New Haven and London, 2008).

3 For the nuns' Persian carpet, see H. Hills, 'The housing of institutional architecture: searching for a domestic holy in post-Tridentine Italian convents', in S. Cavallo, ed., *Domestic Institutional Interiors in Early Modern Europe* (Farnham 2009), p. 134. Lorenzo Lotto is known to have owned a Turkish carpet, such as that shown in the *Portrait of the Giovanni della Volta Family* (see chapter 6, text.2.ii).

4 On these and the ensuing areas, see Fortini Brown 2004 and articles in Ajmar-Wollheim and Dennis, especially M. Ajmar-Wollheim, 'Sociability', pp. 206–221, B. Preyer, 'The Florentine *casa*', pp. 34–49, and P. Fortini Brown, 'The Venetian *casa*', pp. 50–65.

5 P. Aretino, *Sei giornate*, ed. G. Aquilecchia (Bari, 1969), p. 217.

6 Thornton (1991), pp. 354–8.

7 S. Chojnacki, *Women and Men in Renaissance Venice* (Baltimore, 2000), and others have noted women's propensity to leave both articles of clothing and small religious objects to female relatives and close friends. Though primary concerned neither with Italy nor with women, the most stimulating account of the crucial roles played by dress in the Renaissance is A. R. Jones and P. Stallybrass, *Renaissance Clothing and the Material of Memory* (Cambridge, 2000).

8 C. Klapisch-Zuber, *Women, Family and Ritual in Renaissance Italy*, trans. L. G. Cochrane (Chicago and London, 1985), p. 118.

9 J. M. Musacchio, *The Art and Ritual of Childbirth in Renaissance Italy* (New Haven and London, 1999) and *Art Marriage and the Family in the Florentine Renaissance Palace* (New Haven, 200); A. Bayer (ed.), *Art and Love in Renaissance Italy* (New York, 2008).

10 On Isabella as a determined innovator in dress, see E. Welch, 'Art on the edge: hair and hands in Renaissance Italy', *Renaissance Studies*, 23:3 (2009), pp. 241–68.

11 M. A. Morse, 'Creating sacred space: the religious visual culture of the Renaissance Venetian *Casa*', *Renaissance Studies*, 21:2 (2007), pp. 151–84.

12 C. Frugoni, in 'Female mystics, visions, and iconography', in D. Bornstein and R. Rusconi, eds., *Women and Religion in Medieval and Renaissance Italy* (Chicago and London, 1996), pp. 130–64.

13 For these and other work at S. Zaccaria, see G. M. Radke, 'Nuns and their art: the case of S. Zaccaria in Venice', *Renaissance Quarterly* 54:2 (2001), pp. 430–59.

14 See also A. Martini, *Manuale di metrologia, ossia misuri, pesie monete in uso attnalmerte e anticamerte presso tutti i popoli* (Turin, 1883): indexed by city. Available online: http://www.braidense.it/dire/martini/indice.htm.

PART I

THE MATERIAL WORLDS OF WOMEN

The objects women used in their everyday lives – the contents of houses, furniture and furnishings, the clothes they wore, the jewels with which they adorned themselves, the books they held in their hands and read – seem familiar to us when we see them in museums, or represented in contemporary paintings. What could be more straightforward than a bed, or an engraved wooden box, or a dress? And yet, if our point of reference remains our own modern world and the relationships we ourselves have with the objects we buy and use, if we forget the centuries which divide us from those women, we miss a vast range of meanings, experiences and realities. In order to understand any object which survives from the past, we have to understand the way people related to each other and to their material surroundings. What did they notice, and why? What did certain objects connote? Until a couple of generations ago, for example, in Italy, a matrimonial bed was the symbol of the union between two people and two families, the object in the house which most represented 'life'. It was the place where babies were born and where the elderly died. It was something which was kept from the beginning of a marriage right until the end of a couple's life, and not thrown away because fashion changed. Many of these links with the distant past have now gone. So we have to listen to the voices from that past.

These first three chapters deal with material environments, with everyday objects, and with the women who used them – young and old, ladies from aristocratic or wealthy families, women from the lower ranks, prostitutes and nuns. In some cases their voices can be heard through letters to friends, husbands and family members. In other cases we can find out from inventories or from payment records what they owned, bought and used. Detailed descriptions invite us to 'see' their surroundings, or how they were dressed. Some texts are enticingly personal, while others are factual documents, but they are all carriers of meaning. The delight in commissioning luxury objects shown by Isabella d'Este, for example, conveys not only the pleasure of shopping by proxy, or her cultured enjoyment of beauty, but also the awareness of her social position. As Marchioness of Mantua, Isabella had the duty to surround herself with objects which demonstrated her *magnificenza*. For the highest ranks, contemporary treatises identified a private virtue called *splendore*, which enhanced private life and brought beauty into it.[1] *Splendore* expressed the refinement in one's life and was manifested through household furnishings and decorative objects, as well as through the care and elegance of one's person. Ostentation of wealth and luxury on the part of ruling families and the mercantile and banking elites were expected also by the lower ranks of society, since it was seen to bring honour and distinction to their city.

Those who wrote letters, inventories and descriptions had a discerning eye for objects, and could assess their monetary value. They had a good knowledge of materials, textiles and fabrics, as well as of the specialist vocabulary by which they were known. They also possessed a special awareness of different colours and textures which they noticed and described in detail. It was important to make all this information known. During the fifteenth century, this would have been done by letters, read aloud to the members of relatively restricted court circles, or through ambassadorial reports. Later, during the next two centuries, descriptions of court or civic ceremonies would have had a larger circulation through printed sources available to a wider public.

We are constantly struck by the way in which people in early modern society showed curiosity and interest in 'appearance' and 'things'. Theirs was a world where rank controlled the way in which people lived their lives. Even in convents differences in rank mattered, and the daughters of the elite had well-appointed cells, while poorer nuns acted as their servants. Nothing illustrates better the importance of social rank than sumptuary laws. In every city and in the countryside legislators tried to regulate the way women (and men too) should be dressed and adorned according to their rank, or how much they were allowed to spend on the occasion of weddings and other festivities, or what kind of table vessels they should use. There was, of course, social and moral criticism of luxury, when preachers warned against the dangers of wealth and a selfish use of money. During the early fifteenth century, however, humanists began to justify luxury and wealth, which, they wrote, should be connected to liberality and magnanimity in order to bring benefits to subjects and citizens.[2]

The inventories and wills of the lower ranks tell a different story, of a much more frugal life where a few indispensable pieces of furniture, household objects and clothes, many of these bought second-hand, were kept and certainly treasured, and then passed on to others, even if wealth and consumption patterns and habits may have increased the wages and spending power of some artisans and shopkeepers.[3]

All conduct literature of the period stressed the duty of the wife and then the widow to conserve and keep in order the goods of the marital household. In commissioning and acquiring household objects and ornaments, in caring for what they received as part of their dowry or as gifts, and in the way they disposed of them in their wills, women were clearly aware both of these duties and of the role of objects as symbols of their social status, as well as repositories of memories and emotions.

Notes

1 E. Welch, 'Public magnificence and private display: Pontano's "De Splendore"', *Journal of Design History*, 15 (2002), pp. 211–28.

2 On this controversy, and on changes through time, see R. A. Goldthwaite, *Wealth and the Demand for Art in Italy, 1300–1600* (Baltimore, 1993), pp. 204–12.

3 Apart from works cited in the Introduction, see also: Goldthwaite (1993), pp. 47–8; M. O'Malley and E. Welch (eds), *The Material Renaissance* (Manchester, 2007), Introduction, esp. pp. 1–4; M. Ajmar-Wollheim, F. Dennis and A. Matchette (eds), *Approaching the Renaissance Interior: Sources, Methodologies, Debates* (Oxford, 2007); P. Tinagli, '"Donne splendide": Some thoughts on women's acquisition of useful and ornamental objects in the Renaissance', *Acta ad Archaeologiam et Artium Historiam Pertinentia*, new set., 8:22 (2009), pp. 149–69.

BUILDINGS AND INTERIORS

The study of women's possessions, as documented in letters, inventories and wills, has not been confined to recent feminist historians. In the last two decades, however, scholars have begun to ask more questions about the socio-economic significance of buildings and the objects they contained and about the ways in which these combined to shape the identities of their owners.[1] Significant changes occurred between the fifteenth and the seventeenth centuries. Economic and social transformations produced different types of buildings within urban and rural spaces, and a much greater variety of objects within them. While these changes were most spectacular for the ruling houses of Italy, families from mercantile, professional and even artisan classes shared in them to some extent. A shift in attitude towards acquiring and arranging goods for the house can also be detected, articulated in writings from the later fifteenth century onwards.

Gender, of course, plays a very important role in all this. Several historians of art and of material culture recently have been especially concerned not only with documenting what women owned or used in their daily lives, but with exploring women's relationships with the spaces they inhabited, spaces which they normally shared with men, and which contained these objects. The differences between male and female social roles, duties and upbringing in medieval and early modern society affected the arrangement and use of rooms in women's homes, and the furnishings and objects, both decorative and utilitarian, that these dwellings housed. What were the conventions that had become almost second nature to women and men, and that guided their choices and decisions about their material worlds?[2]

This chapter provides the reader with some examples of the spaces in which women of different social ranks lived, and of their basic furnishings. These spaces, except for nunneries, were of course usually in buildings owned or designed by men, and the documents often give little indication of the extent to which female occupants might have adapted them according to their own preferences.

IDEAL SPACES

1. Men, women and their living spaces

In Book V of his *De Re Aedificatoria*, Leon Battista Alberti describes how rooms and apartments in palaces and villas should be organised according to their function and to the gender of those who occupy them. As we shall see in a number of sources, it was common to have a matrimonial chamber for both husband and wife, but also separate rooms for each.

> Leon Battista Alberti, *L'Architettura*, ed. P. Portoghesi, trans. G. Orlandi, 2 vols (Milan, 1966), 1, pp. 342, 426.

i. On rulers' palaces

In a royal palace the quarters of the wife, the husband and the servants should be kept quite distinct, so that each should have its own services and also whatever will show dignity and magnificence, and the large number of servants should not cause confusion . . . Each apartment should therefore be allocated its own area, and have its own separate roof. The different areas of the palace, however, should be linked by covered walkways and have their own entrances, so that when servants and household staff perform their tasks, they should not seem to arrive from a nearby house, but be always ready at the command of the master. The prattling and noisy groups of children and housemaids should be kept separate from the men, and the master and mistress should have no contact with the uncleanliness of servants.

. . . The apartment of [the prince's] wife should be entirely separate from that of her husband, except for the most private room where the marriage bed is. Their apartments should be reached by a single door, guarded by a single keeper.

ii. On villas

. . . Certainly, to my mind, the rooms where women live ought to be treated as though dedicated to the cult of chastity. Young girls and maidens should have comfortable apartments worthy of them, so that their delicate and sensitive minds should be disturbed as little as possible. The lady of the house should be where she can monitor all that happens in the house . . .

Husband and wife must have separate bedrooms, not only so that the husband is not disturbed by his wife when she is giving birth or when she is ill, but also so that both of them can sleep better even in the summer, if they so wish. Each room should have its own door, and also a small door [between their apartments], so that they can communicate without being seen. Next to the wife's bedroom should be a dressing room (*guardaroba*), and next to the husband's, a library.

WOMEN'S APARTMENTS

The allocation and arrangement of rooms in the palaces of ruling families and the urban elite followed different traditions and customs in various parts of Italy, even if ideals concerning property, and the ownership and preservation of material goods, were common to all the upper ranks of society.[3]

This section considers only apartments belonging to aristocratic women. They, as well as women from the minor aristocracy, had their own separate apartments in the family palace, where they lived with their maids of honour, ladies-in-waiting and servants.

2. The apartments of two Este wives, Ricciarda da Saluzzo (1410–74) and Margherita Gonzaga (1418–39)

Ricciarda da Saluzzo, third wife of Niccolò III d'Este, arrived in Ferrara in 1431. Her apartment in the Castello had a balcony looking on to the city's main square. The inventory of 1436 lists about ten rooms, which Ricciarda shared with her ladies-in-waiting, her laundresses and Niccolò's daughter Lucia. To indicate Ricciarda's role as Marchioness of Ferrara, some of the rooms were decorated with Este heraldic devices, while her bedroom was painted with unicorns, a symbol of chastity appropriate to a lady.[4] Margherita Gonzaga was the wife of Niccolò's son Leonello. The following lists are extracts from the 1436 court inventories.

> G. Bertoni and E. P. Vicini, *Il castello di Ferrara ai tempi di Niccolò III. Inventario della suppellettile del castello (1436)* (Bologna, 1906), pp. 71–6, 117.

i. . . . The rooms where our illustrious Lady Ricciarda, wife of our illustrious Lord, lives with her women, that is, in the room in the tower.

The *guardaroba* of the Marchioness
The balcony of the tower, on the main square
The white hall in the tower
The long hall in front of the said hall
The small hall in front of the said hall
The small hall in front of the chapel
The chamber in the pavilion, where Tarsia and her fellow washerwomen live
The kitchen in the pavilion
The Chamber of the Wheels where the illustrious Lady Lucia, daughter of our Lord, lives
The Chamber of the Columns where the Lady Fiorenza lives
The Chamber of the Unicorns where our illustrious Lady lives.

ii. In the Chamber of Lancelot where the Lady Margherita lives
In the small hall near the chapel
The Chamber of the Helmets and of the Wheels where the Lady Paganina from Mantua lives
The *guardaroba* of the said chamber
The large chamber where the maid of honour of the Lady Margherita lives
The chapel
The small hall facing the chapel
The Hall of Columns
The chamber where Margherita's servant, Giovanni da Ravenna, lives

The anteroom of the room where Rizzo from Germany, Margherita's servant, lives.

3. A sung mass for guests in the rooms of Beatrice d'Este in Venice, 1493

Married ladies used their rooms to receive important visitors. In May 1493, Beatrice d'Este was in Venice for an official visit on behalf of her husband, Ludovico (il Moro) Sforza. She stayed along with her mother Eleonora of Aragon, her brother Alfonso and his wife Anna Sforza in the palace the Este owned in Venice. Beatrice received three gentlemen in her rooms where they heard mass, sung by her court singers.

J. Cartwright, *Beatrice d'Este Duchess of Milan 1475–1497. A Study in the Renaissance* (London and New York, 1926), p. 196.

Beatrice d'Este from Venice to Ludovico Sforza, 28 May 1493
. . . This morning, as soon as I was dressed, I heard mass sung in my own rooms. Messer Cordier [a Flemish tenor] sang, and, as usual, did his part admirably, which pleased me greatly, both on account of the rare delight which his talent gives me, and because on this occasion the gentlemen who had been sent to me by the Doge were also present, and expressed the greatest admiration for his singing.

THE CONTENTS OF HOUSES AND PALACES

These texts highlight the great differences between the quantity and quality of objects and furnishings in the houses and palaces of the aristocracy and of the mercantile and banking elite, and the rooms of their servants or the abodes of artisan families, which, in contrast, were very sparsely furnished.[5]

4. The belongings of a Florentine textile worker and his wife, 1427

This extract from the 1427 Florence tax declaration lists the contents of the house of Giovanni di Antonio Dini, a wool worker, and his wife. The value given to their bed can be compared with the price of the bed commissioned by Vincenzo Politi (see chapter 2, text 3). Their clothes were the most expensive items among their belongings.

> E. Conti, A. Guidotti and R. Lunari (eds), *La civiltà fiorentina del Quattrocento* (Florence, 1993), p. 56.
>
> A feather mattress with two pillows, valued at 4 florins
> A bed cover and two pairs of sheets, 3 florins
> A bed with a chest and a platform, 3 florins
> Three benches and a chest, and a chest with locks, 2 florins
> A flour chest and a flour barrel, 1 florin and 1 *lira*
> A table with its trestles and four stools, 1 florin
> A loom for weaving wool cloth, with its furnishings, 2 florins
> Four earthenware basins, 2 *lire*
> A chain and a large cooking pot, a frying pan and a trivet, and other small things, 3 florins
> A dark brown overdress (*cioppa*) and a woman's dress (*gamurra*), 10 florins
> Two faded surcoats and two man's cloaks, 14 florins.

5. Widows in Rimini: the contents of their houses
These three inventories give a good impression of the furniture owned by two widows of the middle rank, and that belonging to the wealthier Sacramoro family. It is interesting to note how many different names were given to various kinds of large and smaller chests and boxes, such containers being by far the most common type of furniture.[6]

> O. Delucca, *Artisti a Rimini fra Gotico e Rinascimento. Rassegna di fonti archivistiche* (Rimini, 1997), pp. 700, 715, 729.
>
> **i. 11 January 1504**
> Inventory of the lady Bartolomea, daughter of the late Giovanni di Vincenzo di Battiferri di Mercatello, and widow of Pietro Paolo, son of the late Paolo Dini, merchant in the *contrada* di S. Maria in Corte.
>   In the upper floor room next to the long hall at the top of the stairs: an image of Our Lady painted and gilded on panel, in a wooden chest (*cassa*). In the same room: a painted terracotta crucifix. In another room next to the long hall: a blue

cloth curtain with gold decorations, old; a long painted chest (*cassa*) of pine wood, in the Venetian style, old; a pair of old chests (*cofani*), painted with stories and gilded, in the antique style; an image on panel of the Virgin Mary, gilded, new.

ii. 2 May 1514
Inventory of the lady Ginevra daughter of Master Pietro, son of the late Santo de Manzaroli di Croce, and widow of Giovanni Battista, barber, son of the late Master Paradiso . . .
In a room on the ground floor: an image painted on panel of the glorious Virgin Mary and some saints, gilded, old; a small painted terracotta crucifix, in the round. In a room on the upper floor, towards the street of Apelles: a bed curtain of black cloth, with its iron bar; two long pine wood chests, painted in green and yellow, used; a long bench, or rather two chests placed together, with their *spalliera*, also painted in green and yellow, used; a white long box (*scatola*); two other long small boxes, painted; a small round box, painted; a glass mirror with its round gilded frame around it, used; a chest, partly in common wood and partly in walnut, painted green, used; a hinged diptych, gilded, on which are painted the images of the crucifix and of Our Lady and of other saints, old; a small painted casket (*cofanetto*) for women's head ornaments; a small painted chest (*cassetta*), used; a small, low table top in pine wood, with its small *credenza* in the Venetian style, used.

iii. 15 July 1532
The lady Elisabetta, daughter of the late Rinaldo de Simonetti and widow of Vincenzo, son of the late Giovanni, son of the late Antonio Sacramoro.
A harpsichord with its box painted green . . . A painted *cappellinaio*;[7] another *cappellinaio* in carved wood, used; a mirror with its triangular gilt frame; a gilded mirror-frame without mirror; a mirror in a square frame; two large chests (*cofani*) painted and gilded in the antique style; three painted chests (*forzieri*); two long chests (*casse*) painted with the coats of arms of the Sacramori and the Belmonti; a square walnut box (*cassetta*) in the Venetian style; a small carved cypress box (*cassettina*); a carved *credenza* in the Venetian style for the hall; a painted cypress cradle for babies.

6. The sumptuous apartment of Lucrezia Borgia, 1508

After arriving in Ferrara early in 1502 as the wife of Alfonso d'Este, Lucrezia Borgia had to wait until the death of her father-in-law, Duke Ercole I, in January 1505, before making radical changes to the ducal residences and decorating her own new apartment in the style and richness of materials suitable to a duchess. A large number of artisans were called to Ferrara from as far away as Spain to gild the coffered ceilings of her rooms.

In April 1508, the Gonzaga ambassador in Ferrara, Bernardino Prosperi, visited Lucrezia, who had given birth to the heir to the title. He describes Lucrezia's apartment in a letter to her sister-in-law, Isabella d'Este.

N. Forti Grazzini, *L'arazzo ferrarese* (Milan, 1982), p. 56.

Bernardino Prosperi to Isabella d'Este, April 1508

This is how the rooms are appointed: in the first hall there is nothing but a large carpet over a table, with a *spalliera* and a bench. In the large antechamber are the bed furnishings in dark reddish-brown (*morello*) satin, embroidered with bunches of houseleeks, which used to belong to your mother of happy memory [Eleonora of Aragon]. Around this room, from floor to ceiling, are some very beautiful wool and silk hangings. Amongst them there is one with the Judgement of David [*sic* – Solomon] with the child, when he said 'Divide the child into two', and so on.

. . . In the *camerino* where she [Lucrezia] is, there is now a *sparviero* canopy[8] made of silver cloth, with a fringe of gold thread and silk at the head of the bed. There are sheets of fine cambric, decorated with braids made some time ago by the Greek lady Maddalena. Around the walls of this small chamber are hangings made of *morello* and crimson velvet, and of cloth of gold.

7. Preparations for the apartment for a new duchess, Mantua, 1531

For his wedding to Margherita Paleologa, Federico Gonzaga commissioned an apartment for his bride from the painter and architect Giulio Romano. The *Palazzina*, an extension of the Castello, faced the lake on one side and a small garden on the other. The architecture of the exterior was very simple, but decorated with frescoes. The interior was embellished with *grottesche* and wood panelling, while paintings from the Gonzaga collection were moved into the new apartment. Isabella d'Este and her son supervised the furnishings of the rooms.

i. F. Hartt, *Giulio Romano* (2nd edn, New York, 1981), p. 262.

Federico Gonzaga to his cousin Francesco Gonzaga, May 1531

At the moment we are having building work done to the Castle here in Mantua, towards S. Giorgio. We are adding a few rooms, that is, a small hall and two small chambers, which we want to furnish with gilded leather hangings like those Your Most Illustrious Lordship had made in Rome. We would like [ours] to be worked like yours, in gold and turquoise. I wish them to be made in this colour more than in any other, but if this is not possible, then we would be satisfied, as long as each room had hangings all of the same colour.

ii. M. S. Ahrendt, 'The cultural legacy and patronal stewardship of Margherita Paleologa (1510–1566), Duchess of Mantua and Marchesa of Monferrat', Ph.d. dissertation, Washington University, St Louis, 2002, pp. 93–4.

The court secretary Gian Giacomo Calandra to Federico Gonzaga, 21 October 1531

The most illustrious Lady [Isabella d'Este] is beginning to prepare all the most beautiful hangings we have in order to decorate the rooms. Today I have been to the court to see Her Excellency. She had sent for me, and showed me some very beautiful *sparvieri* canopies such as I had never seen. She then showed me all the bed canopies and hangings, and she told me how the rooms should be prepared. She will then come to the castle to arrange things as she wants, everywhere in the rooms.

8. The *Appartamento degli Elementi*: furnishings for Leonora di Toledo, 1574

In 1574, Leonora di Toledo (1553–76), the niece and daughter-in-law of Eleonora di Toledo, was living in the sumptuous apartment on the second floor of the Palazzo de' Priori [Palazzo Vecchio], which had been refashioned by Giorgio Vasari and decorated with mythological subjects during the 1550s and 1560s. The 1574 inventory of its contents does not specify what was located in each of the five rooms and *studiolo*. The large quantity of bedding may indicate that Leonora's ladies-in-waiting would often sleep there.

Archivio di Stato di Firenze, Guardaroba 85, fol. 75r–v.

Objects in the new rooms where the Lady Leonora lives
20 June 1574
One inlaid walnut chair decorated with red velvet, with two
    bars for carrying it
One tapestry carpet measuring about eight *braccia*[9]
One chest for storing hangings
One wooden table about six *braccia* long
One wool mattress covered with ticking
One bolster, as above
Bed cover in yellow and blue cloth, stuffed with cotton wool
One linen bed sheet, in bad condition
Three planks of wood for the said bed[10]
One carpet measuring about six *braccia*
One wooden table about five *braccia* long
Two marble heads placed on a large marble base with two
    bronze fixtures
Two andirons with brass supports
Two small tapestries with the arms of Duke Alessandro [de'
    Medici]
'Pavilion style' bed hangings in red *ermisino* [a light silk
    fabric], with a bed valance
Red light taffeta coverlet in Levantine style
Two small wooden tables with decorative feet
One painting of Our Lady with gilt frame
Octagonal [table] of ebony and ivory, with its feet
A low walnut chair, decorated in red velvet
Milanese-style andirons with supports
Six wool mattresses [covered] with ticking
Two wool bolsters
Wood supports for a walnut bed and its wooden board

A small carpet measuring about three *braccia*
Four wool mattresses covered with ticking
Two wool bolsters, as above
One bed cover in red wool
One bed cover in red taffeta
One wood *carriuola* bed[11] with its handles
Two wool mattresses covered with ticking for the said bed
A white bed cover stuffed with cotton wool
Two linen sheets for the said bed
A painting on canvas with St John baptising Christ
One picture [representing] Lord Virginio Orsini[12]
One wooden table five *braccia* long, without its trestles
Two wool mattresses, for the Lady Maria Minerbetti
Wooden bed trestles and their board
Ten wool mattresses covered with ticking
Two tow mattresses covered with canvas
Six wool bolsters, and a feather one
Six pallets [13]
Five white bedcovers stuffed with cotton wool
One white bedcover, as above.

BEDROOMS

In palaces belonging to the higher ranks, the largest number of furniture was kept in bedrooms. These were not private places where people slept: Palladio wrote that in the *camere* 'one sleeps, eats, and receives visitors'.[14] Women spent much time in their bedrooms with other women of the household, members of the family, and servants, and also received friends and visitors there, just as men did. On special occasions, such as the birth of a child, formal and informal visits to the new mother took place in her bedroom.

In palaces belonging to ruling families and to the banking and mercantile elite matrimonial bedrooms represented the union of husband and wife. There the head of the family slept, sometimes with his wife. Matrimonial bedrooms were usually more sumptuously furnished than women's own bedrooms. As might be expected, servants' bedrooms and those of the lower ranks were very sparsely furnished.[15]

9. The bedroom of a new mother from the Venetian patriciate, 1494

It was the custom for new mothers to receive their friends and relatives in bed, after childbirth. The following text, by the Milanese Pietro Casola, conveys his interest in the ceremonies of the Venetian patriciate on such an occasion. The presence of ambassadors who marvel at the magnificence of the decoration and furnishings is particularly interesting.[16]

Viaggio a Gerusalemme di Pietro Casola, ed. A. Paoletti (Alessandria, 2001), pp. 272–3.

We went together by boat to visit the wife of a gentleman of the Dolfin family who had just given birth. I think the visit had been arranged by Don Girolamo [Zorzi, Venetian ambassador to the Holy See], in order to show the pomp and magnificence of those Venetian gentlemen to those magnificent ambassadors, especially the King of France's. The King's ambassador said that neither the Queen of France nor any other French lord would have shown such pomp, and the ducal ambassador said that our most illustrious Duchess [of Milan] also would not have displayed such luxury on a similar occasion.

The ducal ambassador chose me to enter with him, especially because the room was not large enough for so many people, so that I might see and report elsewhere what I had seen. . . It was estimated that the decoration of the room where we were, and where was the lady who had given birth, and I mean the room itself and not the moveable furnishings, had cost more than 2,000 ducats, although it was not longer than 12 *braccia*. There was a fireplace made of Carrara marble, as shiny as gold, carved so finely with figures and foliage that neither Praxiteles nor Phidias could have done better. I cannot express how beautifully decorated was the ceiling with gold and ultramarine blue, and the walls as well . . . There was so much gold everywhere, that I do not know whether in the times of Solomon, King of the Jews, when silver was esteemed to be worthless, there would have been such abundance as here. I prefer not to speak about the ornaments of the lady's bed, that is, coverlets and pillows, of which there were six, and the draperies, because I doubt I would be believed.

10. The bedrooms of a lady and of female servants in a Florentine palace, 1557

The contents of the palace belonging to Lorenzo di Giuliano Scala were listed in an inventory drawn up in February 1557, just after his death. Here the furnishings of the room used by Lorenzo's widowed mother Francesca Villani are contrasted with those of the matrimonial bedroom she had shared with her husband Giuliano, and with those of the household's female servants.

A. Bellinazzi and F. Martelli, 'Il palazzo di Pinti dagli Scala ad Alessandro de' Medici e ai Della Gherardesca' in A. Bellinazzi (ed.), *La casa del cancelliere. Documenti e studi sul palazzo di Bartolomeo Scala a Firenze* (Florence, 1998), p. 167.

In the *camera* of the lady Francesca, upstairs:
one bed with pallets, feather mattress, mattress and *sparviero*
    bed canopy, of green and dark purple cloth, damaged
one day-bed (*lettuccio*) with its thin mattress and cushions
three chests with locks, and a chest
a pair of fire irons
a crucifix

Large *camera* upstairs, used by Giuliano:
One bed with pallets, a feather mattress (*coltrice*), mattresses
    and red hangings
a pair of chests
one day-bed
two chests with locks
two *spalliere* and one door hanging (*portiera*)[17]
two Flemish paintings on canvas
a crucifix
one chest covered in leather

In the antechamber of said *camera*:
A bed for the [women] servants with pallets and mattress
A pair of chests, with a damaged chest with locks, covered in
    leather
A distilling bell

In the [female] servants' bedroom:
A bed suitable for servants with pallets and mattresses, all
    damaged, and a cupboard
Seven padded bed covers.

11. The female servants' bedroom in a villa
The brief list of the contents of the female servants' spartan bedroom, from the May 1609 inventory of the contents of 'Il Riposo',
the Vecchietti family villa near Florence.

> M. Bury, 'Bernardo Vecchietti, patron of Giambologna', in *I
> Tatti Studies. Essays in the Renaissance*, 1 (1985), p. 30.

In the bedroom of the women servants:
    A bed with wooden supports, a feather mattress with a
bolster, also filled with feathers. Three wool mattresses and
two straw pallets, with two white cloths, and one padded bed
cover lined with ticking. Three small and low chests lined
with walnut. One wooden chest.

PAINTINGS AND SCULPTURES IN WOMEN'S BEDROOMS
When paintings and sculptures are listed among the contents of wom-
en's bedrooms, they are usually religious images. These will be examined in chapter 8. Inventories however show that works of art with
secular subjects could be found in matrimonial bedrooms.[18] It should
be remembered that many items of furniture, such as beds, chests,
spalliere and *restelli* [mirrors with complex shelves and adjuncts]
would have been painted with allegories or mythological narratives.[19]

12. Devotional images for the women of an extended
family, 1449
As was often the case, the sons and daughters-in-law of Puccio
Pucci lived together in the family palace in Florence. In the bedrooms which the Pucci sons shared with their wives there were
images of the Virgin.

> C. Merkel, *I beni della famiglia di Puccio Pucci: inventario del
> secolo XV illustrato* (n.p., n.d.), unpaginated.

Piero's bedroom [shared with his wife, Caterina Milanesi]:
One panel with Our Lady, 8 florins
One woman's prayer book, valued at 5 florins

Francesco's bedroom [shared with his wife, Bartolomea Spini]:
One Our Lady, with a candle-holder

The bedroom of the lady Mea [Bartolomea Spinelli, Puccio
  Pucci's widow]:
One small silver altar-piece, 3 florins.

13. Works of art in a matrimonial bedroom, 1493
As well as religious images, Andrea Minerbetti and his wife had two
portraits in the matrimonial bedroom of their Florentine palace.
They also had a birth tray (*desco da parto*)[20] and what seems to be
the heraldic figure of a falcon. The following is an extract from the
1493 inventory.

A. Schiaparelli, *La casa fiorentina e i suoi arredi nei secoli XIV
e XV* [1908], 2 vols (Florence, 1983), 1, p. 184.

One painting of Our Lady with its gilded frame
One painted birth tray with a gilded frame
One painting, a portrait of Alfonsina, with a gilded frame
One painting with a gilded frame
One terracotta relief representing a woman
One painted tabernacle with a female saint
One painted tabernacle with a relief of St. John
One falcon in gilded copper
Three small wax figures, gilded.

**14. Religious sculptures and paintings in the room of a
Florentine lady**
An extract from the April 1502 inventory of movable goods which
Benedetto Frescobaldi bequeathed to his widow Costanza.[21]

Archivio di Stato di Firenze, Magistrato dei Pupilli, 183, fols.
2v, 3r

In Costanza's bedroom
. . .

2 plaster heads with their haloes, that is, a St John and a
Christ
One Virgin Mary painted on panel and gilded, with the coat
of arms of the Ridolfi and Frescobaldi families
One St Jerome painted on canvas with its stretcher
. . .
One wooden crucifix
. . .
One large painting on canvas with its stretcher.

15. Paintings and wall hangings in a Roman bedroom
The following extract from the inventory of Palazzo Altoviti in
Rome, 20 December 1644, lists paintings and wall hangings in the
room of Caterina de Ricci Altoviti.

> A. Chong, D. Pegazzano and D. Zikos (eds), *Ritratto di un
> banchiere del Rinascimento. Bindo Altoviti tra Raffaello e
> Cellini* (Milan, 2004), p. 450.

The following room on the second floor, towards the river
[Tiber] where Caterina de Ricci Altoviti sleeps now:
[The room is decorated with] six tapestries with a wood and
dogs, used, and underneath [there are] old leather hangings
A picture of St Mary Magdalen
. . .
A small picture at the head of the bed, with the Magdalen in
ecstasy.

CONVENTS AND NUNS' POSSESSIONS

Nunneries were an important feature of cities during our period,
because of the very large number of young women destined to the
convent by their parents – perhaps approaching half of the girls
from the urban elites.[22] Many such high-ranking nuns often lived
in their convents as they had in their palaces, in expensively furnished cells decorated with beautiful objects, while poorer nuns or
lay women (*converse*) often acted as their servants. These high-born
nuns continued to have relationships with their families and relatives, and kept in touch with artistic developments in their cities.

After the Council of Trent, following the trend towards religious reform, visitations from ecclesiastical authorities tried to stamp out luxuries in convents, and to introduce a stronger emphasis on poverty and devotion, as well as a stricter enclosure. Guidance was given about what objects for personal use nuns were allowed to keep in their cells.

16. Buildings and images for the convent of Corpus Domini, Venice

This chronicle of the convent of Corpus Domini, Venice (after 1436), is mostly concerned with stressing the moral virtues of the institution, founded and expanded as a result of the heavenly visions and pious actions of its supporters. Accordingly, though one gains a clear sense of the gradual physical consolidation of the convent, references to its images are perfunctory, although in the course of the fifteenth century it came to house notable works of art.

Sister Bartolomea Riccaboni, chronicle of the convent of Corpus Domini, Venice, in Giovanni Dominici, *Lettere spiri-tuali*, ed., M. T. Casella and G. Pozzi (Freiburg, 1969), pp. 265, 269–71; *Life and Death in a Venetian Convert*, ed. and trans. D. Bornstein (Chicago, 2000), pp. 33, 37–40.

It would be impossible to convey how much charity and devotion our Father [Giovanni Dominici] showed that day for his daughters. Having allocated the cells with their altar-pieces, he blessed them with holy water . . .
And through his good reputation, devotion to our convent increased in many people and especially in many gentlemen who embellished the sacristy with chalices, vestments and hangings and all it needed . . . And other people with great devotion and charity took care that walls were erected and windows opened in cells, and vineyards planted. Then Sister Margherita Paruta, the second vicaress, built the new dormitory and the parlour and Sister Geronima dei Cancellieri, who was the second prioress, had the parlours constructed within the sacristy, and Sister Isabetta Tommasini, who was the third prioress, had the chapter room decorated with narrative scenes, and Sister Andriola had the Last Supper painted in the refectory . . .

For the building of the said church the same Messer Fantin paid four thousand ducats, and His Reverence [the Patriarch of Venice, Lorenzo Giustiniani] gave many other alms and goods to our convent. . . Once the church was built, the Prioress Sister Margarita Bocco had the grilles made around our inner church with the money taken from the entry of new sisters, and also the two altarpieces of Our Lady.

17. The convent of S. Chiara in Naples, 1509

Built next to a church and a friars' convent, the Clarissan nunnery of S. Chiara was constructed far from the densely populated centre of Naples, enjoying fresh air and a beautiful view from its hill site. It became one of the largest and richest convents in Naples, housing six hundred nuns by the end of the sixteenth century, most of them from the wealthiest Neapolitan families. In 1508 they asked the King of Naples, Ferdinand II, to look into the contents of the convent, investigating possible cases of nuns owning illicit objects, or selling their possessions. The following is an extract from the report, describing the layout of the convent.[23]

M. Gaglione, 'Quattro documenti per la storia di S. Chiara in Napoli', *Archivio Storico per le Province Napoletane*, 121 (2003), p. 431.

From the inventory by Antonio Sanfelice, delegate of the Regio Cappellano Maggiore, 8 November 1509

Then we entered the convent of the said nuns, where are four upper dormitories: the dormitory of St Anthony on the east side, the dormitory of St Clare on the south side, the dormitory of St Francis on the west side, and the dormitory of St Louis on the north side, with four cloistered complexes with loggias above and below, with an infirmary . . . and a large refectory, with another infirmary called the Virgin Annunciate, and another dormitory on the ground floor, and another house called 'the Saracens' house', with the grilles formerly used for confession, and a cemetery where the nuns are buried. Then there is a cloister, where is a large garden measuring four *moggi*. Outside the said cloister there is a passage towards the church, where are the grilles and the wheel. In this passage are lodgings and stables for the wheel supervisors, the mule drivers, and for the servants of the convent. There is then a garden called *l'Orticello* (the small vegetable garden), where chickens for the convent are kept. There are other chickens in what is called *l'Orto de le galline* (the vegetable garden where the hens are). There is another passage where the door of the store-room is located, with some houses and a small garden to house the baking room. From there is the large covered store-room and one storage room with an upper granary. There are also more chicken-runs behind the kitchen. Then there is a large kitchen with all that is necessary for it. Noteworthy are four bronze or copper cauldrons, which are worth much money . . .. There is also a food storage room. Then there is an area with a furnace to distil water, and a large garden called *lo jardino della Abbadessa* (the garden of the Abbess), with an old bath-house.[24] There is another part called *La Torre* (the Tower), where there are two more gardens.

18. The oratory of the nuns' dormitory in S. Caterina da Siena, Florence

The record book of the Florentine convent of S. Caterina da Siena, among the luxurious refurbishment work for the oratory of the nuns' dormitory, mentions a painting by Sister Plautilla Nelli and her assistants.[25]

J. Nelson (ed.), *Suor Plautilla Nelli (1523–1588) the First Woman Painter of Florence* (Florence, 2000), p. 115.

I record that on 13 May last [1586] we finalised expenditure for the oratory of the Virgin Mary, in the dormitory. Here we placed the altarpiece with its frame, which cost 30 *scudi* without the painting which was done by the hand of our Mother Sister Plautilla and her assistants. In this altarpiece is God the Father with Angels, our Father St Dominic, our Mother St Catherine [of Siena], and two angels at the foot of the panel. They look as if they were supporting the tabernacle with the Virgin Mary, which is placed in the middle of the altarpiece, as one can see. We also had *spalliere* and seats made of pine wood with a walnut veneer, which cost R 42, and the stone altar with its small columns. All this was R 86, as one can see in detail, recorded as a debit in the book marked D, at folio 125. We also had a crown made for Jesus and the Virgin Mary, which is in gilded silver, and it cost R 5 without the pearls and the precious stones mounted on it. This all was done [on the advice of] our Reverend Father Confessor, Fra Cipriano de' Servi of blessed memory, [and paid for] from offerings given to the nuns for that reason by their relatives, in honour of God and of the Holy Virgin . . .

NUNS' PERSONAL POSSESSIONS

19. Luxury objects for the cells of Este nuns, mid-fifteenth century

The following extracts from the account records of the Este court list payments for a series of objects and works of art given to three Este nuns.

Verde was one of the illegitimate daughters of Niccolò III d'Este, and the gifts given to her for her profession were worthy of a princess. The subject matter of the painted *cassoni* was appropriate for a nun, and her father's coat of arms indicated her aristocratic birth. The two paintings, too large for a cell, would have almost certainly been placed either in the nuns' church, or in the convent's common spaces.

Sister Laura and Sister Domitilla were daughters of Meliaduse d'Este.

A. Franceschini, *Artisti a Ferrara in età umanistica e rinascimentale. Testimonianze archivistiche. Parte I dal 1341 al 1471* (Ferrara and Rome, 1993), pp. 394, 415, 643, 660.

i. Sister Verde
22 March 1453
Today 22 March, Master Andrea from Vicenza [Andrea Costa], painter, is paid fifty *lire marchesane* for his labour and expenditure on gold and good pigments, and other materials used to paint a pair of large chests, commissioned through Antonio dei Banchi for the illustrious lady Sister Verde, the

sister of the most illustrious lord our Duke [Borso d'Este], for her profession, which will take place soon. On the chests he painted the story of St Catherine, and gilded the frames at the front, made the lids [decorated] with gilded tin,[26] and on the front and back [he painted] the coat of arms and the devices of our said lord, according to the agreement between him and Galeotto dell'Assassino for the agreed price L50

Today the said [painter] is due fifteen *lire marchesane* for his labour and expenditure on fine gold and pigments used to gild and paint a large panel painting, with a frame carved with fretwork and foliage, made through the offices of the said Antonio, for the profession of [Sister Verde]. In the middle [of the painting] is Our Lady with a triumph of angels around her, with God the Father above, and St Dominic, and [a portrait of] the said lady, Sister Verde. The rest of the panel is all gilded L15

ii. Sister Laura

18 November 1454

A panel, painted and gilded, for her own room. For the work on the said painting, recorded on book S on 18 November L15

A pair of chests, painted and gilded, for her room. For the work on the chests, recorded on book S on 18 [November] L50

iii. Sister Domitilla

26 November 1465

To Master Gerardo, painter . . . For painting a large chest for clothes, with an image of the Annunciation of Our Lady on the front, and [a figure of] Jesus between the Virgin Annunciate and the angel, and with the old coat of arms of the Este House, made for Sister Domitilla, daughter of the illustrious Lord Meliaduse d'Este, who is a nun in S. Antonio, expense recorded L4.

18 November 1466

To the illustrious Sister Domitilla d'Este, nun in S. Antonio, a picture on which is painted the image of St Jerome, in relief, gilded. It is in the hands of Agostino Bressano, administrator of the nunnery of S. Antonio.

20. Rules concerning nuns' cells and personal possessions

After a visitation to the Milanese convent of S. Apollinare in 1571, Carlo Borromeo expresses his concern at the nuns' conduct, advising stricter observance and punishments for infringements. Among his decrees, the following were intended to prevent nuns having small luxuries in their cells, and to impose the keeping of goods in common.

P. Sevesi, 'Il monastero delle Clarisse di S. Apollinare, Milano', *Archivium Francescanum historicum*, 19 (1926), p. 84.

19. Vessels made of glass, earthenware or tin should not be kept in cells, apart from those necessary for bodily needs. Likewise, neither carpets nor any other frivolous object unbecoming to the monastic state should be kept.
20. A small altar, suitably adorned, should be kept in the cell. It is also permitted to keep devotional pictures, and only one chest.
21. All monies, whether belonging to or earned by individual nuns, must be immediately handed over to the abbess, who shall put it in the common fund as soon as possible, so that everything is held in common. All necessities for the nuns' upkeep, clothing and illnesses will be equitably provided for from the common fund, as ordered by the Provincial Council.
22. All clothing, both linen and woollen, should be kept in a communal place, under the custody of a convent office-holder, except for two chemises, two wimples, kerchiefs and *scalfini* (stocking soles), which may be kept in individual chests. All this must be enforced in its entirety within one month.

21. The Poor Clares of S. Spirito, Salerno

In the inventory written on the occasion of his visitation to the Franciscan convent of S. Spirito in Salerno in 1573, the Vicar General for the diocese of Salerno listed the contents of the cells where seventeen professed nuns, seven novices, six lay sisters (*converse*), and a servant lived. Archbishop Marsilio Colonna, on whose behalf the visitation was carried out, wanted to bring the convents in his diocese in line with the pronouncements of the Council of Trent, but encountered difficulties since many of the nuns came from powerful aristocratic families, and were used to living in comfort.

These extracts list the contents of the cells of two nuns, a novice and a lay sister. While the two nuns had more possessions, all of them had, as well as some luxury objects, the necessary ingredients for having their own meals cooked and served 'in private'.

M. A. Del Grosso, *Donna nel Cinquecento tra letteratura e realtà* (Salerno, 1989), pp. 197–8.

The belongings of Sister Beatrice Aversana: first of all two wool mattresses; a pallet, new; a coverlet padded with cotton wool, used; a walnut table with two benches; a coloured wool bed-hanging, used; a *sparviero* canopy of tow cloth; two pair of canvas sheets; four pillows; three tablecloths; five chemises made of tow cloth and linen; six cloth caps; five linen head-bands; three large tablecloths, used; a copper basin; a small copper portable brazier, used; a medium-size copper cauldron; a copper fire-pot; an iron trivet; a small frying pan; a lined chest; four walnut boxes; a large chest; fifty plates; an earthenware mug; an earthenware flagon; two earthenware salt cellars; fifty [earthenware] bowls; two small straw chairs; a wooden chair; six small cheeses from Calabria; two mild cheeses; a piece of lard; half a cheese; seven empty small barrels; an empty cask; a small container full of vinegar; small and large baskets.

The belongings of Sister Delia Dentice: first of all a wool mattress; a cloth *sparviero* canopy; four pillows; one bed valance; one copper basin; a brazier; nine tablecloths; nine tablemats; fifty plates; two used dresses and one new, not yet thread-bare; three Sardinian cheeses and two mild cheeses; two rolls of lard; a small coverlet; five chemises; two wooden chairs; one stool; a walnut table; two measures of wheat; a chest for storing bread; forty soup plates and plates; two earthenware bowls; an earthenware salt cellar; two flagons; a chest containing *caciocavallo* (a type of cheese), two Sardinian cheeses and two mild cheeses; a piece of lard; a silver ring; two crystal cups; a tablecloth; ten baskets; a walnut chest where she stores food; two brass candlesticks.

A list of the belongings of Porzia Dalmazio, a novice: a mattress, a pallet and a small coverlet; three pairs of new sheets; a pillow; a cloth *sparviero* canopy; seven canvas chemises; seven aprons; seven tablemats; five caps; five tablecloths; three hand-towels; a brass basin and a portable brazier; a pan for making pastry; two brass candlesticks; a lined chest; two small wooden chests; two cheeses, one mild and the other from Sardinia.

A list of the belongings of Marzia de Rienzo, a lay sister: a cloth *sparviero* canopy; two pairs of sheets; a small coverlet; a mattress and a pallet; a wooden chest and a small walnut chest; five fine tablecloths; three aprons; a small portable brazier . . . two pieces of lard and a Sardinian cheese; eight plates and six earthenware bowls; a bed.

22. The convent of S. Matteo in Arcetri in two letters by Sister Maria Celeste, 1629–30
Sister Maria Celeste (Virginia Galilei, 1600–34), a nun in the Poor Clares' convent of S. Matteo at Arcetri, near Florence, kept up a constant correspondence with her father, Galileo Galilei. Her letters vividly convey both the simple pleasures one could enjoy in the convent and the hardships caused by poverty and strict enclosure. The nuns of S. Matteo did not have the material comforts of those living in the sister convent of S. Spirito in Salerno.

E. Viviani della Robbia, *La figlia di Galileo* (Florence, 1942), pp. 42–3, 61–2.

Sister Maria Celeste to Galileo Galilei, 8 July 1629
I know that you have some idea of the discomfort I have suffered since being here, because of the inadequacy of my cell. Now I shall explain in more detail. I have had to give Sister Arcangela my small cell, for which two or three years ago,

as customary among us nuns, we paid thirty-six *scudi* to our mistress . . . Therefore I find myself at night in the bothersome company of my mistress . . . and by day I am almost a pilgrim, since I have no place where I can withdraw even for a single hour. I do not wish a large or a very fine room, but just a small one. Now I have the chance to get a small cell, which a nun wants to sell in order to get some money. Because of the recommendation from Sister Luisa, this nun would prefer me to the many others who would like to buy [her cell]. But I cannot afford it, as it costs 35 *scudi*, and I only have ten, which I got from Sister Luisa, and I expect five from my income. In fact, I fear that I will lose it, if you do not help me with the sum I need, which is 20 *scudi* . . .

10 September 1630

. . . Now that it is a bit cooler, Sister Arcangela and I, together with our dearest [sisters], are planning to work in my cell, which is quite large. But the window is very high up, and it needs to be covered with waxed cloth to have a bit more light. I would like to send you the frames, that is the shutters, so that you could fix them for me with some oil cloth which, when it is old, I don't think will be a nuisance.

Notes

1 See R. A. Goldthwaite (1993).
2 See Select Bibliography. See also K. McIver (2006), esp. pp. 107–67, and 'Why did some women build? The case of Ippolita Pallavicina-Sanseverina', *Source*, 25:3 (2006), pp. 16–21; S. Chojnacki, *Women and Men in Renaissance Venice. Twelve Essays on Patrician Society* (Baltimore and London, 2000).
3 See Ajmar-Wollheim and Dennis (eds), (2006), Part 1, 'Defining the casa'.
4 See also T. Tuohy, *Herculean Ferrara: Ercole I d'Este (1471–1505) and the Invention of a Ducal Capital* (Cambridge, 1996), p. 55.
5 See S. Cavallo, 'The artisan's *casa*', in Ajmar-Wollheim and Dennis (eds), (2006), pp. 66–75. For contents of the house of a wealthy courtesan, see C. Santore, 'Julia Lombardo, "Somtuosa Meretrize": a portrait by property', *Renaissance Quarterly*, 41:1 (1988), pp. 44–83, and D. Davanzo Poli, 'Inventario delle cose di Giulia Leoncini, cortigiana di Venezia nel secolo XVI', in D. Liscia Bemporad (ed.), *Il costume nell'età del Rinascimento* (Florence, 1988), pp. 273–85.

6 P. Thornton, 'Cassoni, forzieri, goffani and cassette: terminology and its problems', in *Apollo*, 120:3 (1984), pp. 246–51.

7 See Ajmar-Wollheim and Dennis (eds), (2006), pp. 122–3.

8 For *sparviero* and *padiglione* canopies, see Thornton (1991), pp. 124–9.

9 Carpets were often used to cover tables.

10 These planks supported the mattress.

11 A low bed on wheels, stored under a larger bed and pulled out at night.

12 Son of Leonora's sister-in-law, Isabella de' Medici.

13 A pallet (*saccone*) was a hard mattress, placed on top of the bed-frame. On it a *materasso* was placed, filled either with wool, horsehair or tow. Lastly, a feather mattress (*coltrice*) would be added in wealthier households.

14 See *I quattro libri dell'Architettura di Andrea Palladio* [Venice, 1570] (Milan, 1980), Book II, p. 4.

15 See C. Paolini, *I luoghi dell'intimità: la camera da letto nella casa fiorentina del Rinascimento* (Florence, 2004).

16 See P. Allerston, '"Contrary to the truth and also the semblance of reality"? Entering a Venetian "lying-in" chamber (1605)', in Ajmar-Wollheim, Dennis and Matchette (eds), 2007, pp. 7–17.

17 A *spalliera* was an ensemble of wooden panels, either painted or decorated with intarsia, which was placed above the wainscoting. A *portiera* was a hanging, either a tapestry or made of tooled leather, covering a door.

18 See J. K. Lydecker, 'The Domestic Setting of Arts in Renaissance Florence' (PhD dissertation, Johns Hopkins University, 1987).

19 The courtesan Giulia Leoncini, as well as religious images, owned a portrait of a woman with its curtain, one of a man in armour, and one of a knight, a painting representing a battle, two female nudes, and a bronze statuette. See Davanzo Poli (1988), pp. 275, 279, 283.

20 On *deschi da parto* see J. M. Musacchio, *The Art and Ritual of Childbirth in Renaissance Italy* (New Haven and London, 1999).

21 I thank Suzy Knight for this extract.

22 As well as the works cited in the Introduction, on convents see: H. Hills, 'The housing of institutional architecture: searching for a domestic holy in post-Tridentine Italian convents', in S. Cavallo and S. Evangelisti (eds), *Domestic Institutional Interiors in Early Modern Europe* (Farnham, 2009), pp. 119–50; S. Strocchia, *Nuns and Nunneries in Renaissance Florence* (Baltimore, 2009); S. Weddle, '"Women in wolves' mouths": nuns' reputations, enclosure and architecture at the convent of Le Murate in Florence', in H. Hills (ed.), *Architecture and the Politics of Gender in Early Modern Europe* (Aldershot, 2003),

pp. 115–29; K. J. P. Lowe, *Nuns' Chronicles and Convent Culture in Renaissance and Counter-Reformation Italy* (Cambridge, 2003); Rogers and Tinagli, *Women in Italy*, pp. 210–14, 222–5: M. Laven, *Virgins of Venice* (London, 2006).

23 See H. Hills, *Invisible City: The Architecture of Devotion in Seventeenth-Century Neapolitan Convents* (Oxford, 2004).

24 Roman baths (second half of first century AD).

25 See S. Evangelisti, 'Art and the advent of clausura: the convent of Saint Caterina of Siena in Florence', in J. Nelson (ed.), *Suor Plautilla Nelli (1523–1588) The First Woman Painter of Florence* (Florence, 2000), pp. 67–82.

26 See *The Craftsman's Handbook 'Il Libro dell'Arte' Cennino di Andrea Cennini* (New York, 1960), pp. 61–2.

❧ 2 ❧

BEAUTY, QUALITY AND ELEGANCE: OBJECTS IN THE HOUSE

This chapter deals mostly with objects owned, commissioned and acquired by women of the elite for whom the beauty and elegance, and sometimes the novelty of the furnishings and objects they used were of the greatest importance. Beds, tables and chairs, containers and cabinets, objects in glass, ceramic and silver, bring to our attention the special care these women devoted to their making and their acquisition. Many of the documents in this chapter demonstrate that quality, materials and craftsmanship were important for ornamental objects, *oggetti ornamentali*, bought more for aesthetic than for utilitarian reasons, for the embellishment of one's own surroundings. They were also important for *suppellettili*, objects for everyday use. It is often difficult, however, to separate the two categories: ceramic services, glass vessels and silver tableware could be works of art in their own right. The same is true in the case of extraordinarily valuable tapestries, which were prized decoration as well as having the practical function of insulating rooms.

Several Renaissance writers, starting with the Neapolitan Giovanni Pontano in his late fifteenth-century series of moral treatises,[1] stressed that *splendore, magnificenza* and *liberalità* could be 'virtues' or even duties for aristocratic women, who might appropriately surround themselves with beautiful and elegant objects. Other writers of treatises throughout the Renaissance, dealing with women of the wealthy middle ranks, stressed different duties, but agreed that both their person and surroundings should demonstrate the standing of their native and marital families.[2]

WOMEN, DUTIES AND *SPLENDORE*

1. Isabella d'Este: an example of *liberalità*, 1524
In this dialogue, Giangiorgio Trissino extols the virtues of Isabella d'Este and describes her as a perfect woman, exceeding the famous women of antiquity in those virtues appropriate to a great aristocratic lady. She is beautiful and accomplished, obedient and modest, and also possesses justice, fortitude and moderation. Here, Isabella's munificence is illustrated by the way in which she surrounds herself with fine and precious objects.

> *I ritratti di M. Giovan Giorgio Trissino* (Rome, 1524), unpaginated.

> . . . In our time munificence (*liberalità*) is manifested in her alone. Who better than she knows how to spend on what is praiseworthy and on what is necessary? Her munificence is shown by her magnificent clothes with their splendid ornamentation, and by the fine, delightful and almost divine buildings, her most harmonious *camerini* full of the rarest books, the finest pictures, the most wonderful antique and modern sculpture which rivals the antique, and cameos, *intagli*, medals and the finest gemstones. In short, there are so many precious and rare objects, that those who see them feel both astonishment and great delight.

2. Everything in its place, 1542
In a treatise published in 1542 and reprinted many times, Alessandro Piccolomini gives advice to his friend, the poetess Laudomia Forteguerri, on the upbringing of her son. Piccolomini includes a chapter on the duties of married women in the management of the household.[3]

> Alessandro Piccolomini, *Della institutione di tutta la vita de l'homo nato nobile e in città libera* [1542] (Venice, 1545), fols 259r–260r.

> As to the running of the house, after the father of the family has provided for a comfortable abode, having bought one or

built a new one, the prudent woman must diligently make sure that everything is in its proper place. Everything needed in the various rooms of the house must be well arranged and tidy. She has to organise everything appropriately for each object, room and place. After a woman has been instructed for the first time, she shall not leave this task to her husband: every time something is brought into the house, she shall find the right place for it . . . This order must be observed not only for the produce of the estate, but also for everyday useful objects, that is, those possessions needed by the whole household for the management of the house. The right place should be found for each object, that is, the kitchen for what is needed there, and another place for what is destined to the chambers. And of those objects to be placed in the chambers, bedding must be put in a different place to table furnishings, and, finally, articles for personal adornment . . . and clothes should be in yet another place, whilst a woman must keep her rings, jewels, necklaces, bracelets and other valuable things in the most secret place in her bedchamber.

BEDS

Beds (*lettiere*) were the most imposing amongst the pieces of furniture in the dwellings of the elite and of middle-ranking families, and symbolised important events, such as the union of two families and the procreation of children. These beds were provided with headboards and sometimes with columns, and furnished with hangings fashioned in various ways.[4]

3. A contract for a *lettiera* and a *lettuccio*, Pistoia, 1488

This is very detailed contract, written and signed in front of a notary, for the commission of a matrimonial bed and a day-bed (*lettuccio*). The document is very specific about the inlaid decoration, which includes coat of arms of both husband and wife. Vincenzo Politi was the son of a notary, and therefore belonged to the wealthy middle ranks of the Tuscan city of Pistoia.

G. Milanesi, *Nuovi documenti per la storia dell'arte toscana dal XII al XV secolo* (Florence, 1901), p. 119.

12 January 1488

Niccolò di Jacopo Onofrio Paoletti, woodworker in Pistoia, promises and agrees with Vincenzo, son of the late Ser Niccolò di Bartolomei Politi of Pistoia, to make a bed with its chests and all suitable accessories, and a day-bed, for the chamber of the said Vincenzo, in the house of the said Vincenzo, fashioned in this way, that is:

The headboard [should be made] of white poplar wood, well seasoned, with a walnut veneer, surrounded by decorative frames with a carved inlaid spiral motif. In the middle panel of the said headboard [there should be] a garland, that is a marquetry swag made of spindle-wood, held by two putti, and in the said garland [there should be] the marquetry coat of arms of Vincenzo and his wife. All this should be smoothly planed, with a frieze, cornice and architrave, in the modern fashion as is the custom today. The board at the foot of the bed should be all white, that is white poplar, framed all round . . . The side facing inwards should be all white, and should be framed all around with walnut. The chests around the bed should be all veneered in walnut, with decorative frames, and a carved and inlaid spiral motif, all framed, all smoothly planed, with a base and skirting, with the usual inlaid spiral motif, all smooth, all round the bed.

The day-bed should be lined with white poplar and veneered with walnut, with decorative frames and inlaid spiral patterns, and with spindle-wood marquetry. It should have two armrests decorated in walnut, and it should be similar to the bed, with a large cornice and a frieze and an architrave at the same level as the bed's. [Both should be] similar to the day-bed belonging to Master Lorenzo Politi, which is in the bedroom of the said Master Lorenzo, and with a similar work intarsia and marquetry, the difference being that the cornice is without brackets and does not turn like that one, but it is all on one plane. The height is *braccia* (. . .) [gaps in the text], the length *braccia* (. . .), and the bed is *braccia* (. . .) in height, *braccia* (. . .) in length, *braccia* (. . .) in width, according to the agreed measurements.

All this work must be made well and finished, made in the right way according to the judgement of a honest and intelligent man, knowledgeable about art. It has to be delivered at the end of the next month of May, completely finished in the best possible way, to the house and bedroom of the said Vincenzo. This should be done by the said Niccolò, to whom Vincenzo promises to give for the bed and day-bed twenty-three large gold florins in gold.

4. Isabella d'Este commissions a bed, 1502

Letters exchanged from April 1502 to February 1504 between Isabella d'Este and her agent in Venice, the instrument-maker and musician Lorenzo da Pavia, document the various stages in the commission of a bed. Isabella knew what she wanted, but she was also ready to listen to and follow expert advice. A number of drawings and various sets of measurements were sent back and forth from Mantua to Venice. The bed was finally finished at the beginning of January 1504, and was sent to Mantua by boat. We do not have Isabella's letter with her final comments, but she must have been satisfied, as Lorenzo da Pavia wrote to her in February: 'I have been very pleased that Your Ladyship liked the bed . . .'

C. M. Brown, *Isabella d'Este and Lorenzo da Pavia: Documents for the History of Art and Culture in Renaissance Mantua* (Geneva, 1982), pp. 65–6.

Lorenzo da Pavia, from Venice, to Isabella d'Este, 22 May 1502
Most Illustrious Lady, I enclose with this letter a small drawing of the bed for Your Ladyship. First of all I would like to let you know how much it will cost, as it is my concern that the bed should be made with all possible care by the best master in Venice.

First of all, the columns cannot be worked in stucco, as the result will not be good. They, and everything else, need to be carved. The columns are very high: perhaps your measurement is wrong. The master says that the price will be less than 20 ducats for the wood. It will be gilded and painted with a good-quality blue for 15 ducats. The head and footboards will be decorated with some stories painted in gold powder, and that will look lovely since there is somebody here who will do a good job for 12 ducats. There are masters here who have asked much more than that. They are friends of mine, and I shall do what I like, but Your Ladyship may be assured that it will be beautiful, especially when placed in the *camerino*, it will be outstandingly beautiful. I am sure when it is finished you will be very pleased with it, and the money will have been well spent to your advantage.

Isabella d'Este to Lorenzo da Pavia, 10 June 1502
Lorenzo, we are sending back to you the drawing of the bed [*carriola*], which I like, so that it can be finished. We enclose a paper with the measurements. Having shown it [the drawing] here to some who are experts, they say that it should cost no more than forty ducats. So do what we hope you should do, both about its price and its beauty.

ASSORTED FURNITURE

These texts document examples of other pieces of furniture found in women's (and men's) bedrooms, rather than the larger tables, cabinets or sideboards found in the more public rooms of the house. The most common of these were containers of various types. Chests (*cassoni, casse* or *forzieri*, known also by other names in various parts of Italy) were often commissioned for brides, either by their fathers or by husbands and their family. They could be decorated with painted *istorie*, or worked in relief with gesso and then gilded (*a pastiglia*). From the end of the fifteenth century, chests *a sarcofago*, with *all'antica* sculpted decoration and lion's feet, became fashionable. As we know from inventories, chests were used to store clothes, bedclothing, hangings or all kinds of small objects. They could also be used as seats, especially when placed around the bed.[5] Small boxes and caskets (*cassette*) could be simply decorated, painted or worked *a pastiglia*, or they could be much more ornate, such as the one commissioned by Vittoria Colonna and described in the letter included here. Various new types of chairs developed, some of them becoming much more comfortable thanks to the use of leather or soft fabrics. Mirrors were elaborately worked, often forming part of a toilet set with shelves, hooks and other containers.[6]

5. Gilded *cassoni* for Barbara of Brandenburg, 1462

The painter Marco Zoppo writes to the Marchioness of Mantua, Barbara of Brandenburg (wife of Ludovico II Gonzaga), explaining why he cannot accept a commission from her.

W. Braghirolli, *Lettere inedite di artisti del secolo XV cavate dall'archivio Gonzaga* (Mantua, 1878), pp. 9–10.

Marco Zoppo, from Bologna, 16 September 1462
The reason for this letter is to let Your Ladyship know that today I have received a letter from you, with one from Master Giovanni da Lucca. I understand that Your Ladyship would like me to come and make two pairs of chests. I am letting Your Ladyship know that I would be very happy to come, but according to what the bearer [of the letter] told me, the chests should be made by Christmas. This is not possible, because to do a good job there would hardly be enough time to gild them, as winter is coming. And I too would like to gain credit for that work, because I would come [to Mantua] to show that I am able to make something good not so much for gain, as for the honour and affection for the master of His Lordship [Andrea Mantegna, the Gonzaga court painter]. Making works which could be compared to his would be enough for me, but this is not possible in such a short time, also because I am making a pair of chests here for a lady of this city. They have been gilded and now have to be painted. If Your Ladyship can wait till these are finished, I shall serve you with great pleasure, and, if you like, I shall also come to discuss an agreement with Ladyship.

6. Eleonora of Aragon commissions chairs from Milan, 1492

The Este accounts allow us to follow the commissions of Eleonora of Aragon from 1474 onwards. She provided her apartments with many pieces of furniture and ornaments, among which tables, carved screens, chairs of various sizes and shapes, painted and carved chests, and painted boxes. All these objects have to be seen in the context of the work commissioned throughout her life in Ferrara for the refashioning and the decoration of her apartments in Castel Vecchio. Here Bernardino Prosperi, the Gonzaga ambassador in Milan, reports to Girolamo Gilioli, Master Chamberlain responsible for the *guardaroba*.

F. Malaguzzi Valeri, *La corte di Ludovico il Moro*, 4 vols (Milan, 1913–23), 1, p. 83.

Bernardino Prosperi from Milan, to Girolamo Gilioli, 5 June 1492
There are no ready-made chairs. I have spoken about this to a master who also works for the Court and has made chairs for our Duchess [Isabella of Aragon], but they are elegant and covered in silk. There are some low chairs for women, covered in leather, but they have silk fringes and the backs are painted and gilded. He asks six Imperial and five small *lire* for the large folding [chairs], made in the way you indicate, all in leather with leather fringes, with many bosses, and made with good wood, with well-made joints. The other women's chairs, similar to those used in the palace, square and covered in leather, cost fifty Imperial *soldi*, but with a valance all round, also in leather, he wants three *lire*. They also make similar ones, not with wooden backs but made of leather, which is comfortable for the back. They also make folding chairs, and ask three *lire* also for these. Do let me know at once what you want me to do, both about the price and the type which the Lady [Eleonora] prefers, so that I can commission them.

7. A *cassetta portaprofumo* for Vittoria Colonna, c.1525–33
Vittoria Colonna (c.1490–1547) writes from Ischia to her friend and relative, the *letterato* Bernardino Rota, asking him to commission for her a very ornate casket.

I. Di Majo, 'Vittoria Colonna, il Castello di Ischia e la cultura delle corti', in P. Ragionieri (ed.), *Vittoria Colonna e Michelangelo* (Florence, 2005), pp. 27–8.

Most Magnificent Lord, I am giving you much trouble, but I shall repay you as I can: I still owe you some perfumes, which I shall send to you. I would like a casket of the same size as the other three, to be made for me as soon as possible.

It should be made in the shape of the Colosseum, with brilliant white colonnades. The columns, capitals and everything should be gilded where possible, but this should be done quickly enough to be ready on Monday or Tuesday, since Vittez is going to Vico. Nobody in the world must know about this. Don't ask me any more, but do this very quickly. It should be filled with medicinal perfumes, but they should be highly refined. The vials inside should be very small. Because I am in a great hurry, perhaps they can be found already made. I leave this all to you, as long as it is very beautiful. I would like to spend thirty *scudi*. See what the Marquess and other knowledgeable men think. And since Messer Tommaso Cambi[7] gave 15 or 20 *scudi* from the Marchioness of Vasto [Maria of Aragon] to this master for a casket in the form of a labyrinth, which was not made, the lady will agree that the money should be used for my own casket. I shall explain this to Her Ladyship and send the rest of the money together with yours. Do let me know at once, so I can deal with this as soon as possible, that is by Thursday. Please, do let me know immediately, and indicate that you are in a great hurry. And if you think that it could be fashioned as a temple, then do it, as long as it is decorated and with beautiful columns, and the remainder finished as you and my Epicuro [the humanist Marcantonio Epicuro, Bernardino's tutor] please. Without repeating myself, get [him] to work day and night, but not during feast days. I remain at your command, and I trust you. Do let me know whether I should send the rest of the money, and I shall send it immediately.

8. A cabinet decorated with *pietre dure*, 1620s

The Grand Duchess of Tuscany, Maria Maddalena of Austria (1589–1631), enlarged and embellished a villa on a hill just outside the Florence city walls, calling it 'Poggio Imperiale' to stress her own rank. The 1625–29 inventory, from which this extract is taken, lists the impressive furnishings and works of art which she collected there. The ornate cabinet described here was in her bedchamber. It is a perfect example of the later Renaissance fashion for ebony furniture with architectural elements such as small columns and pediments, decorated with gilded silver or bronze, and enriched by the very expensive *commessi di pietre dure* – intarsia panels of semi-precious stones. This was a much prized technique developed in Florence at the end of the sixteenth century.[8]

P. Barocchi and G. Gaeta Bertelà (eds), *Collezionismo mediceo e storia artistica. II. Il cardinale Carlo, Maria Maddalena, Don Lorenzo, Ferdinando II, Vittoria della Rovere, 1621–1666*, 3 vols (Florence, 2005), 2:1, pp. 279–80.

An ebony cabinet in the shape of a tabernacle, with its front supported by two balls and two small vases, with a base shaped like a step, with three small landscapes [in *pietre dure*], and above a surface with panels in speckled wood, with four finials in the shape of masks and two small scrolls in the shape of snails which we think are made of gilded silver, with panels of various kinds of stones. Above, at the front [there are] two pictures and a half oval, with landscapes of *commessi di pietre*, and similar small pictures at the sides, with columns in the middle flanking an oval of mottled aquamarine and pilasters of a similar stone, with small bases and capitals which we think are made of gilded silver. Above the oval is an ebony pediment and above it are two figures representing two Virtues, Faith and Hope, which we think are of gilded silver. Above is a panel in semi-precious stones, and above it a balustrade with four pomegranates, which we think are of gilded silver. Above there is a decoration in the shape of a tabernacle, with panels of semi-precious stones, and above it are four small agate vases with their handles, and flowers which we think are of gilded silver. Above, in the middle, is a large agate vase, similar in shape, with a bunch of flowers which we also think [is of gilded silver].

HANGINGS AND TAPESTRIES

Rooms were given richness, colour and texture by many types of hangings in tapestry, leather and several kinds of patterned or embroidered cloth. Though they were functional, as they served to insulate rooms, they were beautiful objects and a demonstration of prestige.

The importance of tapestries, the most costly of these hangings, in the eyes of contemporary observers is obvious, since they figure very prominently in written descriptions and letters. Together with other types of wall and bed hangings, tapestries were often given to aristocratic brides as part of their dowry. When Eleonora of Aragon arrived in Ferrara in 1473, she brought with her from Naples tapestries woven with gold and silver threads. Among these were the 'five gold and silk curtains, originally commissioned by Alfonso King of Naples [Eleonora's father], to the value of 150,000 ducats, together with other *spalliere* and fine tapestries' mentioned in Zambotti's *Diario ferrarese* as part of the decoration of the Sala Grande of Castel Vecchio.[9] Often showing the coat of arms of the bride's birth family, tapestries would signal the dynastic alliances achieved through marriage. They would have important familiar connotations, charged with emotional meaning for the young women who had left their surroundings to live in a new environment.

9. Lucrezia Borgia and her tapestries, 1502–3
It took 150 mules to carry the clothes, jewels, silverware and precious textiles, including a large number of tapestries and bed furnishings, when the daughter of Pope Alexander VI, Lucrezia Borgia, travelled from Rome to Ferrara as the bride of Alfonso d'Este. The Gonzaga agent in Rome valued all these objects at approximately 300,000 gold ducats, and her tapestries would have been among the most expensive items.[10] The following is an extract from Lucrezia's *Inventario della guardaroba*, 1502–3. The subjects of the tapestries listed here were either from the Old Testament, or from the life of the Virgin. Lucrezia also owned some *arazzi da letto*, tapestries woven in such shapes and sizes for use as canopies, bed hangings or bed covers.

G. Campori, 'L'arazzeria estense', *Atti e Memorie delle Reali Deputazioni di Storia Patria per le Provincie Modenesi e Parmensi*, 1:8 (1876), p. 467: repr. as facsimile monograph (Sala Bolognese, 1980).

1. One tapestry with figures, with the story of the Judgement [of Solomon], 9 *braccia* high and 6 ½ wide
2. One tapestry with the same story, of the same height and width

3. One tapestry with the figures of King David and Uriah, 5 *braccia* high and 4 wide

4. One tapestry with the figures of King Salem [Melchisedech] and Abraham, 6⅓

5. One large tapestry with figures, with the story of the Virgin, 13½ *braccia* high and 6⅛ wide

6. One large tapestry with figures, with the same story, 10⅓ *braccia* high and 6 wide

7. One tapestry with figures with the said story, 10¼ *braccia* high and 6 wide

8. One tapestry with the said story, 10¾ *braccia* high and 6 wide

9. One tapestry with the figures of Saul and Jonathan, 16 *braccia* high and 5½ wide

10. One set of bed hangings with figures, with the story of Merades, that is two curtains and a parament above the bed with swags, all with the said story, and a canopy

11. One *portiera* with figures, with the story of the Great Judge [Solomon], 4½ *braccia* high and 3½ wide

12. One *portiera* with figures, similar to the story of the Great Judge, 4 *braccia* high and 3 wide

13. One Tapestry with the story of the Conception of Our Lady, 10 *braccia* long and 5 wide

14. One tapestry coverlet with the story of Abraham and the Pharaoh, 7 *braccia* in length and 6 in height

15. One *portiera* of fine red wool embroidered with the Borgia arms.

10. Silvia Piccolomini and her hangings, Siena, 1566

A direct descendant of Enea Silvio Piccolomini (Pope Pius II), Silvia was a learned woman, well known for her poems. On her marriage to the fourth duke of Amalfi she brought with her a very large dowry, estates and palaces, and a large collection of art objects and books. In her will she bequeathed to her daughter Constanza all her possessions, among which were also various tapestries and leather hangings.

E. Novi Chavarria, *Sacro, pubblico e privato. Donne nei secoli XV–XVIII* (Naples, 2009), pp. 218–19.

. . . Twenty tapestries, used, with foliage, plants and birds, 13 hands high, which are in three wood chests made for storing tapestries

Leather hangings, 9 hands high, of a reddish-brown colour (*leonato*), with friezes and pilaster strips of blue leather and gold, with some Latin words, eight pieces in all of the same format, and for each of the corners, upper pieces in the Moorish and Turkish fashion, four pieces each.

Four other leather hangings to be used in the same way, tooled in gold and silver, with different [types of] foliage, about 11 hands high. Two are made of five pieces, one of six and the other of four.

Eight leather hangings, used, of reddish-brown colour, worked in gold with friezes and pilaster strips, 9 hands high, five are made of five pieces, one of seven, one of three and the other of two.

Another hanging of reddish-brown colour in four pieces, without pilaster friezes, but with a frame worked in gold all around.

Two other leather hangings worked in gold and silver, similar to those mentioned above, one in five pieces, the other in four.

Four other pieces of leather, used, 9 hands high, in reddish-brown leather tooled in silver with a frame around, one in six pieces and the others in four. These pieces of leather are all inside two wooden chests made for storing such items.

GLASSWARE, CERAMICS AND SILVERWARE

By the end of the fifteenth century drinking vessels, vases of various shapes and sizes, and bowls and plates made of Venetian glass were becoming increasingly fashionable.[11] This was partly because of the special skill of Venetian artisans, who could manufacture glass of extreme lightness and colourless transparency which imitated the much more expensive rock crystal. Glass objects connoted refinement and luxury because of the glass-makers' skill and because of their intrinsic beauty. Furthermore, they also required elegance of gesture, grace and dexterity by those who used them at the dinner table.

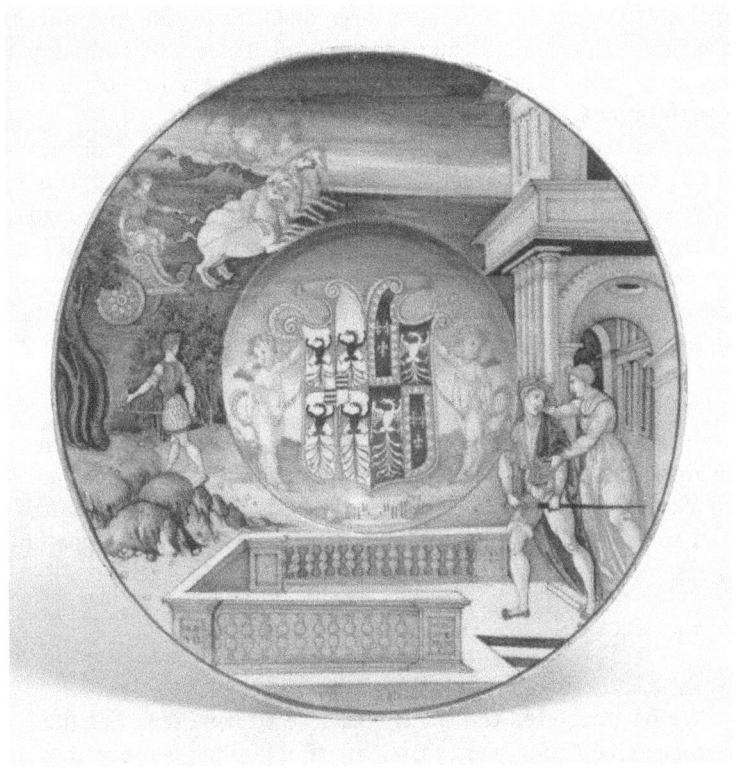

7. Nicola da Urbino, tin-glazed earthenware (majolica) dish, with scene from the story of Hippolyta and Phaedra, c. 1524 (London, Victoria and Albert Museum).

Ceramic plates, jugs, vases and basins were, with some notable exceptions, relatively inexpensive household objects. They were used at the dining table, but could also be luxury objects for display.[12] Ceramics, both colourful historiated pieces (**figure 7**) or fashionable 'white on white' ware, were appreciated for the skills of the ceramist and painter. They too connoted elegance and refinement of manners at the dining table: foreign visitors to Italian courts remarked on the custom of eating from ceramic plates, while north of the Alps pewter plates were still the norm.[13] Women played an important role in the promotion of ceramic workshops, commissioning whole services from artisans and artists in various parts of Italy. Isabella d'Este bought large quantities made in Mantua, Ferrara and Urbino, while Eleonora di Toledo commissioned ceramics from Venice, but also bought the very expensive and sought-after Chinese porcelain.[14]

Silverware was much more expensive than majolica or glassware, and therefore a signifier of wealth and *splendore*.[15] This is why stepped sideboards (*credenze*), loaded with silver and gold vases, ewers, basins and plates, were one of the highlights of displays prepared for guests. They are always described in the *sale* decorated for receptions and banquets, and are often represented in paintings and prints showing these events.

11. Glassware for Isabella d'Este

Isabella's knowledge of what glass-making masters could achieve is evident in the many letters she wrote during the years to her agents in Venice, describing in detail the kinds of glassware she wanted. Her pleasure in planning and her attention to detail are apparent in the following letters.

i. Brown (1982), pp. 119–20, 214.

Isabella d'Este to Giorgio Brognolo, April 1496
We have received the twenty glasses you have sent. We like their height, but their shape has no elegance because they are as large at the bottom as they are at the top. Therefore we want you to get twenty more made, of the same size, but tapering towards the bottom, and at the top no larger than the first ones. They should be without a lip, like those. Ten of them must be made with gold around the rim, that is, from the gold upwards there should be no clear glass showing. The gold rim should not be wider than it is in the other ones. The remaining ten must be made unadorned, without gold. Make sure that the glass is clear and beautiful and that they are elegant.

Isabella d'Este from Mantua, to Lorenzo da Pavia in Venice, 1 July 1510
Master Lorenzo, the other day we wrote that we wished you to commission about six vases of different shapes for drinking water . . . in whatever style you like, but as beautiful as possible, because those who do not drink wine seek this fash-

ion and novelty. Perhaps you have not received our letter, and therefore I am writing again. When these vases are finished, please send them with a note of the price.

ii. D. Bini, 'Isabella d'Este e la cultura del cibo', in D. Bini (ed.), *Isabella d'Este la primadonna del Rinascimento* (Modena, 2001), p. 231.

Isabella d'Este to Jacopo Malatesta, Gonzaga agent in Venice, 2 May 1529

. . . I know that in the glass-masters' shops for this Ascension Day there will be some fine new vases, please find for me about ten or twelve drinking vessels of various shapes: cups and glasses, with pure white filaments, without gilding.

12. A ceramic service from Montelupo, 1518

In 1518, Clarice de' Medici Strozzi commissioned a ceramic service from Lorenzo di Piero di Lorenzo, a well-known artisan from Montelupo, a well-established Tuscan centre for the production of ceramics. The set was decorated *alla porcellana*, a blue pattern on white background imitating the very expensive Chinese porcelain. The prices are indicated in *lire* and *soldi*.

M. Spallanzani, 'Un "fornimento" di maioliche di Montelupo per Clarice Strozzi de' Medici', *Faenza*, 70 (1984), p. 381.

Recorded [expenses for] household items, thirty-six *lire* and eleven *soldi* in cash, paid to Lorenzo di Piero di Lorenzo, potter in Montelupo. They are for a ceramic service *alla porcellana* for [the villa] Le Selve, commissioned by the Lady Clarice for the house, listed below:

11 plates, large, at 20 *soldi* each, as agreed	lb 11
12 plates, medium size, at 4 *soldi* each	lb 4/4
25 plates, medium size, at 7 *soldi* each	lb 8/15
16 soup bowls, large, at 7 *soldi* each	lb 5/12
16 small bowls, all for 3 lb	lb 3
4 large jugs, at 20 *soldi* each	lb 4
Total, as agreed	lb 36/11
Paid for the transport to Mariotto di Spigliato, cart driver, from Montelupo to the Selve	lb 0/14

13. Historiated ceramics from Eleonora Gonzaga, 1524
Eleonora Gonzaga shows herself to be aware of issues of decorum and conventions dictating what was suitable in different settings and circumstances when she refers to the decoration of the ceramic service commissioned for her mother (see **figure 7**), which was suitable for the less formal gatherings at Isabella's villa at Porto Mantovano. The use of the word *credenza* to mean not the article of furniture, but the tableware it was designed to display, should be noted.

M. Palvarini Gobio Casali, *La ceramica a Mantova* (Ferrara, 1987), pp. 211–12, n.29.

Eleonora Gonzaga, from Urbino, to Isabella d'Este, 15 November 1524
As I am thinking of visiting Your Excellency with something typical of these parts which you would like, and not finding anything which would suit, I have commissioned a ceramic service (*credenza*). I am sending it to Your Excellency through my steward Battista, the bearer of this letter. The masters in this area are renowned for their work, and I shall be very glad if Your Excellency likes it and will use it at [the villa of] Porto, since it is suitable for a villa. I hope you will accept it with the good will with which I am sending it.

14. Silverware: an asset in times of financial difficulties, 1516
Silverware and gold vessels were valued not only for their craftsmanship, but also for the intrinsic value of the metal. The large quantities of silverware which were part of aristocratic women's dowries, or which were commissioned by them after their wedding, could be used to supply cash in difficult times. In 1516, Elisabetta Gonzaga and her daughter-in-law Eleonora had to escape from Urbino and seek refuge in Mantua. Being short of money, they decided to part with their silverware.

A. Bertolotti, 'Le arti minori alla corte di Mantova', *Archivio Storico Lombardo*, vol. 5, anno ser. 2, 15 (1888), p. 495.

Benedetto Capilupi from Mantua, to Isabella d'Este, 7 July 1516

My Ladies the Duchesses of Urbino told me the other day
that they needed to break up some of their silverware,
among which two basins with two bronze handles. They
are very beautiful, in the antique manner, and designed
by Raphael. They are oblong, gilded, and I think Your
Excellency would like them. They told me that if Your
Ladyship could give them money or silver objects to melt
down, they would rather give them to you than destroy such
wonderful pieces. They also have other pieces and vases
which I could not see because the man in charge of the keys
was not there. If Your Ladyship would like to take some
of these silver objects, you could let me know, and I shall
arrange to obtain and send them, so that you can see if there
is anything you like.

15. A silver salt cellar for Isabella d'Este, 1525

As in the Middle Ages, in the Renaissance salt cellars were large
and ornate objects used as centre-pieces for the dining table.
Here Francesco Gonzaga writes to his cousin Federico about
a commission from Isabella d'Este. Giulio Romano eventually agreed to be paid 20 ducats for the manufacture. The salt
cellar was sent to Mantua in March 1526, and was very much
appreciated.[16]

A. Bertolotti, *Le arti minori alla corte di Mantova nei secoli
XV, XVI, XVII* (Milan, 1889), p. 69.

Francesco Gonzaga from Rome, to Federico Gonzaga,
November 1525

Today I showed the drawing of the salt cellar for Her
Ladyship, in order to find out the cost and the time it would
take. Master Giulio Romano, the painter, says that it will
take at least three pounds of silver, which will cost about
25 ducats, and it will take more than six gold ducats, and
he asks 30 ducats for the workmanship, even if I think he
would agree to 25. He will not take more than two months to
make it.

16. Benvenuto Cellini and a gold vase for Eleonora di Toledo, 1545

Benvenuto Cellini *La Vita*, ed. G. Davico Bonino (Turin, 1973), p. 393.

During this time I had some kidney trouble, and because I could not work I gladly spent the time in the Duke's [Cosimo I de' Medici] *guardaroba* in the company of some young goldsmiths, Gianpaolo and Domenico Poggini. I asked them to make a small gold vase, all worked in relief with figures and other fine decorations. This was for the Duchess, and Her Excellency had commissioned it to drink water from. She also asked me to make her a gold belt, and this work also was very richly decorated, with precious stones and with some delightful *invenzioni*, such as small masks and other things.

BOOKS

The examples in this section deal with aristocratic ladies' devotional books as works of art. These were made precious by illuminations and gilding, and by bindings and covers in silk or velvet, often adorned with silver clasps.

17. An illuminated Book of Hours for Cecilia Gonzaga

Franceschini (1993), p. 738.

10 June 1469

Today, 10 June, Master Guglielmo, the illuminator, is due eight florins in gold for his illumination for a small Book of Hours of Our Lady which the most illustrious Duke our lord [Ludovico III Gonzaga, Cecilia's uncle] has commissioned for the Lady Cecilia Gonzaga, daughter of the late Lord Messer Carlo. The illumination consists of four initial letters worked with figures, animals and foliage all round, and eight capital letters for the seven beatitudes and charity, worked in gold and with the brush; fifteen letters decorated with foliage which are at the beginning of the Hours, and two hundred and ten letters with leafy scrolls at the beginnings of the psalms and of the prayers, and a thousand three hundred and thirteen small letters in gold and blue. [He is also due payment] for the binding of this Book of Hours. It was bound with left-over boards, and sewn together with silk. For all this, as by agreement, 8 florins. The said book was covered with crimson cloth of gold from the *guardaroba Lire* 22/4

18. A precious binding for Eleonora Gonzaga

G. Gronau, *Documenti artistici urbinati* (Florence, 1936), p. 267.

Francesco Maria della Rovere, from Pesaro, to his ambassador in Venice, Giangiacomo Leonardi, 10 November 1530
The Duchess, our wife, commissioned the writing of a beautiful Book of Hours, and she would like to have it bound accordingly. The binding must be done with boards, covered in black velvet and finely decorated with lapis lazuli [panels] set in gold. The lapis lazuli should be carved with figures of saints in relief, or arranged harmoniously in a group. The covers must be of the same size as the enclosed paper.
   You will have with you Valerio da Vicenza [Valerio Belli], a master in his craft. After you have discussed this matter with him, you will ask him to make a drawing of such a cover, according to his imagination. You will send us the drawing as soon as possible, so that we can send it back with our requests. Then he can begin to make it, now that we have decided to commission this work from him. If it seems better and faster, I would add that that he could make relief figures in gold and set them in the lapis lazuli, without having to carve the figures into the stone.

GIFTS

This final section groups together texts dealing with objects given as gifts, where the personal relationship may be more important than the actual value of the objects.

19. Wedding jewellery for the bride of a slave

In some households, servants and slaves were considered part of the family. Francesco Datini, the 'Merchant of Prato',[17] and his wife Margherita Bandini paid all the expenses for the wedding of one of their slaves, and gave gifts to his wife-to-be. Probably respecting sumptuary laws, none of the gifts were of high value, as Francesco explains in his letter to Margherita.

Le lettere di Francesco Datini alla moglie Margherita (1385–1410), ed. E. Cecchi (Prato, 1990), p. 246.

Rosso is bringing you a garland, which costs 22 *soldi piccoli*, two rings which together cost 30 *soldi piccoli*, and two larger rings, which are in fact of a smaller size, both costing *soldi* 40. The price is written on each of them. Take the ones you want and send the others back to me. I also sent you two imitation brass belts: each costs three *lire* and sixteen *soldi piccoli*. I am not sending you any silver ones, as it is impossible to find one for less than about three gold florins. So, the slave should choose what he wants. Send me back the others with Argomento.

20. A secret love gift for a lady, 1505

Pietro Bembo sends an Agnusdei (a wax or metal roundel, with the image of the Lamb of God) to Lucrezia Borgia as a love token – a provocatively erotic function for a religious image.

Pietro Bembo, *Lettere*, ed. E. Travi, 4 vols (Bologna, 1987–93), 1, p. 141.

Venice, 10 February 150[5]
... Now I kiss that sweet hand of yours which clasps my heart tight. Beside that, if you allow me to be so bold, I kiss one of those most beautiful and bright and sweet eyes of yours which have wounded my soul: the first and lovely reason, and yet not the only one, of my ardour. I shall not fear fortune's blows, nor any harm it may do to me, if I know that I am in your thoughts and in your love. I want no other happiness in this life but you, the harbour and sweetest repose of my troubled ship. If you cannot wear by day the enclosed Agnusdei, which I once wore on my breast, I pray you to wear it sometimes at night, so that the dear refuge of your precious heart could at least be touched by that circle, which touched for so long the shelter of my own. Your heart. If I could kiss it only once, I would trade my life for it. Keep well.

21. Childbirth gifts: a drawing by Francesco Salviati for a *desco da parto*

Deschi da parto were round tray-like wooden objects painted almost always on both sides, given to women after childbirth, or also as wedding presents. They were decorated with a great variety of subjects, often apotropaic.[18]

> Giorgio Vasari, *Le Vite* [Florence, 1568], ed. G. Milanesi, 8 vols (Florence, 1906), 7, pp. 20–1.

As Francesco [Salviati] had made friends with the Florentine goldsmith Piero di Marcone, and as he had become his close friend, he gave as a gift for his wife, after she had given birth, a very beautiful drawing for a painting [to be done] on one of those circular trays which are used to carry food to women after childbirth. In this drawing there was a square, and arranged above and below was the life of man, that is, all the stages of human life, with very fine figures. These were reclining over swags appropriate to the age and the season. In the square there were, in two long ovals, the figures of the Sun and of the Moon, and in the middle was Isais, a city in Egypt [*sic*], asking for wisdom in front of the temple of the goddess Pallas. This means that one should pray for wisdom and goodness for newborn children more than for anything else.

22. A spurned lover's gifts for a courtesan

Much of the satirical and moralising writing against courtesans and prostitutes in the early modern period stress the voracious appetite for acquiring the most expensive or unusual luxury goods becoming available at the time. This extract from a letter by the Venetian *poligrafo* Andrea Calmo to one of his mistresses is a light example of this genre.

> Andrea Calmo, *Delle lettere di M. Andrea Calmo* (Venice, 1572), Book 4, 26r–27v.

Dear Madam Brunella
Lady, full of traps, tricks and snares, . . . now that I have spent and squandered money, and almost thrown away my

mind, not mentioning how I have suffered, you have left me, banished me, and declared me your enemy. We shall see if your new lover lets himself be worn to the bone and runs to do your bidding like a servant, as I have done . . . And with all this, I have been kicked out and never looked at again. I won't mention the *spalliere*, the carpets, the damask bed hangings, the gilded bed, the painted chests, the guinea-pigs from Brescia, and the pewter kitchen vessels, nor the clothes: they are nothing. The pearls are nothing, and the rings trifles. And to cap it all, you castrated my purse every night I slept with Your Excellency.

Notes

1 G. Pontano, *I libri delle virtù sociali* [1498], ed. F. Tateo (Rome, 1999). On Pontano, see J. Lindow, 'Splendour', in Ajmar-Wollheim and Dennis (eds) (2006), pp. 306–7; P. Fortini Brown, *Private Lives in Renaissance Venice: Art, Architecture and the Family* (New Haven and London, 2004), esp. pp. 91–121 for a Venetian context, with references to sixteenth-century treatises.

2 See M. Rogers, 'An ideal wife at the Villa Maser: Veronese, the Barbaros and Renaissance theorists of marriage', *Renaissance Studies*, 7:4 (1993), pp. 379–97.

3 See C. Fahy, 'Love and marriage in the *Institutione* of Alessandro Piccolomini', in C. P. Brand, K. Foster and U. Limentani (eds), *Italian Studies Presented to E. R. Vincent* (Cambridge, 1962), pp. 121–35.

4 For different types of beds and hangings, see P. Thornton, *Italian Renaissance Interiors 1400–1600* (London, 1991), pp. 111–46. On designs for *lettiere*, see H. Burns, 'Letti visibili e invisibili nei progetti architettonici del Rinascimento', in A. Scotti Tosini (ed.), *Aspetti dell'abitare in Italia tra XV e XVI secolo: distribuzione, funzioni, impianti* (Milan, 2000), pp. 131–41. In the same volume, P. Kehl, 'Letti smontabili e letti fissi nelle dimore principesche estensi o, per dirlo meglio nella mia lingua: wie man sich bettet, so liegt man', pp. 155–67. On painted headboards, see A. Braham, 'The bed of Pierfrancesco Borgherini', *Burlington Magazine*, 121 (1979), pp. 754–65.

5 See P. Thornton, '*Cassoni, Forzieri, Goffani* and *Cassette*: terminology and its problems', *Apollo*, 120:272 (1984), pp. 246–51. See also: C. Paolini, D. Parenti and L. Sebregondi (eds), *Virtù d'amore: pittura nuziale nel Quattrocento fiorentino* (Florence, 2010), with bibliography; C. Paolini, in Ajmar-Wollheim and Dennis (eds) (2006),

pp. 120–1; C. Baskins, A. Chong, J. M. Musacchio and A. W. B. Randolph (eds), *The Triumph of Marriage: Painted Cassoni of the Renaissance* (Pittsburgh, 2008); C. Campbell, *Love and Marriage in Renaissance Florence: The Courtauld Wedding Chests* (London, 2009).

6 P. Thornton, 'The restello, what was it?', *Furniture History*, 26 (1990), pp. 174–82.

7 A Florentine banker who lived in Naples and promoted Tuscan artists.

8 See A. M. Giusti, *'Pietre Dure' Hardstones in Furniture and Decoration* (London, 1992).

9 See M. Rogers and P. Tinagli, *Women in Italy, 1350–1650. Ideals and Realities. A Sourcebook* (Manchester, 2005), pp. 124–6.

10 See N. Forti Grazzini, *L'arazzo ferrarese* (Milan, 1982), p. 55.

11 See P. Hills, 'Venetian glass and Renaissance self-fashioning', in F. Ames-Lewis and M. Rogers (eds), *Concepts of Beauty in Renaissance Art* (Aldershot, 1998), pp. 163–77, and Fortini Brown (2004), pp. 144–8.

12 See R. A. Goldthwaite, 'The economic and social world of Italian Renaissance maiolica', *Renaissance Quarterly*, 42:1 (1989), pp. 1–32, 23–7.

13 See C. Benporat, *Cucina e convivialità italiana del Cinquecento* (Florence, 2007), pp. 63–101.

14 See M. Spallanzani, *Ceramiche orientali a Firenze nel Rinascimento* (Florence, 1978), and *Ceramiche alla corte dei Medici nel Cinquecento* (Modena, 1994).

15 For price comparisons, see Spallanzani (1978), pp. 131, 186.

16 Giulio Romano designed vessels and jewellery for Isabella d'Este. For his silverware designs, see F. Hartt, *Giulio Romano*, 2 vols (New Haven, 1958), 2, plates 130–147. Major artists like Giulio, Raphael and Cellini designed silver objects for the table, but ceramists and glass-makers used their own painters, or copied prints from major artists.

17 I. Origo, *The Merchant of Prato* ([1957], Harmondsworth, 1963).

18 See Musacchio (1999), pp. 70–1.

❧ 3 ❧

CLOTHES: LEGISLATION, DESCRIPTIONS AND USES

In early modern Italy, descriptions of clothes in letters and chronicles, as well as in printed treatises and pamphlets, were even more numerous than those of furnishings, of which we have seen some examples. Women could signal their identity, social status and taste through their clothes and personal ornaments, expressing the much-sought virtues of elegance, harmony and grace through movements and gestures.[1] Both commentators and legislators were well aware that clothes defined women's (and men's) social rank, and treatises recognised the powerful signals of clothing, advising women of different ages and rank to dress appropriately.[2] Churchmen, humanists, *letterati* and legislators, however, complained about women's vanity and tried to curb the ostentation of fashions which they censored as frivolous or dangerous for feminine virtue. It was important to be able to tell honest women from prostitutes who were meant to wear clothes appropriate to their trade, but very often did not.

The enormously costly clothes worn by the elite, with their bright colours obtained only from expensive dyes, would offer a vivid spectacle compared with the grey-browns of the lower ranks. Even simple clothes were expensive, and most people, at times even women from the banking and mercantile elite, would have worn used clothes, turned inside out or refashioned. People of lower ranks bought their clothes at second- or third-hand, or worn those bequeathed to them by friends or employers.

SUMPTUARY LAWS

As well as trying to curb expenditure on fabrics, clothes and jewellery, sumptuary laws were concerned with differentiating social ranks by indicating what women and men could wear, the kind of fabrics they could use, and the quantity and quality of ornaments and jewellery.[3] Fines were applied to those who broke the rules. These regulations must have been extremely difficult to enforce, because sumptuary legislation was constantly changed and updated in all Italian cities.[4]

1. Sumptuary laws in Rome: jewellery and clothes for brides, 1471

Marco Antonio Altieri, 'Li Nuptiali', ed. E. Narducci (Rome, 1873), p. xliv.

We decree and command that brides should be allowed to wear a crown according to custom, from the evening when they are promised in marriage to the evening of the consummation of the marriage, and during the ceremony of thanksgiving. This crown must be valued at no more than 40 ducats. The fine will be of twenty-five *talleri*.

2. Artisans' wives and daughters in Bologna, 1474

L. Frati, *La vita privata di Bologna dal secolo XIII al XVII* (Bologna, 1900), pp. 281–2.

The daughters and wives of master woodworkers, shoemakers, builders, smiths, furriers, tailors, barbers, booksellers, tanners, fishermen, shearers, dyers, embroiderers, and members of similar minor guilds, or those who belong to other inferior guilds not listed here, are allowed to wear one or more pair of sleeves of silk or fine silk or wool fabric in dark reddish brown (*morello*), and not in any other fabric. But they are not allowed to have or wear other garments or bodices in silk of any colour, or garments made of *grana* fabric [a colour from dark crimson to orange], or of any other fabric, or with open sleeves, or embroideries, or fastenings of gold or silver brocade, or pearls, jewels of other types, or anything more than this, but less. They are allowed to wear buckles, thin cords of gold and collars, as long as they are valued at no more than ten ducats, but leaving them with half of the dowries.

3. A novice runs foul of sumptuary law

This text is an example of what could happen when sumptuary laws were not obeyed. Caterina Bellini, a novice in the Florentine convent of Annalena, was arrested while out on a visit because she was wearing too much jewellery instead of the stipulated two rings and one gold necklace. Her jewels were confiscated. The Abbess of Annalena, Clemenza de' Bardi, belonged to an ancient Florentine family, and she used her considerable power, skilfully arguing Caterina's case with the authorities.

G. Calvi, 'Abito, genere, cittadinanza nella Toscana moderna, secoli XVI–XVII', *Quaderni Storici*, 110 (2002), p. 498.

8 September 1639
Yesterday I sent [on a visit] to the Lady Lucrezia one of our maidens who has been accepted as a lay sister. I allowed her to go out as she is going to make her profession in a few days. As she felt she was a bride [of Christ], she dressed as best as she could, and accepted the ring of her marriage, not thinking that she was doing something against the rules. I hear that she was followed by some guards who made her take off her rings with rough words, in contempt of the maiden and this convent. This has caused me much sorrow. I am now turning to Your Lordship, entreating you to allow me to make clear to the Chancellor that this business should be concluded today, and not to wait till tomorrow for his judgement. This maiden is dedicated to God, and [I hope that] he can use some justice, and not follow the rules.

DESCRIPTIONS: AN 'ENCYCLOPAEDIA' OF CLOTHES

4. Cesare Vecellio and women's clothes, 1590

Perhaps the most famous book on clothing was Cesare Vecellio's illustrated *De gli habiti antichi et moderni*, printed in 1590 and republished many times. Vecellio describes the fashions characteristic of various parts of Italy, and the clothes worn by women of all ranks of society.[5]

Cesare Vecellio, *De gli Habiti Antichi et Moderni...* [1598], *La moda nel Rinascimento*, ed. M. F. Rosenthal and A. R. Jones (London, 2008), pp. 87, 92, 405.

Women citizens, or wives of Roman merchants
Roman merchants' wives are dressed sumptuously and magnificently. They wear dresses with a very low bodice, leaving the breasts exposed and adorned with many gold necklaces and pendants. Their overdresses are made of very finely worked damask or brocade, reaching to the ground and decorated with beautiful stripes of gold brocade. Under these they wear taffeta or silk gowns, and cover their arms with sleeves of silk net, with a light gold or silver lining underneath. They wear their hair in ringlets on the forehead, while the rest is dressed under a long veil reaching to the ground.

Peasant women in the Rome area
In the fortified villages around Rome and in all places owned by Roman lords and barons, most women wear dresses of turquoise or green cloth, reaching down to their feet, decorated with a velvet band all round, and with a low-cut bodice leaving the neck uncovered. They decorate the bodice with rather large silver studs. They wear fringed linen aprons, and shoes similar to little boots, tied with laces. On their head they wear a piece of linen hanging down at the back.

Neapolitan maidens
Neapolitan maidens wear their hair dressed beautifully, with various ringlets, and adorned with a string of pearls. They wear fine high ruffs, and gowns of white damask reaching to the ground, with a band of gold brocade at the hem, and open sleeves leaving free their arms which are covered with sleeves of patterned silk. They have a short train and carry fans in their hands. They do not use make-up to make themselves beautiful, and they do not show themselves much. Not only aristocratic women dress like this, but also plebeian women and prostitutes.

WOMEN AND THEIR CLOTHES: ADVICE AND COMMENTS

What women wore provoked all kinds of comments. From admiration to strong criticism, from serious advice to satire, the words of preachers and *letterati* show how important this matter was in the eyes of contemporary society. Women were criticised for fashions considered bizarre or too expensive, but they were also complimented for the same things, since fine clothes were a sign of their social position or, as in the extract from Lucrezia Marinella's book, of the superiority of the female sex.

5. St Bernardino of Siena criticises women's provocative outdoor clothes, 1427

In his lively sermons to women St Bernardino often criticised their ornaments and fashions which he saw as demonstrations of frivolity and lack of dignity. In these extracts from a sermon addressed to Sienese women he makes fun of those who wore overly decorated outer garments, and warns them not to dress like prostitutes.

Bernardino da Siena, *Prediche volgari sul Campo di Siena. 1427*, ed. C. Delcorno, 2 vols (Milan, 1989), 2, pp. 1071–2.

The exterior [appearance] shows what the interior is. From the exterior you can know the interior. I want to say that when a woman wears the clothes of a prostitute, I may not know what she is really like, but from the exterior I can see something dirty. It seems to me that you are a . . . I don't want to say that word, but you understand my meaning. How do you dare to wear that dress, you silly thing? Have you got no sense? . . .

You trail your overdress (*giornea*) among nuns, sisters-in-law and relatives, and every roguish act is reflected in it. Because of this, one can reach certain conclusions. Have you ever thought what the *giornea* looks like? It looks like a horse's cover, with fringes at the sides and at the hem, so that you wear the garment of an animal. From the exterior, one could say that you are an animal. From seeing that you are dressed like an animal, I deduce that inside you are like one . . .

Therefore you, woman, must not look like a prostitute either by what you wear or by the way you walk. You should wear clothes made in a suitable way, so that you are judged to be good and honest. Tell me: if someone told you, while you walk down the street: 'Oh, you look beautiful, just like a whore!', what would you think? I don't think you would like that. Therefore, remove the reason for these words: act so that you do not look like that.

6. Canon Pietro Casola observes Venetian women, 1494

From their hair to their jewels, from their exposed flesh down to their shoes, a curious but mildly disapproving Pietro Casola describes in his travel diary the ways in which Venetian women of different ages show themselves in public. As a Milanese, he is obviously intrigued by the different customs of Venice.

Casola, ed. Paoletti (2001), pp. 100–2.

Almost all their women seemed to me to be very small, because if they weren't, they wouldn't use such high slippers. In fact, I have seen some [slippers], either worn by someone or on sale, which are almost ½ a Milanese *braccio* high, so that some women look like giants, and others are so unsteady that they have to be well supported by their slaves. As to the way they dress their hair, at the front it is so high that at a first glance they look more like men than women. Most of their hair is false. I say this with certainty because I have seen hair sold by yokels in Piazza San Marco, hanging from poles, and I have even enquired about it, pretending that I wanted to buy some, in spite of my long white beard.

To continue on this subject: Venetian women, especially those who are beautiful, try as much as possible to show their chests in public, I mean their breasts and shoulders, and seeing them I was often amazed that their clothes did not fall off. Those who can, and also those who cannot, wear ostentatious clothes and have large jewels and strings of pearls in their hair and around their neck. They wear many rings on their fingers, great balas-rubies, rubies and diamonds. I said 'those who cannot', as I have been told that many rent them.

Their faces and what is on show look very artificial, because they want to look more beautiful. In general, those women who go out and are not young and beautiful, are all covered up and dressed mainly in black right up to their head, especially when they go to church, so that at first I thought they were all widows. Sometimes, on entering a church during a religious ceremony, it seemed to me that they were all nuns of the order of St Benedict. Young women who are not yet married also dress like that. It is impossible to see their face for anything in the world, and they are so covered up that I cannot understand how they can walk. At home, however, young or old, Venetian women take much pleasure in being seen and looked at, and they have no fear of being bitten by flies. They are in no hurry to cover up when a man comes suddenly upon them. I notice that they don't spend much money on kerchiefs to cover their shoulders. Others may like this habit, but I do not: I am a priest, and I did not want to enquire much more into their lives.

7. A *letterato's* view of women's clothes, 1539

In his youth, Alessandro Piccolomini (1508–79) was a member of the *Accademia degli Intronati*, a group of aristocratic Sienese men who wrote and performed humorous and elegantly erotic plays for women of the upper ranks. The first extract, a witty dialogue from his play *La Raffaella*, pokes fun at women who make themselves ridiculous by what they wear and how they behave. The second extract is from his treatise *Della institutione di tutta la vita de l'homo . . .*written later in his life. He explains the way in which women must dress appropriately to their social status, and stresses the important concept of 'proportion'.

i. Alessandro Piccolomini, *La Raffaella, ovvero Dialogo della bella creanza delle donne* [Venice, 1539], ed. G. Alfano (Rome, 2001), pp. 47–9.

RAFFAELLA: I say that splendour in dressing depends very much on carefully seeking out silks, light and thicker wools, or other fabrics of the best possible quality, the best that one can find. Because to use thick fabrics, as for instance the lady Lorenza does, who had a dress made in a material which looks almost monastic, is to be defined as 'miserable fashion'.

MARGARITA: Why do you say 'almost'? It is monastic, utterly monastic!

RAFFAELLA: So much the worse! Besides, dresses must be full and generous, but not so that they are uncomfortable. This is very important, because there is nothing worse than seeing some of our ladies who go around Siena wearing miserable tight dresses made with less than sixteen *braccia* of fabric, with little cloaks that don't reach their arse, and they wrap one bit around the neck, holding another bit in their hand with which they cover half their face, and go around as if they were wearing a mask. With their other hand they pull up their dress behind, so that it doesn't get frayed trailing on the ground, and they go down the street in a hurry, banging their slippers on the ground in such a way that it seems they have got the devil between their legs. Perhaps they keep their dress raised to show their lovely feet, and a little bit of their dashing little legs? In reality, they show ugly wide feet, badly cared for, with some ghastly slippers, old and scuffed. But I shall discuss this later, when we come to it.

MARGARITA: It seems to me that you have described my cousin to a T, even if she told me that she does not walk around like that because she is silly, but because she is elegant.

RAFFAELLA: They all say that, and out of necessity they make a pretence of gracefulness and that they have given thought to what in truth they do either because they are stingy, or poor, or inept.

I think that dresses, ample, as I have said, should be full of bands, slashes, little cuts, embroideries and other such things. In other occasions, however, they should be very simple, because variety in one's clothes demonstrates great magnificence and much that is good.

RAFFAELLA: Above all, Margherita, splendour in dress can be seen by always wearing different garments, and not by keeping the same one on, not just for weeks but even for months on end . . .

I say that it is very bad to wear the same clothes for a long time, but it is even worse when others can see that a dress has been made using the fabric of another, either by dyeing it, or by turning it inside out, or in other ways. This is what the wife of a man who is now in the government did. As a bride, she had a dress made of white damask. After she had worn it for many years, since it was quite filthy, she turned it inside out, and she wore it like that for five years, Sunday in and Sunday out. As it was becoming quite threadbare, she had it dyed in a colour between yellow, red and brown (*giuggiolino, leonato*), whatever we want to call it, because she wanted to show that she had changed her dress, and because it is impossible to tell whether a dress in that colour is threadbare, and also because at her age white was not suitable any more. Now, some years later the dress started to tear, and so she decided to take it apart. She used some of it to make fringes for I don't know which other dress – a purple one. Then she made sleeves out of another bit. These sleeves were soon falling apart, and she covered them with a piece of cut linen, and this is what they are like today. We'll have to see what happens now. I think that before the poor damask is dead and buried, it will have to atone for its sins in one shape or another for a few years more.

ii. Piccolomini, *Della institutione di tutta la vita de l'homo nato nobile e in città libera* (Venice, 1545), Book 10, Chapter 4, 254r–255r.

Having at heart the love of her husband, a woman must hold dear everything pertaining to him. Because of this, she has to consider first of all what can be afforded with his wealth, without endangering or diminishing it at all. She has to seek what is appropriate for the decoration of the rooms in the house, and especially of her chamber, as well as her own clothes and ornaments, according to what can be afforded. It would be very foolish indeed if, without considering their means and being discontented with four dresses of good cloth a year, she were to have eight or ten made. If their income did not allow this, their wealth would be squandered, and the family would lack other necessary things. If a woman is married to a noble gentleman, it would be loathsome and obnoxious if she appeared dressed in a way better suited to a duchess or a queen than to a gentlewoman and wore brocade or cloth of gold, embroidered with pearls or decorated with precious stones and other ornaments inappropriate to her status. In fact, beauty resides in the proportion of all the parts to each other and to the whole, and ugliness is caused by lack of proportion, and disorder of all the parts . . . And what I have said about the adornment of one's person is true also about the adornment of one's house, and particularly of one's own bedchamber, which has to be in proportion to one's wealth and social rank.

8. The farthingale: an uncomfortable contraption, 1583

The farthingale (*guardinfante*) was a contraption used in the late sixteenth century, worn under the skirt to keep it stretched in the shape of a bell. It was made of connected circles of various materials: saplings, strips of wood or iron rods, smaller near the waist and larger towards the hem. The term *guardinfante* refers to the protection that such a cage would provide for the belly of a pregnant woman. This extract from the *Ragionamento di nobili fanciulle genovesi* (1583), a fictitious dialogue between six young women from Genoa on their way back from a religious ceremony, makes fun of this fashionable item of underclothing.

L. T. Belgrano, *Della vita privata dei genovesi* (Genoa, 1875), pp. 169–70.

FIAMMETTA: I still do not like farthingales, especially some of the large ones which look like the great bell of S. Lorenzo. Even if they say they are very comfortable for walking, because the legs are freer from the skirts, I still do not like them, and I have never wanted to wear them because I hate them so much on other women. I have seen some of these women trying to get through a door with great effort, so large were their farthingales. And they are extremely uncomfortable when you sit down, as you have to fiddle about with them if you don't want to make a public exhibition of yourself.
CLELIA: It is for this reason that young men like them, because they can often enjoy a good spectacle!

9. Lucrezia Marinella (1571–1653) on women's dress

According to this late sixteenth-century writer, not only aristocratic women but also the wives of members of the lower ranks dressed lavishly by this date, giving honour to their city and their sex thereby. This is doubtless exaggerated, in view of the fact that, as we have seen, in Venice as elsewhere in Italy strict, if unenforceable, sumptuary laws restrained the luxury of both dress in public and furnishings in the home, and one of Marinella's goals may have been to criticise such laws. Given that her book would have been read by her fellow citizens, though, her account of the richness of Venetian women's dress, which was used by her as an argument for the superiority of the female sex, cannot have been total fantasy.

> Lucrezia Marinella, *Nobiltà et l' eccellenza delle donne, co' difetti et mancamenti de gli uomini* (Venice, 1621), p. 37.

> So women gain honour by the use of adornment which far exceeds that used by men, as we can see. It is a wonderful thing to see in our city the wife of a shoemaker, a butcher or a porter dressed in silk with gold chains round her neck, with pearls and costly rings on her fingers, accompanied by a couple of women supporting her on either side and giving a hand, and then, on the contrary, to see her husband chopping up meat all soiled with beef blood and shabbily dressed, or loaded up like a donkey, dressed in sackcloth. At first sight it seems grotesque, and the husband looks so very rough that often he seems like her servant or workman. But if one reflects on it carefully, it seems reasonable, for it is necessary that women, however base and lowly, be adorned with such clothing by virtue of their natural dignity and excellencies, and that man, like a servant and donkey, born to serve them, should be less so.

PRECIOUS GOWNS AND ACCESSORIES

Ladies of the elite took great personal interest in their clothes and ornaments. These texts show the care with which they discussed these matters.[6]

10. Precious fabrics for Barbara of Brandenburg

In the Autumn of 1459, Barbara of Brandenburg was preparing for a visit to Milan and needed fabrics for her new clothes. The correspondence on this subject with the Mantuan ambassador in Milan, who was trying to find what the marchioness wanted, continued for months.

> I. Lazzarini (ed.), *Carteggio degli oratori mantovani alla corte sforzesca (1450–1500)*, 15 vols (Rome, 1999–2003), 1, *1450–59*, p. 351.

> Vincenzo della Scalona from Milan, to Barbara of Brandenburg, 28 September 1459.
> Most Illustrious Lady, Your Illustrious Ladyship should not wait for me to send that *morello* damask brocaded in gold for a dress. We have looked and looked in all the shops and workshops, and could not find enough to make a bodice. I am sorry that I am not able to satisfy Your Excellency, and I recommend myself to her good will.

11. Getting ready for a visit: Beatrice d'Este and an embroidered dress

In April 1493, Ludovico il Moro and his wife Beatrice d'Este were planning a visit to Ferrara, and Beatrice was busy preparing new clothes and jewels. In this letter to her mother she asks advice about a pattern by the Spanish embroiderer Master Jorba.

> A. Venturi, 'Relazioni artistiche tra le corti di Milano e Ferrara nel secolo XV', *Archivio Storico Lombardo*, ser. 2, vol 2, anno 12 (1885), p. 253.

> Beatrice d'Este, from Milan, to Eleonora of Aragon, 10 April 1493
> Tonight I have received the design of the *camora* made by Jorba, which I admire very much. As Your Highness advised, I have shown it to my embroiderer. He advised me that, using the drawing [for the embroidered flowers] as it is, all of the same size for the top and bottom, the pattern will not work, as the *camora* will be cut narrower above than below. The flowers should be smaller in the upper part of the *camora*, so

that they are proportional to each part of the dress. I have not yet decided what is the best thing to do, but thought I would report to Your Excellency what my embroiderer said, so that you could let me know as soon as possible what you think. Then I shall do what Your Excellency thinks best.

12. Fine fabrics for Isabella d'Este's chemises, 1496
A very fine linen fabric woven in Reims, *tela di renso*, was used for chemises. Here Isabella asks Giorgio Brognolo, her agent in Venice, to look for some in that city.

> C. Zaffanella, 'Isabella d'Este e la moda del suo tempo', in Bini (ed.) (2001), p. 216.

> Isabella d'Este to Giorgio Brognolo, 5 August 1496
> We wish to have six or eight *braccia* of *tela di renso*, which should be so fine and beautiful that it cannot be equalled, because we [already] have great quantities of the common kind. We want you to look in all the shops in Venice in order to find the finest one, and to show it to your wife because she'll be more expert than you. If it is not possible to find as much as I want, and there is a small piece left measuring two or three *braccia*, send it to me, and do not worry about the price, because, even if it costs one ducat a *braccio*, we shall not mind that.

13. Embroidered devices
The clothes of aristocratic ladies were sometimes embroidered with devices and mottoes. Here Isabella d'Este wears the device of the 'musical pause', which was one of her favourites, embroidered on a *camora*.

> G. Malacarne, 'Il segno di Isabella: stemmi, motti, imprese', in Bini (ed.) (2001), p. 195.

> The Marchioness of Cotrone to Francesco Gonzaga, 2 February 1502
> The Lady Marchioness your wife, accompanied by many ladies, went to the house of the Master of Taxes to see the entry of the bride [Lucrezia Borgia, bride of Alfonso

Gonzaga]. She was dressed with a beautiful *camora*, embroidered with the device of [musical] times and pauses.[7]

14. Two ladies and a marten fur

Margherita Paleologa writes to Giovanna Gonzaga about one of the fashionable luxury objects for women used during the sixteenth century, a *zibellino* (marten, sable or ermine) fur adorned with a gold and jewelled head and attached to a chain, which was carried either across the shoulder or held in the hand. This letter allows us to understand some of the ways in which these furs could be fashioned, and also how the highest ranking ladies looked for something novel.[8]

S. Hickson, 'Diplomazia e pellicce nella Mantova del Rinascimento: Margherita Paleologo e uno *zibellino* per Maria d' Aragona', *Civiltà Mantovana*, 129 (spring 2010), p. 101.

Margherita Paleologa, from Mantua, to Giovanna Gonzaga, 6 December 1541
. . . I shall go ahead and commission the gold marten head about which you have written to me. I shall not, however, commission it from Master Niccolò, since he is dead, but I shall ask another goldsmith. I shall have it made without lining as mine was, so that the fur inside can be seen. This is a very beautiful style, and difficult to find: there are very large numbers of those [heads] which are lined, as most of them have been made in this way. They are very beautiful and could not be better, but it does not seem appropriate to me to send you something which everybody is wearing. After all, if you do not like it without lining and would like it lined instead, one could get a gold lining inserted: any good goldsmith would be able to do that, and it would look very good.

As to the marten fur, I shall endeavour to find the best, even if this is the worse season for such things. Perhaps it will be difficult to find a suitable one, but I shall do all that is possible . . .

Postscript: Since Your Ladyship does not seem to be in a hurry, in order not to get something you may dislike, I have thought not to commission the gold head until you let me know whether you want it all lined, as it is fashionable here, or without lining so that the fur can be seen, as mine is, the latter being of a kind which is not seen here. In the meantime I shall try to find a goldsmith who will be able to do a good job, whatever shape we decide. Again I recommend myself to you.

MOURNING AND BURIALS

Customs about what should be worn after the death of a relative, and how long the period of mourning should last, were regulated by different conventions and legislations in different parts of Italy.

Burial clothes were usually very simple, and many men and women of high ranks requested to be buried wearing the habit of a religious order.

15. What Sienese women should wear during mourning, 1460

Originally, not all women were allowed to wear mourning clothes: in early fifteenth-century Perugia, for example, the only women permitted to do so by law were widows and those belonging to religious orders, even if in fact most women did not follow this rule. The following is an extract from a Sienese 1460 law regulating the use of mourning clothes.

> E. Casanova, 'La donna senese del Quattrocento nella vita privata', *Bollettino Senese di Storia Patria*, 8:1 (1901), p. 95.

It is decreed that in future no man or woman will be allowed to wear mourning unless in the following categories: for the [death of the] father, mother, wife, older or younger brother, or if related as follows: an uncle on the father's side, the grandfather on the father's side, or a relative of the son, if aged twenty or more.

In the case of the death of the above mentioned relatives, black or reddish-black (*perso*) clothes can be worn, according to present custom, and cloaks reaching a quarter [*braccio*] from the ground in length, or shorter, as wished.

It is decreed that these mourning clothes cannot be worn for more than a year. Women can wear dresses or cloaks without trains in similar fashions and circumstances.

Widows are allowed to wear black clothes, that is, a cloak with a train a quarter [of a *braccio*] long, and one *cioppa* only. They can wear veils costing not more than one florin, that is four *lire di denari*, each.

No woman is allowed to wear a cloak with a train longer than a quarter [of a *braccio*].

The fine for any man or woman who contravenes [this law] is fifty *lire*.

16. Mourning clothes for Beatrice d'Este, 1493
A description of what Beatrice wore after the death of her mother.

Zaffanella, in Bini (ed.) (2001), p. 216.

Leonardo Aristeo to Isabella d'Este, 25 October 1493
. . . She wears a gown of black cloth, with sleeves of black cloth, and above it a very long cloak also of black cloth. On her head [she wears] a cap of black silk, with veils, neither yellow nor grey, but white.

17. Funerary clothes for Anna Sforza and her baby daughter, 1497
The first wife of Alfonso d'Este, Anna Sforza, died after giving birth to a still-born baby. For her funeral she was dressed in the habit of Augustinian nuns. Dressing the corpse in a religious habit was a common practice for both women and men.

T. Tuohy, *Herculean Ferrara: Ercole d'Este (1471–1505) and the Invention of a Ducal Capital* (Cambridge, 1996), p. 331, n. 172.

13 December 1497
Duke Ercole [d'Este] left his palace in the main square in Ferrara and went to the palace of S. Francesco [residence of Alfonso d'Este and Anna Sforza], where was the body of the most illustrious Lady Anna, his daughter-in-law, on a bier covered in black cloth. She was dressed with the habit of the nuns of S. Vito, and at her side was her baby girl, also dead, dressed in white damask.

DOWRIES, GIFTS AND BEQUESTS

a. Dowries

18. Clothes and accessories for Nannina de' Medici, 1466

On the occasion of the wedding of Nannina, daughter of Piero de' Medici, and Bernardo Rucellai in June 1466, her family gave the bride rich garments and accessories.

Giovanni Rucellai ed il suo Zibaldone, 'Il Zibaldone Quaresimale', ed. A. Perosa (London, 1960), pp. 32–3.

1 overdress (*cioppa*) in light pink and *paonazzo* [a purple-greenish colour] cloth, embroidered with pearls

1 overdress (*giornea*) of *alessandrino* [a shade of deep blue] satin, decorated with threaded pearls

1 *giornea* of white and crimson damask, with fringes and pearls

1 *cioppa* of grey fabric, with its sleeves embroidered with gold thread

1 gown (*gamurra*), *paonazzo* and light pink, with gold, silver and pearls

1 gown (*cotta*) of *alessandrino* light silk with brocade sleeves

1 *gamurra* of white cloth with light damask sleeves

1 silk underdress with white and red damask sleeves

1 *gamurra* in *paonazzo* cloth with silk sleeves decorated with silver

1 green and black underdress *a uccellini*, double, fine

20 *braccia* of *panno lucchesino* [a red cloth from Lucca] with a wide weave, in one piece

A batch of material for 13 towels and 1 piece of thin cloth and 4½ *braccia* of fine *panno lucchesino* for a small dress

12 embroidered chemises in fine light fabric

1 crimson headdress embroidered with pearls

1 cap embroidered in silver and pearls

1 cap in *alessandrino* satin embroidered with diamond shapes.

19. Clothes and linen for a painter's sister, 1543
An extract from a list of objects given to Anna, sister of the painter
Jacopo da Ponte [Bassano] as part of her dowry. The value of the
goods, mainly clothing of a less luxurious kind, was assessed by two
tailors, one chosen by each of the two families.

F. Signori (ed.), *La famiglia di Jacopo nei documenti d'archivio*
(Bassano, 1992), p. 28.

29 November 1543
. . .

One underdress in light wool cloth, new	*lire* 22 *soldi* 18
One orange underdress	*lire* 18 *soldi* 18
One tunic of red wool	*lire* 17
	176 *soldi* 12

One white cotton bodice, with its sleeves	*lire* 19 *soldi* 10
One pair of sleeves of yellow light satin	*lire* 6
One pair of sleeves of purple satin	*lire* 12
One embroidered band [to be worn around the waist]	*lire* 15
One pair of sleeves in red-brown light fabric	*lire* 2 *soldi* 10
One lamb fur coat, new	*lire* 18 *soldi* 10
Four woman's chemises, new	*lire* 28
One mirror kerchief	*lire* 3 *soldi* 5
One striped silk kerchief	*lire* 3 *soldi* 10
Another linen kerchief	*lire* 2 *soldi* 8
. . .	
A fine silk kerchief	*lire* 5 *soldi* 10
Three aprons, new	*lire* 3 *soldi* 10
Two aprons	*lire* 5 *soldi* 10
	133 *soldi* 19
	176 *soldi* 12
	310 *soldi* 11

b. Gifts

20. A nun gives a precious dress to her convent, 1512
On 19 March 1512, Paola Vimercati, a member of an ancient
Lombard family, gave a dress of cloth of gold to the Poor Clares'
convent of S. Apollinare in Milan, where she was going to become
a professed nun. The luxury fabric was to be used to make church
vestments.

> P. Sevesi, 'Il monastero delle Clarisse di S. Apollinare, Milano',
> *Archivium Franciscanum Historicum*, 18 (1925), pp. 552–3.

> I leave . . . to the convent the dress made of gold and crim-
> son silk on my behalf, and worn by me. In this used garment
> there are 29 *braccia* of cloth of gold, estimated at about 23
> Imperial *lire* for each single *braccio*, as above. And this dress
> has sleeves made of cloth of gold . . . of light turquoise silk,
> valued at 700 *lire* in good current Milanese money. And this
> shall be given to the Abbess and the nuns of S. Apollinare
> fifteen days after my profession. And from this garment of
> cloth of gold, for 700 Imperial *lire*, I wish the Abbess and
> the nuns to make one beautiful and honourable chasuble in
> cloth of gold and crimson for the mass.
> I wish and order that the remaining fabric from this gown,
> or the money left over after making the chasuble, should be
> used to make two beautiful, honourable and praiseworthy
> crosses of gold or silver brocade for the said chasuble and
> to repair the convent's organ, or to make a new fine and
> praiseworthy organ.

21. A wedding dress for a servant, 1582
A Milanese lady gives as a gift to one of her female
servants everything needed for her wedding dress. Here is the
list of the items and their prices, expressed in *lire*, *soldi* and
denari.

> P. Venturelli, 'L'abito delle dame di Milano tra il 1539 e il
> 1599. Ornamento e colore', in A. G. Cavagna and G. Butazzi
> (eds), *Le trame della moda* (Rome, 1995), pp. 371–72.

Milan, 2 October 1582
The lady Antonia Torta owes
For the making of a whole dress in grey silk *grossagrana* [*gros grain*] for the bride, who was her young servant, with embroidery, lined with grey S. Gallo silk, with a border and a small band *Lire* 6

And for a ¼ of cloth for borders for the said dress at lire 4 *soldi* 10 per *braccio*	*Lire* 1 s 2 d 6
And for the embroidery	*Lire* 6 s 8
And for ¾ of grey silk at 30 *soldi*	*Lire* 1 s 2 d 6
And for ¼ of stiff cloth for the collar	*Lire* – s 2 d 6
And for hooks and eyes	s 4
And for the making of a coat in crimson silk *grossagrana*, top-stitched and slashed	*Lire* 2 d 2
And for ⅓ of silk for the above at *soldi* 30	*Lire* – s 20
And for 3 ounces of cotton wool	s 4 d 6
And for ⅔ of stiff cloth for the lining and collar	s 4
The total is	*Lire* 18/9

c. Bequests

Used clothes were often mentioned in wills: it was customary for both women and men to bequeath their old clothes to relatives or friends, or to ask that they should be sold to provide alms for the poor.

22. The will of an artisan's wife, 1483

Lucia Bischizzi, the wife of Master Paolo, a window-maker, bequeaths her clothes to female friends, and leaves to the poor the money obtained from the sale of other clothes.

A. Franceschini, *Artisti a Ferrara in età umanistica e rinascimentale. Testimonianze archivistiche. Parte II, Tomo I, dal 1472 al 1492* (Ferrara and Rome, 1995), p. 301.

From the Archivio Notarile of Ferrara, 14 April 1483
The testatrix bequeaths to Bernardina, widow of Master Antonio from Venice, a painter, for the soul of the said testatrix, a dress in green cloth with *morello* velvet sleeves, three women's chemises, one [piece of] used linen cloth.

The said testatrix bequeaths to Criseide, daughter of Master Gerardo, a painter, one of her dresses of fine red wool, without sleeves, lined in silver, for the soul of the said testatrix.

. . .

The testatrix wants and commands that through her executor named below her clothes and goods listed should be sold, and through him the money should be given and distributed amongst the poor and unfortunate people, for the soul of the said testatrix.

23. The will of a Dominican tertiary, Vicenza, 1593

The poetess Maddalena Campiglia (1553–95), a Dominican tertiary well connected with *letterati* and members of aristocratic families in the Veneto, dictated her will while living in the house of her cousin Vincenzo Negri. Being childless and separated from her husband, she made a number of bequests to her nieces (Emilia, Vittoria and Polissena), to her cousin's wife, to her servant, and to the nuns of the convent of Acella. Among her bequests are luxury clothes, jewels, household linen and fine furniture. Because of her semi-religious state, she had been unable to use these items. The following are extracts from her will.

B. Morsolin, *Maddalena Campiglia poetessa vicentina del secolo XVI*, (Vicenza, 1882), pp. 68–70, 73–4.

6 October 1593

. . . She bequeaths to the said lady Emilia twelve of the best chemises of fine silk in possession of the said testatrix, and twelve aprons, twelve handkerchiefs, a quite old walnut bed which is usually in the kitchen, with its canopy of dark reddish colour (*roano*) decorated with black bows, with its feather coverlet, mattress, pallet and pillow, and a pair of pillow-cases, a pair of sheets of fine silk embroidered with couching work, and a pair of hemp sheets embroidered in a similar manner. All these objects cannot and shall not be given to Emilia until she marries, and in the meantime they must be kept by the gentlemen mentioned below as executors.

She bequeaths ten ducats from her own monies to Marietta di Spezzati, who is now her servant, as well as what the said testatrix owes her for her wages . . .

She bequeaths to the said [Marietta] a pair of chemises and a pair of aprons, for the love of God.

. . .

She bequeaths all her dresses and fabrics, that is, embroidered linen used for decoration for women's clothes, to the lady Vittoria and her sister the lady Polissena, her nieces, daughters of her brother Signor Francesco Campiglia, when they marry, to be divided equally between them. In case of one of them dying or becoming a nun, all these [objects] will go to the other.

The said testatrix bequeaths some of her lovely and elegant objects, which she keeps in a strongbox (*forziero*), to the magnificent lady Lavinia [Gualdo], her cousin, wife of the magnificent Signor Vincenzo Negri, who can choose and receive as a gift everything she would like. All that will be left in the said strongbox, together with all the rest of her [the testatrix's] moveable goods which have not been disposed of, and which are in the house at the time of her death, will be listed in an inventory with great care and precision, and should be given to the care of one of the executors mentioned below until the time when her undermentioned heirs will have the rest of the inheritance . . .

[On 7 January 1595, just before her death, Maddalena Campiglia added a codicil to her will. She indicated some more bequests, and cut out her niece Emilia from the inheritance.]

She bequeaths her green *spalliere* decorating the bedroom in which she is lying to the reverend nuns of Santa Maria Nova, for the love of God, and for the decoration of their church.

She bequeaths to the said Reverend Mothers all those things in their possession at the time of her death, because she wishes the Reverend [Mothers] to have them without being obliged to return them or to answer for them to anyone.

She bequeaths all her chemises, handkerchiefs, aprons and kerchiefs for the head, made of fine cloth and other fabrics, to the lady Calidonia Cozza, so that they will be hers, and she shall be able to do with them whatever she wants. She wishes the said lady Calidonia to keep all those things in her possession at the time of the said lady Maddalena's death with a good conscience, without being obliged to return them or to answer for them to anyone, because they are bequeathed to her.

. . . This codicil cuts, cancels, revokes and declares void all those parts in her previous will which benefited Emilia, daughter of Signor Antonio, her brother.

USED CLOTHES

Mending clothes and using old fabrics to make 'new' garments was very common, and not only among the members of lower ranks. Poorer people, for whom new clothes would have been too expensive, would buy second-, third- and fourth-hand clothes.[9]

24. Old clothes and a family argument, 1461
The Strozzi belonged to the higher ranks of republican Florence, but their men had been exiled for political reasons. Here the widow Alessandra Macinghi Strozzi writes to her son Lorenzo, who was living in Bruges, about a relative, Lucrezia Cavalcanti, who had just been widowed. Alessandra complains about the tight-fisted Niccolò Strozzi, who was not providing for Lucrezia and her daughters' clothes.

Alessandra Macinghi Strozzi, *Tempo di affetti e di mercanti. Lettere ai figli esuli* (Milan, 1987), p. 147.

Alessandra Macinghi Strozzi, from Florence, to Lorenzo Strozzi, in Bruges, 25 August 1461
. . . [Niccolò] hasn't done anything yet to dress them, and also Lucrezia. The mother complains a lot because they had to deal with everything by themselves, in relation to Margherita's illness and other expenses, and had no help from him. The cloth he has given for their *cioppe* is not enough, and he does not want to hear about the *gamurre*, of which those two girls need one each. He says they had some of them from you, and that they are good. This is not so,

because they are already threadbare, and they can be worn only at home. The clothes arriving from Bruges [inherited by Lucrezia from her husband] are not good enough to be reused, Lucrezia says, since they are so shabby.

CLOTHES FOR THE LOWER RANKS

25. Shoes for a wet-nurse at the Este court, 1475

Eleonora of Aragon wanted the wet-nurse of the infant Isabella d'Este to look more like her ladies-in-waiting. The following is an entry from the records of the ducal chamberlain.

> L. A. Gandini, *Isabella, Beatrice e Alfonso d'Este infanti. Documenti inediti del secolo XV* (Modena, 1896), p. 17.

> On the said day [the last day in December] five *lire* and two *soldi marchesini* for 12 pairs of shoes at 5 *soldi* the pair, and 6 pairs of slippers at 7 *soldi* the pair, given to Isabetta di Gasparino dell' Angelo, wet-nurse to our Lady Isabella from the beginning of the year till now. [This is] the order of Her Ladyship, who wants her dressed and shod like her ladies-in-waiting.

26. The clothes of a peasant woman, 1630

This brief description from a court report concerning a dead peasant woman in Bologna reminds us that poor people were dressed in muted colours, and that their clothes were without ornaments.

> O. Niccoli, *Storie di ogni giorno in una città del Seicento* (Rome and Bari, 2002), p. 79.

> . . . A dress of linsey-woolsey of *morello* colour; an apron of mediocre material, black; a pair of rough socks, grey; a canvas shawl on her shoulders, a veil on her head and a chemise.

COURTESANS AND PROSTITUTES: THEIR APPEARANCE AND CLOTHING

Many courtesans aspired to dress much like affluent respectable women, causing confusion which sumptuary legislation from several cities tried to prevent. Other prostitutes, however, adopted certain features of men's dress, especially breeches, whether to signal specialised sexual practices, or merely to lend themselves an attractive piquancy.[10]

27. Prostitutes in public places, Venice, 1598
Vecellio (2008), p. 202.

The common prostitutes who inhabit places of ill repute do not dress all in the same way . . . they dress rather like men, since they wear doublets of silk or linen or other material, according to how rich they are, and these are trimmed with large fringes and padded out like those of young men, and even more like Frenchmen's garb. Over their bodies they wear men's shirts, again varied in delicacy and refinement according to their spending capacity, above which in hot weather they place a bodice or apron of silk or linen down to their feet, and in cold weather a fur-trimmed coat of velvet or silk, whichever suits best. The clogs they wear are over a quarter of a *braccio* high, but decorated with fringes, and on their feet they wear silk or velvet stockings, embroidered, as are the Roman-style slippers on their feet. Many of them wear breeches like men's of *ormesino* or other cloth. By these signs, or by their wearing of little roundels of silver coins, they are easily made out. What is less easy to describe is the way they dress their hair, nor are they to be seen at the windows since they frequent the doorways and the streets instead to catch the passer-by in their web.

Legislation

Most large Italian cities sought to regulate and contain prostitution: they were not unrealistic enough to seek to abolish it. In the sixteenth century, allegedly because of the increased number of prostitutes, their opulent dress and their increasingly brazen behaviour, several states felt a need to legislate against them. These extracts, taken from statutes issued in various parts of Italy, show that civic authorities were concerned also with the misuse of resources on the luxuries associated with these women.

28. The Venetian Senate decrees on what courtesans are forbidden to wear, and why, 1543

A. Barzaghi, *Donne o cortigiane?* (Verona, 1980), p. 138.

The prostitutes in this city have risen to such an excessive number that they have put aside all embarrassment and shame, and go around the streets and churches and elsewhere so well dressed and adorned that often our noble and citizen women are mistaken for them, the good for the bad, not only by foreigners but also by native inhabitants, since they are not dressed differently. This is a wicked, evil example for the women who live amongst them and observe them, with considerable grumbling and causing scandal to all. So we lay down this law, which is pleasing to Eternal God, in order to remove this bad example and scandal and to remedy their excessive expenditure in clothing . . . Be it declared that no prostitute living in this land may wear gold, silver or silk anywhere on her person, apart from her cap which may be of pure silk, nor wear necklaces, pearls or rings with or without stones . . . By 'prostitutes' we mean those women who, though not married, have commerce and relations with one man or more, and also those who do not live with their husbands, though they have them, but live separately and have commerce with one or more men.

29. What prostitutes can or cannot wear in Florence, 1546

C. Carnesecchi, *Cosimo I e la sua legge suntuaria del 1546* (Florence, 1902), p. 21.

Prostitutes are not allowed to wear silk dresses, nor silk of any kind, but they can wear as many jewels and as much gold and silver as they want. On their head they must wear a veil, or napkin, or kerchief, or any other cloth, which should have a band one finger wide, made of gold, or silk, or other yellow material, in a place where it can be seen by everybody. They must wear this sign so that they are distinguished from good women who live an honest life, under the penalty of ten gold *scudi* in gold, each time they transgress.

Notes

1 See M. G. Muzzarelli, *Guardaroba medievale: Vesti e società dal XIII al XVI secolo* (Milan, 1999).
2 See J. Bridgeman, "*Condecenti e netti . . .*": beauty, dress and gender in Italian Renaissance art', in F. Ames-Lewis and M. Rogers (eds), *Concepts of Beauty in Renaissance Art* (Aldershot, 1998), pp. 44–51.
3 For the clergy's objections to luxury, see D. O. Hughes, 'Sumptuary laws and social relations in Renaissance Italy', in P. Findlen (ed.), *The Italian Renaissance: Essential Readings* (Malden, MA, 2002), pp. 124–50.
4 See C. Kovesi Killerby, 'Practical problems in the enforcement of Italian sumptuary law, 1200–1500', in T. Dean and K. J. P. Lowe (eds), *Crime, Society and the Law in Renaissance Italy* (Cambridge, 1994), pp. 99–120, and by the same author, *Sumptuary Laws in Italy 1200–1500* (Oxford, 2001). See also Rogers and Tinagli (2005), pp. 100–01, 147–8.
5 See T. Sherrill, 'Who was Cesare Vecellio? Placing "Habiti Antichi" in context', *Medieval Clothing and Textiles*, 5 (2009), pp. 161–88.
6 See E. Welch, 'Art on the edge: hair and hands in Renaissance Italy', *Renaissance Studies*, 23:3 (2009), pp. 241–68.
7 This device, a stave with time signature, notes and pauses, was used also in Isabella's apartment as decoration. It signified a silent time necessary for meditation.
8 I am very grateful to Sally Hickson for allowing me to read her article before publication, and to use one of the documents. See also S. Tawny, 'Fleas, furs and fashion: *Zibellini* and luxury accessories of the Renaissance', *Medieval Clothing and Textiles*, 2 (2006), pp. 121–50.
9 See P. Allerston, 'L'abito usato', in C. M. Belfanti and F. Giusberti (eds), *Storia d'Italia, Annali*, 19, *La moda* (Turin, 2003), pp. 561–81, and E. Welch, 'New, old and second-hand culture: the case of the Renaissance sleeve', in G. Neher and R. Shepherd (eds), *Revaluing Renaissance Art* (Aldershot, 2000), pp. 101–19.
10 On prostitutes, courtesans and their possessions, see T. Storey, 'Clothing courtesans: fabrics, signals, and experiences', in C. Richardson (ed.), *Clothing Culture, 1350–1650* (Aldershot, 2004), pp. 95–107, and *Carnal Commerce in Counter-Reformation Rome* (Cambridge, 2008). See also Rogers and Tinagli (2005), pp. 279–82.

~ 4 ~

CEREMONY AND TRAVEL: FEMALE PARTICIPANTS AND SPECTATORS

The previous chapters have been concerned with the domestic spaces and surroundings of women, and the everyday appearance of women as seen on the street and in social gatherings. The following chapter deals with women as they participated in major public events in the cities of Italy, such as the weddings, births or funerals for members of ruling houses or the ceremonial welcomes given to visitors. The accompanying spectacles, which became more lavish and complex during the time-span covered by this book, had several facets[1]. The costumes and adornments of the main aristocratic protagonists and their entourages would demonstrate the political significance of the events, as would the dress of upper-ranking members of city who formed welcoming parties or spectators. Sumptuary laws would be suspended so that their elegant clothes, jewels and deportment might serve to communicate the wealth, culture and virtue of the state. The buildings and spaces of the city between the gates and the centre of government would be embellished by garlands of foliage, luxury textiles and temporary architectural constructions and serve as the sites for *tableaux vivants*, dramatic performances or sporting competitions. Elaborate feasts inside or outside the main palace would allow the display and use of fine and often innovative vessels and tableware, as well as more ephemeral artefacts such as coats of arms in jelly or sugar statuettes. The accompanying *intermezzi* involved fantastic costumes and the introduction of allegorical, astrological or mythological themes of relevance to the event. By the end of our period, these would be evolving into full theatrical and operatic performances.

Such spectacles, then, provided food for both wonder and thought for viewers of both sexes at all social levels. Lengthy descriptions of them are preserved, initially in letters addressed to members of other courts but also, like newsletters, intended to be read by their associates[2]. These texts catered to an already existing demand for information and vicarious enjoyment, and would have fostered a competitive desire among ruling regimes to display their own magnificence and ingenuity on future occasions. Later, with the advent of publishing, pamphlets on particular ceremonies could reach a more general audience. These had propaganda purposes, but must also, like the guidebooks or costume studies of a similar period, have helped to spread awareness of new developments in dress and in the decorative and performing arts, and understanding of the meanings of the mythology-based political allegory that became increasingly prevalent in the later sixteenth and seventeenth centuries. The necessarily brief extracts given here show different features of these ceremonies. Some of them reveal women as not merely passive, bejewelled pawns in the status games of political authorities but, as the examples written by females make clear, as close observers of what seemed to them visually noteworthy.

Pursuing the theme of women's awareness of sites and objects outside the home, some writings by women on their travels have been included in the last part of the chapter. Though women in general were less able to move freely beyond their city states or even their city quarters than were men, upper-ranking women did leave some record of the novel or noteworthy sights observed on their voyages. In broadening perspectives, both personal experience and literary descriptions could enrich individual women and potentially aid them if they became patrons in their own right.

COURTLY AND CIVIC SPECTACLES

a. Weddings

1. Eleonora of Aragon entertained as she passed through Rome, 1473

Letters, diaries and historical works provide lengthy descriptions of the marriage of Eleonora of Aragon (1450–93) and Ercole I d'Este in 1473 and the ceremonies staged for it in the cities through which she passed in her journey northward through Italy. Eleonora's own account of the varied entertainments in Rome was written on 10

June 1473 to a correspondent in Naples (perhaps her tutor and spiritual director, Diomede Carafa). She was received by Pietro Riario, the Cardinal of S. Sisto, who organised trips to the Vatican, theatrical performances and elaborate banquets at the Piazza SS. Apostoli, the seat of his palace. *Intermezzi* were based on mythological figures relevant to the nuptial pair; items of food were given the shapes of birds and fish.

F. Cruciani, *Teatro nel Rinascimento a Roma 1450–1550* (Rome, 1983), pp. 157–60.

Having entered Rome, we arrived to dismount in the SS. Apostoli district at the dwelling of the Reverend Cardinal of S. Sisto, which we found well prepared, furnished and decorated as follows.

In the piazza in front of the palace was a ceremonial stage fifty feet long and the same across, decorated with silk hangings and covered with six pieces of red, green and white cloth above. On one side of the stage was a grand, ample dais, its floor covered with carpets and cloths of (. . .) with an awning of crimson velvet. On the other side, a *credenza* with eight tiers thirty palms wide, decorated with silk at the front, furnished for the banquet. On the other side of the piazza was another platform, well decorated to allow various displays, with the arms of His Majesty [her father, the King of Naples], the illustrious Duke of Ferrara and the above-mentioned Cardinal throughout.

On mounting the staircase we found a medium-sized room decorated with silk; from that room we passed through one chamber and entered the main decorated chamber where there was a bed hung with blue Venetian silk. From there we entered the second furnished chamber where there was a bed hung with crimson silk and above the bed a coverlet of gold brocade with a lining of wolf- and deer-skin of about a palm in breadth, and a flounced trim of marten, and two cushions of crimson gold brocade . . .

On Sunday morning at the invitation of our Holy Father we went to St Peter's to see Mass . . . After vespers the Cardinal of S. Sisto put on a play of the story of Susanna, something truly fine and worthwhile, and so passed Sunday.

On Monday the Cardinal of S. Sisto hosted a banquet to which we were invited, and held the banquet on the dais and the *credenza* I mentioned before, well provided with silver on all its tiers.

When we came to table we remained on our feet for a little, our shoulders facing the table, and there came a meal with ten confections with imperial eagles formed of sugar, and a confection of sugar and candied and gilded pomegranates and vessels of malmsey wine.

[There follows lengthy description of the different food courses, some worked into decorative or symbolic shapes, and followed by short *intermezzi*, as for example:]

Five dishes of jellied capons, and the arms of the Cardinal formed in the garnish, within the gelatine, certainly cleverly done . . .

Ten confections with ten ships made of sugar filled with garlands and sugared roses, and ten cups with pine-nut tartlets shaped like different kinds of fish. Cutlery and salt-vessel of silver, and silvered bread; elderflower fritters, and elderflower cordial in ten silvered cups.

Five dishes of eels, mashed up and silvered, three whole sturgeon, ten soups of almonds and white sauce . . .

After the meal, the dance of Hercules with five men and nine women. Amongst the dance came centaurs and fought a fine battle. The centaurs were defeated by Hercules and returned to perform a handsome dance.

This banquet lasted from 12 to 18 hours of the night, so well organised, with such fine entertainment and abundant goods that it would be impossible to recount them all.

On Tuesday after dining S. Sisto had a play performed on a miracle of the consecrated Body of Christ.

The Wednesday morning, accompanied by the Very Reverend Cardinal of Naples we went to visit His Holiness Our Father where we found S. Sisto. His Holiness gave a gracious audience and handed out a great quantity of Agnusdei to us and to all the company.

With the permission of His Holiness, accompanied by the above-mentioned Cardinals of Naples and of S. Sisto we viewed the [relic of the] Holy Face[3] and returned home.

2. Allegorical chariots at the 1475 wedding of Costanzo Sforza and Camilla of Aragon
Accounts of the very elaborate wedding celebrations survive in Marchigian and Tuscan, including an illustrated luxury version. The *tableaux vivants* can be compared with contemporary paintings with which women would have been familiar, such as 'Famous Women' cycles. Later, *Pudicitia* [Modesty], probably played by a young man, addresses Camilla: another *Pudicitia* made of spun sugar appeared later at the banquet.

> Anon., *Le nozze di Costanzo Sforza e Camilla d'Aragona celebrate a Pesaro nel maggio 1475*, ed. T. de Marinis (Florence, 1946), pp. 5–6.

When the said lady [Camilla] entered the town she met, almost at the gate, a great and magnificent chariot of Modesty, entirely covered in silver with painted ornamentation and fringes, carrying putti and vases all gilded and silvered. The chariot was 18 feet high, and on top of it was a lady garbed all in silver and with a golden palm in her hand, who represented Modesty, and around the middle of the chariot on six seats were six women famed for their chastity. In front of this chariot was a small rectangular chariot, not very high, all gilded and silvered, on which were a group of girls dressed in white with loosened hair, who represented Modesty's companions, each holding a lily in their hands, and one of them had a flag of light green silk, on which was depicted an exquisite ermine with a jewelled collar.

3. Beatrice d'Este describes the wedding of Bianca Maria Sforza (1472–1510) in Milan to Maximilian, King of the Romans
This letter of 28 December 1493 by Beatrice d'Este (1475–97) to her sister Isabella in Mantua places some emphasis on the antique imperial elements in the decoration, appropriate for a marriage between members of the Imperial family and a dynasty founded on the military prowess of Francesco Sforza.

> A. Luzio and R. Renier, 'Della relazioni di Isabella d'Este Gonzaga con Ludovico e Beatrice Sforza'. *Archivio Storico Lombardo*, ser. 2, vol. 7, anno 17 (1890), pp. 384–8.

On the final day of last month . . . for the ceremony in the main church of the city of Milan, a porch was constructed above the main door on the front of the facade with columns beside it, above which was hung a decorative canopy of dark red decorated with doves, suspended from high up. Inside the church both sides were covered with hangings of brocades up to the beginning of the choir, in front of which a triumphal arch on huge columns was erected, with the figure of the illustrious late Duke Francesco [Sforza, first Sforza duke of Milan] on horseback with the ducal insignia painted above, and the arms of the serene King of the Romans above. This triumphal arch, rectangular in shape, was decorated with pictures of antique festivities, and the side facing the altar had the imperial insignia on top. Above were the arms of the illustrious lord my consort. Beneath this arch at its end began the staircase ascending to the great tribune built at the high altar; on this tribune was a small tribune draped with gold brocade on the left, beside the altar, where one ascended to sing the Gospel, and on the right side another small tribune decorated with silver brocade. Beside these tribunes were seats for the service covered with fabrics for the councillors and other feudatories and gentlemen.

The route through which one went to the ceremony was richly decorated. The street from the fortified tower of the castle up to the bottom of the piazza was lined with columns entwined with ivy, and with decoration in the antique manner made with foliage between each column and in their roundels, with arms of the Empire and of this ruling house [the Sforza] in the middle and attached to the awning of Sforza cloth which covered the street from the castle to the cathedral. Many doors themselves had columns decorated in like fashion, as there would have been in the season of May. On both sides of the street the walls were covered with tapestries, except where there were the new paintings just frescoed on some of the houses of Milan, which were no less lovely to see than tapestry . . .

At the seventeenth hour, that is, at 17, the illustrious Queen mounted the triumphal chariot which our late mother of happy memory gave me when I was in Ferrara, drawn by four white steeds. Our serene Queen had a dress of crimson silk, richly embroidered with gold silk, with the headdress full of jewels, the train extremely long, and the sleeves shaped in a fashion resembling two wings, which made a fine sight. On her head she wore an ornament of the finest diamonds and pearls, and to enhance the occasion Messer Galeazzo Pallavicino was appointed to carry the train, and Count Conrad of Lando and Count Manfredo Torniello each of the sleeves . . .

The most serene Queen sat in the middle of the chariot, the illustrious Duchess Isabella [Isabella of Aragon, wife of Gian Galeazzo Sforza] on one side on the right, and myself on the left. The Duchess wore a gown of crimson silk with gold ribbons threaded on, as they were on a gown of mine of *beretino* cloth, as I may remind Your Excellency that you have seen in my wardrobe. I myself wore a gown of dark red velvet with a border with the motif of knots in gold, the background enamelled in white and the knots in green, as is appropriate. These knots were half a *braccia* high, and were also worked on the bodice in front and behind, and the sleeves were also worked with knots, and the robe was decorated with inserts of gold cloth, and on top it had a girdle of St Francis of large pearls, at the end of which, instead of buttons, was a beautiful uncut balas . . .

[After the crowning, the guests departed to the door of the cathedral and the Queen placed under a baldacchino of white damask trimmed with ermine.]

The baldacchino was again carried by the doctors, dressed as previously described, and beside the Queen followed the illustrious Duchess Isabella and myself, the relatives, the courtiers and lady guests, all on horseback, and likewise the ladies of the Queen and of the Duchess and my own ladies, dressed so they made a lovely sight, and above the others the Queen with the crown on her head. Nothing but gold and silver brocade was to be seen, and those less well dressed were in crimson velvet which was certainly marvellous, as were the numerous chains worn by the horsemen and others, and in the opinion of all so fine a spectacle was never seen, and the Russian Ambassador, who was there to observe, said that he had never seen such splendour.

4. The impressive appearance of a bride, 1502

Nicolo Cagnolo da Parma, Governor of Pescara and member of the retinue of the French Ambassador, describes Lucrezia Borgia, her clothes and jewellery on her arrival in Ferrara. The opulence of these, together with her costly dowry, were meant to impress an old-established ruling house, the Este, with the power of the Borgia family.

> 'Diario ferrarese dall'anno 1409 sino al 1502 di autori incerti', ed. G. Pardi, in *Rerum italicarum scriptores*, vol. 24, pt 7 (Bologna, 1928–37), p. 282.

> The most illustrious lady Lucrezia Borgia is more or less twenty-five years old [she was actually twenty-two], not very tall and of quite delicate build. Her face is rather long, the nose is sharp and beautiful, her hair is golden, the eyes blue. Her mouth is quite large, with very white teeth. Her neck is slim and white, and lightly flushed. She is always happy and smiling. She was dressed with a gown in crimson satin trimmed with bands of gold brocade, with a cloak of *morello* satin lined with very beautiful marten fur. On her head was a gold bonnet decorated with pearls, and around her neck a necklace of large pearls with a very beautiful pendant of great price hanging on her breast.

5. Citizens and people participate in the welcome of a royal bride, 1598

The passage through Ferrara in 1598 of Margherita of Austria (1584–1611) to marry Philip III of Spain in 1599 occasioned not only splendid dress, the viewing of relics, religious plays and a concert by nuns (Margherita was very pious) but popular festivities, including a regatta of women.

> Il Cavalier Reale, *La felicissima entrata della serenissima regina di Spagna, Donna Margherita d'Austria, nella città di Ferrara il 13. Novembre MDXCVIII* (Ferrara, 1598), unpaginated.

> In the evening wonderful festivities were held in the great hall, to which came a great number of Ferrarese ladies, masked and beautifully dressed. On their arrival, while they

were ascending the staircase hand in hand, they were greeted by a large number of trumpets and drums, and in the hall musicians and various fireworks.

On Monday Her Majesty went to Santa Maria in Vado to see the miraculous blood, and then to S. Vito, where she heard a lovely musical concert by those Reverend Sisters.

After a late dinner, on the following day thirty ladies from Comacchio rehearsed a wonderful regatta for the following day in six barges on the moat of the Castle. They were dressed in silk in six different combinations of five livery colours, that is green, red, yellow, yellow and turquoise, white, and white and turquoise, with feathers in their hair of similar colours. Some sounded trumpets, and sang in their customary fashion, making a cheerful sight.

The same Monday, in the evening, in the room of our lord's guard in the Castle a play of Judith and Holofernes in Latin was rehearsed, which was performed the following day to our lord by the pupils of the Jesuit Fathers.

b. Childbirth

6. Teodora degli Angeli describes the furnishings of the rooms in the Castello at Milan where Beatrice d'Este received visitors after childbirth

Teodora degli Angeli, lady-in-waiting to Eleonora of Aragon, in a letter to Isabella d'Este of 4 January 1493 describes the ceremonies following the birth of Massimiliano Sforza, the son of Beatrice d'Este and Ludovico Sforza (Il Moro) on 25 January of the same year. These were much more lavish than those following the birth of the son of Duke Gian Galeazzo and Duchess Isabella the previous year, in this reflecting Ludovico's ambitions. Teodora describes the sumptuously appointed rooms in which Beatrice received visitors, showing particular interest in the heraldic and emblematic aspects of the textile decorations, as well as in their great cost. Another letter of 24 February describes the later festivities.

A. Portilioli, 'La nascità di Massimiliano Sforza', *Archivio Storico Lombardo*, ser. 1, vol. 9, anno 9 (1882), pp. 328–9.

On today, Sunday, the ladies, lords, ambassadors, councillors and all the gentlemen began to visit my illustrious Lady of Bari [Beatrice] after childbirth, and today all the decoration is on show. First in the great Room of the Treasury, which serves as an antechamber for the illustrious lady after childbirth. The doors in the tribunal were opened to show vases of silver, two footmen at the first exit, then at each exit a footman and a distinguished major-domo, dressed in turquoise and silver brocade, showed them the chamber, and the ceremony due to ambassadors, lords, ladies and so on. As well as the silverware, this first chamber was furnished with a curtained bed draped with white hangings embroidered in deep red, with the device of the 'Manara' of stars and a yoke, then towards the fireplace was set out anther bed [*lontirolla*], all gilded, with four columns, with a *lettuccio* decorated with a coverlet and curtains of white damask with a large fringe around it, very splendid.

On the right of the beginning of the exit of this chamber was a curtain woven in gold with a man on horseback in perspective, and each bed had two guardians beside it, and each bed had four cushions embroidered like the hanging, two on the curtains and another two on the ground and on the coverlet, since the coverlet hung to the ground on three sides.

From there one entered the childbirth room, which had three beds, one large one in the middle, of velvet embroidered in gold and (. . .) and with a large device in the middle of two serpents entwined one against the other attached to a silver pole, and at the top of the pole was a letter B, as your ladyship has well seen, and then there were four cushions or more. To guard this, to which access is not barred, were two pages of the illustrious lady, then towards the fireplace the bed where my illustrious lady lies, with the illustrious Lady Duchess of Ferrara [Eleonora of Aragon] always in attendance, with a large number of ladies, and very many women and girls. This bed had side benches around it of deep red brocatelle, covered with a canopy of crimson satin all ornamented with raised gold letters and rosettes. Some of the letters spelt LUD and the others BEATRICE, delightfully done and both with an ornamental rosette, and likewise its superstructure, with a lovely golden apple around the canopy, and beneath it a large gold fringe. It is said that this cost about 8,000 ducats and that the tapestries and hangings amount to 7,000 ducats.

From this room one enters the baby's, where as before there were marshals, guards and footmen, where there was set out a large bed furnished with hangings with Sforza emblems of white and turquoise and the falcon and sun on the red ground, above a panther and birds, all embroidered in gold and with borders around.

Then towards the fireplace the baby's area, where he continually lies, covered with beautiful silks. Inside, the baby is completely covered with brocade, and the chamber is decorated inside with crimson. Then in another part of this chamber was set out a cradle made here in Milan, extremely elegant and all gilded, with four colonettes and a charming canopy, made of gilded cords and turquoise silk with gold rosettes between one cord and the other, really lovely, with its base fabric covered with brocade up to the canopy: truly it was rich and elegant in every way.

c. Ceremonies of welcome and triumph

7. Beatrice d'Este describes her reception on entering Venice in 1493

In a series of long letters to her husband, Ludovico il Moro, Beatrice d'Este describes the sumptuous festivities laid on for her and members of her Ferrarese family, at a time of political alliance between Milan, the Papacy and the Republic of Venice. In the following, written on 27 May, she describes the boats welcoming her at her entry into the city, evidently understanding the political messages conveyed through mythological allegories concerning the wisdom and the friendship of the two states.

P. Molmenti, *Storia di Venezia nella vita privata*, 3 vols (Bergamo, 1905–8), 2, pp. 627–8.

. . . We[4] set out again on our journey, meeting an infinite number of elaborately decorated galleys, boats and barges.

Among them there were figures of Neptune with his trident and Minerva with a spear. Next to them was a mountain, with a rock close by on top of which were the arms of the Pope and our illustrious lord [Duke Gian Galeazzo], together with your own and those of the *Signoria* of Venice. Neptune began to leap about, dancing and gambolling, and then Minerva did the same, and they met and danced together. Next Minerva struck the mountain with her spear and an olive tree came out: Neptune did the same with his trident, and out jumped a horse. There were other people next to the mountain with books, which signified the decision they had to make on the name of the principal city on the mountain, and they decided in favour of Minerva. So one was meant to conclude from this representation that states are maintained by coming together in peace, and moreover that those who perform such deeds will perpetuate their name there, as Minerva did in naming Athens, where, according to what is said, learning was founded.

Moving further on, more armed galleys and finely decorated boats appeared, amongst which was a galley armed by Milanese with a Moor on a seat with a weapon in his hand like a battleaxe, and shields with the ducal arms and your own, with banners attached to the stern and prow. Around him were figures of Wisdom with sceptre in hand, Fortitude, Temperance and Justice, which made a fine spectacle, together with gunshots, cannon-shots and rockets which were all quite splendid.

Next there were many barges finely decorated by all the trade guilds, which represented their crafts and made a fine sight. And thus we entered the Grand Canal, where the illustrious Doge, who had earlier behaved very graciously towards us, speaking on many subjects, took great pleasure in showing us the palaces of this city and especially the young ladies, who, as well as the 130 who were in the ducal barge, embellished with countless jewels, stood at the windows, all of them also finely decked out, and certainly it was an absolutely wonderful sight to behold.

8. The entry to the Ducal Palace in Venice of Dogaressa Zilia Dandolo, 1557

Occasionally, Venetian ceremonial afforded some public role to the Dogaressa.[5] Here, Zilia Dandolo, the consort of the newly elected Doge, Lorenzo Priuli, swears her own allegiance to the Venetian Republic. Much attention is given to the clothes of the Dogaressa and of the ladies accompanying her to San Marco, in line with the near-princely status of her husband and the wealth of the city. The displays in the Doge's Palace laid on by the leading trade guilds are also emphasised, and there may be the implication that the Dogaressa was expected to patronise and encourage the artisans producing goods such as luxury fabrics, metalwork or paintings.

Francesco Sansovino, *Venetia città nobilissima et singolare* [Venice, 1581], reprint (Bergamo, 2002), fs 154r–157r.
[After a display by the butchers near S. Marco, involving canvases showing their trade and symbols of St Mark and the arms of the ducal pair, the Doge and his retinue took the state barge, the *bucintoro*, to meet his wife at S. Barnaba.]

They boarded the *bucintoro* by a wooden bridge made with boats as is customary, and went to the house of Girolamo Priuli, a procurator of San Marco and brother of the Doge, which is situated in the area of S. Barnaba, on the canal. Here was a great display of gold hangings of the greatest beauty. They mounted the staircase, and were met by the Princess [the Dogaressa] dressed in her state robes in cloth of gold, with large sleeves, and with a brocade gown. On her head she wore a dazzling white veil of Cretan work which covered her shoulders. Over that she wore a crown or a horned [Doge's] cap of the same cloth of gold, and slightly curved. After the due salutations, she was asked to swear obedience to her duties. She did so, and then gave to the councillors, according to the old custom, a bag of gold bouclé fabric, and another one to the Grand Chancellor . . .

[Then a regatta organised by the various guilds began on the Grand Canal, after which the Dogaressa was escorted to S. Marco with a cortege of ladies dressed according to age and status.]

After these, 235 young gentlewomen followed, two by two, dressed in satin, damask or white moire silk. They were all adorned with pearls of great size and beauty, and they had collars and headdresses of various fashions, studded with pearls and precious stones of inestimable value. Among these were six brides, with their hair and gold threads spread on their shoulders. Behind these there were 21 older ladies dressed in black, with veils on their heads. The last of these was the wife of Vittorio Grimani, a Procurator of S. Marco, dressed in black satin, with long sleeves in the ducal fashion, since she was the wife of a procurator. The secretaries and the Grand Chancellor followed, and then the two sons-in-law of the Prince, and between them the son of the Prince, dressed in crimson in the ducal fashion. After them, the two daughters of the Prince followed, separated from the other ladies so that they could be recognised. They were dressed in bouclé brocade over white velvet. One was the wife of Antonio Morosino, the other of Pietro Cappello . . .

[The Dogaressa then entered the Ducal Palace, within whose decorated corridors elaborate displays had been set up by the main guilds, such as the barbers, goldsmiths, tailors, mercers, painters and others.]

Moving further on, she was received by the chief official of the goldsmiths . . .They were situated near the barbers, and on the first side of the wall were many tapestries with figures, delicately made, in panels with friezes in different colours, a wonderful sight, and in front they had an elaborate *credenza* for silverware, with many other ornaments all in gold and solid silver. And, changing direction, she entered a big corridor looking over the Piazza, whose ceiling was completely covered from one side to the other with a turquoise blue canvas with gilt stars, and on the inner side decorated with the finest tapestries, and on the outer with exquisite hangings. And the columns and the balustrades, 136 in number, were also covered in the same way, apart from the four columns flanking the Office of the Criminal Magistrates, as they were covered with hangings of crimson and gold damask, with twelve excellently decorated with different motifs, and each vault had its own festoon, with the arms of the Dogaressa . . . Walking further along, she came to the Office of Foreign Affairs, where the mercers had their stand, very finely decked out with silk hangings, with an awning covered with brocade worked in various colours. And above the doorway there were embroideries of gold thread and pearls, extremely rich, and above a column a tapestry of green silk with gold work, with many lovely festoons as ornament . . . Arriving at the Grand Salon adorned with brocade hangings, she took her seat on the ducal throne, and sat there amidst the councillors, the heads of the Council of Forty, Matteo Dandolo, the Cavalier Cappello, and her son Pietro dressed in crimson silk, and on her right were all the matrons . . .

[There followed feasting, dancing, and fireworks in the courtyard of the palace, with bullfights and other festivities in the Piazza on the subsequent day.]

WOMEN TRAVELLING AND SIGHTSEEING

Although moralists advocated that women, at least of the higher social classes, should leave their houses infrequently, women did go out to church and to social functions within their cities. Though they travelled further afield much less than did men, they might also stay in the country in the summer months, visit their relatives or friends in other towns, or attend shrines and pilgrimage sites. All of these could have provided attentive female spectators with opportunities for observing unfamiliar styles of architecture or art. However, only a few surviving letters demonstrate them doing so.

9. Beatrice d'Este views S. Marco and its Treasury, Venice, 1493

Beatrice evidently enjoyed the less official aspects of her stay in Venice. For her, as for other observers, the Basilica and Treasury of St Mark's demonstrated the longevity and piety of the Republic, while the shopping streets and the magnificently dressed Venetian ladies exhibited its wealth. But, as she conveys in this letter to her husband of 30 May 1493, she was also well aware of her own duty to display the wealth and luxury of Milan, with her spectacular dress and jewels.[6]

Molmenti (1905–8), 2, p. 628.

This morning the illustrious lady my mother, Signor Don Alfonso, Madonna Anna and I, with all our party, set out to go and hear Mass at S. Marco, where the Doge had invited us with our singers, and to show us the Treasury. But before we reached S. Marco we disembarked at the Rialto and went on foot through the streets called 'the Mercerie' where there were shops selling spices and silks and other goods, all well displayed, and which from the huge quantity and quality of different goods of other crafts made a wonderful sight, so that they caused us to linger to see now one thing, now another. We would not have minded if we had never reached S. Marco. Arriving there our trumpeters sounded above the church on a loggia in front. We found the Doge who came to meet us at the door of S. Marco and placed himself between my mother and me, according to the order observed on other occasions, and led us to the altar where we found the priest beautifully turned out. The Prince and our party knelt and our confessions were heard, and then we went to the seats reserved for us and heard Mass, which the priest sang solemnly with his other assistants, and our singers embellished, pleasing the Prince and the others greatly with their song, especially Cordiero who has always taken great care to give honour and satisfaction to Your Lordship. Once Mass was over we went, still with the Prince, to the Treasury, where we endured the worst trouble in the world in entering, owing to the great crowds of people which were gathered, as they also were in the streets, although everything was done to make us room, even the Doge crying out. The Doge had to give up because of the great crush of the crowd, and just a few of us got in and even then with great difficulty. Once in, we saw the treasure one piece at a time, which was a great delight both in its vast extent and in the beautiful jewels and splendid vessels. Going out we went through the Piazza S. Marco around the stands for the Ascensiontide fair, where we were amazed by the abundance of fine glassware we found, and here we were forced to stay a long time, and seeing it was late we went back home to dine as it was the seventeenth hour. I was dressed in an embroidered overdress of burgundy cloth with the reverse of the bodice decorated with caduceus; I had a string of pearls at my neck and a ruby on my bosom. These jewels, and especially the ruby, were much gazed at so that people said: 'She hasn't worn the same ones twice!' – some of their eyes nearly touched my breast while gawping at them. And seeing such avidity I said I would willingly show it to them, if they would come to the house.

10. The travels of Isabella d'Este, 1494–1525

The travel letters of Isabella d'Este show a development over her adult life: as a young woman she remarks on luxurious or novel details, but later on is more impressed by classical buildings, which stimulate her desire both to acquire and to emulate them.

i. Isabella d'Este in Urbino to Francesco Gonzaga, 16 April 1494
Il palazzo di Federico da Montefeltro, ed. M. L. Politecchi (Urbino, 1985), doc. LXXVIII, pp. 372–3.

Our most noble Lord,
And so you may keep informed of all our doings, I can tell you that we left Gubbio on Friday and came to Caglio. First we came to a castle called Cantiano which was all decorated with arches and festoons of foliage with Gonzaga and Feltre arms and devices, and a fine meal was provided, and all the streets vied with each other with countless arches and doorways decorated with greenery. We remained there all Saturday. On Sunday we went to Casteldurante whose honours surpassed all the others, not only with decorations with arms and arches like those at Caglio but with all the streets covered with white cloth, and in the middle of the piazza there was a triumphal chariot with the Seven Virtues, who recited verses. We stayed put all Monday so we could go to the Park, but the rain prevented it. We did go yesterday after a meal and much enjoyed chasing and killing a

deer. I cannot describe the loveliness of the place. I think I recall on other occasions it being drawn to Your Excellency's attention if we should spend time here at Urbino. At Urbino I found the palace much more beautiful than I had expected from its reputation. Apart from its inherent beauty, they decorated it richly with tapestries and furnishings and silver tableware.

ii. Isabella d'Este writes to Francesco Gonzaga on the Roman ruins at Sermione, 20 March 1514
Isabella's letter to her husband during her travels around Lake Garda refers to his recent illness.

A. Pedrazzoli, 'La Marchesa Isabella d'Este Gonzaga a diporto sul Lago di Garda colla sua corte', *Archivio Storico Lombardo*, ser. 2, vol. 7, anno 17 (1890), pp. 866–78, p. 873.

My Illustrious Lord . . . Yesterday I went to the mountains to see the ruins, and entered the caves to have a good look. They are truly marvellous, especially to me, not having visited the Roman ones. I am not surprised the Romans liked this place and revelled in it, for it is really beautiful and deserves wonderful buildings. If God grants you health and we can enjoy such places in peace, we could build some sort of small house above them, not for the fame that might befit our state, but for our pleasure and relaxation. I spent all day, on foot and on horseback, contemplating the ruins and the site.

iii. Isabella d'Este from Rome to her son Federico Gonzaga in Mantua, 18 May 1525, describing a dinner reception at the Villa Madama
J. Shearman, *Raphael in Early Modern Sources 1483–1602*, 2 vols (New Haven and London, 2003), 1, pp. 792–3.

On last Monday we were given a most sumptuous and delightful supper at His Holiness's *vigna*[7] at which were executed all the ceremonies which, according to everyone, would have been performed in the presence of His Holiness himself: served with the silverware and his personal servants down to His Holiness's cup-bearer, and while the meal lasted there were different types of music which we much enjoyed. But what was most delightful was the building itself: even though it was unfinished it looked exquisite, in a very lovely site and rich in many wonderful antiquities, which we have often longed to have at one of our own places.

11. Cities of Italy compared: Moderata Fonte, *The Worth of Women*, 1600
In the dialogue by the Venetian writer Moderata Fonte (1555–92), seven fictional women from patrician or citizen backgrounds assess the attractions of different cities. The male relatives of such women would have been involved in the government of the Venetian mainland territories, so that their female kin could have visited or stayed in the cities mentioned. Although it comes from a 'literary' text, it is plausible that such conversations could have taken place.

Moderata Fonte, *Il Merito delle donne* [1600], ed. A. Chemello (Mirano and Venice, 1988), pp. 101–2; *The Worth of Women*, ed. and trans. V. Cox (Chicago, 1997), pp. 155–6.

'And I', said Leonora, 'feel affection for the Adige, since when I was living in Verona with the [Venetian] authorities I had an enjoyable time on the river with many ladies who accompanied me'.
    'Certainly', said the Queen,[8] 'that is indeed a fine and distinguished city, as is Vicenza, through which the gentle river Bachiglione flows, a city which, though not very large, is well-populated and rich, and full of fine buildings and graceful gardens. But the city of Verona is very old, dating from the time of the ancient Romans whose colony it was, and there remain several ruins there, like the Arena called the amphitheatre and many other buildings. Despite it having been many times sacked by the barbarians, nowadays it flourishes more than ever'. . . .
    'Whatever you others may say you like', Corinna then said, 'to me the city of Brescia seems more flourishing and prosperous than the other Italian cities and its territory

extremely fertile. I used to stay with my grandfather in the government there, and the countryside is very gentle, although on one side it has mountains and is full of many castles and important fortresses.'

'The river Arno', said Cornelia, 'still deserves to be placed above them all'.

'Yes, certainly', replied Corinna, 'since it is the celebrated river dividing the fair city in which such wonderful intellects flourished: Dante, Boccaccio and the supreme Petrarch, and others both past and present whom it would take too long to mention. Apart from which, at present it is so abundant in fine buildings, lovely gardens and illustrious citizens that it could be called unrivalled in the world.'

Notes

1 A vast bibliography by theatre and music as well as social and political historians exists on Renaissance spectacles, with varying attention to their female participants or viewers. Wide-ranging works are R. Strong, *Art and Power: Renaissance Festivals 1450–1650* (Woodbridge, 1984); E. Muir, *Civic Ritual in Renaissance Venice* (Princeton, 1981); F. Cruciani, *Teatro nel Rinascimento a Roma 1450–1550* (Rome, 1983); B. Wisch and S. Scott Minshower (eds), *"All the World's a Stage...". Art and Pageantry in the Renaissance and Baroque*, 2 vols (University Park, PA, 1990).

2 An appendix listing many of the published accounts of major festivals in Europe from 1494 to 1641 is in Strong, pp. 175–79. Discussion of later Florentine texts, with translated extracts, are in A. M. Cummings, *The Politicized Muse. Music for Medici Festivals, 1512–1537* (Princeton, 1992), and J. M. Saslow, *The Medici Wedding of 1589* (New Haven and London, 1996); for Ferrara see B. Mitchell, *1586, a Year of Pageantry in Later Renaissance Ferrara* (Binghamton, NY, 1998), and for Venice, P. Fortini Brown, 'Measured friendship, calculated pomp: the ceremonial welcomes of the Venetian Republic', in Wisch and Scott Minshower (eds), 1, pp. 136–86.

3 The supposed veil of St Veronica, retaining the imprint of Christ's face, was a very well-known and revered relic.

4 Beatrice, her mother the Duchess of Ferrara, and her brother-in-law Alfonso I d'Este and his wife.

5 For the roles played by the Dogaressas of Venice, see Holly S. Hurlbert, *The Dogaressas of Venice 1200–1500. Wife and Icon* (New York, 2006).

6　For discussion of this letter, see Welch (2005), pp. 183–4.
7　The Villa Madama outside Rome, begun by Raphael and his workshop, and then owned by Pope Clement VII.
8　A courtesy title given to Adriana, as the oldest woman of the group.

PART II

WOMEN, SECULAR ART AND ARTISTS: COMMISSIONING, BUYING, PRESERVING

We have seen how many women from the highest ranks of society were able, and ready, to spend considerable amounts of money on expensive objects. Money is also the unspoken protagonist in many of the passages included in Part II, which is dedicated to sources concerning women's patronage of secular buildings and their decoration, to their patronage and use of portraits, and to their relationships with artists. The women who could afford to build palaces and villas, who commissioned painted cycles to decorate these buildings, and who collected objects and works of art, came from reigning families or from the aristocracy. In the society of early modern Italy these were the only women who could rely on large sums of money: their own personal allowances, gifts, investments, systems of credits and loans, and even, contrary to popular misconception, their own personal earnings.[1] This was the case, for example, with the extraordinarily wealthy Eleonora di Toledo, who had the monopoly of the wheat trade in the Duchy of Tuscany.[2]

Commissioning buildings and gardens and buying works for their collections were for these women not only pleasurable occupations, but also duties which were part and parcel of the life and role of an aristocratic lady.[3] Their *splendore* and *magnificenza* had to be shown publicly by their architectural surroundings. As we have seen, aristocratic women and, later, women belonging to other ranks, gained a knowledge of architectural styles based on the buildings of ancient Rome, and came to understand the language of allegory. Sure in their own taste and requirements, they became skilled in their dealings with artists, commissioning buildings and decorative cycles, at times supervising the construction from a distance with the help of agents, or acquiring works of art.[4]

They might also gain an awareness and appreciation of the different characteristics of contemporary artists, perhaps acquiring a more articulate language to describe them. On a smaller scale, portraiture became an artistic genre with which women were familiar, which was emotionally important to them, and on which they confidently expressed their opinions.

Notes

1 See E. Welch, 'Women in debt: financing female authority in Renaissance Italy', in L. Arcangeli and S. Peyronel (eds), *Donne di Potere nel Rinascimento* (Rome, 2008), pp. 45–65. On the social power of aristocratic women, see, in the same volume, C. Antenhofer, 'Il potere delle gentildonne: l'esempio di Barbara di Brandenburgo e Paula Gonzaga', pp. 68–87. See also Welch, 'Women as patrons and clients in the courts of Quattrocento Italy', in L. Panizza (ed.), *Women in Italian Renaissance Culture and Society* (Oxford, 2000), pp. 18–34.

2 On Eleonora di Toledo's finances and patronage, see B. L. Edelstein, 'Nobildonne napoletane e committenza: Eleonora d'Aragona ed Eleonora di Toledo a confronto', *Quaderni Storici*, 104:2 (2000), pp. 295–319.

3 See B. Borrello, 'Protezioni di donne. Mogli aristocratiche e patriziato cittadino (Gubbio, Rome and Siena), XV–XVI secolo', in Arcangeli and Peyronel (eds), (2008), pp. 223–45.

4 See K. McIver, 'Two Emilian noblewomen and patronage networks in the Cinquecento', in S. E. Reiss and D. G. Wilkins (eds), *Beyond Isabella: Secular Women Patrons of Art in Renaissance Italy* (Kirksville, MO, 2001), pp. 160–76, and 'Matrons and patrons: power and influence in the courts of Northern Italy in the Renaissance', *Artibus et Historiae*, 22:43 (2001), pp. 75–89.

⮞ 5 ⮜

THE BUILDING AND
EMBELLISHMENT OF PALACES,
VILLAS AND GARDENS

After the possession of adequate finances, fashion and taste were the prerequisite for commissioning palaces and villas: a building had to show knowledge of what was fashionable in the architectural practice of the time, as well as of the principles of antique architecture. The vast majority of palaces and villas were commissioned by men, but recent research has brought to light the contribution of women.[1] Husbands and wives also commissioned palaces and decorative schemes together, so that it is often difficult, but also unhelpful, to separate their roles, unless they are clearly documented.[2]

Building a palace was traditionally the most public affirmation of power: it was a monument to the individual and to his lineage. It was also considered to increase the beauty and glory of a city, and therefore was an act of civic homage to the city itself and to its inhabitants. Villas denoted another important aspect of the lives of the elite: that of time spent in *otium* away from *negotium* and the duties and preoccupations of government. Surrounded by the comforts and beauty of the villa, in the middle of the tamed nature of a garden decorated by fountains and grottoes, enjoying the colours and smells of fruit and flowers, mind and spirit would be open to music-making, poetry and *civil conversatione*. Some of these gardens became the subject of literary works in verse or in prose: the garden of Caterina Cornaro at Asolo, which surrounded her villa and also included a wood for hunting, was celebrated, probably with a degree of literary licence, by Pietro Bembo in his *Asolani*. Villas were often given to women as gifts which they would then enlarge and embellish, and which they in turn bequeathed to their female relatives.

Such buildings required decoration of various kinds. The largest proportion of historical, mythological or allegorical paintings commissioned by aristocratic women were cycles in their palaces or villas, many of which celebrated womanly virtues.[3] The final section of this chapter includes documents on the collections of works of art and objects which were part of the surroundings of women of the elite. These were again a sign of their wealth and refinement, but could also have a special sentimental value.

PRESTIGE AND SPLENDOUR: PALACES

1. Caterina Piccolomini's palace in Siena

Just after Enea Silvio Piccolomini became Pope Pius II in 1458, his sister Caterina, a widow, begun to acquire land to build a palace for herself in Siena (**figure 8**). Documents mention the Sienese Antonio Federighi, and a 'Magister Bernardus', traditionally identified as the Florentine architect and sculptor Bernardo Rossellino. The three-storey palace has an impressive Florentine-style façade in rusticated travertine, almost completely rebuilt after a fire in 1523.[4]

S. Borghesi and L. Banchi, *Nuovi documenti per la storia dell'arte senese* (Siena, 1898), pp. 201–2.

15 October 1460
Before the magnificent and powerful Lords Priors, Governors of the Commune, and the Captain of the magnificent city of Siena, the Lady Caterina de' Piccolomini, sister of His Holiness Pope Pius II, humbly prays Their Lordships to see fit, with appropriate recommendation, to allow the following: that she or others in her name should be allowed to bring into Siena travertine and any other type of stone which is necessary for the palace which she is constructing anew, both for the façade and for any other part of the building, without having to pay tax to the Siena Commune, despite any law or regulation stating the contrary. [She prays] Their Lordships to waive [the said laws], considering that the Lady Caterina has the intention and the desire to build this

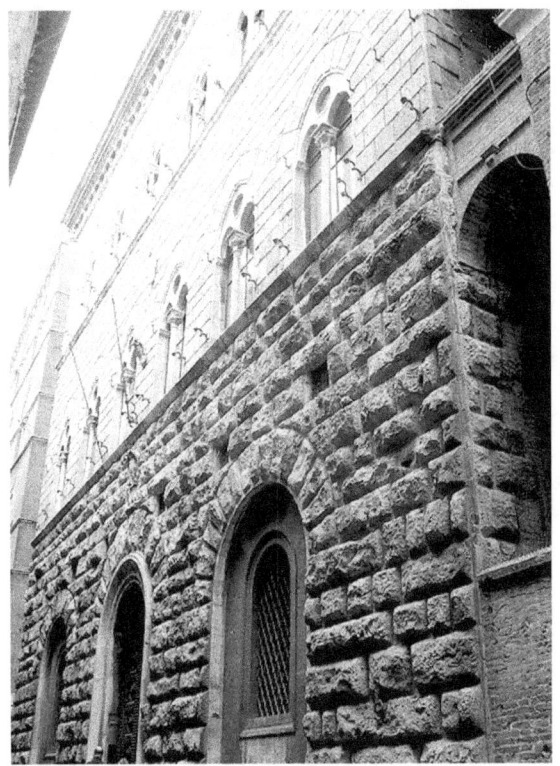

8. Palazzo Piccolomini (Palazzo delle Papesse), Siena, c. 1460.

most praiseworthy palace at great expense, for the honour of this magnificent city and of Their Magnificent and Most Excellent Lordships.

The said Lady Caterina has had a highly skilled master design the said palace, and he has advised her that if the façade is to look good, she would need to occupy the alley-way next to the palace, which goes down towards the Campo. Also, if the street behind the palace were to be left as it is now, the building would seem lacking. Therefore the Lady Caterina, following the advice she has received, petitions to be allowed to occupy the alley, completely or in part, according to the opinion of the said master, and to be allowed also to occupy the street behind it, towards Piazza Manetti, also according to the opinion of the said master. The Lady Caterina offers to restore the said street to the present width, within two years from obtaining this permission, in spite of any law or regulation to the contrary. All expenses will be paid for by the exceptional generosity of that lady.

2. Eleonora di Toledo and the Pitti Palace

In 1549 Eleonora di Toledo paid 9,000 gold *scudi* from her own dowry for the large unfinished palace which Luca Pitti had begun to build during the previous century on a hillside on the left bank of the Arno. Eleonora also bought a large area in front of the palace and some land on the hill behind. Work was begun on the gardens and then on the palace itself. One of Eleonora's favourite artists, Bartolomeo Ammannati, was given the commission to enlarge the palace and to build a spectacular courtyard open towards the gardens. In the following letter, another favourite, the sculptor Baccio Bandinelli, compliments Eleonora for her expertise, and explains why princes and good architects need each other.[5]

G. Gaye, *Carteggio inedito d'artisti dei secoli XIV, XV, XVI*, 3 vols (Florence, 1839–40), 3, p. 4.

Baccio Bandinelli, from Florence, to Eleonora di Toledo, 30 May 1558
Most Illustrious and Excellent Duchess, I have been to the Pitti Palace, as Your Excellency asked me to do, and I have looked at the addition you have commissioned, which brings the old and the new together very comfortably and conveniently. Architecture has no other objective, one so useful that he who can achieve it makes possible the pleasure, happiness and life of all men, since the building itself has the excellent proportions of a human body. Therefore wise princes have always tried to have the best and most able master to devise fine plans. Since in the construction of a building a master has to manage many different artisans in different trades, he must, if he wants to be feared and respected, set an example

of upright morals, and above all be extremely vigilant and careful, because in this way time is not wasted and neither is the Prince's money . . .

3. Margherita of Austria (1522–1586) and the Palazzo Farnese in Piacenza

As a young widow, Margherita of Austria, the illegitimate daughter of Emperor Charles V, married Ottavio Farnese, grandson of Pope Paul III. In 1558 Margherita, by then Duchess of Parma and Piacenza, begun to built a palace in Piacenza, paid for with money from the inhabitants of that city.[6] The commission was first given to Ottavio's court architect, Francesco Paciotto, and from 1560 to Jacopo Barozzi da Vignola, court architect to Cardinal Alessandro Farnese. Margherita, who had been appointed Governor of the Netherlands in 1559, followed the work from Brussels. She did not see her commission completed: the work was interrupted in 1568, when, just after her return from Brussels, she retired to her estates in Abruzzo. Here she demonstrates her detailed knowledge of building work.

i. A. Lodovisi and G. Trent (eds), *I Vignola: Giacomo e Giacinto Barozzi* (Vignola, 2004), pp. 76–7.

Margherita of Austria, from Brussels, to the *podestà* of Parma, Gabriele Boccabarile, 30 August 1561
We are very grateful for your letter of the 17th past with the detailed information about the building work. We are extremely pleased that everything is proceeding promptly, which, as you know, is what we wish . . . We would have liked to keep the drawing sent to us by Messer Giacinto [Jacopo Barozzi's son],[7] so that we might follow closely the progress of what is being built. However, since it is absolutely necessary for you to have the plan, we are sending it back so that you can give it to Bosello [the master-of-works Giovanni Boselli]. Please do this without losing any time.
We very much wish to know if it is possible to have a similar [plan]. You could ask Bosello on our behalf to have another one made, and send it to us as soon as possible . . .

ii. B. Adorni, 'Il ruolo di Margherita d'Austria nella costruzione del Palazzo Farnese a Piacenza', in S. Mantini (ed.), *Margherita d'Austria (1522–1586): costruzioni politiche e diplomazia tra corte Farnese e monarchia spagnola* (Rome, 2003), p. 113.

Margherita of Austria, from Brussels, to Giovanni Boselli, 13 November 1561

. . . Let us come to the modifications which you say are necessary for the rooms facing North, as between these and those facing West there are more exposed walls than comfortable rooms. We think that your considerations are very sound and appropriate. It is quite clear that we would gain many comfortable and salubrious rooms, which, in winter, will not be bad for our person.

We also liked the place you have designed with good judgement for the *guardaroba*. Since all this can be done without changes to the cross-section of the building, or to the exterior of the palace, we think that all the above should be done as you say. However, we would like you to discuss all this with the Duke [Ottavio Farnese], who agrees with the changes, so that everything can be done without delay. We would like you to communicate all the above to Signor Pietro Vitelli,[8] who has a good understanding of such things, and hear what he thinks.

The other point I want make is this: if dressed stones were used for the slits in the small basement rooms, it would be extremely expensive. We suggest you to think about this matter, so that we do not end up wasting money: since those slits are below ground level and therefore will not be seen, why should dressed stones be used instead of bricks? We, however, lack the expertise that you and others in the trade possess, and therefore we would like to have your opinion both about this matter, and about anything else which may come to your attention. Tell us frankly what you think, communicating first of all with His Excellency, so that everything can be carried out for the good of the building. We especially entrust the care of the building to you . . .

For the basement slits, do not leave them as they are, but continue with the doorways and the windows in brick till you reach the first floor.

RELAXATION AND ENJOYMENT: VILLAS AND GARDENS

4. Isabella d'Este and Porto Mantovano

The Palazzo di Porto was one of the Gonzaga villas close to Mantua. It had always been a retreat for Gonzaga wives, and Francesco Gonzaga gave it to his wife Isabella d'Este as a gift. Isabella commissioned building work to make the villa more beautiful and comfortable. Porto Mantovano became one of her favourite places, and from 1490 till her death in 1539 Isabella spent much time there, in the company of her court and her guests. The copious correspondence about the new buildings at Porto demonstrates Isabella's knowledge and care in dealing with all the stages of the work. It also shows how Isabella was still in very close contact with the Este court and how much she relied on her brother's advice.

C. M. Brown, "'Al suo amenissimo Palazzo di Porto" Biagio Rossetti and Isabella d'Este', *Atti e Memorie. Accademia Nazionale Virgiliana di Scienze, Lettere ed Arti*, new ser., 58 (1990), pp. 44–6, 48.

Isabella d'Este from Mantua, to the Este court official Girolamo Ziliolo, 29 July 1511

While our major-domo was there in Ferrara, we informed the most illustrious lord the Duke [Alfonso I d'Este], our most honoured brother, that we wished to build a palace, and that we wanted His Excellency to send an engineer to design it. My request was satisfied. We could not, however, build it in the way we desired, because we could not divert a river: our Lord [Francesco Gonzaga] said that it would damage that area of the town. Therefore we decided to have a smaller building and, accordingly, we made the drawing of a fanciful small building (*casino*). For this I do not need an engineer, but a builder who must be a good master, able to work well with his own hands and also capable of leading a team of builders, as well as building vaults and making a good job. Therefore, as you are with His Excellency, we would like you to ask him if he can find such a builder, and send him to us by this messenger. He could then see the drawing, and we could discuss with him whether he is willing to take on this work, and provide him with every-thing necessary. We have written at length about this to Bernardino Prosperi [a Mantuan court official]. He should be with you, as I also want to give him the task to find out whether we could borrow, or buy, a few columns there, to save some time.

Girolamo Ziliolo, from Ferrara, to Isabella d'Este, 1 August 1511

In reply to what Your Ladyship asked me to do, the most illustrious lord the Duke sends you the engineer Master Biagio Rossetti, even if I made it clear that Your Ladyship did not need him because the idea for the project has been changed. With him is Master Bartolomeo Tristano, the builder, expert in his craft, especially vaulting. [The Duke] has instructed them to serve Your Ladyship as well as pos-sible. His Excellency wanted to send you the engineer so that you shall be entirely satisfied.

Isabella d'Este, from Mantua, to Alfonso I d'Este, 9 August 1511

Your Excellency knew my needs better that I did, since he sent me Master Biagio, your architect, together with the builder I had requested. Truly, it has been the right thing to do, because, even though I had already made a drawing of my building, which I liked, nevertheless he has done a new drawing which I like much more. I give Your Lordship all my thanks for this. I send Master Biagio and the builder back to you, as we did not agree about the price, as Master Biagio will tell you. Your Lordship will give to Geronimo Ziliolo the task of making a deal either with this master builder Bartolomeo, or with another who would be able to serve me well. [Ziliolo] should tell the builder with whom he makes the deal that he and Master Biagio should come here, because I want them to start with the foundations as soon as possible. The sooner they come, the more pleased I shall be.

[The planting of the gardens of Porto Mantovano was supervised by Isabella with the same care and interest as the building work. She used all kinds of plants, amongst which were fruit trees, poplars, cypress trees, mulberry trees, vines and various flowers, in order to turn the gardens into a delight admired by all.]

Biagio Rossetti, from Ferrara, to Isabella d'Este, 5 November 1511
I am sending to Your Ladyship, by Jacopo, your bailiff, four hundred and seventy cuttings. Amongst them are: sixty-eight pear trees of various species, all good; three hundred and ninety apple trees, also of various kinds, and good; twelve apricot trees of excellent kind. I am absolutely sure that Your Ladyship will be well served. I have written to Master Bartolomeo Tristano to prepare the orchard and to plant the cuttings according to your wish. I recommend Your Ladyship to let me know how many more she needs if the cuttings don't take root, and I shall send you more.

5. Eleonora Gonzaga (1493–1550) and the Villa Imperiale, Pesaro

From 1529 onwards, the Duchess of Urbino, Eleonora Gonzaga, commissioned the restructuring of a villa near Pesaro as well as the building of a new villa attached to the old one.[9] The architect Girolamo Genga was put in charge of the building work. He also supervised the decorative schemes for the interior of the old villa, as well as the creation of the gardens. With the new fresco cycles, the elegant new building and the gardens, Eleonora turned the Imperiale into a beautiful and comfortable place for pleasure and relaxation, dedicated to her husband, Francesco Maria della Rovere. On the exterior, an inscription by Pietro Bembo states the function of the villa, as well as glorifying the military virtues of the Duke: FR. MARIAE DUCI METAURENSIUM A BELLIS REDEUNTI / LEONORA UXOR ANIMI EIUS CAUSA VILLAM EDIFICAVIT. / PRO SOLE PRO PULVERE PRO VIGILIIS PRO LABORIBUS / UT MILITARE NEGOTIUM REQUIETE INTERPOSITA / CLARIOREM LAUDEM FRUCTUSQUE UBERIORES PARIAT.

These letters, selected from the large number written during the work, demonstrate how Eleonora followed the example of her mother Isabella d'Este, giving great attention to practical matters. The extract from Bembo's letter provides a contemporary insight in the perception and understanding of the architectural qualities of the villa.[10]

i. G. Gronau (1936), pp. 135, 138–9.

Stefano Vigerio, Governor of the State of Urbino during the absence of Francesco Maria della Rovere, from Pesaro, to Eleonora Gonzaga, 14 October 1537

Today I was at the Imperiale to carry out what the most illustrious Lord asked me to do. The window-panes were removed, and the shutters and doors of the rooms of the Lord and Her Excellency closed. The upstairs room, where Your Ladyship's ladies-in-waiting live, are occupied by stone-cutters and builders, and Genga tells me that it cannot be done otherwise.

The citron trees are fine, and there is a wonderful one from Savona which produces a lot of blossom. If the winter does not damage it, I hope that when you return there will be fruit.

The pergolas, espaliers and the other plans of this new gardener, are taking a long time, and there will be major continuing expenses. He could look after the gardens that need to be made and the citron trees by himself, especially as a fair number of these could be planted as espaliers in the enclosed garden, where there is water stored. Others could be accommodated at the Imperiale as necessary: there is no need to dig these in, but to arrange them among the gardens and the trees.

Stefano Vigerio, from Pesaro, to Eleonora Gonzaga, 4 November 1538

Ricciardetto has ordered 220 plants of bitter oranges from Fermo. For the espaliers in the enclosed garden I would like Genga to change the [irrigation] canals so that they bring water to the cistern. Messer Geronimo is not happy about this, so I have told him that he should first see if the trees stand up to the cold and the wind in the area where there are no canals, as we can always change them. Personally, I very much doubt that they will bear it as easily as he believes. If you think it necessary, you should mention this to the most illustrious Lord [Francesco Maria della Rovere].

Eleonora Gonzaga, from Venice, to Stefano Vigerio, 10 February 1538 [1539]

About the gardener's plan to change the canals which bring water to the cistern, we did not want to discuss it with the most illustrious Lord, as we believe His Excellency would not have liked it, and neither do we. In fact, doing it would cost money and time, more than is necessary, since His Excellency's greatest wish is to be able to enjoy those fountains when he is in the palace. You will, however, get together with Genga, and, considering the matter together, you will arrive at a decision about it that seems possible and will work well.

ii. G. Bottari, S. Ticozzi, *Raccolta di lettere sulla pittura, scultura e architettura*, 8 vols, [Milan, 1822–1825], (Bologna, 1979-80), V, pp. 196–8.

Pietro Bembo, from Gubbio, to Eleonora Gonzaga, 19 December 1543.

... I then went to Pesaro, where I was received with much honour by order of the Lord Duke. I saw Your Excellency's Imperiale with immense pleasure, because I very much wished to see it, and also because it is a building which has been conceived and executed with true knowledge of the art [of architecture], both in its antique manner, and in its beautiful and graceful *invenzioni*, better than in any other modern building I have seen. For this I deeply congratulate Your Ladyship. Certainly, my friend Genga is a great and rare architect, and has greatly exceeded my expectations.

6. A fountain for the gardens of Palazzo Pitti

The task of creating a new large garden behind Palazzo Pitti was given to Niccolò Tribolo, who had already designed the garden and the fountains for the Medici villa at Castello. The intention was to provide a splendid setting to the palace, transforming it into a spectacular residence. While Palazzo Pitti had the architectural characteristics of a town palace, its garden setting turned it into a *villa urbana*. After Tribolo, the project was continued by Bartolomeo Ammannati, and then by Bernardo Buontalenti.[11]

Here the ducal steward Luca Martini, on behalf of Eleonora di

Toledo, asks the Medici court sculptor Baccio Bandinelli to design a fountain for the *prato* just behind the palace.

L. A. Waldman, *Baccio Bandinelli and Art at the Medici Court* (Philadelphia, 2004), p. 455.

Luca Martini, from Pisa, to Baccio Bandinelli in Florence, 25 January 1501
Most Magnificent and Excellent Knight,[12] etc. I have not written to you earlier in order not to disturb you, but now I am writing following the wish of the most illustrious and excellent lady, the Duchess . . .

Coming to the task which the most illustrious Duchess has given me, I am letting you know that she wants you to make a model as soon as possible for a fountain to be placed in the middle of the meadow in the garden of the Pitti [Palace]. In the basin there would be only four *braccia* of water, at fifty barrels an hour. As the space is very large, she would like a fountain which is correspondingly large. She has asked me to urge you [to make a drawing], and to send it to her as soon as possible. Since I know that you take Her Illustrious Excellency's business to heart, I shall say no more, apart from offering myself [to your service] and recommending myself to you.

7. The delights of a garden
The poetess Chiara Matraini (1515–1604), author of a number of religious treatises as well as poetry, also wrote letters intended for publication. While her description of the pleasant pastimes in a garden might be fictitious, similar events would have certainly taken place in villas such as those in this section.

Lettere di Madonna Chiara Matraini (Venice, 1597), fols 22r–25r.

To the lady Batina Centuriona
On delightful recreation
Most illustrious, virtuous and esteemed lady, on the 15th of last month I received your dear and affectionate letter, from which I learnt with the greatest pleasure that you had been in the villa at Peio to enjoy the company of many gen-

tlemen and honourable ladies. I rejoice with you at all your pleasures and delights, as I know you would do the same for me. Therefore, as you have confided in me and trusted me with the tale of your pleasurable entertainment, I shall now tell you about the virtuous pleasures I had in the company of a merry crowd of young ladies and their husbands in the villa belonging to one of them.

Well then, one day, during the month of May, I was strolling together with three most noble ladies some way out of town . . . As we walked, joking and laughing about one thing and another, without noticing we found ourselves near a fine and ornate palace on a small hill. On entering its spacious and beautiful courtyard, we saw before us a large and charming garden, with long paths covered with pergolas heavy with citron and orange trees in blossom. Their rich scent was mixed with the smell of roses and jasmine with which the hedges were interlaced, and all together they diffused perfumes of the most intense sweetness. We all sat down in the middle of the garden, in a pleasant and fragrant shade, next to a lovely fountain from which poured cool, clear water. While we enjoyed its marvellous beauty and were further soothed by a sweet breeze blowing gently through the flowers and foliage, tables were set with many delicacies and excellent, cool wines. We stood up and, after washing our hands, we began to eat, while birds, vying with each other in joy, were singing. When we finished eating, we went back to sit around the lovely fountain, in the pleasant shade . . .

[More friends arrive, and time passes].

Young men and young ladies began to dance. Afterwards, as it was time for dinner, to everyone's pleasure it was decided to eat there. The servants were ordered to lay white tablecloths all covered with flowers onto the soft green grass beside a cool stream which flowed nearby, and bring various and dainty dishes. We dined happily next to the clear, murmuring waters of the stream which ran across the middle of the valley. After this, as it was quite late, we stood up and walked towards our rooms, singing the following song as befitted such a happy time and place . . .

As we finished singing, we found ourselves in a fine chamber, and as everybody had their own room, we reposed in white and soft beds till dawn.

DECORATION OF PALACES AND VILLAS: WALL PAINTINGS AND HANGINGS

8. A view of Naples for the balcony of Eleonora of Aragon in Castel Vecchio, Ferrara

Used to the luxury of the Neapolitan court, Eleonora of Aragon took care of much rebuilding and decorative work at Castel Vecchio in Ferrara, where she arrived in 1473 as the bride of Ercole I d'Este. In this northern city often enveloped in thick fog, she commissioned a painting of her native Naples to decorate a balcony next to her rooms. The court payments to the painter Giovanni Trullo include a detailed description of the lively landscape, incorporating unknown personages.[13]

Tuohy (1996), pp. 416–17.

31 December 1485
Lire 45 due for painting the back wall of a balcony which is covered in lead, in the Castello, with a frieze above illusionistic columns, with [a view of] Naples, that is the city represented as it is, with the harbour and the Castel Nuovo, the San Vincenzo quarter and the Castel dell'Ovo, with ships and galleys, and the sea, and small figures of people in the city, with a giraffe, the donkey of Jenyalta, an ox and a sheep, with the mountain above Naples, the Castel Sant'Elmo, and the gardens of Naples, and the blue sea . . . represented as if they were real, with a border painted like a garden, with roses and carnations, and bushes underneath and around the said balcony with Zoltera. There is a cupboard painted in green and fine blue with three window-frames and glass painted in green and blue.

9. Decoration of the apartments of Villa Imperiale, Pesaro

The decoration of the old Villa Imperiale apartments for Francesco Maria della Rovere and for Eleonora Gonzaga was carried out under the guidance of Girolamo Genga by a group of six painters:

Dosso and Battista Dossi, Raffaellino del Colle, Bronzino, Francesco Menzocchi and Camillo Mantovano. The paintings reflect the different social roles of husband and wife, but in both sets of rooms the military career of Francesco Maria and his achievements were the inspiration for the subject-matter. Eleonora was frequently at the Imperiale during May and June 1530 in order to follow the work.

S. Eiche, 'Prologue to the Villa Imperiale frescoes', *Notizie di Palazzo Albani*, 20 (1991), p. 118.

Eleonora Gonzaga, from the Villa Imperiale, to the ducal agent in Venice, Giangiacomo Leonardi, 10 May 1530
We have begun to have some of our rooms here at the Imperiale painted, and wish them to be finished by the same master, that is Master Francesco da Forlì [Francesco Menzocchi]. He is not very eager to remain here, since he has to finish certain work which he has begun in that city [Venice] for Messer Gerolamo Badoer and Messer Battista Zeno. In order that the said Master Francesco can attend to our own work, you should not fail to impress on them, on our behalf, as you will easily be able to do, that in spite of this master's commitments to them, they should be content with him remaining here at our service for at least three [more] months . . .
    We are enclosing a list of colours which we need you to send from there, and you will endeavour to obtain everything according to what Genga advises in his list. And you will send them as promptly as you can, so that the work will not be left unfinished for want of these colours.

10. Margherita Paleologa (1510–66) and her tapestry *spalliere*
Flemish tapestry weavers had been employed during the early fifteenth century at the court of Urbino by Battista Sforza. The 1548 correspondence between Margherita Paleologa and one of the most famous weaver, Nicholas Karcher, suggests that she was commissioning from him tapestries for her bedroom.[14] This extract from her will records some of her tapestries of various kinds, one set of which was bequeathed to Ludovico Gonzaga di Nevers.

C. M. Brown, 'Ricordi dell' archivio', in G. Delmarcel and C. M. Brown (eds), *Gli arazzi dei Gonzaga nel Rinascimento* (Milan, 2010), p. 257.

One *spalliera* made of eleven pieces of Flemish tapestry, large and small, woven with foliage with a variety of birds. This *spalliera* belongs to the most illustrious and excellent Duke of Nevers.

A Flemish *spalliera* made of eight pieces of tapestry, with landscapes and figures and various kinds of animals. Some of the pieces are large and some are small.

Eight pieces of Flemish tapestry with figures and narratives, with the story of Elijah, with two *portiere*.

Five more pieces of Flemish tapestry with the stories of Gideon.

11. A dream of tranquillity for Christine of Lorraine: La Quiete, 1630

Christine of Lorraine (1565–1636/37) was brought up at the court of her grandmother, the Queen of France, Caterina de' Medici. She married Ferdinando I de' Medici in 1589, and acted as a regent after the death of her husband in 1609. In 1627, towards the end of her regency, she bought for 6,000 *scudi* a villa outside Florence. Christine envisaged it as a retreat from the busy and stressful court life where she could live in peace and tranquillity, as the name of the villa indicates. The iconographic programme for the decoration was written by the Florentine poet and academician Alessandro Adimari in 1630, and published two years later with the title *La Quiete. Ovvero sessanta emblemi sacri*, an extract of which is included here. Christine commissioned Giovanni da San Giovanni to paint an allegory of Tranquillity for the ceiling of an enclosed *loggia* on the first floor. The painting shows some difference from Adimari's programme.

C. Pizzorusso, 'La Quiete. Giovanni da San Giovanni e Alessandro Adimari', *Artista*, 1 (1989), pp. 87–8, 91, 92, 95.

La Quiete should be a woman of a certain age, because Rest and Tranquillity are more appropriate to the elderly than to the young. She should be sitting on a rich gold chair, dressed in a sumptuous and severe blue and gold gown, denoting that real tranquillity depends on serene conscience and purity of mind: this costume does not wear out with the passing of time . . . She should hold a flame above her head, as if it were flaming hair, denoting that the tranquillity of the soul is like a clear flame unmoved by the winds. The flame rises without difficulty, signifying moral purity. [*La Quiete*] should lean her head on her hand, as if resting but not sleeping, with her elbow on the armrest. Under her feet should be a cube, a [geometrical] form which always comes to rest on one side, whichever way it is thrown. To her side should be, like a hieroglyphic, a heifer returning to the stable, with the yoke on the ground . . . At the four sides of the chair the four principal winds should be chained, that is Zephyrus, the East Wind, the West Wind and the North Wind, wearing their usual garments, half-hidden amongst the clouds, signifying that one must curb the four passions of the soul in order to enjoy Tranquillity. These passions in fact, heavily panting around the clear flame of wholesome thoughts, either blow it out or do not allow it to become stronger. On the contrary, they draw up monsters from the vast sea of our hearts, similar to that commotion seen by Daniel.[15] On the two sides of the cube which is under her feet, two images could be painted. On one side an halcyon, with half a verse from Tibullus referring to Tranquillity, 'Haec reparat Vires'. . . On the other, the scales, well balanced, . . . with the motto 'Quies in aequo'. If this pleases Your Most Serene Highness, I would also like to widen the concept with two *imprese*, painted over two shields on both sides of the framing of this figure. On the first there should be a Syrian bow with the string hanging only from one tip, with the motto 'Quiete defensus'. . . On the other shield there should be a lyre or a violin with loosened strings, resting in its case, with a motto taken from a verse by Dante, 'Non fia men dolce'.

BEQUESTS

12. Caterina Cornaro (1489–1510) bequeaths her villa and estate at Asolo to her brother, to be kept in her memory, 1500
There are no contemporary descriptions of the *Barco* which Caterina Cornaro built at Altivole, near Asolo, a small town in the

Veneto hills. Her villa, completed in 1491–92, had also a garden with fountains and waterworks. The following is a partial description from the first of Caterina's two wills (1500 and 1508).[16]

L. Comacchio, *Storia di Asolo*, 16 vols (Asolo, 1980), 2, pp. 197–8.

We have gifted, bequeathed and transferred to the Magnifico [Giorgio Cornaro], our only brother, and to his heirs, our park in the territory of Asolo, surrounded by walls, with all the properties pertaining to it, and all the houses and buildings which have been erected up till now and which will be built in the future, together with the palace and dwelling house which we have built, God pleasing, and will be finished for the dwelling of ourselves and of our court in future times and in our memory. [We bequeath it with] all the streams and brooks which run and will run within the confines of our park and around it, with the watercourse that is to arrive from the villa at Crespignano to the said park. The said streams and watercourses must not be directed away from our park in any way, nor must they be given to others, nor must they be removed by anybody without the permission of the said Magnifico, my brother, or his heirs. [The same applies] to all household objects and furnishings, made or bought, or which will be made or bought for the use and decoration of the said park and dwelling. The same applies to all the cattle and everything in the said park, buildings or movable objects, and also any property and land which we have bought up till now, or will buy in the future, in the territory of Asolo or elsewhere.

We reserve our life interest in all and each of the properties and goods. The Magnifico, our brother, and his heirs, may at their pleasure dispose of the entire estate, and of each and all of the goods gifted them above.

13. A peaceful retreat for Medici princesses
In her will of 9 April 1630, Christine of Lorraine set out her intention for the villa La Quiete to be a place where the Medici princesses could live peacefully, away from the bustle of Florence. Her youngest daughters, Maria Maddalena (1600–33), who had severe

disabilities from birth and lived as a recluse in the convent of the Crocetta in Florence, and Claudia (1604–48), wife of Archduke Leopold V of Austria, are mentioned as her heiresses. Christine's granddaughter Maria Cristina (1609–31), also with disabilities, was meant to inherit the villa after them. In fact, in 1650 the villa was bought by Eleonora Ramirez di Montalvo, who established a confraternity of lay women, and turned the villa into a school for young girls from good families.

> C. Corsani, 'Le transformazioni architettoniche del complesso della Quiete', in C. De Benedictis (ed.), *Villa La Quiete. Il patrimonio artistico del conservatorio delle Montalve* (Florence, 1997), pp. 20–1.

We wish the dwelling which we have built for us at the Crocetta, next to that belonging to our daughter Princess Maria Maddalena, and the villa which we call La Quiete, next to the convent of Boldrone, to be enjoyed and occupied by the said Princess Maria Maddalena, together with all the furniture and objects of all kinds, which are there for the use and ornament to the dwellings at the time of our death. These [buildings] are the Crocetta, where she will continue to live, and the villa, where she can go from time to time for relaxation. The income from the villa and its estate is due to her during her lifetime. If the Archduchess Claudia came back to Florence to live, she could and should partake of a half of the said dwelling, furnishings, and income. When one of my daughters has succeeded the other and both are dead, and, if God wills, my most beloved granddaughter Maria Cristina is still alive, we want her to inherit the said dwellings, furnishings and income during her lifetime, after Princess Maria Maddalena, and even during the lifetime of Archduchess Claudia if she is not living there . . .

As for the ownership of the dwelling of the Villa La Quiete and its estates, at the death of the said three princesses we wish it to remain in perpetuity with the Princesses of Tuscany for their recreation, while they are not yet married. If among these there are some who want to retire to the convent, the villa should belong to them only during their lifetime. If, during our lifetime, the villa should not be entirely paid for, or the building designed and begun by us were not finished as we intend, we want our Most Serene heir [her grandson Ferdinando II] to finish it, so that the said princesses may enjoy everything freely without any burden.

COLLECTIONS: PAINTINGS AND *OBJETS D'ART*

When does an assortment of paintings and objects, acquired in widowhood or as bequests, become a 'collection'? Collecting requires first of all an intention to bring together works of art and/ or objects, with the guidance of one's own taste and connoisseurship. Collections of paintings as well as of small precious objects such as cameos, *intagli*, statuettes, were a feature of aristocratic palaces and houses of wealthy bankers, merchants and scholars.[17] These collections were placed in cabinets, on shelves and pedestals in small rooms (*studioli*). Towards the end of the sixteenth and during the seventeenth century, collections of pictures by contemporary or near contemporary painters might be assembled and shown together in *sale* or *gallerie*, or, in the case of Venice, in the large *sala* or *galleria* known as the *portego*. In these picture galleries religious subjects were placed next to portraits or historical and mythological paintings. These pictures might not be commissioned for a specific place, or with a specific function, but were bought or commissioned purely as 'works of art', and collected for their fashionable subject-matter or for the fame of the artists who painted them.

While men's collections of paintings and sculptures, both contemporary and ancient, are well documented and have been extensively studied by scholars, the same cannot be said for the much less numerous collections begun by women, or received as bequests and cared for by them. [18] Isabella d'Este's collections in her *studioli* and *camerini* are of course an exception, and so are those belonging to women who had gained important positions in seventeenth-century papal Rome.[19]

14. Isabella d'Este and her famous collections
Isabella d'Este occupies a very special place in the history of collecting. She lovingly stored her collection in small rooms in her apart-

ments: from the early 1490s she had a *studiolo* and a room called a *grotta* on the second floor of the Castello di San Giorgio. Later, a new *studiolo* and a *grotta* were built side by side in her apartment on the ground floor of the Corte Vecchia. These small rooms were like precious caskets, with coffered and gilt ceilings and elegant marble door frames.The *studiolo* and *grotta* in the Corte Vecchia were next to Isabella's small private garden, enclosed by the walls of the palace. Here an inscription declared her ownership and stated her lineage: ISABELLA ESTENSIS, REGUM ARAGONUM NEPTIS, DUCUM FERRARENSIUM FILIA ET SOROR, MARCHIONUM GONZAGARUM CONIUX ET MATER, FECIT A PARTU VIRGINIS MDXXII. Her correspondence with agents, relatives, friends and artists survives almost in its entirety. It vividly shows her as a discriminating, knowledgeable and insatiable patron and collector. Her desire to acquire works of art and objects of different kinds, from antique and contemporary sculptures in bronze and marble, to antique cameos and gems, from vases made of semi-precious stones to glassware, crystals and porcelain, was legendary.[20]

i. Isabella commissions a turquoise with an intaglio carving with a Victory, one of her *imprese* which can also be seen on the reverse of her portrait medal in Vienna. This is one of the many letters exchanged between Isabella and the Mantuan ambassador Giorgio Brognolo on the subject.

Zaffanella, in Bini (ed.) (2001), p. 219.

3 January 1496
As we very much wish to commission a turquoise with an intaglio carving with a whole figure of a Victory, and not with a head, as the other was, we wish you to meet Francesco de Nichino, and together select a fine, perfect and not too large turquoise, suitable for engraving. There is no particular hurry, but we would be very grateful if you got it soon. When you have found it, you will have it engraved with a 'Victory', as we have already written. There should be no need for you to urge Francesco to do a good job: both for his own reputation as an excellent master, and for the affection he bears me, he would certainly do this, but he has too many

commissions. The concern you show towards him will be an incentive to complete this commission soon.

ii. The following letters are two amongst the many written by Isabella from the late 1490s onwards in her constant search for antique sculptures. The Cupid and the Venus mentioned here had been taken from Urbino by Cesare Borgia, probably in 1496. He returned them to the Duke of Urbino, Guidobaldo della Rovere, but took them again when he conquered Urbino in 1502. Isabella used the authority of her brother, Cardinal Ippolito d'Este, to obtain the two sculptures. With her expertise, she immediately recognised the Cupid (by Michelangelo) to be a modern work.

A. Venturi, 'Il Cupido di Michelangelo', in *Archivio Storico dell'Arte*, 1 (1888), p. 4.

Isabella d'Este, from Mantua, to her brother Cardinal Ippolito, 30 June 1502
The Duke of Urbino, my brother-in-law, had in his palace an antique marble Venus, small but excellent, according to its fame, and also a Cupid which before he had given as a gift to the most illustrious Duke of Romagna [Cesare Borgia]. I am sure that these objects, together with others, are now in the hands of the Duke of Romagna because of the changes in the Duchy of Urbino. I have taken much care in collecting antiquities to bring honour to my *studio*, and I greatly desire to have them. I do not think this thought should cause a contretemps, since I hear that His Excellency is not particularly delighted by antiquities, and so he can give pleasure to others. Since, however, I am not on such familiar terms that I could be sure of receiving this favour without an intermediary, I thought I could make use of the authority of Your Most Reverend Lordship. So I pray you to ask him [Cesare Borgia], through letters and messengers, to give me pleasure by making me the gift of the Venus and the Cupid I desire.

Isabella, from Mantua, to her husband Francesco Gonzaga, 11 July 1502
Yesterday the muleteer arrived with the Venus and the Cupid sent by Duke Valentino [Cesare Borgia]. Messer

Francesco, his *cameriere*, gave them to me, and today, after taking leave from me, he left . . . I am not writing about the beauty of the Venus because I think that Your Lordship has seen it. The Cupid, as a modern work, is without equal.

iii. From 1496 to c. 1530, Isabella commissioned a series of mythological allegories to decorate the walls of her *studiolo*. The paintings she commissioned from Mantegna, Perugino, Lorenzo Costa and Correggio alluded to her virtues. Looking for paintings for her *studiolo*, Isabella writes to the Vicar General of the Carmelite Order in Florence, asking for information about Leonardo's activities in that city.

A. Luzio, 'Nuovi documenti su Leonardo da Vinci', *Archivio Storico dell'Arte*, 1 (1888), pp. 45–6.

Isabella d'Este from Mantua to Fra Pietro da Novellara, 27 March 1501
If Leonardo, the Florentine painter, is in Florence, would you please inform me what he is doing, whether he has started on any commission, as has been mentioned to me, and what commission it is, and whether you think that he is going to remain there for some time. Then find out if he would undertake to make a picture for our *studiolo*, and if he would, we could leave the subject-matter and time-scale to be decided by him. But if you find he refuses, see at least whether you can get him to make a small picture of Our Lady, pious and sweet (*devoto e dolce*) as the subject demands.

iv. Writing to the humanist Paride da Cesarea, Isabella praises him for his *invenzione* for Lorenzo Costa's *Coronation of a Lady*, but complains about the difficulties of dealing with the painters from whom she was commissioning works for the new *studiolo*.

A. Luzio and R. Renier, 'La coltura e le relazioni letterarie di Isabella d'Este Gonzaga', *Giornale Storico della Letteratura Italiana*, 34 (1899), p. 89.

Isabella d'Este, from Mantua, to Paride da Cesarea, 15 November 1504.

Messer Paris, I could not like your *invenzione* more. We praise your promptness and your elegant idea, and congratulate you for the diligence and speed with which you have served me. We would wish all painters to serve us as well, but wish in vain: we have to accept what they want or are able to do. We shall send you a painter to sketch out the story according to your intention, so that the Bolognese [Lorenzo Costa] will not make mistakes. Keep well.

v. Contacts between Isabella and Francesco Francia begun in 1505 and continued till 1511, but the only works she got from him were a portrait of her son Federico and a lost portrait of Isabella herself. The painting discussed in these letters was not executed.

E. Negro and N. Roio (eds), *Francesco Francia e la sua scuola* (Modena, 1998), p. 117.

Francesco Francia to Isabella d'Este, 11 January 1511
Most Illustrious Lady, I understand from your letter to Girolamo Casio that Your Most Illustrious Ladyship would like to know whether I am ready to paint the canvas for Your Ladyship's *camerino*, commissioned from me by our Casio some time ago. I want, as much as I can, to make something that Your Ladyship will like. If you can let me have the canvas, the measurements and the lighting conditions, so that I should not make mistakes, I shall begin, and work on the painting carefully and promptly, to please and honour Your Ladyship.

Isabella d'Este, from Mantua, to Girolamo Casio, enclosing a letter for Francesco Francia, 6 February 1511.
We have the canvas for the picture we wish to have painted by your hand. We would have sent it already, if these difficult times had not prevented us. When things are more settled we shall send it to you, with the measurements and the right lighting. In the letter to Geronimo Casio we asked him to find out whether the *invenzione* for the picture was to your liking. As we have heard nothing from you about it, I ask you to let me know your point of view and opinion

before we send you the canvas. We think that we should always follow your judgement, and are always receptive to your wishes.

15. A lady with a collection of antique cameos

The Countess of Caiazzo, Barbara Gonzaga, was a widow with a considerable collection of antique cameos which she had very probably inherited from her father. The cameos were mounted on twenty-one gilded silver sheets, fixed on a support covered in velvet. The countess's financial situation after the death of her husband was very difficult, and, when in need of money, she would sell her cameos. Isabella d'Este, her cousin-in-law, was one of her creditors. Being unable to pay her back, Barbara offered the Marchioness some of her cameos. Isabella, driving a hard bargain, offered to buy just four of them.

> C. M. Brown, *'Per dare qualche splendore a la gloriosa città di Mantua', Documents for the Antiquarian Collection of Isabella d'Este* (Rome, 2002), p. 309.

Isabella d'Este to Barbara Gonzaga, 15 April 1533
I have read what Your Ladyship writes in the letter of 7 April, with your excuses since you cannot repay me by Easter the 200 ducats which you owe me, according to what was agreed between us some months ago. You offer me four of your cameos to cover [a repayment] of 100 *scudi*. I am still of the same mind and disposition as I always have been, and I want to please you as I think of you as my own sister. It would have been more convenient for me to have the money, for which I had already made some plans, but for your own convenience I am glad to accept a number of cameos from you up to the value of 200 ducats, according to an estimate done by experts whom we trust. I would not be happy to accept the four cameos you have sent to cover 100 *scudi*, because, according to someone who has examined them carefully and who has an excellent understanding of such things, they are not even worth 80 ducats.

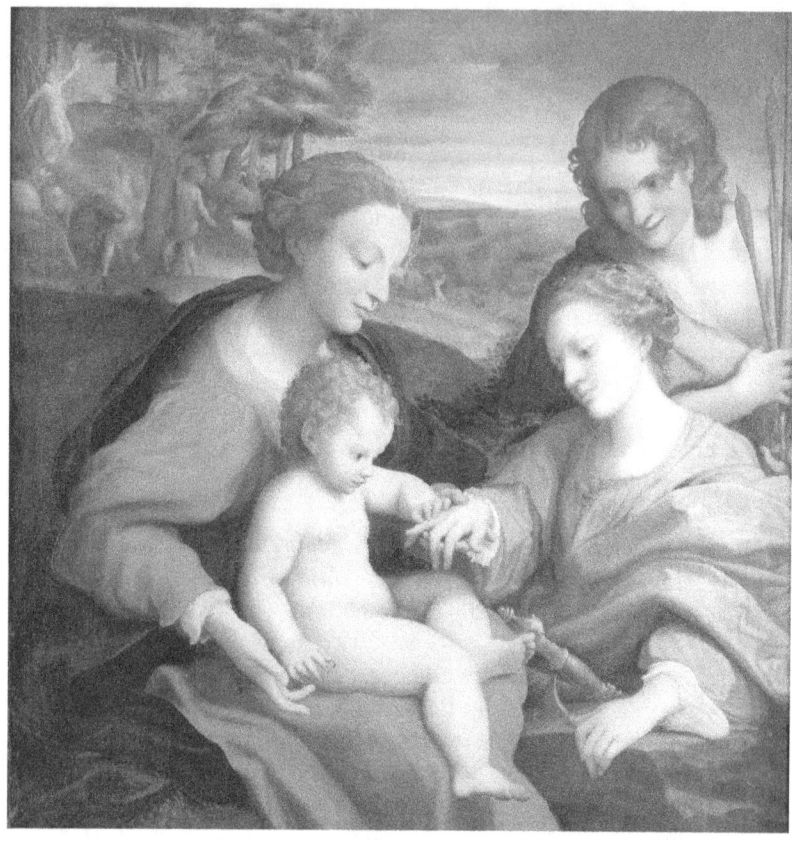

9. Correggio, *The Virgin with St Catherine and St Sebastian/ Mystic Marriage of St Catherine*, c. 1525–30 (Paris, Musée du Louvre)

16. A much-prized collection of paintings

Caterina Nobili Sforza, Countess of Santa Fiora (1535–1605), a wealthy widow, spent the last decades of her life in her palace in Rome, surrounded by her collection of paintings.

i. The countess had been trying to obtain a picture by Correggio, the *Madonna with St Catherine and St Sebastian* (Paris, Louvre). The painting was still in the possession of the Grillenzoni family from Modena who had commissioned it, and they were very reluctant to part with it. Finally Cardinal Luigi d'Este succeeded in obtaining the painting, and gave it to the countess as a present (**figure 9**).

L. Corsini Sforza, 'La collezione di Caterina Nobili Sforza contessa di Santafiora', *L'Arte*, 1 (1898), p. 277.

Caterina Nobili Sforza from Parma, to Cardinal Luigi d'Este, 15 May 1582

When the Governor of Modena returned here after eight days, he gave me the painting by Correggio from you. As it was impossible to obtain it another way, I had asked you, through Ambassador Cortile, if you with your authority could ask the owners for it. Since then I had not heard by letter anything from anybody about it.

Now, understanding that your magnanimity has obtained such a special gift for me, I am writing this letter to give you all my thanks, and to let you know that I am indebted to you forever. My lowly condition will entail no other significant consequence, [but] I will always recognise my firm and deep desire to serve you. Now, in order not to trouble Your Most Illustrious Lordship further with my writing, and relying on your connection with Signor Pierfrancesco, my brother, I humbly kiss your hands, and I pray Our Lord God to grant you all well being.

ii. While in Rome during the 1590s, looking for paintings for Emperor Rudolf II, the deputy chief minister Rudolf Coradusz visited a number of collections. One of these belonged to the Countess of Santa Fiora. Here is what he saw in the palace of the elderly countess. He did not succeed, however, in buying any paintings from her.

L. Urlichs, 'Beiträge zur Geschichte der Kunstbestrebungen und Sammlungen Kaisers Rudolph II', *Zeitschrift für Bildende Kunst*, 5 (1870), pp. 50–1.

An Our Lady with St Catherine and St Sebastian, by the hand of Correggio.

The portrait of a lady of the Osse family from Ferrara, dressed in an old-fashioned way, half-figure, with a similar one on the opposite wall, by the hand of Correggio. These two paintings are something unique and divine.

A Christ in the garden, a small picture by the hand of Correggio.

A naked woman, portrayed from life, half-figure, by Raphael.

A small picture of Our Lady, by Parmigianino.

A cartoon with another Our Lady, in *chiaroscuro*, by the hand of Parmigianino.

iii. Lodovico Cremaschi, the agent for the Mantuan princes in Rome, was looking for paintings for his master, Duke Vincenzo I Gonzaga, and put out feelers to the Countess of Santa Fiora. He was particularly impressed by two pictures, which he describes in his letter to the duke. As Cremaschi recounts, the spirited response of the elderly countess was that these paintings were to be preserved as solace for herself and for a legacy to her descendants. She bequeathed her collection to her daughter, Costanza Sforza Buoncompagni (1550–1617).

Corsini Sforza (1898), p. 273.

Rome, 22 February 1597
I looked for the Countess of Santa Fiora, and when I found her, I was taken into a room full of paintings, amongst which I saw the half-figure of the naked Venus, with black hair and eyes, with a bracelet on her left arm, on which is written 'Raphael Urbinas'. When I turned my eyes, I saw a larger picture with the beheading of St John the Baptist, painted in this way: the figure of the executioner, who, with a brutal action, with his hand in the hair, holds above a stone basin the head of the saint which is spurting blood, his face pale and ashen, his lips colourless, and his hair dishevelled. Next is the figure of Herodias, with a contented expression on her face and a smile on her lips. With her left hand half open and placed above the basin, she seems to display the holy head, and it seems that she is rejoicing and taking pride in this event. This painting is truly miraculous, and made with great skill, and it was among the delights of Galeazzo Sforza, perhaps amongst the finest and most marvellous to view.

After that, in order that I could pick out the pictures to be bought, after a few days I let the Countess know that my lord the Duke [Vincenzo Gonzaga] wanted to purchase those two paintings, and that it did not matter if the price was very high. However, we needed her willing agreement.

She asked Cavalier Ramazzotti to let me know that she was now of such advanced age, that she had retired from the world, and she kept those and other pictures for herself as consolation and comfort in the weary life which remained to her, with the intention of leaving them to her descendants as witnesses of the decorum, reputation and nobility of the Sforza family. For these reasons she valued them more than money and other precious objects, and she knew how to look after them and keep them, because she had owned them for so many years. She therefore begged His Highness to allow her to enjoy them for the short time she had left to live. I did not refrain from asking her more than once, but the more I offered reasons to persuade her to accept the wishes of Your Highness, the more resolutely, in fact stubbornly, she persisted in the answers she had given. I have explained to Your Highness how resolute she was because nothing can be obtained from her hardened soul, and because I want it to be known that I have spared no effort or diligence in attempting to buy those pictures.

17. A *wunderkammer* for Christine of Bourbon (1606–63), after 1619

Natural specimens collected for their oddity and displayed together with scientific instruments and works of art were fashionable in aristocratic households from the second half of the sixteenth century, and became a prerequisite for seventeenth-century collectors. In this letter a gentleman close to the Savoy court advises Christine of Bourbon, the daughter of King Henri IV and Maria de' Medici, and wife of Vittorio Amedeo I, Duke of Savoy, on how to arrange *cose curiose* in a *wunderkammer* in the palace of Venaria, near Turin. From 1632, Christine was the patron of Giovanna Garzoni (see chapter 11, texts 16 and 19).

M. Di Macco, 'Arredo di palazzo e collezionismo di corte. La quadreria', in M. Di Macco and G. Romano (eds), *Diana trionfatrice. Arte di corte nel Piemonte nel Seicento* (Turin, 1989), p. 98.

From Giovanni Tarino in Turin, to Christine of Bourbon
In this room shall be kept all the curiosities which may be obtained, both from the realm of nature and from the realm of art, such as birds, fish, four-footed animals, minerals and half-minerals, interesting stones, ingenious mechanical objects, ancient and modern weapons, singular war machines, curious books and other such things which are worthy of admiration. I have seen such a room in Bavaria, in the palace of His Most Serene Highness the Elector, and in Bologna, in the houses of the Aldrovandi. It will be for this interesting, delightful and worthy concept that foreigners full of curiosity will come to the Venaria Reale. It will be a remarkable [place], especially since it was born from the fertile mind of Your Royal Highness.

18. The collection of a painter: Fede Galizia disposes of the paintings in her possession
The painter Fede Galizia (1578–1630) died in Milan during a terrible plague which halved its population. She had written her will at the beginning of the 1620s, during a previous bout of pestilence. In this extract she takes care of her collection of paintings.

F. Caroli, *Fede Galizia* (Turin, 1989), pp. 20–1.

21 June 1623
I, Fede Galizia, as the only owner of all the movable goods in my house, being free to dispose of the said goods, intend to dispose of them in the following way, for the good of my soul, and of my cousin Anna Galizia and my nephew Carlo Enrico, who are the heirs of part of the said goods.

After my death I bequeath six pictures to the Reverend Fathers of S. Antonio. They are: a St Thomas touching the wound in Christ's side, with the other apostles; a St Catherine, by Luini; a Gipsy Woman, by Correggio; a Christ in the Garden, by Correggio; an Our Lady of the Basket, by

Correggio; a Christ carrying the cross, with a carved frame. I bequeath these six paintings with the request that thirty Masses of St Gregory should be celebrated three times. I bequeath all the other paintings to be divided between the said Anna and Carlo Enrico. After their death, they should be bequeathed to the Reverend Fathers, as above.

If Carlo Enrico, when he reaches the right age, enters a religious order, I wish him to bequeath his paintings to that Order.

[...]

I, Don Alessandro Porro, Provost of the Regular Clerics of S. Antonio, declare receipt of the six paintings listed above. Ninety Masses shall be celebrated.

Notes

1 See K. A. McIver, 'Why did some women build? The case of Ippolita Pallavicina-Sanseverina', *Source*, 25:3 (2006), pp. 6–21.

2 See K. A. McIver, 'Love, death and mourning: Paola Gonzaga's Camerino at Fontanellato', *Artibus et Historiae*, 18:36 (1997), pp. 101–8; McIver, 'Women of power: what women say as builders of secular architecture in early modern Italy', in *Acta ad Archaelogiam et Artium Historiam Pertinentia*, 22:8 (2009), pp. 171–92. Also, B. L. Edelstein, 'Bronzino in the service of Eleonora di Toledo and Cosimo I de' Medici: conjugal patronage and the painter-courtier', in Reiss and Wilkins (eds) (2001), pp. 226–61, esp. pp. 232–4.

3 See for example Maria Maddalena of Austria's work at Poggio Imperiale, in I. Hoppe, 'Uno spazio di potere femminile. Villa del Poggio Imperiale, residenza di Maria Maddalena d'Austria', and R. Spinelli, 'Simbologia dinastica e legittimazione del potere: Maria Maddalena d'Austria e gli affreschi del Poggio Imperiale', both in G. Calvi and R. Spinelli (eds), *Le donne Medici nel sistema europeo delle corti, XVI–XVIII secolo*, 2 vols (Florence, 2008), 2, pp. 681–9 and 645–79. See, in the same volume, A. Galdy, 'L'appartamento di Eleonora di Toledo in Palazzo Vecchio: la scena della nuova Isabella la Cattolica', pp. 615–26. On the same apartment, see P. Tinagli, 'Eleonora and her "Famous Sisters": the tradition of "illustrious women" in painting for the domestic interior', and P. J. Benson, 'Eleonora di Toledo among the famous women: iconographic innovation after the conquest of Siena', both in K. Eisenbichler (ed.), *The Cultural World of Eleonora di Toledo Duchess of Florence and Siena* (Aldershot, 2004), pp. 119–35 and 136–56.

4 See A. L. Jenkens, 'Caterina Piccolomini and the Palazzo delle Papesse in Siena', in Reiss and Wilkins (eds) (2001), pp. 77–91.

5 See B. L. Edelstein, 'Palazzo Pitti e il Giardino di Boboli: l'*hortus* albertiano come prototipo della reggia', in V. Arrighi and G. C. Rombi (eds), *Palazzo Pitti* (Florence, 2006), pp. 31–44.

6 See McIver (2009), pp. 188–90.

7 The plan of the basement, sent from Giacinto Barozzi on 25 May 1561, together with other drawings of the palace.

8 One of Ottavio and Margherita's courtiers, and Governor of Parma.

9 See C. King, 'Architecture, gender and politics: the Villa Imperiale at Pesaro', *Art History*, 29:5 (2006), pp. 796–826. King discusses the 'gendered design' of the villa in relation to fifteenth- and sixteenth-century treatises on women's behaviour.

10 See A. Pinelli and O. Rossi, *Genga architetto* (Rome, 1971).

11 For a view of palace and garden at the end of the sixteenth century, see the lunette by Justus Utens (Florence, Museo di Firenze com'era). The enclosed garden on the left-hand side, with its geometric beds, and the Grotticina di Madama, with a fountain with sculptures by Baccio Bandinelli and Giovanni Paolo Fancelli, built between 1552 and 1555, were commissioned by Eleonora di Toledo.

12 Bandinelli was a Knight of the Order of St James.

13 See Tuohy (1996), pp. 100–1.

14 See M. S. Ahrendt, 'The Cultural Legacy and Patronal Stewardship of Margherita Paleologa (1510–1566) Duchess of Mantua and Marchesa di Monferrato', PhD dissertation, Washington University, St Louis (2002), pp. 141–5.

15 A reference to Daniel's vision of the four great beasts, Old Testament, Book of Daniel, Chapter 7.

16 See S. Hickson, 'Caterina Cornaro in Asolo: the Art and Architectural Patronage of a Renaissance Queen (1489–1510)', MA dissertation, Queen's University, Kingston, Ontario (1995). See also L. Puppi, 'La corte di Caterina Cornaro e il barco di Altivole', in ed R. Maschio, *I tempi di Giorgione* (Rome, 1994), pp. 230–5.

17 On women's *studioli*, see D. Thornton, *The Scholar in his Study: Ownership and Experience in Renaissance Italy* (New Haven, 1997), pp. 90–7. On Ippolita Maria Sforza's *studiolo*, see E. Welch, 'Women in debt: financing female authority in Renaissance Italy', in L. Arcangeli and S. Peyronel, eds, *Donne di Potere nel Rinascimento* (Rome, 2008), pp. 45–65, esp. p. 57, and 'Between Milan and Naples: Ippolita Maria Sforza, Duchess of Calabria' in D. Abulafia (ed.), *The French Descent in Renaissance Italy (1494–1495)* (Aldershot, 1995), pp. 123–36.

18 See S. Bracken, A. M. Galdy and A. Turpin (eds), *Women Patrons and Collectors* (Newcastle upon Tyne, 2012).

19 The collections of Olimpia Aldobrandini (1567–1637), niece of Clement VIII Aldobrandini, and Olimpia Maidalchini (1594–1657), sister-in-law of Innocent X Pamphili, were particularly important.

20 On Isabella d'Este's collection, see the following works by C. M. Brown: 'I camerini di Isabella d'Este in Corte Vecchia: ipotesi e certezze', in F. Trevisani and D. Gasparotto (eds), *Bonacolsi l'Antico: uno scultore nella Mantova di Andrea Mantegna e di Isabella d'Este* (Milan, 2008), pp. 98–103; 'A Ferrarese lady and a Mantuan marchesa: the art and antiquities collections of Isabella d'Este Gonzaga (1474–1539)', in C. Lawrence (ed.), *Women and Art in Early Modern Europe: Patrons, Collectors and Connoisseurs* (University Park, PA, 1996), pp. 53–71; '"Our insatiable desire for antiquities": the collections of Greco-Roman art of Isabella d'Este Gonzaga', *Center – National Gallery of Art, Center for Advanced Study in the Visual Arts*, 13 (1993), pp. 47–8.

~ 6 ~

WOMEN ACQUIRING AND USING PORTRAITS

By the mid to late fifteenth century women from aristocratic houses would have been used to living with portraits of themselves and of their family members and associates, whether in panel paintings, in manuscripts, in medals or, less frequently, in fresco cycles, or in busts.[1] By the end of the century women from families associated with the nobility, or from mercantile or professional classes, might own portraits, usually of their menfolk, although the situation varied from city to city. By the mid-to-late sixteenth century, however, some prosperous artisans and their wives seem to have had themselves portrayed, as certain entries in Lorenzo Lotto's account book attest.

This chapter will focus on portraits where women were certainly the primary patrons, and also include those where there is likely to have been some input from women during the commissioning or execution, as with images of a married couple, a family, or a group of women such as confraternity members. In these cases husbands or other males might be named in documents, but females' wishes would be likely to have been taken into account to some degree. The chapter will also deal with women as givers, receivers or spectators of portraits, and women as the collectors, conservers or arrangers of such images, usually those of family members.[2] The wider topic of women as the subjects of portraits will not be addressed unless the images fall into one of these categories.

PORTRAITS AND LIFE-CYCLES

The extracts in this section record women involved in the commissioning of portraits at different stages in their own, or their family members', life-cycles.

a. Betrothals

As is well known, marriage negotiations between aristocratic houses in different cities often involved the making of portraits of future brides or grooms to be sent to their proposed spouses and their families for their interest and approval. Once the match was finalised and attendant ceremonies had taken place, more portraits might be made, perhaps commemorating the clothing and jewels bought for the occasion, which might be vastly more expensive than the paintings. Plenty of extant images, of both aristocratic and patrician sitters, seem to be of this kind, although the latter are rarely documented like the courtly examples.[3]

1. Eleonora of Aragon has a portrait made for her stepdaughter's betrothal, 1479

Prior to her marriage in 1472, Eleonora of Aragon had been sent portraits by the Ferrarese court painter Cosimo Tura of her betrothed, Ercole I d'Este, Duke of Ferrara (1431–1505), and his illegitimate daughter Lucrezia. When Lucrezia was herself betrothed to Annibale Bentivoglio of Bologna in 1479, Eleonora is recorded in the ducal accounts as having ordered Tura to make a portrait of her.

Franceschini (1995), and no. 269, p. 188.

27–28 January 1479
By the order of the Illustrious and Excellent Lady Eleonora of Aragon, Duchess of Ferrara . . . to be given to Cosimo the painter four gold florins, in gold, for his painting from life and for all his expenses for the portrait of the illustrious lady Lucrezia d'Este, the daughter of our illustrious Lord Duke and the betrothed spouse of the magnificent Lord Annibale Bentivoglio, which our said illustrious Lady is sending to Bologna to the magnificent and generous Lord Giovanni Bentivoglio, father of the said Lord Annibale, and the sum put to the expenses of their Highnesses.

b. The married state

As more portraits in general were produced from the later fifteenth century onwards, it seems to have become more common for married women to be shown several years after their weddings, in paintings celebrating the union, its fruitfulness or the virtues of the women.

2. Lorenzo Lotto paints female sitters in the 1540s

Lotto's notebook of accounts for work done in the 1540s and 1550s records several portraits of women from modest social strata. These were the wives or widows of merchants and artisans, sometimes the friends or associates of the painter, as with his landlords, the della Volta family, where the wife helped him find a housekeeper. The sitters were portrayed sometimes with their spouses or, more unusually, with children. Although the notes are much briefer than those recording transactions in aristocratic circles, they may imply some intervention from these women in the commissioning process.

Lorenzo Lotto, *Il 'Libro di spese diverse'*, ed. P. Zampetti (Venice, 1969), pp. 132, 98.

i. Portrait of Marietta Novella, wife of Tommaso da Empoli, September 1541
Venice, . . . September 1541. Given by Madonna Marietta Novella, wife of Messer Tommaso Empoli, the Florentine jeweller, for the stretcher and the canvas to make a large portrait for her, 3 *lire* down payment to make a good start, with no further price or negotiation.

ii. Portrait of the Giovanni della Volta family, 1546 (London, National Gallery)
20 May, 1546. Messer Giovanni della Volta, the owner of my house, according to the account made 6 months ago, contracted with him in his study, with his wife present, 10 ducats, as appears in his own handwriting in my rent book . . .

23 September, 1547. Given by the said Messer Giovanni della Volta, the owner of my house, for a painting with his por-

trait from life together with his wife and two children, four altogether. The painting was judged to be excellent in merit and in colour, and with its cover and framework valued at 50 ducats or more by disinterested parties; and we gave each other what was due and I was content with 20 ducats.

c. Childbirth and children

3. Beatrice d'Este sends a portrait drawing of her son Ercole (b. 1493) to her mother, who sends it on to her other daughter, Isabella d'Este
i. Venturi (1885), pp. 227–8.

Beatrice d'Este, from Villanova, to Eleonora of Aragon in Ferrara, 16 April 1494
My most Illustrious Lady Mother. Your Excellency must excuse me if I've delayed somewhat in writing to you: the reason has been that I was hoping every moment that the painter would bring me the portrait of Ercole, which My Lord and I are sending to Your Excellency. We can assure you he is much bigger than the portrait as he has grown in the eight days since it was made. We are not telling Your Excellency his height because it is said to be unlucky to talk about sizes in case he grows up differently.

ii. Luzio and Renier, vol. 7, anno 17 (1890), p. 368, n. 3.

Eleonora in Ferrara to Isabella in Mantua (undated)
I enclose a drawing sent from Milan showing that our little boy is doing well. Even though we hear he is flourishing, this gives a truer picture as he is presented almost as though speaking when he sees you. We will say no more as to whether the portrait is good, except to mention the sender and the artist, ensuring that 'it will be judged very well'.

4. A portrait of Isabella d'Este as a girl is copied because it resembles the newborn Anna d'Este, 1531–2

This exchange of letters shows Isabella, as a widow, wishing that younger members of the Este family should have, as she said, 'some memory of me' in portrait form, and perhaps that the

French-born bride of her nephew, Duke Ercole II of Ferrara, should feel a greater connection with her new extended family. When the Duchess Renée gave birth to a daughter, Anna, a resemblance was seen between the baby and Isabella when young, and a longstanding associate, Girolamo da Sestola known as Cholgia, suggested that the mother should be sent a copy of a portrait of Isabella as a girl.

A. Luzio, *La galleria dei Gonzaga venduta all'Inghilterra nel 1627–28* (Milan, 1913), appendice B 'I ritratti d'Isabella d'Este', p. 184.

Girolamo da Sestola in Ferrara to Isabella d'Este in Mantua, 16 November 1531
My illustrious lady,
Our Lady the Duchess went in a litter to the jousting at the Schifanoia, and called for me and asked me about her baby girl, who seemed to me to be doing excellently, both beautiful and large. She told me her lord had said the child looked rather like Your Excellency when you were small. I replied that I thought so too, and that I'd seen a portrait of Your Excellency at Mantua that seemed rather like. At once he told me to write to Your Excellency asking you to have it sent and he would return it to Your Excellency later. The portrait is one I saw at the house at La Borgna . . . The portrait was made when Your Excellency was a girl and, if I remember rightly, with a garland or branch around the head and a feather in the middle, and I believe Your Excellency gave it to La Borgna since you showed it to me when we were in your house . . .

Isabella to Girolamo, 31 January 1532
I gladly send the Excellent Duchess the portrait of me, which I thought was the one you wrote about, made when I was about three years old. You may safely judge whether it is at all like Her Excellency's little girl. If it pleases God that, in the opinion of the Duke, she resembles me it would give me immense pleasure. I have given the painter another portrait of me, made after I was married, to freshen it up – if it turns out all right I will send it. I will then be well pleased when both are dispatched.

5. Portraits of deceased children, 1629–32

The accounts of the seventeenth-century Venetian painter Tiberio Tinelli, little known today but fairly successful in his own lifetime, record many commissions from women for portraits of themselves. Several of them show women wishing to preserve the memory of children who had died young.

> *Libretto dei conti del pittore Tiberio Tinelli (1618–1633)*, ed. B. Lanfranchi Strina (Venice, 2000), documents 190, 289, pp. 39, 51.

On the 10th day of the same month [May 1629]. Received from the most illustrious lady Maria Moresini, for a portrait head of her dead son, 7 *scudi* worth 63 *lire*.

On the 23rd day of the same month [January 1632]. Received from the magnificent lady Antonia . . . the money for the portrait of the late lady Marietta, her daughter, 40 *lire*.

d. Widowhood: maintaining memories

After their husbands' deaths, widows could more easily order portraits, whether of themselves or of their deceased spouse, without the need for male intermediaries. They also retained portraits of their late husbands or of their associates in their dwellings. A painting by Bernardino Licinio in the Castello Sforzesco, Milan seems to depict a widow treasuring such a memento.[4]

6. Portraits of family members owned by a widow from Rimini, 1532

Outside the circles of courts, and of patrician elites in certain centres, there seems to have been little tradition of portraiture until the sixteenth century. Records of the household goods of widows in Rimini between 1416 and 1539 reveal widespread ownership of devotional images, or painted furnishing items, but mention portraits only in one household apart from that given below, which was unusually rich in the number of paintings it contained. Even here, images of male family members greatly exceed those of women.

Delucca (1997), p. 729.

15 July 1532. [For] Lady Elisabetta, daughter of the late
Rainaldi de Simonetta and former wife of Vincenzo son of
Giovanni son of Antonio de Sacramoro, of the *contrada* of S.
Maria a Mare.

... A painted panel where are portrayed the figures of the
late Giovanni Sacramoro and his wife; another painting on
wood in which is portrayed the figure of Messer Antonio
Sacramoro the elder; another portrait panel with the figure
of the said Vincenzo Sacramoro; another large picture in
which is portrayed Messer Antonio, son of the said late
Antonio; a panel painting of a Venus; another canvas painting of a *Fortune* ...

7. A widow from Ancona orders a portrait from Lorenzo Lotto, 1552

Lotto records a portrait commission from a widow in Ancona. The
'de naturale' means the image is most likely to be of the woman
herself rather than of her dead husband, although the Italian is
ambiguous.

Lotto, ed. Zampetti (1969), p. 144.

In Ancona, the (. . .) day of April, 1552, Madonna Maria,
widow of the late Messer Antonio Durante dal Monte gave
... for a portrait from life [*de naturale*], for the stretcher and
canvas and having it framed ...

She had the portrait as arranged and it is valued at a good
price of 8 gold *scudi*, in gold.

8. A widow in Florence takes delivery of her husband's portrait, painted after a death mask, 1583

I. B. Supino (ed.), *I Ricordi di Alessandro Allori* (Florence,
1908), pp. 21, 30.

From Madonna Lucrezia Capponi de' Torrigiani 245
[*lire*] for the remaining payment for the portrait of Messer
Raffaello Torrigiani and for a portrait of the Virgin
Annunciate, one *braccio* high and 2 *braccia* wide ...

I record that on this day of 29 July [1583] I delivered to Madonna Lucrezia Capponi de' Torrigiani a portrait of Messer Raffaello her husband, made after his death, 2 *braccia* high and correspondingly broad, with as much time taken with the clothing as with the head, for which I had only a small clay mould which I made shortly after his death a few months ago, the said portrait and its price related to the time and effort being thirty gold *scudi.*

THE COMMISSIONING PROCESS AND ITS MOTIVATIONS

Only widows or women from the a city's ruling house were legally entitled to order portraits, or other works of art, without the intervention of a male associate. This section is mainly concerned with such commissions, often documented because of the use of intermediaries between female donors and artists based in different cities. Letters between these parties illuminate the practical problems involved, the commissioners' actual or professed motivations, and their concerns that artists should capture likenesses or achieve a good aesthetic standard. In addition, there must have been many joint husband-and-wife commissions where women's initiatives, or preferences as to choice of artist, setting or costume would have been important, though not documented.

a. Negotiations and enquiries

9. Isabella of Aragon requests an antique bust, 1498

Widowed in 1495 after the death of her husband, Duke Gian Galeazzo Sforza, Isabella of Aragon (1470–1524) was kept under close guard by Duke Ludovico il Moro. She turned for support to her relatives at the court of Mantua, from whom she requested several portraits. Amongst these was an antique bust Mantegna had brought from Rome, which Isabella wished to acquire because it was thought to resemble her physically. Although this might not be a scholarly antiquarian motivation, Isabella states firmly that she does not want a cast version, but the original antique.

C. M. Brown, 'Little known and unpublished documents concerning Andrea Mantegna, Bernardino Parentino, Pietro

Lombardo, Leonardo da Vinci and Filippo Benintendi' (Part One), *L'Arte*, 6 (1969), p. 145; P. Kristeller, *Andrea Mantegna* (Berlin and Leipzig, 1902), document 149, pp. 564–5.

Isabella of Aragon, in Milan, to Isabella d'Este, in Mantua, 26 February 1498
As the Reverend Father Messer Pietro da Novellara had come to this city, he came to visit us on behalf of our illustrious Lord Marquis and of Your Ladyship, and with many affectionate words conveyed us how strongly you both desired to make an agreeable gesture. So the Lord Marquis would order a bronze cast to be made of that antique portrait, as it had a defect in the marble around the nose, and send it to me. For this we thank Your Ladyship with all our heart and are greatly obliged, as we have already written to the Lord Marquis, but ask His Lordship to send the marble one rather than the bronze cast, as it would delight us more, being antique. And so we ask Your Ladyship also that this wish of ours should be satisfied as soon as possible, together with the copy of the portrait from life which His Lordship has of His Majesty the Lord King of happy memory, our brother [King Ferrante of Naples], because those two things would be as pleasing as any other which Your Lordships are capable of granting.

Isabella d'Este, to an unknown correspondent in Milan, 28 February 1498
A few days ago the illustrious Duchess Isabella, through Fra Pietro da Novellara the Dominican, asked if we would be willing to let her have an antique head which Andrea Mantegna had brought from Rome, saying that it resembled her. As we wished to be kind, feeling affection for her, we at once put it to Mantegna. But he valued this head greatly for its high quality and as a scholar of antiquity, and did not want to relinquish it either beforehand or now, and wanted to cast it in bronze, giving away the cast and keeping the original for himself. In the end we were so insistent in person that we would not be satisfied with the cast that he gave up the antique marble head, which we are sending by the present muleteer. For our part, we wish to make a gift

of it to Her Ladyship as it gave her such pleasure, telling her how very glad we are to have done her this service, as we think the head much resembles her and those who have seen it have rated it highly.

10. Isabella d'Este wants a portrait of her son, captive in Rome, 24 May 1512
Isabella writes from Mantua to her agent, Matteo Ippolito, in Rome, asking him to have a portrait made of her twelve-year-old son Federico, then a hostage in the Vatican. Concerned for artistic quality as usual, she wants Raphael, or the next best artist. Raphael accepted, and there are several later letters by Isabella and her correspondents about the costume Federico was to wear, which was sent from Mantua.

Shearman (2003), 1, pp. 158–9.

Matteo. Because the portrait of Federico our son which was made at Bologna has been given away, we wish to have another of him, especially if we find a more graceful and beautiful one. I would like you to see if Raphael, the son of Giovanni Santi of Urbino can be found in Rome, and ask him if he would portray him chest length, in a suit of armour. And if Raphael is not there, find the next best one, as we don't want a minor painter, wishing to have the handiwork of a good master. We will treat him with courtesy and honour, as you know is our custom. Tell him to show him life size, and as swiftly as possible, and that he could do nothing more pleasing. Greet Federico on our behalf, and take care to get well again.

11. Pietro Aretino solicits Lucietta Saracina to let the young Alessandro Vittoria make her portrait medal, 1552
During his 1547–53 residence in Vicenza, working mainly on stuccoes for the Palazzo Thiene, Alessandro Vittoria made several medals of women.[5] These included Aretino's mistress Caterina Sandello and illegitimate daughter Adria. The sculptor was known to him as a former pupil of his friend Jacopo Sansovino. Here Aretino addresses the Vicentine noblewoman Lucietta Saracina as

someone able to persuade her husband to order a portrait image of herself by his protégé, flattering her that it will convey her virtues, and appealing to her competitive sense by mentioning the excellence of Vittoria's other likenesses of ladies of Vicenza. The outcome of this letter, perhaps always intended for publication, is not known.

P. Aretino, *Lettere sull'arte di Pietro Aretino*, ed. E. Camesasca, 4 vols (Milan, 1957–60), 2, DCXXXVIII, pp. 412–13.

Pietro Aretino in Venice to Lucietta Saracina in Vicenza, 1552

As I do not know how to give grateful recompense to the greetings sent me by the mouth of your lord, Gasparo, a consort devoid of lying or deceit, it remains my office and my duty prayerfully to commend to Alessandro Vittoria, who recently has come to Vicenza, the idea of making a likeness of your head. My task has been to make this excellent sculptor want to portray you, since the merits of your behaviour, which adorn you with illustrious praise, demand that anyone who understands their virtue should honour you in works . . . To agree to thus please me, the young man, who is beginning to convey his artistic personality in marble, wishes to add your modest and noble image to the abundant similar ones from his hand, seen in lively relief. Already showing equal talent in this type of art, he is also thinking of portraying in medal you, who are worthy of it, with just the enthusiasm that he has depicted Maximilian, Prince of Piedmont and of Spain, as well as his father, brother and nephew and other gentlemen and prelates, in Trent. So that the care taken by him in expressing the gentleness, the gravity and the grace of the sublime Caterina Chiericati will equally be seen by you in his imitation of the sweetness apparent in the charming daughters of the much-loved Count Marcantonio Thiene.[6] To conclude: if it is doubted whether the follower of Sansovino Phidias in style could rival his great master in fame, firm proof is given (apart from the head depicted by him of the distinguished matron Maddalena Liomparda) by the majesty which lends glory to the expression and face of the great, magnanimous Duke of Atri.[7] Or so I consider. I kiss your right hand with fatherly charity and an affectionate desire to serve.

b. The work in progress: costume

In a culture highly sensitive to clothing and accessories as markers of status, worth and affluence, and often as bearers of symbolic meanings, the garbing of sitters for portraits was no light matter.[8] It was not unusual for articles of dress to be sent by the sitter to the artist's workplace, and the loan of costly items might be carefully noted by the relevant court employees. At a lower social level, it would be felt important that religious images including female donors should show them modestly dressed and with pious demeanour.

12. Group portraits within religious work, 1541

The confraternity devoted to the Madonna at the church of S. Pietro di Fonte in the province of Bassano included females as well as males. The contract for their altar-piece of 27 November 1541 was made between a local painter, Francesco da Milano, and named male members in the presence of 'molti altri confratelli', perhaps including women. The subject was the Madonna with saints and angels and members of the confraternity, whose dress was specified.

M. Muraro, *Il libro secondo di Francesco e Jacopo dal Ponte* (Bassano, 1992), p. 326.

And beneath these saints we wish the confraternity [to be shown] with the banner, the crosses with the candles and the brothers gathered in undershirts and scourges and the sisters with black veils on their heads and with short candles in their hands.

13. The costuming of Titian's portrait of Giulia Varano, Duchess of Urbino, 1546–47

Several letters over 1543–47 between Duke Guidobaldo della Rovere of Urbino, his Duchess, and their agent in Venice, Leonardi, reveal that a portrait by Titian of the Duchess, Giulia Varano (1523–47), was done from another image, supplemented with costume items sent from Urbino. It seems that Titian had requested the Duchess be clothed in crimson velvet, but as she did not possess a velvet dress of this colour, crimson silk garments were dispatched. These the artist transformed to velvet in the finished painting in the Palazzo Pitti, Florence, in what was possibly an unusual instance of an artist's colour preferences taking precedence over the realities of the sitter's wardrobe. Two of Giulia's letters complain of Titian's delays, usual with the artist.

Gronau (1936), pp. 96–8.

Giulia Varano to Leonardi, Fossombrone, 8 July 1546
In order that Titian has no more excuses to hold up the execution of our portraits, we are sending the sleeves he wanted by another post.

Giulia Varano to Leonardi, Fossombrone, 7 August 1546
If Titian would reply in deeds rather than words, we think we would possess the portrait this very moment, and that you would already have ordered the barge . . .

Paolo Mario [a courtier at Urbino] to Leonardi, Fossombrone, 8 February 1547
One of the Lady Duchess's dresses is being sent to you, by the coach coming from Madama Marietta, so that you may pass it on to Titian, to whom we could say that we would have sent a richer gown had he not demanded one of crimson or rose velvet, and as Her Excellency did not have one, I thought that this one, in the same colour in damask, would accord with his wishes.

14. Alessandro Allori records his return of the items used in a portrait of the Grand Duchess of Florence, Bianca Cappello, 1580–81
When portraits of high-ranking ladies were produced by court artists, much attention was often paid to the careful and authentic rendering of rich clothing. Several surviving images of Bianca Cappello show a similar precise depiction of costume.

Supino ed. (1908), pp. 24, 26.

I record that this day of 14th November [1580] I consigned to
. . . the *guardaroba* of the Grand Duchess and to the brother
of Piero, her wardrobe-master, several garments of cloth that
I had . . . for the commission of the Grand Duchess, namely,
an over-dress of silver fabric with turquoise velvet detailing,
a dress with a low neckline in gold tabby-weave with a gold
fringe . . . a doublet of cloth-of-gold, trimmed, with sleeves,
and likewise the over-dress with long sleeves down to the
ground, all lined in an orange-yellow taffeta.

I record that this day [28 January 1581] I despatched a garland or headdress of pearls of the Grand Duchess's, which
Her Serene Highness gave me with her own hands for her
portrait to be sent to Venice: and I consigned the same headdress, in which there were ten rosettes with ten diamonds, to
Monna Lena to give to Signora Pietra.

I record this 11th day of April [1581] how My Lady the
Grand Duchess Bianca Cappello has to give me 90 *scudi* in
coins, this for a portrait of His Excellency the Grand Duke
Francesco on canvas 3⅙ high and 2 *braccia* wide, the colours at my expense, painted full length, seated, with coat
and hose of grey and waistcoat of black silk; and this portrait
was priced at 35 *scudi*, and the portrait of the Lady Grand
Duchess at 55 *scudi*, which is the same size as the first, with
overdress of cloth of silver and turquoise, that is with cut-
velvet work; and in the portrait there is also my Lord Prince
seated, full length, dressed in white silk, and the portrait of
the Marquis Don Antonio her son in the same place, dressed
in white silk . . . consigned this day to M. Corsini, master of
the household, who packed them in cases to send to Venice
to the Illustrious and Excellent Signor Bartolommeo, father
of the Lady Grand Duchess, costing 630 *lire*.

c. Concerns over likeness and quality

By the end of the fifteenth century, if not earlier, female patrons
from aristocratic circles seem to have shown confidence in their

judgements on the quality of portraits, especially in regard to their resemblance to the sitters and the liveliness of the image. Various means were tried to ensure the images proved satisfactory, or compensation was sought if they were not.

15. Malatesta donor portraits of poor quality, 1496
Elisabetta Aldobrandini Malatesta, the mother of Pandolfo IV, Lord of Rimini, had apparently in 1493, on behalf of her son, ordered Domenico Ghirlandaio to produce an altarpiece for the Malatesta family chapel in S. Cataldo, Rimini (now in the city's Pinacoteca Comunale). As well as saintly figures, the panel included four kneeling donors: Elisabetta, her sons, Pandolfo and Carlo, and Pandolfo's wife. Following Domenico's death in 1494 the painting was completed by his brother, Davide. Elisabetta refused to pay the total agreed price, 130 florins, on the grounds of its inferior quality, and the case went to arbitration. The arbiter, Pandolfo da Leonardello, issuing his conclusion to the Episcopal Court in Florence, upheld Elisabetta's judgement, pointing out the lack of resemblance of the portraits to the sitters (something Elisabetta herself must have noticed), and decreasing the sum owed to Davide.

J. K. Cadogan, *Domenico Ghirlandaio. Artist and Artisan* (New Haven and London, 2000), document 45, p. 378.

[Pandolfo da Leonardello of Rimini issues his judgement on 14 November 1496:]
As we find, and is stated to us, the said panel for the above-mentioned place by Domenico, who was a fine master of his craft, was not and is not finished by the said Domenico, since his death prevented him from finishing it, but was and is finished and put in place by Davide, the brother of Domenico, together with other painters, so that because of these other workers it looks different. The testimony of many experts in the art of painting tells us this, and even looking with our own eyes we see from the quality of the panel how far its execution falls short. And it is clear that the figures in it which should have been taken from life of the illustrious lords of Rimini hardly conform to their appearance at all.
Thus, basing our opinion on just and reasonable grounds,

we pronounce, sentence, discern, declare, refer and arbitrate that the said Davide of the same name should be awarded credit by the most illustrious Lady Elisabetta and Tommaso her agent only to the total sum and quantity of 10 Florentine gold florins in gold, for the remainder of the said panel.

16. An unsatisfactory portrait of Isabella d'Este improved, 1511
These extracts from her correspondence show that Isabella had enlisted the help of her half-sister, Lucrezia, the wife of Annibale Bentivoglio of Bologna, to check on a portrait by Francesco Francia, who was based in Bologna and working from an earlier image.[9]

Negro and Roio (1998), pp. 117–18.

Lucrezia Bentivoglio to Isabella d'Este, 7 September 1511
Most Illustrious and Excellent Lady, and my most honoured sister. The next day I went dutifully to the house of the painter Francia, to see how far the portrait of Your Excellency made by him resembled your natural appearance. I will speak the truth and not be evasive. It doesn't seem to me like you at all, appearing more sombre and gaunt: another person, another image – not Your Excellency. In so far as it did suggest the real person, I made him aware of all its shortcomings, begging him, for the sake of his own honour and my satisfaction, to journey to Mantua to see the image of Your Excellency in life, so that his portrait might seem a similar living image. But I could not persuade him to promise to do so: he said it would be too dangerous to expose himself both to fortune and to art in making a portrait from life. However, he told me that he wanted to redo it, and then change it and rechange it following my opinion, and perhaps he might be able to achieve a better likeness. However, without seeing Your Excellency I rather doubt it will be as lifelike as if taken from the living person, had he been persuaded to come and see you at Mantua.

[Eventually the portrait was delivered. Isabella wrote to Francia that he had made her 'more beautiful than had Nature', but asked him to make alterations to achieve greater likeness, to which Lucrezia reported his reaction.]

> Lucrezia to Isabella, 9 December 1511
> Most Illustrious and Excellent Lady and my honoured sister. Messer Francia our painter behaves as though he's in heaven, he is so pleased to have satisfied Your Excellency with his portrait, especially as you write him that his art has made you more beautiful than has Nature. But he would not be so boastful about his skill in painting as to believe he could surpass Nature, that irreproachable mistress – that would be too arrogant. Still, in truth this conceit coming from a lady such as you does not displease him! However, he does have doubts about the changing of the eyes from dark to blue, lest the existing good parts should be spoilt, and the certain lost for the uncertain. He would be reluctant to run the risk, claiming he would need to change the shading of the whole painting to suit the colour of the eyes, and that then he would need to varnish it once more, and that were the positioning of the eyes to be adjusted just a little the picture could lose all its grace.

SETTINGS AND FUNCTIONS

Inventories and letters give us some idea of the hanging and display of portraits in the Renaissance.[10] Some portraits, such as those within palace fresco cycles, devotional works or tombs, were not easily moved. The larger-scale images of important family members that became more common in the sixteenth century would be prominently displayed in the more public rooms of dwellings. Special collections made to celebrate the socially or intellectually distinguished might have their own room or gallery. Small examples, though, which often had covers which are now lost, seem frequently to have been shifted between their owners' different dwellings and rooms. Sometimes this was connected with the ways in which they were used by women, often compensating for absences of family members or friends, whether dead or alive. The following extracts suggest a range of settings, and sometimes illuminate female spectators' responses to them.

a. Images of friends and family

17. Court ladies at leisure portrayed in their dining room, Pavia, 1469

Several fifteenth-century sources mention frescoed decorative cycles in palaces which incorporated portraits of ladies of the courts, such as the lost cycle featuring Eleonora of Aragon at the Palazzo Schifanoia, Ferrara. Some of these paintings ornamented suites of rooms predominantly used by court ladies, as here in the Castello at Pavia, where the restoration (or repainting) of existing frescoes was ordered by the Duke of Milan, Francesco Sforza, in 1469. His architect Bartolommeo Gadio was to oversee the work.

M. Caffi, 'Il Castello di Pavia', *Archivio Storico Lombardo*, ser. 1, vol. 3, anno 3 (1876), p. 547.

In the room where the ladies dine [are painted], our illustrious Lady, the illustrious Lady Isabella, who play at ball or at the game of *poma*[11] with their ladies-in-waiting. And with them are Virgilio, Don Biagio and Gianantonio the jester: the female dwarf turns round in surprise to My Lady. In the chamber in the tower the illustrious Lord and My Lady in Turkish dress with the wife of the mayor and the illustrious Count of Pavia, and her ladies embrace them and tell her the news.

18. A portrait kept with religious objects, 1498

When female members of aristocratic families were under political pressure, as was often the case, assembling portraits of their relatives might not only give psychological support, but serve to remind their captors of the women's influential kin. At a time when she was humiliated by the ascendancy of her enemies in Milan, the widowed Isabella of Aragon took consolation from a portrait of her brother, the King of Naples.

A. Dina, 'Isabella d'Aragona duchessa di Milano e di Bari', *Archivio Storico Lombardo*, ser. 5, vol. 8, anno 48 (1921), p. 376.

Isabella of Aragon in Milan to Francesco II Gonzaga, 10 April 1498
Illustrious kinsman, most honoured like a brother,

We have received the portrait from life of the Lord King our brother, sent by Your Excellency, which has greatly pleased and satisfied us. Owing to the great affection we have for him, we have not been able to contain our tears in seeing him and contemplating him, and so we have moved it to the place where we keep some objects of devotion which we wish to look at frequently. So we give all possible thanks to Your Excellency.

19. A portrait of a friend kept in a chamber, 1627
Here, Livia della Rovere, Duchess of Urbino (1585–1641), writes to Maria Maddalena of Austria, Grand Duchess of Tuscany (1589–1631), on 22 June 1627. She refers to her granddaughter Vittoria della Rovere (1622–94), the eventual heir to the della Rovere collections.

Barocchi and Gaeta Bertelà (2005), p. 341.

I cannot fully express, nor can Your Highness imagine with what delight the Lord Duke [Cosimo II de' Medici] and I beheld the portrait which Your Highness sent us to give us pleasure. Princess Vittoria and the Lord Duke have praised it highly, judging that the German outfit suits you very well. I have placed it in my chamber and I look at it all the time, with a great longing one day (whenever your Highness may be pleased to grant me the favour) to be able to be both rewarded and pleased by the presence of the real original.

Your Serene Highness's most devoted servant, Livia, Duchess of Urbino.

20. A portrait collection in an aristocratic *guardaroba*, 1650–52
An aristocratic wife might retain portraits of members of her family of birth in her personal apartments. As well as expressing and maintaining ties of affection, these might also reinforce her status at court, evoking her illustrious lineage. Inventories made over the years 1646–52 of the paintings in the *guardaroba* of Vittoria della Rovere, Grand Duchess of Tuscany, include works she inherited from Urbino, with 20 portraits out of a total of 42 paintings, many of them well-known and on display in the Uffizi and Pitti galleries.

Barocchi and Gaeta Bertelà (2005), pp. 712–13.

14 June 1650

4. A painting on copper, ¼ *braccio* high, depicting Cardinal Giulio of Urbino, with a gilded copper setting

26 March 1652

7. A panel painting, 1½ *braccia* high and 1½ broad, depicting Pope Julius II, by Raphael of Urbino.

8. A painting on canvas, 1⅔ *braccia* high and 1¼ broad, depicting a lady dressed in black in old-fashioned style, which is said might be Duchess Eleonora of Urbino, by Titian.

9. A painting on canvas, 1 *braccio* high and 1⅗ broad, depicting Marquis Ippolito Della Rovere, by Baroccio.

10. A painting on canvas, 2 *braccia* high and ⅘ broad, depicting Monsignor Giuliano della Rovere, by Baroccio.

4 April 1652

15. A painting on canvas, 1⅞ *braccia* high, 1⅔ broad, depicting a lady in old-fashioned dress, said to be of the Varano house.[12]

16. A painting on canvas, 1½ *braccia* high, 1¼ broad, depicting a Duke of Urbino, by Giorgione.

17. A painting on canvas, 2 *braccia* high, 1¾ broad, depicting Francesco Maria I, Duke of Urbino, in armour, by Titian.

18. A painting on panel, 1⅞ *braccia* high, ½ broad, depicting a Duke of Urbino with his hand on the head of a dog, by Baroccio [in fact, by Bronzino].

c. *Women using portraits as gifts*

Aristocratic and other women are recorded using gifts of portraits to maintain a friendship, seek or reciprocate a favour, or make a personal statement.

21. Eleonora di Toledo commissions a portrait gift for Pope Julius III, 1550

It was intended that Giovanni (1543–62), the second son of Eleonora and Cosimo de' Medici, should be made a cardinal, and the portrait mentioned below served to remind the Tuscan

Pope, who had been elected pontiff earlier in the year, of the Ducal couple's hopes.

Archivio di Stato di Firenze, Mediceo del Principato, vol. 1176, insert 1, fol. 16, www.medici.org.

Cristiano Pagni, secretary to the Duchess Eleonora, writes from Pisa to the Major-domo Pier Riccio in Florence, 8 December 1550.

My Duchess has told me to write to you order Messer Bronzino to come to her, so that he can make a portrait of Don Giovanni to send to the Pope, which she wants despatched as soon as possible.

22. Veronica Franco presents her portrait to King Henri III of France, 1580

When the new King of France, Henri III, came to Venice in 1574 he visited Veronica Franco (1546–91), one of the cultivated courtesans of the city. Franco's *Lettere familiari a diversi* (Venice, 1580) included a fawning dedication letter and two sonnets to the King, recording her presentation of her portrait to commemorate this high point in her career. Her literary ambitions – allegedly encouraged by the King – are also drawn to the attention of her readers. The work, whether a miniature to be worn on the person or a medallion to be displayed in a cabinet, would have suggested her refined taste.

B. Croce (ed.), *Veronica Franco. Lettere dall'unica edizione del MDLXXX con proemio e nota iconografica* (Naples, 1949), pp. 7–8; Veronica Franco, *Poems and Selected Letters*, ed. A. R. Jones and M. E. Rosenthal (Chicago, 1998), pp. 24–8.

To the most unvanquished and Christian King, Henri III of France and Poland
To the supremely high favour that Your Majesty, coming to my humble abode, deigned to show me by taking my portrait away with him in exchange for the living image of his heroic virtues and divine courage left deep in my heart – an exchange too fortunate and happy on my side – I am able to reciprocate neither in thought nor desire . . .Yet just as the

whole world can sometimes be drawn in the small space of
the narrowest page, I have, in these few verses which I reverently send to Your Majesty, set down a sketch, however
crude and limited, of my gratitude and my immense and fervent desire to celebrate beyond the limits of any earthly hope
the innumerable and superhuman gifts lodged in your generous breast, to their good fortune. And, with devoted and
deep affection, I bow down reverently, I embrace your sacred
knees.

As once, benignly, Jove descended
from heaven beneath a humble roof amongst us,
and, lest the lofty sight smite earthly eyes,
took human form:
so to my poor shelter,
without regal pomp which blinds and dazzles,
came Henri, elect by fate to such dominion
that no single world can contain or vanquish.
Even disguised thus, straight to my heart
a ray he struck of his heavenly merit,
such that my innate vigour was extinguished.
So, not unaware of this emotion,
he took my painted and enamelled image
on his parting, in kind and liberal spirit.

Take, O King, supreme and perfect in virtue,
that which my hand extends to give you:
this sculpted and coloured likeness,
in which my living being is conveyed.
And, if your blessed gaze is unaccustomed
to so base and faulty a depiction,
reflect on the cause, not the effect.
A tiny spark may a mighty flame alight.
And as your divine, immortal courage,
tested a thousand-fold in peace and war,
filled my soul with lofty wonder,
so the longing felt in a woman's heart
to exalt you above the heavens, far from this world,
observe in this likeness, expressed and sure.

23. Caterina de' Medici sends her portrait to nuns in Florence, 1588

Caterina de' Medici favoured the convent of Le Murate in her native city, and here she sends notice of the dispatch of her portrait to be exhibited in its church to encourage the nuns prayers for herself and her family. She had earlier intended a portrait in marble.

Lettres de Cathérine de Médicis et al. ed. H. de la Ferrière-Percy, 11 vols (Paris, 1880–1943) vol. 9, p. 321.

Caterina de' Medici to the Abbess and nuns of Le Murate, Florence
I will give orders to have sent to your convent, as I promised, not a marble statue, for that would be too difficult, but a portrait from life of myself, very well painted, which should be placed and exhibited in a short time in your church, recommending to your prayers the good health of the King my son and the Queen my daughter, and that it may please God to give them children. I pray God, my ladies the abbesses and nuns, that he has you in His holy and noble regard.

d. Portraits as inspiration

The belief that portraits as executed by good masters could convey virtue and excellence as well as likeness, which was held throughout the Renaissance but spelt out much more clearly in the sixteenth century, encouraged the viewing or collecting of images of distinguished or saintly personages: see chapter 9, text 13, and chapter 12, text 10. [13] It should be remembered that the term *ritratto* was often used to refer to non-narrative images of saints or historical personages as well as to portraits in the modern sense.

24. Isabella d'Este borrows portraits of great Tuscan poets from Bernardo Bembo, 5 January 1504

Isabella d'Este was unusual amongst women collectors in trying to acquire images of persons of distinction: not just the 'Famous Women' conventional for women's contemplation, but male writers or philosophers. The following letter implies she was having the images of the Tuscan poets copied by a painter at court.

R. Iotti, 'Phenice unica, virtuosa e pia. La corrispondenza culturale di Isabella', in Bini (ed.) (2001), p. 173.

Lord Bernardo Bembo. We send to Your Magnificence the portraits of Dante, Petrarch and Boccaccio that you lent us: if we have been dilatory in returning then, attribute this to the slowness of the painter, and exonerate us as not guilty of lacking care. We thank Your Magnificence for granting us this convenience, offering ourselves as always ready to give similar or greater favours to him.

25. Vittoria Colonna praises the powers of portraiture, c1540.

The long speech by Vittoria Colonna (c. 1490–1547) in de Holanda's First Dialogue praises the art of painting as educational and elevating, treating portraiture as a prime example, moving seamlessly from discussing images of religious or historical personages to those of people of recent times. Though Colonna would not actually have spoken these words, the author must have thought it plausible that she could do so. The sentiments accord with the poet's own writings and the advocacy for morally praiseworthy portraiture by later Catholic Reformation moralists, and indeed by another female writer, Veronica Franco, in 12.10.

Francisco de Holanda, *Dialogues with Michelangelo* [c. 1540–48], ed. D. Hemsoll, trans. C. B. Holroyd (London, 2006), pp. 58–9.

[Painting] represents to us the constancy of the martyrs, the purity of the virgins, the beauty of the angels, and the love and ardour with which the seraphim burn, better than in any other way, and lifts up our spirit and plunges our mind into depths beyond the stars . . . it leaves a memorial of the present times for those who come after . . . it places before our eyes the image of any great man who should be seen and known because of his deeds, and likewise the beauty of a woman who is separated from us by many leagues, a thing on which Pliny reflects much. To one who dies it gives many years of life, his own face remaining behind painted, and his wife is consoled, seeing daily before her the image of her deceased husband, and the sons who were left little children rejoice when men to know the presence and the aspect of their dear father, and fear to shame him.

Notes

1 Several studies on portraiture in media that tend to be less studied are in N. Mann and L. Syson (eds), *The Image of the Individual* (London, 1998).

2 Few of the many general works on Renaissance portraiture consistently devote space to women's involvement in the commissioning or collection of portraits. For female artists' self-portraits, see J. Woods-Marsden, *Renaissance Self-Portraiture* (New Haven and London, 1998), pp. 187–222, with bibliography. For female patronage of portraits by Lavinia Fontana, see C. P. Murphy, 'Lavinia Fontana and Le Dame della Città: understanding female artistic patronage in late Sixteenth-century Bologna', *Renaissance Studies*, 10:2 (1996), pp. 190–208.

3 This type of portrait has been much discussed, with some consideration of the role of brides' female relatives. See recently E. Fahy, 'The marriage portrait in the Renaissance, or some women named Ginevra', and J. M. Musacchio, 'Wives, lovers and art in Italian Renaissance courts' in A. Bayer, ed., *Art and Love in Renaissance Italy* (New York, 2008), pp. 17–28 and pp. 29–41, with bibliographies.

4 For portraiture of widows, including donor portraits, see C. M. King, *Renaissance Women Patrons* (Manchester, 1998), especially pp. 129–83; Murphy (1996), pp. 198–200 and essays in A. Levy, *Widowhood and Visual Culture in Early Modern Europe* (Aldershot, 2003).

5 F. Cessi, *Alessandro Vittoria medaglista (1525–1608)* (Trento, 1960).

6 A bronze medal inscribed 'Caterina Chieregata' is in the Museo Correr, Venice, illustrated in Cessi, pl. 5a, but the images of the Thiene daughters are not known.

7 The medal of Maddalena Liompardi, a *cortigiana onesta* of mature years, is shown in Cessi, pl. 4.

8 For textiles in portraits, L. Monnas, *Merchants, Princes and Painters* (New Haven and London, 2008), pp. 181–215.

9 For this episode and its context, see S. Hickson, '"To see ourselves as others see us": Giovanni Francesco Zaninello of Ferrara and the portrait of Isabella d'Este by Francesco Francia', *Renaissance Studies*, 23:3 (2009), pp. 288–310.

10 See especially J. Fletcher, 'The Renaissance Portrait: Function, Uses and Display', in *Renaissance Faces. Van Eyck to Titian*, eds. L. Campbell, M. Falomir, J. Fletcher and L. Syson (London, 2008), pp. 46–65.

11 A game akin to tennis.
12 Likely to have been the portrait of Giulia Varano by Titian in text 13.
13 Into this category should be placed many portraits of nuns kept in their converts, a little-studied topic for which see K. I. P. Lowe, 'Elections of abbesses and notions of identity in fifteenth- and sixteenth-century Italy with special reference to Venice', *Renaissance Quarterly*, 54:2 (2001), pp. 389–429.

❧ 7 ❧

RELATIONSHIPS WITH ARTISTS

While contracts between artists and patrons, as legal documents, deal with the hard facts of an agreement between the two parties, the texts in this chapter allow us to discover a fuller picture of the intriguing, and sometimes less known, connections between them. A number of texts show how close these relationships could be. This was especially so in the context of a court, when patrons and artists were in everyday contact with one another, and often lived in the same building. The texts chosen here are mostly letters from artists and their patronesses, or from friends, secretaries and agents, but also include personal or official records. They bring to life stories of money, illness and rivalry, as well as of trust and friendship.

The tone and language of many of these letters to powerful women will strike the modern reader as servile and at times sycophantic, being more formal than the mode of address used between members of the same family or very close friends. Etiquette and respect for formality, however, were second nature to members of a society based on hierarchy and rank.

LETTERS OF INTRODUCTION

The letters in this section show how both artists and patrons relied on a network of kinship and friendship. Artists' skills were certainly considered in a recommendation, but personal qualities and character traits were also very important. An artist, especially in court service, was required to follow codes of courtly behaviour, and this held true throughout our period. These qualities were less relevant for artists usually working for the open market.

1. A talented artist needs no recommendation, 1490

Isabella d'Este arrived in Mantua as the bride of Francesco Gonzaga in February 1490. A few months later, the humanist Battista Guarino wrote this letter recommending Andrea Mantegna, who had already worked for the Gonzaga.

Kristeller (1902), pp. 506–7.

Battista Guarino from Verona to Isabella d'Este, 22 October 1490

Most Illustrious Lady, Andrea Mantegna insisted that I should recommend him to Your Excellency, believing that you will heed my words. I told him that talented men such as he do not need to be recommended to you, because you are much disposed to prefer and favour those who deserve it, but that nevertheless I would do it. And so I pray you to cherish and think highly of him, because, as well as being most excellent and unequalled in his art, he is also a gentleman. His concepts and plans will produce many excellent results for Your Ladyship. He will bring honour to the Most Illustrious Lord and to the city. I recommend him to Your Excellency.

2. Elisabetta Gonzaga introduces a sculptor to her brother, 1495

The 'Adriano Fiorentino' Elisabetta Gonzaga recommends to her brother Francesco II Gonzaga, is the sculptor Adriano di Giovanni de' Maestri (c. 1450/60–c. 1499). In 1493 he was in Naples, working at the court of King Ferrante, where he produced a number of portrait medals. He left Naples in the Spring of 1495, and stopped briefly in Urbino, where, among other works, he made a portrait medal of Elisabetta.[1]

A. Luzio and R. Renier, *Mantova e Urbino. Isabella d'Este ed Elisabetta Gonzaga nelle relazioni famigliari e nelle vicende politiche* (Turin and Rome, 1893), p. 84.

Elisabetta Gonzaga, from Urbino, to Francesco Gonzaga, May 1495

Because it is my natural instinct to protect talented men, I can do no less with those who are recommended to me. I recommend to Your Excellency the bearer of this letter, Adriano Fiorentino, as highly as I can, and I pray you to accept him into your service. I am certain that his behaviour, as well as his work, will be such that each day you will declare yourself better served and satisfied.

So that Your Excellency is informed about his career, I inform you that for some time he has been on the payroll of the Most Serene King Ferrante. Now he is no longer in his employment, and has been discharged from his position because of bad luck. He has now placed all his hopes in Your Excellency becoming his sole patron during his lifetime, something he strongly desires, especially knowing the strong affection that has always existed between the King and Your Excellency. So that you are aware of his work, I can tell you that he is a good sculptor, and has made some very fine medals. He is also a good writer of sonnets, an expert lyre player, and he improvises very well. I shall end by saying that in the three months he has been here he has given [us] much pleasure. Among his virtues I judge him to be a good person, honest and loyal.

3. Raphael wants to go to Florence, 1504

With this well-known letter, which Crowe and Cavalcaselle believed to be a fake but which is now considered to be authentic, Giovanna Feltria (1463–1514) warmly recommends the young Raphael to the *Gonfaloniere* of the Florentine Republic Pietro Soderini. Giovanna was one of the daughters of Federico da Montefeltro and Battista Sforza, and the widow of Giovanni della Rovere, *prefetto* of Rome and Lord of Senigallia. Raphael and his father, Giovanni Santi, had worked for her and other members of the Urbino court.

V. Golzio, *Raffaello nei documenti nelle testimonianze dei contemporanei e nella letteratura del suo secolo* (Città del Vaticano, 1936, repr. Farnborough, 1971), pp. 9–10.

Giovanna Feltria della Rovere, from Urbino, to Pietro Soderini, 1 October 1504

The bearer of this letter is Raphael, a painter from Urbino. Since he is very skilled in his art, he has resolved to live in Florence for some time in order to learn. His father was a fine

man and devoted to me, and the son too is a sensible and cour-
teous young man, so I am extremely fond of him and wish him
to become perfect in his work. I therefore recommend him
most highly to Your Lordship, as highly as possible, praying
you, for the affection you have towards me, to be willing to lend
him your assistance and favour. All the kindness and opportunities he receives from Your Lordship, I shall regard as if they
had been received by me, and I shall be much obliged to you.

**4. The Grand Duchess of Tuscany praises the qualities of her
court painter, 1627**
Maria Maddalena of Austria writes a detailed letter to the Grand
Master of the Knights of Malta, introducing the Medici court
painter Justus Sustermans (1597 –1681), then in Rome for a short
period of study. Besides describing his skills as a portrait painter,
Maria Maddalena stresses his gentlemanly qualities – an important
consideration for a court artist. She refers to a letter from Pope
Urban VIII, who had recommended Sustermans for admission to
the Order of the Knights of Malta.[2]

Bottari and Ticozzi (eds) (1979–80), 3, pp. 523–5.

Maria Maddalena of Austria, from Florence, to Antonio di
Paola, 18 August 1627
It is now many years that Justus Sustermans has been serving this house to the great satisfaction of us all owing to his
qualities and virtues. As he is firmly committed to painting
and very gifted, some months ago my son the Grand Duke
and I thought he could go for a while to Rome, to see the
famous ancient and modern paintings which are in that city,
and then return to our service. He has also had the opportunity to make his skill known to the Pope [Urban VIII] by
painting his portrait, and His Holiness, as a sign of his satisfaction, suggested his admission to the Order of the Knights
of Malta, as the enclosed letter demonstrates.

Even if I do not doubt that Your Most Illustrious Lordship
shall agree to this request and give the relevant orders, I
would like to recommend Justus to the good heart and kindness of Your Most Illustrious Lordship, and attest that he

not only deserves this honour because of his birth and virtuous qualities, such as dressing and behaving nobly, but
especially for being my special servant. He has been on my
payroll for many years, and [is paid] twenty-five *scudi* a
month, with board and lodging in our palace, and payment
for all the works we commission from him. From the advantage gained from wearing the habit of the Order, he will be
able to live and work more comfortably and also from the
title he received a few years ago from my brother His Majesty
the Emperor [Ferdinand II], who asked him to paint portraits
of himself and the archdukes, his brothers and his son.[3]

From this, one can understand how the honour granted to
him from His Holiness, and which he shall receive from Your
Most Illustrious Lordship, will be well deserved, and I assure
you that he will be worthy of it.

PROBLEMS AND DIFFICULTIES

Disagreements and litigations about works of art were not unusual,
and when an agreement could not be reached informally through
mediators, the matter was referred to the formal arbitration of
judges and magistrates. It is obvious that acquaintance or familiar-
ity with important personages was crucial, as can be seen in both
the examples chosen here.

5. An unsuccessful mediation: Pietro Bembo, Isabella d'Este and Giovanni Bellini, 1505

During the summer of 1505, Pietro Bembo and Isabella d'Este
discussed whether Giovanni Bellini might agree to execute a
painting for Isabella's *camerino*, with an unusual secular subject
to be devised by Bembo. Bellini had earlier, in July 1504, delivered a *Madonna and Saints* to the Marchioness, but at the end it
proved impossible to persuade him, despite the efforts of several
intermediaries and friends in Venice.

Bembo, *Lettere*, ed. Travi, 1, pp. 196, 204.

Pietro Bembo, from Venice, to Isabella d'Este, 27 August
1505

I have not forgotten my promise to Your Ladyship to try and get Giovanni Bellini to paint a picture for Your Ladyship's *camerino*. I have had much help from Paolo Zoppo, who has much regard for Your Ladyship and is a dear friend of Bellini. In short, we have pushed so much, that I think the castle will surrender. To make sure that this happens unconditionally, Your Ladyship should write a warm letter about it, compelling him to please you. Send it in my name, as I am sure it will not be written in vain.

Pietro Bembo to Isabella d'Este, 20 November 1505
Coming back from the Marche, where I have been for a few days, I found letters from Your Most Illustrious Ladyship in answer to my old letters about the painting by Bellini. I have also heard that Messer Paolo Zoppo and Messer Lorenzo da Pavia, good servants of Your Ladyship, have diligently acted on my behalf as required.

Today I have been to see Messer Giovanni Bellini, and have found out that he has decided to satisfy Your Ladyship's wish. I am sure he will do so with much diligence. I am just waiting for the reply from Your Ladyship, about the measurements and the lighting, and about the other things we have discussed.

6. A jeweller who did not keep his word, 1555
Giulia Feltria della Rovere (1531–63) was the daughter of Francesco Maria della Rovere and Eleonora Gonzaga, and wife of Alfonso d'Este, illegitimate son of Alfonso I and Laura Dianti. Here she writes to the judge Camillo Giordani in Bologna, asking him to intervene in a dispute with the goldsmith Giovan Battista Locarno about the costly materials he wanted for a fashionable object she had commissioned, a gold jewelled head for a *zibellino* pelt.

G. Gaye, *Carteggio inedito d'artisti dei secoli XIV, XV, XVI*, 3 vols (Florence, 1839–40), pp. 402–3.

Giulia della Rovere from Ferrara, to Camillo Giordani, 25 May 1555
Most magnificent and esteemed one,
    it is now more than a year since I paid Master Giovan

Battista Locarno, a goldsmith from that city [Bologna], forty-six *scudi* in gold, for a gold *zibellino* head which he promised to make, so that I would have it for the following October, a promise which he did not keep. After two or three months he let me know that, if I wanted him to finish the head, I should send him more gems which he needed. I answered that since he had not kept his first promise, I did not want the contract to go ahead, because I thought he would do a second time what he had already done, and that he should return my money to me, which he has failed to do. Therefore I ask you, as this is a particular concern of mine, to summon him before you, and force him to give you my money, or a reasonable sum as security, on suitable terms. I shall be very much obliged, and I recommend myself to you.

PAYMENTS

7. Part-payment in kind, 1485

Part-payments in the form of land, houses, wine and oil, or, as in this case, fabrics for clothing, were quite common, especially in times of financial crisis, such as the years 1482–84, when Ferrara was at war with Venice. This extract from the Este court registers records that Eleonora of Aragon paid her tailor for fabrics for a *camora* for Pellegrina Agazzi, wife of the sculptor Guido Mazzoni who had undertaken a commission for the eight life-size figures of the *Lamentation over the Dead Christ* for the church of Santa Maria della Rosa in Ferrara.[4]

A. Venturi, 'Nuovi documenti', *Archivio Storico dell'Arte*, 7 (1894), pp. 52–4.

5 May 1485
To Master Tommaso from Naples, tailor of our most illustrious lady, for the following: five and a half *braccia* of grey Florentine cloth which the most illustrious lady gives as a gift to the wife of Master Paganin da Modena [Guido Mazzoni], painter, who made the *Lamentation* in Santa Maria della Rosa, to make a *camora*, at 2 florins a *braccio* [making in total] *lire* 33

... and (. . .) *braccia* of *morello* velvet for a pair of sleeves at 3 florins a *braccio* [making in total] *lire* 9

8. The painter Bernardino Poccetti wants to invest his money, 1609

The painter Bernardino Poccetti writes to Christine of Lorraine, wife of Ferdinando I de' Medici, asking that his remaining payment of 400 *scudi* be paid in a lump sum and deposited in the *Monte di Pietà*. This large sum was probably in payment for a number of frescoes decorating various apartments in Palazzo Pitti. The sum was paid in the manner requested by Poccetti on 22 August 1609.

H. Geisenheimer, 'Spigolature poccettiane', *Arte e Storia*, 28:3 (1909), p. 70.

Bernardino Poccetti, painter, . . . reverently explains [to Christine of Lorraine] that the works made for Your Most Serene Highnesses have been paid by those appointed to do it, and for this sum the creditor is the petitioner. The sum of four hundred *scudi* must be paid from the office of Signor Donato dell'Antella. He, however, cannot pay the said 400 *scudi* all at once, but rather in various instalments. Because of this I cannot use [this money] as capital for my old age. Trusting in the kindness and favour of Your Most Serene Highness, I humbly pray you to have the sum paid into the petitioner's credit on the *Monte di Pietà* so that the petitioner's capital and interest can be paid in full and both credited to him. I shall be very much obliged.

PATRONS AND ARTISTS: A RECIPROCAL RELATIONSHIP

The patron-artist relationship was one of mutual dependence. Patrons needed artists for their skills and their fame, and artists needed the protection of their powerful and rich patrons in a society where influential people could provide the solution to many problems, and protection from the difficulties and vagaries of life. Artists asked for help with law suits which had gone on for too long, with financial and health problems, and, very frequently, in finding a post for a relative.

9. An intercession in a law suit, 1484

The sculptor Guido Mazzoni asks for help from his patroness Eleonora of Aragon with a law suit which, he believes, his opponents are prolonging unnecessarily.

> T. C. Verdon, 'The Art of Guido Mazzoni', PhD dissertation, Yale University, 1975, p. 246.

> Guido Mazzoni to Eleonora of Aragon, 1 June 1484
> Most Illustrious and Excellent Lady, I am making this humble supplication, beseeching you to hear my plea. My adversary with his advocates and other lawyers are in the wrong, and are trying to prolong my suit by any means so that, in this way, they can obtain my possessions . . . I cannot stand such worry and also such intolerable expenses. This does not allow me to work, nor to do anything well.

10. A plea for a painter fallen on hard times, 1505

Antonio Tebaldeo, a poet and secretary to Ercole I d'Este, writes to Isabella d'Este asking her to help Gian Francesco Maineri, a penniless painter from Parma waiting for a court case in Mantua.

> G. Campori, *I pittori degli Estensi nel secolo XV* (Modena, 1886), p. 78.

> Antonio Tebaldeo, from Ferrara, to Isabella d'Este, in Mantua, 2 February 1505
> Gian Francesco Maineri, a famous painter from Parma, is now in Mantua for a certain law suit he has in that city, as I think Your Ladyship knows. Because he is poor and he can hardly afford to live away from home, as he has doubtless told Your Excellency, we beg you to ask that his suit be heard and that he be swiftly granted a good space [in which to live]. I think he deserves it as he is a good person, and we wish him all the best. We would praise any good treatment he may obtain from your interest.

11. A request addressed to Titian, 1549

Argentina Rangoni Pallavicini (1502–50), an aristocratic lady well-known for her poetry and her interest in botany, asks Titian to take on the brother of one of her ladies-in-waiting who, she believes, will make a good apprentice. Rangoni, who was obviously on very close terms with Titian, also mentions a portrait of her daughter Lavinia, which she had commissioned from him and which she would like the painter to finish.

G. Gaye (1839–40), 2, p. 375.

Argentina Rangoni Pallavicini, from Modena, to Titian, 26 April 1549

I would like the brother of one of my ladies-in-waiting to spend some time with you, so that he can learn something. He has a sound basic knowledge of the fundamentals, is willing to learn, and is an honest and sensible young man of eighteen years. I am asking you to take him on for my sake, as I could have no greater favour from you, and I am certain he will please you. Captain Francesco Faloppa will discuss this with you.

I recommend myself to you, and I pray you to finish the portrait of Lavinia: the Trebbiano [a white wine] will not be lacking.

12. Baccio Bandinelli agrees to a request of Eleonora di Toledo, but asks for a reward in exchange, 1550

Baccio Bandinelli writes that he accepts a young Spaniard sent by Eleonora di Toledo to study with him. Bandinelli, who was on very good terms with the Duchess, takes advantage of this occasion to beg for the Duchess's intercession with Duke Cosimo for a good position in his old age.[5] The progress of the Spanish pupil is discussed in a letter of 10 February 1551.

Waldman (2004), p. 442.

Baccio Bandinelli, from Florence, to court secretary Jacopo Guidi, 5 December 1550

I pray you to tell the Most Illustrious Lady the Duchess that I have promised to teach her young man Spagnoletto, and in fact I succeeded at it, as she thought I would. However, he began to do as he pleased, and to make drawings in places away from me, which is a very bad habit as I cannot teach him or correct the mistakes he makes. As I have great affection for him, and he is like a son to me, Her Ladyship can be assured that I shall make him the best draughtsman that ever existed in Spain, if he obeys me . . .

I humbly pray the Duchess, who is a true source of mercy, to speak for me to him whom I adore as my own God [Duke Cosimo], that Spagnoletto deigns to complete the good work he has begun for me. I have now grown old in my long service [to the Medici], and during these last years I wish to sit amongst the high magistrates, being honoured by the other citizens. In this way I shall be able to find husbands for my daughters, since now at my age I have to arrange a settlement for one. With the help of His Excellency, I shall also be helped by God and all the saints.

13. A widow-queen asks Michelangelo to make an equestrian statue of her deceased husband, 1559

After the death of King Henri II of France in 1559, his Florentine-born widow, Caterina de' Medici, hoped to get Michelangelo, who was living and working in Rome, to agree 'despite his advanced age' to make an equestrian statue of her deceased husband. Stressing her desire to give expression to her love and grief and to perpetuate Henri's memory, she also invokes the artist's fame, his service to earlier Medici, and his love for his country. Her intermediary in Florence was to be her relative Roberto Strozzi. Michelangelo, however, did not agree to the commission.

G. Campori, *Lettere artistiche inedite* (Modena, 1866), pp. 37–9.

Caterina de' Medici, from Blois, to Michelangelo Buonarroti, 14 November 1559

Following the bitterest death of the Most Christian and Serene King my Lord, I am left with no . . . greater desire than keep alive his name and my former lawful love and my later, present sorrow. Amongst the other works I have planned for this end, I have resolved to have [an image] made of my Lord on horseback, for the middle of the courtyard of one of my palaces, of a size suited to the court. And as I, like all the world, know how far you surpass all others in that art in our time, and are held in long-standing affection by my house, as witnessed, amongst other things, by the singular works of your hand surrounding the tombs of my kinsmen in Florence, I beg you to wish to undertake this task. Even though I know that your advancing years might serve as an excuse to another person, I believe this would not work with me. At least, do not rule out the task of designing the work, and having it cast and chased by the best masters that money can find. Assuring you that you, above all people in the world, could not undertake anything I would value more, and which I would wish to reward most generously.

14. Titian and a gift for the daughter of Charles V, 1567

Margherita of Austria, Duchess of Parma and Piacenza, the illegitimate daughter of the late Emperor Charles V, here offered an engraving of a painting, *La Gloria* (Madrid, Prado), that Charles had commissioned in the 1550s and greatly loved. The engraving was made by Cornelis Cort in 1566 and formed part of a group of many engravings of Titian's work executed around this times.[6]

Tiziano: le lettere, ed. C. Grandini (Belluno, 1977), no. 184, p. 245.

Titian, from Venice, to Margherita of Austria, 15 June 1567
Most Serene Lady, in these last days I have had printed from a copper plate the design of the painting of the Trinity which was commissioned from me by the Emperor of eternal glorious memory, father of Your Highness. For the devotion I feel and the service I have done to the most august House of Austria, I feel obliged to send some of the first impressions to my patrons. I have not failed to do this to the Most Serene Catholic King [Philip II], and I am now doing the same for Your Highness, humbly presenting a print of the said drawing to you. I pray you to accept it with the benevolence it deserves, as it contains the effigy of such a glorious Emperor, a defender of God's Holy Church. I am sure that Your Highness shall do it, since you are as well-disposed as that saintly Emperor, your father, to accept the smallest gift from your devoted servant.

15. Two Florentine artists write to their patroness requesting good positions for their relatives, 1585 and 1602
i. The Florentine painter Giovanni Bizzelli, a pupil of Alessandro Allori, writes from Florence to Eleonora de' Medici Gonzaga thanking her for her patronage and asking for a favour for his brother. Bizzelli had recently finished a commission from the Duchess for the church of S. Agata in Florence.

> R. Piccinelli, *Le collezioni Gonzaga. Il carteggio tra Firenze e Mantova* (Milan, 2000), pp. 77, 158–9.

Giovanni Bizzelli, from Florence, to Eleonora de' Medici Gonzaga in Mantua, 25 July 1585
With these few lines I again thank Your Most Serene Highness for the great kindness shown to me, for which I shall always be much obliged. I hope to obtain the post of Canon of San Lorenzo for my brother, when this becomes available, because the post for which we were hoping for did not come about. I therefore beg Your Highness for help. I continuously pray Jesus Christ for your eternal health and greatest happiness.

My brother prays [for you] during holy mass and his divine services, adding to this the devout prayers of the nuns of Santa Agata, who have great affection for Your Most Serene Highness.

ii. Writing from Florence, Bernardo Buontalenti asks Eleonora de' Medici Gonzaga to help a relative who is ill in Mantua.

Bernardo Buontalenti to Eleonora de' Medici Gonzaga, 16 August 1602
In reply to a letter from Your Most Serene Highness, to whom I am much obliged and whom I thank again, knowing your infinite kindness, I pray to be remembered to your consort [Vincenzo I Gonzaga], as I am always the most faithful and devoted servant of Their Most Serene Highnesses.

You will excuse me if I am troubling you. A relative of mine is there [in Mantua], and gives me news of Your Most Serene Highness. My relative has written me that he has received much kindness and help from Their Most Serene

Highnesses. He is now ill in hospital, and I pray you, if I may, that Your Highness may have mercy and provide some help for him.

I am always your most faithful servant.

CLOSE PERSONAL RELATIONSHIPS

16. A special friendship: Vittoria Colonna and Michelangelo

Much has been written about Vittoria Colonna, the celebrated poet, and Michelangelo. His biographer Ascanio Condivi was the first to give an account of their deep friendship.[7] Their closeness was based on their similar religious beliefs as well as on their reciprocal respect and admiration for each other's creative powers.

i. Vittoria Colonna on Michelangelo's Crucifixion, 1539–40
Vittoria Colonna shows appreciation for the fine workmanship and grace of the figure of Christ with angels in a drawing, possibly that in the British Museum [1895–9–504, or a variant], which she is uncertain is by the master himself or an associate (**figure 10**). Her careful, connoisseur-like examination might have involved a magnifying glass or a convex mirror. Her literary skill is shown in her elision of the concepts of the grace given to Michelangelo by God and the grace of the Christ in the drawing, and her play on Michelangelo's name. In the second passage, she states her opinion that his artistic skill is a grace given by God; this elevated conception of art is in line with the opinions she is made to express in the c. 1540 dialogues on art of Francisco de Holanda.[8]

S. Ferino-Pagden, *Vittoria Colonna. Dichterin und Muse Michelangelos* (exhibition catalogue, Vienna, 1997), pp. 339–40.

Vittoria Colonna to Michelangelo, c. 1538–41
Michelangelo, unique master and my most particular friend. I have received your letter and seen the *Crucifixion*, which has certainly crucified in my memory any other picture ever seen. No more finely wrought, lively and highly finished image could ever be seen. Certainly, I could never describe how delicately and wonderfully it is done, so that I have resolved to wish it by no one else. So make things

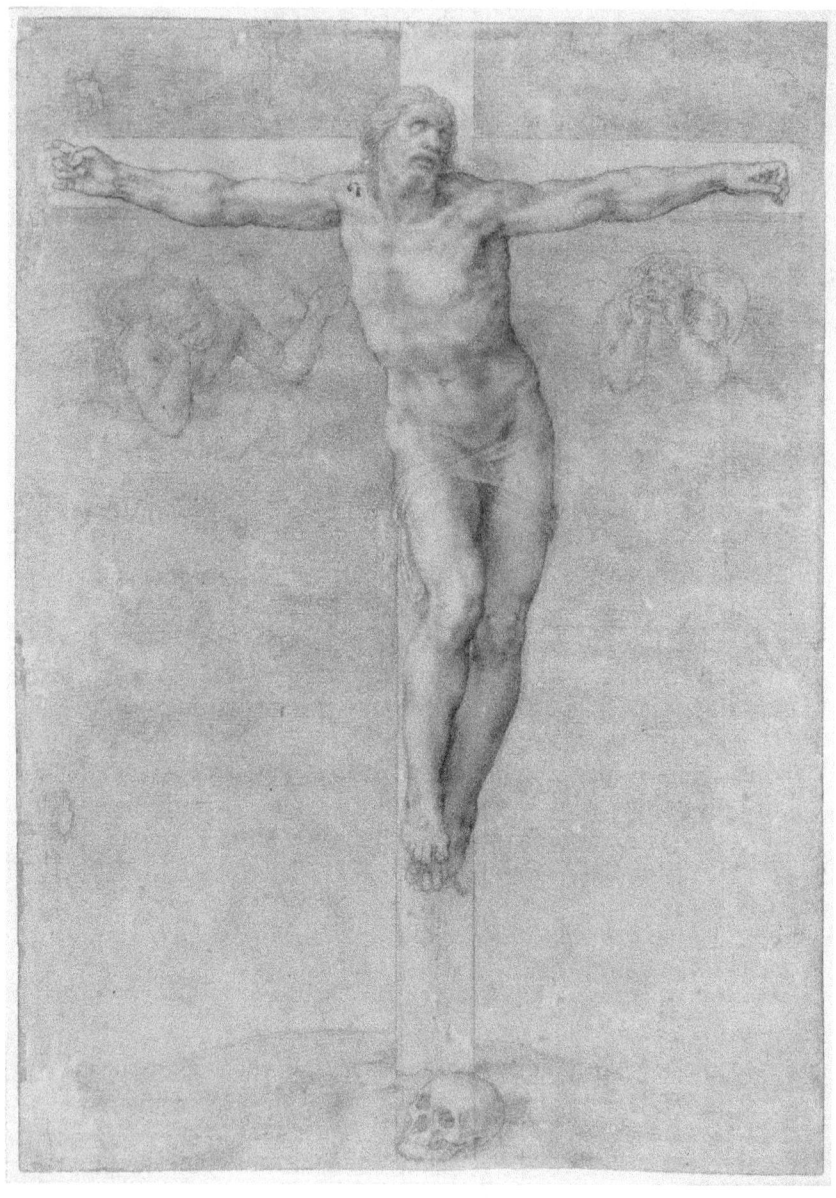

10.   Michelangelo, *Crucifixion*, c. 1538–40 (London, British Museum).

clear: if it is by someone else, never mind; if it is yours, I will certainly take it. But in the event that it isn't yours, and you want to have one made by that assistant of yours, we will discuss it first. Since I know how difficult would be to copy it, I would prefer the other artist to make something else. But if it is yours, be patient if I do not give it back. I have examined it in the light and with a [magnifying] glass and in the mirror, and have never seen anything brought to such perfection.

Your creations perforce demand a response from every viewer, and after more experience of seeing them I spoke of the increase of the bounty of perfect things. And I have seen that 'all things are possible for believers'.[9] I had the utmost faith in God that he would endow you with supernatural grace in making this Christ. Then I saw him [the Christ in the drawing], so wonderful that he surpassed all my expectations in every respect: then, emboldened by your miracles, I longed for what now I see miraculously achieved, namely that in every feature he is utterly perfect, and no more could be wished for, nor could one wish for so much. And I tell you that I am so happy at the beauty of the right-hand angel, since St Michael will place you, Michelangelo, on the right of the Lord on Judgement Day. And thus I know no other means of serving you than to pray to this gentle Christ whom you have painted so well and so perfectly, and to beg you to rule me as yours in everything and for everything.

ii. A friendship in Christ, early 1540s

Vittoria Colonna wrote this letter c. 1541–43, while living in the convent of Santa Caterina in Viterbo. At that time Michelangelo was in Rome, working in the Pauline Chapel on the *Conversion of St Paul*, which had been commissioned by Pope Paul III Farnese. In her letter, she expresses doubts on the possibility of their meeting, in spite of their profound need for the religious comfort they found in each other. Vittoria mentions a now-lost drawing of Christ and the Woman from Samaria which Michelangelo had sent to her, and writes that when they meet again in Rome their faith will be as alive as he had been able to convey in his drawing.

Ragionieri (ed.) (2005), p. 184.

Vittoria Colonna, from Viterbo, to Michelangelo, in Rome, 20 July

I did not reply earlier to your letter, since it was almost a reply to mine, as I thought that, if you and I continued to write according to my commitment and to your kindness, I should have to leave the chapel of St Catherine without being with these sisters at the appointed times, and you would have to leave the chapel of St Paul, and not be there before daybreak and for the whole day, in sweet conversation with your paintings. These, in their own idiom, speak to you as much as the living people who surround me. In this way, I would fail the brides of Christ, and you His VICAR.

Knowing however how stable your friendship is, tied in a Christian knot with secure affection, I think my own letters are inadequate at communicating what yours can, but I shall wait for a good occasion to serve you with readiness in my soul.

I will pray the Lord about whom you talked to me with a humble heart, burning [with such love], before I left Rome, that I shall find you, when I return, with His image renewed and alive in your soul, as you have represented it in my [drawing of the] woman of Samaria.

I recommend myself to you, and also to your Urbino [Francesco dell'Amadore, called 'Urbino', Michelangelo's servant and assistant].

17. A difficult path to tread, c. 1553

This extract from Benvenuto Cellini's autobiography illustrates vividly the problems of a court artist dealing with powerful patrons, and the need to tread cautiously in order not to offend them. Cellini, who often worked in the ducal palace, in very close contact with Duke Cosimo I de' Medici and Eleonora di Toledo, at times found this proximity very difficult to manage.

This is the beginning of a long tale about a pearl necklace, which Eleonora wanted her husband to buy for her. Cellini describes the events in a lively and apparently simple language, using dialogue to convey the immediacy of the situation to the reader. As well as his literary ability and his sense of humour, the passage underlines his skills as a jeweller and as a diplomat. This story, however, ends badly for Cellini: both the Duke and Duchess get angry with him, and he bitterly concludes that, with these powerful patrons, '. . . *non basta l'esser uomo dabbene e virtuoso*' ('it is not enough to be a decent and virtuous man').

Cellini, ed. Davico Bonino, p. 437.

. . . The Duchess came suddenly into the *guardaroba*, and not finding the Duke there, sat down next to us. She watched us working for a while, and then, very pleasantly, she turned towards me and showed me a necklace of large and very rare pearls, and asked me what I thought of them. I told her that they were very beautiful. Then Her Most Illustrious Excellency said to me: 'I want the Duke to buy them for me, so, my Benvenuto, praise the necklace to the Duke as highly and as well as you can.' On hearing these words, I revealed to the Duchess what I really thought, as respectfully as I could, and I said: 'My Lady, I thought that this pearl necklace belonged to Your Most Illustrious Excellency. Now that I know that it does not, I can, indeed I must, say certain things, though prudence would wish me not to. Your Most Illustrious Excellency should know that, because [as a goldsmith] I have an expertise in these matters, I saw that these pearls are full of flaws, and therefore I would never advise Your Excellency to buy them.' At this, she said: 'The merchant would sell them to me for six thousand *scudi*, and if they did not have these little flaws they would be worth more than twelve thousand.' I then said that, even if the necklace were perfect, I would never advise anybody to pay more than five thousand *scudi*, because pearls are not jewels. Pearls are fishbones, and after a time they die. But diamonds, rubies and emeralds, and sapphires, do not grow old. Those four are jewels, and one should buy them.

At these words the Duchess said to me, rather contemptuously: 'I want these pearls now, and so I ask you to take them to the Duke, and praise them as much as you can. And if you think you have to tell a few lies, tell them as a duty to me, since this will be profitable to you.'

I have always been a true friend of truth and an enemy of lies, but it was necessary to do it, because I did not want to lose the goodwill of such a great princess. So, disgruntled, I took those damned pearls, and went into the other room, where the Duke was.

Notes

1 See C. von Fabriczy, 'Adriano Fiorentino', *L'Arte*, 4 (1901), pp. 415–17.
2 The Grand Master did not accept this recommendation. On Sustermans, see M. Chiarini and C. Pizzorusso (eds), *Sustermans: sessant'anni alla corte dei Medici*, exhibition catalogue (Florence, 1983).
3 Sustermans was in Vienna from November 1623 till October 1624, when he obtained a title from the Emperor.
4 See T. C. Verdon, 'The Art of Guido Mazzoni', PhD dissertation, Yale University, 1975.
5 Bandinelli received the title of Knight of St James from Charles V in 1530.
6 See M. Bury, *The Print in Italy 1550–1620* (London, 2001), pp. 91–2.
7 A. Condivi, *The Life of Michelangelo* [1553], ed. H. Wohl (Oxford, 1972).
8 A. Nagel, 'Gifts for Michelangelo and Vittoria Colonna', *Art Bulletin*, 79 (1997), pp. 647–68.
9 Mark, 4:26–7.

PART III

WOMEN, DEVOTION AND ART

During the period considered in this book, religion and the condition of one's soul were important concerns in everybody's life. Everyday existence was so thoroughly permeated by religious practices that it is often difficult to separate religious concerns from those which we would now consider secular: in fact, such a separation would have seemed meaningless.

Crucial was the belief in the afterlife, where the good would be rewarded, while those dying in mortal sin would be condemned to the never-ending suffering of hell. Those who repented before dying, or were guilty of 'venial' sins, would spend a period in a *locum purgatorium*, which could be shortened through the acquisition of indulgences, obtained through pilgrimages, prayers in certain churches during religious festivities, or other practices.[1]

Indulgences could also be applied to the dead, through prayer and Masses, perhaps in conjunction with certain altarpieces. The Church fostered and directed prayer, almost always in front of images of Christ, of the Virgin Mary and of the saints, who were believed to act as intercessors with Christ. The faithful who were standing or kneeling in front of *imagini* (cult images) or *istorie* (narrative scenes), whether viewed at home, in church or in public places, would feel that holy images responded to their prayers and protected them, even when they did not miraculously 'come alive'. Proximity to relics, too, made the faithful feel protected by holy personages, and their collection, their viewing and their embellishment continued to be popular.[2]

From the late Middle Ages onwards, preachers had taught that images and narratives could instruct through empathy and example, and in the age of Catholic reform both they and devotional writers continued to encourage the faithful to use visual images as an aid to meditation through the sense of sight, in works often directed towards women. For their part, painters and sculptors helped the faithful to become more intimately involved and responsive to visual images by making them more concrete and emotive. Female viewers might be assisted not only by visual techniques like gestures or eye contact linking them with saintly figures, or by the positioning of the Christ Child or the dead Christ close to them and tended by holy women, but also by the introduction of dress, settings and artefacts evoking contemporary life.[3]

Notes

1 See J. Le Goff, *La naissance du purgatoire* (Paris, 1981).

2 T. C. Verdon, 'Christianity, the Renaissance, and the study of history', in T. C. Verdon and J. Henderson (eds), *Christianity and the Renaissance: Image and Religious Imagination in the Quattrocento* (Syracuse, NY, 1990), pp. 1-37. See also: S. Ringbom, 'Devotional images and imaginative devotions', *Gazette des Beaux Arts*, 6:73 (1969), pp. 159--70; D. Bornstein, 'Spiritual kinship and domestic devotions', in J. C. Brown and R. C. Davis (eds.), *Gender and Society in Renaissance Italy* (London and New York, 1998), pp. 173–92. On relics, see R. C. Trexler, *Public Life in Renaissance Florence* (Ithaca and London, 1980), pp. 57–61, and S. J. Cornelison and S. B. Montgomery (eds), *Images, Relics and Devotional Practices in Medieval and Renaissance Italy*, Arizona Center for Medieval and Renaissance Studies, Medieval and Renaissance Texts and Studies, 296 (Tempe, Az, 2006).

3 See Trexler (1980), pp. 61–73, 113–15; M. Baxandall, *Painting and Experience in Fifteenth Century Italy* [1972] (Oxford, 1988), pp. 40–56; D. Freedberg, *The Power of Images: Studies in the History and Theory of Response* (Chicago, 1989); J. Shearman, *Only Connect ... Art and the Spectator in the Italian Renaissance* (Princeton, 1992); T. C. Verdon, *Arte della preghiera* (Rome, 2010). Many paintings show the figure of the Virgin 'coming alive' in front of praying men and women (see **figure 5**).

❧ 8 ❧

PRIVATE DEVOTION

What were women's personal relationships with the holy, and with the devotional images and objects they possessed?[1] Women were thought to be morally more frail and mentally less capable than men, hence in greater moral danger of falling into temptation. They therefore needed to be guided, and the use of suitable images as *exempla* was encouraged. Images were also important as a starting point for visualising stories and meditating on their content and meaning.[2] The many stories and 'mysteries' of the life and passion of Christ took first place, while the Virgin was the most powerful intercessor and an important example of chastity and obedience. As well as their own patron saints, that is, the saints whose name they carried, women had particular saints to whom they could pray in special moments in their lives: St Margaret was the patron saint of women in childbirth, and Mary Magdalen an example of penitence. Women who dedicated their life to the care of the sick would follow St Catherine of Siena, while devout women and nuns could be inspired by the mystic visions of St Catherine of Alexandria.

Praying in the quiet and seclusion of one's own room meant following Christ's advice: 'when you pray, go into your room, and when you have shut your door, pray to your Father who is in the secret place; and your Father who sees in secret will reward you openly'.[3] Paintings could be fixed to a wall, with a candle-holder on a bracket in front of them, or protected with shutters, wooden covers, or curtains, as were altarpieces and holy images in churches, since such images were believed to have a special power and could be shown only on special occasions. At home, paintings could also be placed on a table, or on a small portable domestic 'altar'. From inventories and wills we know that in practically every house throughout Italy there were religious images. Paintings and sculptures by well-known artists, engravings, statuettes and crucifixes in ivory, ebony and silver or terracotta, reliquaries and rosaries made by excellent artisans: all had their place in the palaces and houses of wealthy women, either commissioned by them, or received as part of their dowry or as gifts. For the lower ranks there were mass-produced images in terracotta, plaster or papier mâché. Cheap paintings of the Virgin, of the crucified Christ or of local saints could be bought ready made from painters' shops, and prints of religious subjects were also much sought after.[4] Cheap prints were bought from itinerant sellers, so that even low-paid workers and poor widows could all have devotional images in their houses. These prints for private devotion would have been rather small in size.

THE USE OF IMAGES IN PRAYER

Some of these extracts stress the emotional impact of devotional images and illustrate what the attitude of a woman in prayer should be, emphasising a method of meditation guided by the observation of the image itself. Other texts advise and instruct their readers about the role of images in prayer.

1. Prayers in front of a domestic 'altar', 1471
The Carthusian prior Giovanni di Dio wrote his *Decor puellarum* in Venetian dialect, so that this treatise for girls could be understood more easily. He advocates reading a Book of Hours before a domestic 'altar', and structuring the day with prayers.[5] He also wrote similar books addressed to married women and widows.

> Giovanni di Dio, *Decor puellarum: zoe honore de le donzelle: la quale da regola forma e modo al stato de le honeste donzelle* (Venice, 1471), Book 3, Chapter 2, unpaginated.

> Make yourself an altar which you will take delight in decorating with beautiful and pious images, with beautiful ornaments or embroidery or some of your own handiwork. Do it in this way. First, say some short prayers before this altar. Then read a little if you can: those who can't should learn

stories of male and female saints. Then return to prayer at your altar. Then, if you know how, write some pious work. If you really have extra time, so to escape the danger of idleness, you may honour the Lord God by decorating your altar, that is, make a garment for some [image of] Our Lady, embroidery, lace for the altar frontal, or a garment or other decoration for an image of the Virgin Mary to which you are devoted, always alternating this task with prayers until supper time.

2. Praying in front of a crucifix
Representations of the crucifix were found in most households, as they most conveyed the hope for eternal life and repentance for one's sins. These three extracts describe meditations on different aspects of the Passion of Christ.

i. St Antoninus and his advice to Dianora Tornabuoni, 1455
The Archbishop of Florence Antonino Pierozzi (1389–1459) wrote *Opera a ben vivere* (1455) for Dianora Tornabuoni Soderini. Here he teaches her how to pray. Kneeling in front of a crucifix, Dianora is led to visualise Christ's body and his sufferings. Her emotions and pity should stimulate her love for him and the Virgin Mary, and repentance for her sins. The last stage of this meditation brings to mind contemporary paintings representing the Deposition or the Lamentation, where images of the Virgin, female saints or female donors contemplating the body of Christ are placed in the foreground, so that women could identify with them. Implicit in this text is a belief that using 'the eyes of the mind' results in deeper devotion. While monks and more advanced mystics should aim for 'imageless devotion', ordinary folk, and perhaps especially women, might need familiar settings and naturalistic details in devotional paintings.[6]

S. Antonino, *Opera a ben vivere*, ed. C. Angelini (Milan, 1926), pp. 136–9.

'Meditation on the Passion of Christ while reciting fifteen Our Fathers'
Before or after you have heard the mass, or in your own

bedroom, kneel in front of a crucifix and, with the eyes of the mind rather than with your bodily eyes, consider His face. First, think about the crown of thorns penetrating into His head, reaching His brain; then [think] about the eyes, full of tears, blood and sweat; then the nose, full of snot, tears and blood; the mouth, full of gall, dribble and blood; His beard, also dripping with dribble and blood and gall, and full of spit, with its hairs pulled out; then the face, dark, covered in spit, and marked by beatings and lashes, and bleeding. And for reverence of all these, you should say an Our Father and a Hail Mary.

'Meditation on His hands'

Then turn your mind's eyes to His hands, and think deeply in your heart about the way they are torn and bleeding. Think that, for the great weight of the body they supported, they would be much torn and cut open by those nails. Think deeply about how much pain the Son of God must have suffered, because of His love for you! You will then say two Our Fathers and two Hail Marys, that is, one for each hand.

'Meditation on His chest'

Then consider the wound in His side. This meditation, however, should focus more on His Mother than on Him, because He was already dead when He was wounded, but the heart of the Mother, as Simeon had prophesied, was wounded too. And in reverence for His chest, and for His Mother, say two more Our Fathers.

'Meditation on His whole body'

Think then about His wounded body: as Isaiah had prophesied, there was nothing whole in His body, from head to foot. Think deeply in your heart about His wounds: from one, black blood pours out, another shows blood just under the skin, from another water pours, another is bruised. And so think of His body down to His feet, and say another Our Father. Then turn your mind's eyes to His feet, and think deeply about them, how much they bleed, how torn by the nails they are for the great weight of His body they had to support. But the body of Christ was the most beautiful which ever lived and which shall ever live. About this, David prophesied 'You are beautiful, above all men's sons'. And then you'll say another Our Father, so that you will have said seven all together.

[...]

'The burial'

Then think about John the Evangelist, and the Magdalen, and Joseph of Arimathea, and Nicodemus, and the other holy women, anointing Him and wrapping Him in the sheet, with Our Lady of Sorrows holding Him on her lap, soaking Him with tears. Then at last He is placed in the Sepulchre. And you shall say another Our Father.

ii. Sister Maria Maddalena de' Pazzi, a crucifix and her visions, 1584

This second text shows how this kind of meditation could lead to mystic visions. While the female reader of the St Antoninus treatise is encouraged to look and imagine, the mystic Maria Maddalena de' Pazzi, during her visions, used to take down the crucifix from the wall, hold it in her arms and kiss it in a frenzy of love and repentance. Caterina Lucrezia de' Pazzi (1566–1607) entered the Carmelite convent of S. Maria degli Angeli in 1582, taking the name Maria Maddalena. In 1583, while still a novice, she begun to have ecstatic visions of a type experienced by many women from the Middle Ages onwards. These were intense and frequent, taking place every morning after Communion, and lasted two or three hours. Since religious authorities were wary of women's visions and needed to make sure of their divine origin, what Maria Maddalena said during her visions was memorised and then transcribed by a nun, while another would note down her actions. The transcriptions were then shown to the convent's confessor. In this extract, the actions and movements of Maria Maddalena are reported in italics.[7] Sister Maria Maddalena was canonised in 1669.

Maria Maddalena de' Pazzi, *I quaranta giorni*, ed. M. Rolfo (Palermo, 1996), pp. 79–81.

Monday 11 June [1584]

She saw God, totally pure, loving Himself and all His creatures with a pure and infinite love. She saw in a vision all that God had done for His creatures, which are so base. During

this vision she shouted out loudly, so that everybody around her heard her say:
Love, love, oh, God, You who love Your creatures of a pure love, oh, God of love, oh, God of love.

Seeing then that His creatures were so ungrateful, she looked as on the point of bursting with the pain this was causing, and said:
My Lord, no more love, no more love, Lord, the love you feel towards Your creatures is too much! It is not too much, no, for Your greatness, but it is too much for Your base creatures. Why, Lord, do You give so much love to me, to me, who am not worthy of it, and am so lowly? Are there more of Your creatures, or am I the only one? Give, my Lord, this love to Your other creatures. You give it to them, my love, but You see well that those who betray You do not want it. Oh, my Jesus, what led You to this cross, if not Your love?

She was holding a crucifix in her hand and she was talking to it, seeing only with her mind's eyes. She was not aware of anything but the crucifix she was holding. That day she held her eyes fixed on the holy feet of the crucifix, and in them she saw the evil done by human beings, and she said:
My love, who has pierced Your holy feet, if not the evil done by human beings? Last Friday You showed me what now I feel with such pain, that is, that those who lead an evil life have pierced Your holy feet. Alas, my Jesus, why am I not at Your place on this cross? If at least You had not been naked on this cross, for greater scorn! This is what You wanted. Love drove You mad, and You went mad for these human beings, who are so ungrateful. Oh, the blindness, oh, the wickedness of man, faced with so much love! There is nobody in the world, nobody who loves my love! Oh, my love, when shall I be like You? When shall I be at one with You? When shall I love You infinitely? *Ego autem in justitia apparebo conspectui tuo: satiabor cum apparuerit Gloria tua.* My Jesus, enough with love, I cannot stand it any more. And yet, if You want to give me more, give me as much as You want, but give me also the strength to bear it. Oh, holy Virgin, how could you bear this? You knew he was your son, but He was also the Son of God, and you knew that He was

doing this for the love He feels for all humanity! How could you bear this without dying for this pain? I, who did not see it, am split open and I die for this great pain. My Jesus, on Saturday You showed me that she could bear everything.

Turning to the nuns who were there, she proffered them the crucifix she held in her hand, saying:
Love Him, love Him, my Jesus. You have to love Him, because no one else does.

iii. Prayers for a penitent prostitute, c. 1575
The following is an example of how, in front of the image of the crucifix, emotion could help a sinner to repent. Here the *letterato* Sperone Speroni exhorts prostitutes to use the visual power of images of the crucified Christ.

Sperone Speroni, *Contra le cortigiane* (?1575), in *Opere di M. Sperone Speroni degli Alvarotti*, 5 vols (Venice, 1740), 3, pp. 232–3.

If you realise that your way of life is perilous, and don't know how to stop or turn away from it, confess your wrongdoing and humbly devote your mind to prayer. And because I expect that somewhere in your not yet godless house there still are some sacred images, you should go in front of one representing the Crucifixion. Kneel down with your body and soul, and, crying, pray to the Son of God through His image. He did not descend from heaven to earth to die on the cross for you in vain. Add your heart to your gaze, and don't separate it from your words. At first be silent, ashamed at your disreputable life. Look not at the beauty of the painting, which might be fine for a Michelangelo or a Titian, but instead contemplate it devoutly.

EXEMPLARY IMAGES

Teaching by example was considered to be the most effective way of showing the right path leading to virtue and to eternal life. Paintings representing stories from the lives of saints were used for this purpose, both in the instruction of children and as guidance for all. To be effective, however, the paintings had to reach out to the viewer and be able to move her.

3. An exemplary woman and two paintings, 1397

Maria Sturion (c. 1379–99) was the daughter of a wealthy Venetian merchant. After her husband's departure for war, she first returned to her parents' house, but then, moved by the preaching of the Dominican friar Tommaso Cafarini, she dedicated her life to prayer and charitable work, following the example of St Catherine of Siena. Cafarini became her spiritual director, and after her death wrote in Latin 'The Legend of Maria from Venice', which he translated into Italian to reach a large number of women. He presents Maria Sturion as a model for all his readers: pious, modest, chaste and obedient. In this extract Fra Tommaso tells of how Maria acquired an image of St Catherine and used it as a model for another painting, in which she had herself represented in the act of offering her heart to Christ, as Catherine had.

F. Sorelli, *La santità imitabile: Leggenda di Maria da Venezia di Tommaso da Siena*, (Venice, 1984), pp. 182, 188.

Having heard my sermons in [the church of] Santi Giovanni e Paolo and elsewhere about the fervent and immense charity of that seraphic virgin, the Blessed Catherine of Siena, and what she had received from her Blessed Spouse, she [Maria Sturion] was much roused to devotion. [One day] she was passing through the *contrada* of San Luca in Venice, where there are many painters, and saw by chance a small panel with the image of the said Catherine, painted as the Lord had inspired him to do. Prompted by God, she entreated the painter so sweetly that he gave it to her, even if at the beginning he did not want to. After she had obtained that image, with great happiness she began to wear a white tunic over her hair shirt, because she wished to be dressed in the habit of St Dominic for the love of her celestial Spouse, as the Blessed virgin Catherine had done. This desire was such that she had herself painted, in the [Dominican] habit, in an altarpiece among images of saints of our order standing on either sides of the image of the crucified Jesus, holding her heart in her hand, offering it for herself and for other sinners.

4. Beautiful and appropriate images as examples for nuns
Explaining which paintings are appropriate for the spiritual life of nuns, Gian Battista Armenini pays attention to their particular attitudes and requirements. The emotional responses of the viewers are always very important and, he adds, can be best prompted by the work of good painters.

> Gian Battista Armenini, *De veri precetti della pittura* [1587], ed. M. Gorreri (Turin, 1988), p. 196.

> . . . In the nuns' cells it is good to [have sacred images] on the walls and on panel . . . As it is better that [the images] remain pure and devout in their minds, in their cells there should be no other pictures apart from the mysteries of the Crucifix and of Our Lady, then [stories from] the Holy Scriptures and from the lives of young virgin saints, so that the nuns should always keep in mind their martyrdom as example. And so that their emotions are aroused more intensely, I would have them painted only by the best masters. In fact, because the stories are so vivid and the nuns are so full of piety, they would be more moved by suffering and inflamed by the fire of charity and divine love. The pictures made by unskilled painters, in fact, sometimes move their innocence to laughter and to lasciviousness, while those which are vivid penetrate into their heart. In private spaces or in the shared ones [in the convent], I would like pictures of the most honest kind, and all pure and devout, reserving the grandiosity of variety and style for those places which are magnificent and sumptuous.

IN THE POSSESSION OF WOMEN: DEVOTIONAL IMAGES AND OBJECTS

We have already seen a few examples of the devotional images which women from all ranks had in their rooms (chapter 3), and of collections including religious paintings (chapter 5). Having considered in this chapter how women were encouraged to pray, and what their responses to images could be, the texts in this section provide examples of the images or objects women had around them. Their quality depended primarily on their owners' social rank.

Possessions

5. Isabetta Gonzaga's religious books, 1432

When Isabetta Gonzaga married Carlo Malatesta, she brought with her as part of her dowry a large collection of books. In the inventory drawn up at her death in 1432, only a few books were listed among her possessions, most of them prayer books and lives of saints.

> S. L'Occaso, *Fonti archivistiche per le arti a Mantova tra Medioevo e Rinascimento (1382–1459)* (Mantua, 2005), pp. 219–21.

> One small book covered in velvet, with stories from the life of Our Lady, Jesus Christ and other saints
> Another small prayer book, covered in parchment
> Another with the life of St John
> One small Book of Hours, covered in leather
> One small book, with the 'Our Father' in the vulgar tongue
> One book made of parchment, beginning 'Here begin the ten commandments of the law', and ends 'Iste liber est magnifice domine'
> One book in French, beginning 'Cy comenza la via de Madonna'
> [. . .]
> Another one beginning 'The beginning of the prologue of St Elizabeth'
> One book with the miracles of Our Lady

6. Images, holy dolls, rosaries and prayer books for women in a Sienese household, 1483

The inventory of the possessions of the Sienese philosopher and physician Master Bartalo di Tura and of his wife Camilla was drawn up in 1483 after their death. These extracts are from the contents of women's rooms.

The 'small books for women' were prayer books written especially for women, while Books of Hours contained prayers to the Virgin to be recited at appointed times during the day. As well as having a devotional function, they were clearly admired for their beauty and for the quality and material of their binding, which are specified in the inventory. 'Holy dolls' were devotional objects in the form of an infant, which are often listed in inventories of brides' and nuns' possessions.[8] Rosaries were used for prayers but also as ornaments.[9]

C. Mazzi, *La casa di Maestro Bartalo di Tura* (Siena, 1900), pp. 29, 35, 38, 42–3, 49, 62.

Two small paintings, measuring ½ a *braccio*, with Our Lady and St Jerome
Two other paintings, one with the Holy Face, and the other with St Francis receiving the stigmata
Another small picture with St Anthony of Padua
[. . .]
One small book covered in green silk, with the Office of Our Lady
[. . .]
A small book for women, covered in crimson silk, with gold illuminations and two silver clasps, and a pearl button as a bookmark
Another small book for women, with a silver clasp, in a white linen case
[. . .]
A Venetian [holy] child, with his small chemise
A Tuscan [holy] child, with his little dress of crimson silk, with some gold 'Jesus' [medals with the image of Jesus]
[. . .]
A pair of rosaries made of small beads, long, in the shape of acorns, with a button of gilded silver
A pair of crystal rosaries, with a pearl button
Another rosary with small beads made of precious stones
A rosary with beads made of glass paste, black, small
[. . .]
A pair of small panels with Our Lady, in an old-fashioned manner

7. Extracts from two inventories: devotional paintings in the houses of two widows from Rimini, 1532 and 1543
Delucca (1997), pp. 729, 735–6.

15 July 1532. The Lady Elisabetta, daughter of the late Rinaldo de Simonetti and wife of the late Vincenzo, son of the late Giovanni, son of Antonio di Sacramoro

. . . A large canvas painting with the image of Our Lord Jesus Christ in the Garden; a panel painting, gilded and framed, with the image of the Glorious Virgin Mary; another painted with the image of Jesus Christ with the cross on His shoulder; a small wooden *Pietà*; a gilded plaster image of Our Lady, in half-relief, in its box; another image of the Glorious Virgin Mary which can be closed; another small gilded picture with the image of the Glorious Virgin Mary; a large canvas painting with the miracles of St Paul the Apostle; two other panel paintings of the Virgin, which must be given to the church of S. Castaldo in Rimini; a small picture with many figures, hinged in the middle, which can be closed; a painting on canvas with the image of St Jerome; another canvas painting with St Christopher and St Francis.

28 April 1543. Inventory made by the lady Olivia, daughter of the late Santo Giacomo della Gaudenzia, from the *contrada* Rossoleto, and widow of Master Bernardo, shoemaker, son of the late Michele Giorgio, called Micheletto from Friuli, *contrada* S. Silvestro

Two panels with their frame, on which are painted the images of Our Lord Jesus Christ with the cross on His shoulders; another painting with a Nativity; another painting, also with its frame, around which were the images of Our Lord Jesus Christ and the disciples, going to Emmaus; another painting with the image of Our Lady with her baby in her lap; another picture with the image of Our Lord Jesus Christ as a gardener, appearing to St Mary Magdalen, all framed and gilded.

8. A reliquary belonging to Margherita of Austria, 1586
Amongst the precious objects and jewellery listed in the will of Margherita of Austria, 3 January 1586, is this splendid reliquary.

R. Lefèvre, 'Il testamento di Margherita d'Austria, duchessa di Parma e Piacenza', *Palatino* (1968), p. 246.

A silver gilt reliquary, worked all over, with various enamelled figures, with the Passion of Christ, and also figures from the Old Testament. Above is a silver cross with an ivory Christ, and four ivory figures at the foot of the cross. There are also two rubies, three sapphires and two emeralds, all set in gold, seventeen pearls and nine cameos. There are also six figures in relief, made of gilded silver, which act as a pedestal. It weighs twenty-two marks, two ounces and twelve *starlini*.

Dowries

9. Devotional objects in the trousseau of Caterina Pico, 1474

Caterina, daughter of Count Gianfrancesco Pico della Mirandola, married Leonello Pico, Lord of Carpi, in 1474. Among the clothes, household linen and jewellery listed in the inventory of her trousseau, there are also devotional objects. The new bride owned a number of precious Agnusdei, rosaries, Books of Hours and a small container for holy water with an aspergillum, which implies the existence of a small altar, either portable or in a chapel in her new residence.

A. Morselli, *Il corredo nuziale di Caterina Pico (1474)* (Modena, 1956), pp. 97–8, 101–2.

A rosary with sixty-three coral beads and six silver buttons
A mother-of-pearl rosary, with a clasp of mother-of-pearl, with eight agate beads
A small vessel for holy water with its aspergillum, all in silver, and its chain with the coat of arms of Mirandola, weighs 17 ounces
[. . .]
A [small] bone altarpiece with a crucifix and other figures, with gold and fine blue
[. . .]
An Our Lady in plaster, gilded, and with fine blue
A small book with the Office of Our Lady, with illuminations and figures, bound in crimson silk and gold brocade, with corners in gilt silver, with a bookmark with pearls, and a

case made of strong cloth, decorated with gold lace, weighing 4/4/8 ounces

A book of psalms with illuminations and with painted stories, bound in gold and *morello* brocade with its corners in silver *niello*, with its bookmark in silk and pearls, and a case made of strong cloth with gold lace and a girdle of St Francis, weighing 5/4 ounces

[. . .]

A book with the Office of Our Lady, with illuminations, bound in *alessandrino* silk velvet, with corners and clasps of silver *niello*

Bequests and gifts

10. Bequests of Isabetta Gonzaga, 1432

Amongst the objects left by women to their female friends or servants, devotional images and prayer books were certainly much prized because of their strong emotional meaning.[10] In her will of 1432, Isabetta Gonzaga bequeathed her devotional books, images and objects to a female relative and to nuns. The 'Umiliate' were nuns from the convent of S. Matteo, while the 'nuns of the Angeli' were the Poor Clares from the convent of the church of the Angeli in Mantua. It is interesting to note that the scriptures bequeathed to the nuns were in the vernacular. These translated texts were usually for women, as would be the vernacular editions printed from the 1490s.

L'Occaso (2005), pp. 215–16.

. . . She bequeaths to the magnificent Lady Isabella da Polenta, daughter of the Lord Malatesta da Cesena, her Book of Office, on which is painted the coat of arms of the Marquess, that is the eagle and the unicorn.

[. . .]

. . . She bequeaths to the Umiliate nuns a carved *Maestà*, that is Our Lady with her Son in her arms

[. . .]

She bequeaths to Sister Michelina her book of the Gospels in the vulgar tongue.

Also, to the said sister, the Bible in the vulgar tongue.

Also, to the nuns of the Angeli, her books in the vulgar tongue, that is [the life] of St Christina and the Life of Christ, and that of St Joachim, with the letters fully illuminated with the story of Our Lady.

Also, she bequeaths to the Umiliate nuns her crystal [reliquary in the shape of a] *Maestà* in which are kept some relics which are of help to women in childbirth.

11. Mantegna and a religious painting for Eleonora of Aragon

The year after becoming Marquess of Mantua, Francesco Gonzaga corresponded with his court painter Andrea Mantegna about a picture of the Virgin for his future mother-in-law, Eleonora of Aragon. Here are two of the letters exchanged on this matter.[11]

Kristeller (1902), p. 543.

Francesco Gonzaga to Eleonora of Aragon, 6 November 1485
. . . When I heard of Your Excellency's desire to have the painting of Our Lady with other figures by the hand of Andrea Mantegna, which he has not finished, I gave him the commission to complete it with as much care as possible. I hope to visit Your Most Illustrious Ladyship soon, and I shall bring it with me, or send it. I wish to do my utmost to please you. I recommend myself to you, *que bene valeat.*

Francesco Gonzaga to Andrea Mantegna, 6 November 1485
. . . The most illustrious lady, the Duchess of Ferrara, as you can see from her letters which we enclose for you to understand her desires better, would like to have the painting of Our Lady with other figures, which you had begun to paint. In order to satisfy the lady, I would like you to finish it very diligently, using your own skill. We trust you will do that, and do so as soon as possible, so that the illustrious lady will be pleased – something which we want above all else.

12. A wedding gift for Isabella d'Este, 1489

For Isabella d'Este's wedding in February 1490, her parents commissioned a small silver portable altarpiece from a Milanese goldsmith. This letter deals mostly with the cost of its materials and manufacture.

Venturi (1885), pp. 248–9.

Jacopo Trotti to Eleonora of Aragon, 27 November 1489
The drawing of the small altarpiece has been given to Master Alvisio Cagnola. He has been to see me with the goldsmith called Fra Rocco, who is also making other objects. He has promised not only to do everything for Her Excellency, but also to improve on the drawings. He has promised that he will finish everything by next January, with difficulty. They have agreed in my presence that for these objects they shall need about five hundred ounces of silver, plus the gold and the manufacture. According to the said goldsmith, I think this will cost about five hundred ducats. I had estimated to spend about one hundred gold ducats. Now Master Alvisio has begun using some of the money so that the work should not be delayed and can be finished in time.

He wanted to know whether the altarpiece should be made for hanging, or standing on an altar. I answered that I was sure that Your Ladyship wanted it to be hung, because from the drawing it looks too slender [to stand up].

13. A gift from Lucrezia Borgia, 1507
The half-length format of this painting is usual in Bartolomeo Veneto's early Madonnas, which follow the devotional types of Giovanni Bellini.[12] It was a gift for a 'Madama Caterina', who had just got married.

A. Venturi, 'Pittori della corte ducale a Ferrara nella prima decade del secolo XVI', *Archivio Storico dell'Arte*, 7 (1894), p. 298.

16 March 1507
Due from the Duchess [Lucrezia Borgia] to Master Bartolomeo da Venezia [Bartolomeo Veneto], painter, *lire* 20 for the cost of a panel painting, gilded, with gilded columns, with a half-figure of Our Lady with her Son in her arms and a St Jerome and a St John, and a steel mirror of a good size.

14. A banker's gift to his wife, 1543
Bindo Altoviti (1491–1557), the Florentine banker portrayed by Raphael c. 1512 (Washington, National Gallery of Art), com-

missioned a devotional painting from Giorgio Vasari for his
wife Fiammetta Soderini (1497 – post-1566). The painting is now
lost.

Giorgio Vasari, *Il libro delle Ricordanze di Giorgio Vasari*, ed.
A. Del Vita (Arezzo, 1938), p. 42.

I record that on 11 February 1543 Messer Bindo Altoviti
received from me a small picture of Our Lady, painted in oil,
which he gave his wife as a gift. There were five figures, that
is, Our Lady sitting on the ground, covering the child, and St
Elizabeth and St John the Baptist, and St Joseph reading. The
said painting was fifteen *scudi*, [that is] seven *grossi*, that is,
scudi 15.

**15. A gift of a miniature for Eleonora de' Medici Gonzaga,
1605**
The Vicar of an order of hermits sends the Duchess of Mantua
(1567–1611) a miniature of the miraculous image of the Virgin kept
in the church of the SS Annunziata in Florence, which Eleonora
would have known well.

Piccinelli (2000), pp. 178–9.

Fra Bernardino, from Florence, to Eleonora de' Medici
Gonzaga, 26 March 1605
. . . Our fathers here paint and make illuminations. For
the time being we are sending you a small image of the
Annunciation of the Virgin, which should be kept in the
Book of Office of Our Lady. Please accept this small sign of
affection which we, poor hermits, send you without pomp.
We are ready to make other small images, according to your
liking.

Commissions

16. A cover for a *Nostra Donna*, 1508
This extract from a letter from Raphael to his uncle refers to the
cover for a painting of the Virgin belonging to Giovanna Feltria
della Rovere.

Raffaello: gli scritti, ed. E. Camesasca (Milan, 1993), p. 104.

Raphael, from Florence, to Simone di Battista Ciarla, in Urbino, 21 April 1508

. . . The other day I wrote to my uncle the priest [Raphael's guardian, Don Bartolomeo Santi] to ask if he could send me the panel which was the cover for the painting of Our Lady belonging to the *profetessa* [*sic: prefettessa*. Giovanna Feltria, widow of the *prefetto* of Rome, Giovanni della Rovere], but he has not done so. I ask you to let us know when someone comes here, so that I can make the Lady happy.

17. A Mary Magdalen for Vittoria Colonna, 1531
Federico Gonzaga helps Vittoria Colonna to obtain a devotional painting from a great master. Titian's *Penitent Magdalen* exists in two basic versions, the one from this earlier date being semi-nude. It was one of the most popular images he ever produced, appealing to the contemporary taste for emotionally affecting religious works.[13]

J. A. Crowe and G. B. Cavalcaselle, *Titian: His Life and Times*, 2 vols (London, 1877), 1, p. 451.

Federico Gonzaga to Vittoria Colonna, 11 March 1531
I have heard from Signor Fabrizio Maramaldo, who told me that you would like to have a beautiful painting of St Mary Magdalen by the hand of an excellent painter. I have immediately sent a letter to Titian, who is probably the most excellent living painter, and I pleaded him to paint one for me, as beautiful and tearful as possible, and to send it to me soon.

18. A Madonna by Alessandro Allori for a Florentine lady
In his *Ricordi*, Alessandro Allori mentions a painting commissioned by a Florentine lady. It is a version, adapted for private devotion, of Allori's altarpiece, *Christ in the Sepulchre with the Virgin and Three Angels* (Arezzo, Museo Statale) which he painted for the Badia dei Santi Michele e Biagio at Passignano. It shows the Virgin alone, contemplating a chalice filled with Christ's blood, and would have inspired the viewer to meditate on Christ's death in the tranquillity of her bedroom. The inscription NON VI SI PENSA QUANTO SANGUE COSTA (one cannot conceive how much blood this

costs) is a verse from Dante's *Divine Comedy* (*Paradiso*, XXIX, 91), also used by Michelangelo for a *Pietà* for Vittoria Colonna. The entries in this extract show payments in kind as well as in money, a quite common practice.

Supino (ed.), (1908), pp. 17, 28.

1582
From the most illustrious Lady Giovanna [wife] of the Lord Montalvo, silver forks and spoons for the value of forty-five *lire*, for a painting of the head of a Madonna as the one in Passignano. My sister Alessandra collected them on this day, 20 April.

I record on this day that the Lady Giovanna [wife] of the Lord Montalvo has to give seventy *lire* for a painting on canvas of a Madonna as the one for the Badia at Passignano. For this Madonna I have been paid in silverware. [. . .] A dress for my daughter Dianorina, worth 12 ducats or more.

PRIVATE CHAPELS

Though, as we have seen, it was common to have informal foci of devotion at home, with images and other adornments, these were not proper altars. In the fifteenth century private chapels with a fixed, consecrated altar where Mass could be said were the privilege of important members of the clergy and of reigning families. Only rarely was ecclesiastical permission given to other ranks for a domestic chapel, even if, in practice, members of the elite had small chapels in their city palaces.[14] During the Catholic Reformation, these rules became stricter, making it more difficult to obtain permissions for a domestic chapel.

The texts chosen here concern chapels commissioned by wives of rulers, usually built close to their apartment or next to the bedroom.

19. The chapel of Margherita Gonzaga d'Este, 1584–86
Margherita Gonzaga (1565–1618), daughter of Guglielmo Gonzaga, Duke of Mantua, married Alfonso II d' Este in 1579. At the death of her husband in 1597, she returned to Mantua. She

lived in a sumptuous apartment in the Corte Vecchia, where she had a small chapel built.

i. A painting by Andrea del Sarto

S. L'Occaso, 'Margherita Gonzaga d'Este: pitture tra Mantova e Ferrara intorno al 1600', *Atti e Memorie. Accademia Nazionale Virgiliana di Scienze Lettere ed Arti*, new ser., 73 (2006), p. 94.

Margherita Gonzaga d'Este to her brother Vincenzo Gonzaga, November 1584

During the past few days Your Highness wrote to me that you had found a painting by Andrea del Sarto. With this letter I now entreat Your Highness to be so kind as to send me the measurements of its height and width and the theme of the painting, because I wish to begin furnishing my small chapel and I would very much like to have this information for many reasons, but especially for the arrangement of the wall decoration. [I also wish] to find another of a similar size, for a certain plan which I have for the walls.

ii. The decoration of the chapel

This extract from the Gonzaga court records of payments for building works for the period 1581–91 shows that the decoration of Margherita's chapel was exceptionally rich. The dome and the arches were painted, probably *a secco*, and the walls were decorated with a collection of religious paintings which Margherita had received from the Este, or from her father and brother.[15] The glass for the chapel window was commissioned from Murano.

A. Venturi, 'Quadri in una cappella estense del 1586', in *Archivio Storico dell'Arte*, 1 (1888), pp. 425–6.

Today 31 August 1588, the painter Master Bastiano di Filippi [Sebastiano Filippi, il Bastianino] is due the following sum for the following works done in the small palace chapel of the Most Serene Duchess of Ferrara, begun in the year 1586.

First, for the cupola in the vault where he has painted God the Father with Angels and Seraphim in glory, amounts to L 76/0/0

And for painting in the spandrels of the cupola the Four Evangelists with their symbols, amounts to L 45/12/0

And for painting on the underarch a St Francis receiving the stigmata with his companion, with ornaments in gold paint to be included, amounts to L 11/8/0

And on another underarch a penitent St Mary Magdalen, as above L 11/8/0

And on the springing of the said arches four half-figures of male and female saints, as above, amounts to L 30/8/0

And for mounting twenty-three paintings in the said chapel, with stucco and other decorative work in oil, that is: on the entrance wall where the door is, a painting of 'The Washing of the Feet' by Mazzolino, and another with an Our Lady by the same painter, and one with the Woman of Samaria, and one with the Disputation of Our Lord in the Temple, and a Nativity by Andrea Mantegna. On the second wall towards the courtyard, a painting of the Ascension [sic] of Our Lady by Master Gerolamo da Carpi; an Our Lady by the Ortolano; one [painting] with the Magi by Dossi; and a St George by Raphael of Urbino. An Our Lady by Andrea del Sarto; and an Our Lady in an old-fashioned style. On the third wall: an Our Lady by Andrea da Correggio, and a Death of the Virgin by Andrea Mantegna; an Our Lady by Raphael of Urbino; a Judith by Leonardo da Vinci, one by Master Benvenuto; and an Our Lady by Dossi; an Our Lady by Gerolamo da Carpi; a picture by Messer Andrea Mantegna; and one by Master Benvenuto di Garofalo. Everything amounts to L 74/0/0.

20. Two Grand Duchesses and their chapels

i. An altarpiece for the chapel of Christine of Lorraine in the Pitti Palace, 1589

Christine of Lorraine had a chapel built next to her bedroom, in her apartment in the Pitti Palace, where she moved immediately after her marriage to Ferdinando I de' Medici in April 1589. The chapel was decorated by Alessandro Allori with 'small gilded *grottesche* stories', and the altarpiece was also by Allori (Florence, Galleria dell'Accademia).

S. Lecchini Giovannoni, *Alessandro Allori* (Turin, 1991), p. 274.

A panel painting in the niche above the altar, with a St John baptising Jesus Christ, by the hand of Alessandro Allori, height about *braccia* 3, width *braccia* 2, with its gilded frame, with its walnut base with carved gilt roundels, with ovals painted as marble.

ii. *Maria Maddalena of Austria and her Cappella delle Reliquie, 1612–18*

Maria Maddalena of Austria used an octagonal chapel built the previous century in the Pitti Palace to house her large collection of relics, sent by friends and correspondents from all over Italy. She commissioned the decoration of the chapel, including seven stories from the life of her patron saint, St Mary Magdalen. In September 1618 she also commissioned from Fabrizio Boschi, Matteo Rosselli, Giovanni Bilivert and Filippo Tarchiani eight shutters painted with figures of saints for her relic cabinets.[16] The following letter deals with different aspects of the chapel's decoration.

L. Goldenberg Stoppato, 'La Cappella delle Reliquie in Palazzo Pitti', in M. Gregori (ed.), *Fasto di Corte. La decorazione murale nelle residenze dei Medici e dei Lorena*, 2 vols (Florence, 2005), 1, p. 141.

Maria Maddalena of Austria to Piero Guicciardini, Medici ambassador in Rome, 21 December 1612
. . . We have had our chapel in Pitti decorated following an attractive design, with beautiful paintings and with a great number of holy relics. To conduct it to perfection only two pictures are now missing: one, an Assumption of the Virgin, and the other, [the descent of] the Holy Spirit. We would like them painted by skilful artists, such as Cigoli and Passignano. Therefore you should call both of them and give them this commission on our behalf, something which shall please us very much. I enclose with this letter the measurements of the height and width, and you will allocate one of the two stories to each, according to your judgement or their preference. Above all, we wish them to paint them as soon as possible,

as I think they shall do, mainly because these are small-scale works.

Notes

1 On the relationship between women and devotional images, see D. Rigaux, 'Dire la foi avec des images, une affaire des femmes?', in J. Delumeau (ed.), *La religion de ma mère* (Paris, 1992), pp. 71–90. On domestic space, use of religious images and objects, see: M. A. Morse, 'Creating sacred spaces: the religious visual culture of the Renaissance Venetian *casa*', *Renaissance Studies*, 21:2 (2007), pp. 151–84, and 'The Arts of Domestic Devotion in Renaissance Italy: the Case of Venice', PhD dissertation, University of Maryland, 2006. See also: D. Cooper, 'Devotion', in Ajmar-Wollheim and Dennis (eds), (2006), pp. 190–203; P. Mattox, 'The Domestic Chapel in Renaissance Florence, 1400–1550', PhD. dissertation, Yale University, 1996, and 'Domestic sacral space in the Florentine Renaissance Palace', in Ajmar-Wollheim, Dennis and Matchette (eds), (2006), pp. 658–73.

2 On visualisation see C. Frugoni, 'Female mystics, visions and iconography', in D. Bornstein and R. Rusconi (eds), *Women and Religion in Medieval and Renaissance Italy* (Chicago and London, 1996), pp. 130–64.

3 Matthew 6:5–6, cited by V. M. Schmidt in 'Painting and individual devotion in late medieval Italy: the case of Saint Catherine of Alexandria', in A. Ladis and S. E. Zuraw (eds), *Vision of Holiness: Art and Devotion in Renaissance Italy* (Athens, Ga, 2001), p. 23.

4 See M. Bury, *The Print in Italy 1550–1620* (London, 2001), p.127.

5 According to Church law, the term 'altar' is reserved for places containing relics, at which masses can be said. For the relevance of texts such as Giovanni di Dio's for Renaissance art, see R. Kasl, 'Holy households: art and devotion in Renaissance Venice', in R. Kasl (ed.), *Giovanni Bellini and the Art of Devotion* (Indianapolis, 2004), pp. 58–89.

6 See for example the images by Fra Angelico and his assistants in the cells at S. Marco, contrasting with public commissions such as his Great Deposition (Florence, Museo di San Marco). Michelangelo's *Crucifixion* for Vittoria Colonna (**figure 10:** see also chapter 7, text 16. i) was an image demanding an intellectual as well as an emotional response. A similar mental exercise in devotional meditation is in St Caterina Vigri's *Le sette armi spirituali*, discussed in J. M. Wood, *Women, Art and Spirituality: the Poor Clares of Early Modern Italy* (Cambridge, 1996), esp. pp. 128–30.

7 For the vision of the mystic Angela da Foligno, inspired by the *Imago*

Pietatis (a half-figure of the dead Christ in a sarcophagus, supported by the Virgin), see C. Frugoni (1996), p. 163 n. 76.

8 See C. Klapisch-Zuber, 'Holy dolls: play and piety in Florence in the Quattrocento', in S. Blake McHam (ed.), *Looking at Italian Renaissance Sculpture* (Cambridge, 1998), pp. 111–27.

9 See Cooper, in Ajmar-Wollheim and Dennis (eds) (2006), pp. 196–7.

10 See the extracts from wills cited by D. Romano in 'Aspects of patronage in fifteenth- and sixteenth-century Venice', *Renaissance Quarterly*, 46:4 (1993), pp. 712–33, esp. 720.

11 The description has suggested various possible identifications: *Madonna and Child with Cherubs* (Milan, Pinacoteca di Brera); *Holy Family with Sts Elizabeth and John the Baptist* (Fort Worth, Texas, Kimbell Art Museum); and another picture of the same subject (Dresden, Staatliche Kunstsammlungen), all stylistically dated around 1485–86.

12 For example Bellini's *Virgin, Christ Child, and Sts Peter and Sebastian* (Paris, Louvre), or *Virgin and Child, and Two Female Saints* (Venice, Gallerie dell'Accademia).

13 See R. Goffen, *Titian's Women* (New Haven and London, 1997), pp. 177–9.

14 See Lydecker, p. 30. Also A. Lillie, 'The patronage of villa chapels and oratories near Florence: a typology of private religion', in E. Marchand and A. Wright (eds), *With or Without the Medici: Studies in Tuscan Art and Patronage* (Aldershot, 1998), pp. 19–46, esp. pp. 29–35.

15 For the identification of the painting, see L'Occaso, *Fonti archivistiche per le arti a Mantova tra Medioevo e Rinascimento (1382–1459)* (Mantua, 2005), pp. 96–100.

16 See J. A. F. Orbaan, 'Florentijnsce Gegevens IV', *Oud Holland*, 44 (1927), pp. 280–4, and A. Conti, 'The reliquary chapel', *Apollo*, 106:3 (1977), pp. 198–201.

∂ 9 ∞

COMMUNAL DEVOTION:
SPECTACLES, RITUALS,
MIRACULOUS IMAGES AND
PILGRIMAGES

The aspects of public and collective devotion that occupied the lives of women and men during our period were many and multifaceted, and only some have been selected here. The first four sections cover what perhaps were the most emotional among the manifestations of religious belief and devotion. A public demonstration of the trust people had in images, repositories of their hopes during difficult times, would make those who prayed in front of these images feel part of the larger community of the faithful. This of course would be a different experience from praying in the (relative) solitude of one's home.

As we have seen in the previous chapter, images were considered almost 'incarnations' of the divine, or of those men and women who had lived an exemplary life – the saints. People asked an image for help, and if help did come – if, for example, it came alive, spoke or worked miracles – the image would often attract prayers and devotion from great numbers of people. It is not coincidental that all the examples in the section on miracle-working images deal with paintings of the Virgin Mary, the Mother on whom all women could rely. Gifts, in the form of an ex-voto, would often been left as thanksgiving offerings at the sanctuary where the painting or sculpture was housed, and prayers said.

Processions and other ceremonies, such as mystery plays, often performed in churches, would involve women and men, lay and clerics, in public events of great emotional and aesthetic impact. Banners, monstrances containing the Host, reliquaries, paintings and statues would be carried around the city as the focus of people's devotion, and mystery plays would be staged, similar in iconography to paintings and sculpture groups. Men and women would embellish streets and squares, or organise different aspects of these spectacles, and finally observe or participate in these events. These communal occasions had a strong social significance, as they bound together people from all ranks of society, and gave women the possibility of organising and participating in these important events in the life of a city.

Many women of all social classes throughout the period went, or aspired to go, on pilgrimages within Italy and beyond, though their numbers were not nearly as great as those of men, especially for journeys further afield such as the Holy Land or Santiago de Compostela. Pilgrimage centres might be in the immediate locality (perhaps housing relics of a saint or miracle-working images), or might be major centres such as Rome, Assisi, and Loreto, an extremely popular destination at the time. By going on pilgrimages, people would be granted indulgences so that their soul could avoid lengthy periods in purgatory. It should be remembered that pilgrims would face discomfort, danger and possible death in order to visit holy places and churches, and therefore journeys were usually undertaken in groups. Seeing new places and meeting new customs, and relying on the goodwill and charity of others, pilgrims could also achieve a spiritual transformation.

WOMEN AND MIRACLE-WORKING IMAGES

Miraculous images of the Madonna or of saints have long been part of religious devotion. As their miracle-working fame spread, their sites, whether a street tabernacle or a church, attracted the faithful in large numbers. People showed their devotion for a specific image by going on pilgrimages to visit that image, praying in front of it and often leaving offerings.[1]

1. A visit to SS. Annunziata, 1562
Isabella de' Medici Orsini (1542–76), wife of Paolo Giordano Orsini, was the favourite daughter of Cosimo I de' Medici. In 1562, during a period of poor health, she made a vow to one of the most loved miraculous images in Florence, the Annunciation of the Virgin in the church of SS. Annunziata.[2] After her recovery, she

went to the church as she had vowed to do. It is interesting to note that only the Duke could give permission to uncover the fresco of the Annunciation, usually protected by a curtain.

F. Winspeare, *Isabella Orsini e la corte medicea del suo tempo* (Florence, 1961), p. 84.

Isabella de' Medici Orsini to her father, 3 November 1562
With this letter I beseech Your Excellency to be so kind as to forgive my arrogance. Your Excellency should know that, when I was ill, I made the vow to walk to the [church of] Santissima Annunziata. On the evening of All Hallows I decided to fulfil this vow together with some gentle-women. While we were on our way, I sent word to the friars to uncover the Virgin Annunciate for me. They answered that they had been ordered not to uncover it without your permission. I said that I had had permission from Your Excellency, as I knew that if I had asked it, you would not have denied me. Therefore I beseech you to forgive me for this presumption, and I know that you will not refuse. There was nobody at all in the church except for my own entou-rage, and nobody heard about it. Signor Paolo [Orsini] kisses Your Excellency's hands, and thinks that in about ten days he shall come to wait on you as he should. I beseech you to keep me in your favour, and for this I kiss your hands. May Our Lord keep you well, as I desire.

2. Miraculous images in seventeenth-century Rome
The diarist Giacinto Gigli (1594–1671) gives accounts of several miraculous images in early seventeenth-century Rome. Their pop-ularity often stemmed from visions experienced by lower-ranking women: they then became the focus of more general cults, which might be officially sanctioned though later falling into disuse.

Giacinto Gigli, *Diario di Roma*, ed. M. Barberito, 2 vols (Rome, 1994), 1, pp. 167–8; 2, pp. 475–6.

i. A religious woman hears an image of the Virgin on a wall speak to her, 1627

During this month of December 1627 an image of Our Lady painted on the wall of a garden outside Porta Flaminia, which today is called Porta del Popolo, worked miracles. This is how they say it happened. A certain nun or tertiary, passing in front of this image, knelt down to pray. They say that the image spoke to her, saying that it should be honoured by keeping its lamp burning all the time. In fact nobody else had taken care of it after the death of the owner of that land, Cardinal Del Bufalo, who had paid homage to the image with a lamp burning at all times. So the place had become derelict, covered with brambles and weeds. As soon as this event became known, many people arrived and many miracles took place. The nun who had told this story was put in prison to verify the truth of what she had said. The image, which was set into a small niche, was then shielded by a wall, and a burning lamp was placed into the niche. Ex-votos and other objects were hooked on to it by people who had received miracles. After that, on 8 February 1628, the image of Our Lady was brought into the convent of the friars of Santa Maria del Popolo.

ii. An old woman uncovers a painting of the Madonna and Child with Saints in the Pantheon (Santa Maria ad Martyres), 1646

The painting discovered by the old woman is a fifteenth-century altarpiece, still *in situ*, the *Virgin and Child with St Francis and St John the Baptist* by a Peruginesque artist.

On 11 July it was first heard that in the church of the Rotonda there was an image of Our Lady which was working miracles. This is what happened. On the previous morning, that is 10 July, a poor woman, who was believed to be a simpleton, said that Our Lady had appeared to her in a dream, and had ordered her to find an image [of Our Lady] which was in the Chapel of the Crucifix in the said church. The woman asked which chapel it was, and then begun to clean its walls which were so dirty with dust and cobwebs that it was impossible to see any image. She continued, painstakingly cleaning the wall and washing it with the help of another woman who was in the church, so that at last they begun to see a painting. The next day the women went back to do the same thing, and finally an image of Our Lady appeared. She was seated, with her Son in her arms, blessing, with St John the Baptist on one side, and St Francis on the other. The chapel is the nearest one to the High Altar, on the right side, and the image is at the left of the chapel's altar. Many people then came. A possessed man was freed from the Devil, and many ex-votos were brought, and alms given. People kept arriving, for many months now, so that the said image on order of the Church authorities has been covered with a cloth.

Because of this, vergers and those who take care of churches should mend their ways, since they do not keep them clean and let the images of the saints be covered by dust and dirt. These images were made by pious Christians, and now it seems that Our Lady and the saints need to look for poor women to clean them and bring them again to people's devotion.

RELIGIOUS SPECTACLES, CEREMONIES AND PROCESSIONS

3. Eleonora of Aragon views an enactment of Christ's Passion in the court chapel, 1481

The staging of the mystery play described in this text refers to the iconography of the Crucifixion, the Descent into Limbo (Harrowing of Hell), and the Lamentation over the dead body of Christ. As well as words and gestures, singing was also used to achieve emotional intensity. This play, seen by Ercole I d'Este and Eleonora of Aragon, together with 'men and women of the Church', brings to mind the life-size terracotta group of the *Lamentation* by Guido Mazzoni, with portraits of the Duke and Duchess as Joseph of Arimathea and Mary Salome.

G. Ferrarini, *Memoriale estense (1476–1489)*, ed. P. Griguolo (Rovigo, 2006), p. 123.

On Friday 20 April, Good Friday, our Duke Ercole had the Passion of Christ staged in his court chapel. This was certainly an event of great devotion, and took place after the sermon. Among other things, there was a wooden platform in front of the altar, which was as long as the width of the chapel, from wall to wall, and of the right width. There was a great wooden serpent's head which opened and shut: here was the Limbo of the Holy Fathers. There was a well-made rocky mound. First of all Mary Magdalen came out, and said a few words, then [came] St John, in front of the crucifix. Then the Virgin Mary arrived with some women, and went to Christ's tomb and said some words, after which they sat down on the tomb. Then a man dressed as Christ went to the head of the hydra or serpent, which was the Limbo, to take the Holy Fathers away with him. He said '*Atolite portas*' and the throat of the serpent opened up. [The Holy Fathers] came out of it, singing praise to the Lord and kissing the cross.

And it seemed as if there was the Devil, there in that throat . . . There were chains, and flares which reached up to the ceiling of the chapel. After that, Nicodemus arrived to take Christ off the cross, singing some verses which made one cry, and, while singing, he placed the dead body in the arms of his mother, the Virgin Mary. They wrapped him in a cloth and placed him in the tomb. The Duke was high up in the chapel, on the balcony which is above the door of the chapel, watching with his Duchess and various men and women of the Church.

4. The Doge 'marries' the Abbess of Santa Maria delle Vergini, 1506

The ceremony of the Doge 'marrying' each new abbess of the Augustinian convent of the *Vergini* dated back to its medieval establishment. The elegant style of life of the nuns, usually from high-ranking families, was often noted.[3]

I diarii (MCCCCXCVI–MDXXXIII) di Marino Sanuto, 58 vols (Bologna, 1969–70), 6, p. 353.

Sunday [June 14]. The Doge went with ceremonial galleys to wed the Abbess of the *Vergini*. She belongs to the Badoer family, and the Doge comes to marry the abbess in the year of her installation since the church is under his patronage. He was accompanied by the *Signoria* and by patricians. They heard Low Mass and then the patriarch celebrated a High Mass, but the Doge did not stay. And the church was beautifully decorated, more than any other church in the city was ever decorated, at the cost of sixty ducats. It was permitted to go inside [the convent] as far as the refectory, where more than five hundred women and a few men had refreshments. [The display on] the *credenza* was magnificent.

5. A rosary confraternity in Rome celebrates the anniversary of the Battle of Lepanto, 1625

The battle of Lepanto (7 October 1571) between the Turkish fleet and that of the Christian Holy League was seen as a great Christian victory against the Turks, and therefore cause for religious celebration. Giacinto Gigli describes the unusually elaborate procession in the Jubilee year of 1625, organised by the Company of the Rosary, based at the church of S. Maria sopra Minerva in Rome. The members of confraternities dedicated to the Virgin Mary or to the rosary were often both male and female, but women seemed to have no directive functions, and often only their presence is mentioned. The procession was dominated by the male members of the Company who carried paintings of the fifteen Mysteries of the Rosary, but the young girls who were the beneficiaries of the Company's charitable bequests were an important part of the spectacle.[4]

Gigli (1994), 1, pp. 147–9.

The whole church of Santa Maria sopra Minerva was decorated from the vault to the ground with very beautiful and sumptuous hangings of all kinds, and the streets through which the procession was going to pass were similarly decorated. Along these streets [from the Minerva to the church of the Gesù, to the Corso and back again], which were all decorated with very beautiful tapestries and other silk cloths, the procession was composed in this way . . .

[Officials of the Company, trumpeters and Dominican friars bearing gilded candelabra, a cross and the standard of the Company, lead the procession.]

Then came many other members of the Company with burning torches, behind which came a large round picture, which, like the Sun, was surrounded with golden rays, and was carried on two poles by two men walking side by side . . . On the picture was painted the naval battle during which the Turk was defeated, and in memory of this [the victory is celebrated] on this Sunday of October every year, in the most solemn way . . .

[Paintings representing the Mysteries of the Rosary are then carried in procession]

After these, after a multitude of men carrying burning torches, came four trumpet players, and then all the friars of the Preachers' Order, also with burning torches. Then came another music choir, and after that thirty-one poor unmarried girls, dressed in white, who receive dowries from the Company (as is customary on this day). Twenty-four of these dowries were used [for the girls] to get married, the other seven to become nuns. They walked in this order: two ladies, officials of the Company, holding in their hands silver staffs on which they lent, preceded every four couples of unmarried girls; among the last of them was the Signora Costanza Magalotti, wife of Signor Carlo Barberini, the brother of the Pope, and the unmarried girls, who were divided into four groups. Each of the last seven wore a gold crown, which signifies that, as they wanted to dedicate their virginity to God, they had reached such a high rank amongst the other women that they deserved to be considered and honoured as queens.

PILGRIMAGES

What women observed at pilgrimages sites, which had often received much architectural, sculptural or pictorial embellishment, and at places along the route from their homes, is less well documented than the offerings they made, except, as is to be expected, from records concerning women from the highest ranks of society.

6. A request denied, 1423

Paola Malatesta (d. 1449) was a learned woman with a strong religious commitment. In November 1423, on the occasion of the

Jubilee proclaimed by Pope Martin V Colonna, she wrote to her father, the Lord of Pesaro, Malatesta di Malatesta, who at the time was at the papal court. Paola wanted to travel to Rome to obtain the indulgence granted to pilgrims, but the journey was out of the question because of the uncertain political situation. The churches Malatesta mentions in his letter to Paola were the oldest and most important basilicas in Rome, and were in disrepair after years of neglect. The Pope was eager to bring them back to their ancient splendour.

W. Brandmüller, 'Paola Gonzaga e il giubileo di Martino V', in A. Groppi and L. Scaraffia (eds), *Le donne ai tempi del giubileo. 'Con singolar modestia e insolita devozione'* (Milan, 2000), p. 78.

10 December 1423
My dearest daughter, . . . I begged Our Lord [the Pope] to grant you absolution and indulgence in this [Jubilee] year. He replied from his own lips that he was happy to grant it to you and would willingly do it right away, provided that you send to the same churches (St Peter's, St Paul's, St John's [Lateran] and Santa Maria Maggiore) a quarter of what you think you would have spent, had you travelled there for the same purpose. His Holiness did not think that you should be granted absolution without any cost to yourself. I do not know if you would have been able to get this absolution otherwise. In any case I can tell you that, as you are not able to get what you wish through any other means, you should go to confession and repent, making sure during this year to obtain an absolution and indulgence. I send you this news, as I have got nothing else to send you, thinking that you should be grateful and content with it.

7. Angela Merici's pilgrimage to Rome, 1524
Before founding the *Compagnia delle Orsoline* in 1535, the Franciscan tertiary Angela Merici (1474-1540) travelled to the Holy Land. On her return she decided to go on a pilgrimage to Rome. The following is an extract from the evidence provided by her travelling companion, Antonio de Romanis, during her beatification proceedings in 1568.

G. Zarri, 'Sante pellegrine: Orsola e le compagne', in Groppi and Scaraffia (eds), (2000), pp. 69–70.

I tell you that, after some time, she [Angela Merici] wanted to visit those most holy relics which are in Rome. She therefore left with two priests, and went on the journey. When she returned she told me many things about the holy relics. [She told me] that, while visiting them, she was seen by a certain Messer Piero della Puglia, chamberlain to His Holiness, who was also with us on our journey to Jerusalem, and that after many words of praise, he took her to kiss the foot of His Holiness.

8. The pilgrimage of Christine of Lorraine (1565–1636/37) to Loreto, 1593

The basilica of the Holy House in Loreto dates from the middle of the fifteenth century. It was built around a house believed to be the place where the Virgin Mary had received the Angel of the Annunciation, and which had been transported by angels from Nazareth to a hill in the Marche, where it arrived in 1294. The Holy House was enclosed within a marble sanctuary by Andrea Sansovino from a project by Bramante.

Several accounts were published from the later sixteenth century onwards of great ladies going on pilgrimages. Although intended to underscore the piety of members of ruling houses and their favours to holy sites, the emphasis in these writings on the ladies' vast accompanying entourages and the splendour of the welcome laid on for them makes them comparable to other sixteenth- and seventeenth-century publications on other festivities.

Earlier Medici had given generously to the shrine. Christine of Lorraine would make another pilgrimage to Loreto later in her life. As is to be expected, the 'sights' on the towns along the route from Tuscany to the Marche were largely of pious interest, and many opulent reliquaries and some secular works of art were proudly displayed.

F. Grimaldi, 'Pellegrini e pellegrinaggi a Loreto nei secoli XIV–XVIII', *Bollettino Storico della Città di Foligno*, supplement 2 (2001), pp. 428–31.

On 15 September, which was the Wednesday of the Ember Days, the Most Serene Grand Duchess of Tuscany left Florence at 19 hours to go to the Holy House of Loreto, accompanied by priests, by the illustrious and most reverend Monsignor Martelli, by many lords and a large number of ladies, and by a company of horsemen, twenty-five Germans and many others, whose names I omit.

[They passed through Arezzo, Castiglione and Cortona, where they saw the body of St Margaret of Cortona.]

. . . The following day we stayed in Cortona, and Her Highness went with the others to the church of S. Margherita to see the body of that saint which rests in the church. After that, we went to Sant'Agostino, where we were shown the body of Santo Mugolino, and we saw many relics. On the same morning we heard mass in the cathedral and were shown a gold cross full of a large number of relics, which was wonderful to see.

[The company advanced to Perugia and then to Tolentino and Macerata.]

On Monday 22nd in the morning, we went for lunch to Tolentino, where everything was well organised, and in the evening [we arrived] at Macerata, where My Lady was received with great pomp by the Governor, Monsignor Fantini. The main hall was decorated with many beautiful paintings, particularly [portraits of] the House of Medici, and first of all the [portrait of] Grand Duke Ferdinando [Christine's husband]. This gave the Grand Duchess much joy, and she stopped to look at it. The following morning, Thursday 23 September, we lunched in Macerata, having been to mass in the morning. After lunch we continued on our way towards Loreto. Near Recanati Her Highness was met by the Most Illustrious Cardinal Gallo, Protector of the Holy House, together with the bishop of that place, and we reached Loreto all together at 22 hours. We went to the Holy House first of all, and Her Highness knelt in front of the Holy Sacrament for some time. Then she entered the chapel of the Blessed Virgin Mary, and was there for vespers and compline. Then she went to her lodgings.

On Friday 24th we stayed on in Loreto. On this day Her Highness offered to the Holy House a very fine *paramento* in cloth of gold which was decorated with wonderful embroideries. She heard the Mass [celebrated] by Cardinal Gallo, and she took the Holy Sacrament of Communion from him. She then heard a very solemn High Mass. After lunch Her Highness returned to the Holy House and listened to vespers. Then we saw all the silverware, gold vases and precious stones which are all very valuable. In fact, there is a large treasure there. We saw all the cupboards with *paramenti* given by various kings, dukes, princes and lords, all of them quite splendid, one more beautiful than the other. After that, it appeared that the most illustrious Cardinal Gallo is planning a chapel, which Her Highness is thinking of building and endowing, spending 200,000 ducats, and she will take the plan to the most serene Grand Duke. From there we went to bed.

[After hearing mass in Loreto on the 26th, Christine and her entourage departed via Recanati, Macerata, Tolentino and Montefalco, where she saw the body of St Clare and presented a *paramento* of gold fabric to her convent, for Assisi and Perugia.]

In the evening we arrived at Assisi, where we remained for the following day, Friday 1 October. On that day we went to mass at Santa Maria degli Angeli, one mile from Assisi. Monsignor Martelli said mass and gave communion to Her Highness and to the whole entourage, so [they all] obtained the indulgence that His Holiness Our Lord [Pope Gregory XIV] has granted with a letter he sent to Her Highness and to her entourage. After this, we saw the Chapel of the Roses, the place where St Francis granted plenary indulgence. There we saw some rose bushes without thorns: it is said that, when St Francis was tempted by the enemy of mankind [the Devil], he threw himself on the thorns, which changed into roses without thorns, as can be seen. Her Most Serene Ladyship left another *paramento* of gold fabric in this place. After returning to Assisi for lunch, we went to the church of Santa Chiara, where we saw a large number of relics, and in particular the crucifix which spoke to St Francis. Then, going down to the church of St Francis with her entourage, Her Highness heard vespers and compline, and touched the girdle of St Francis with the permission of the prior of that place . . .

On Sunday we were in Perugia, and in the morning the bishop of that city said mass for Her Highness in the cathedral, where we saw the ring of the Virgin Mary, a relic unique in the world. She went back to her lodgings, accompanied by many gentlewomen, and had lunch. In the evening she went for vespers to [the church of] St Francis, where we saw a thorn from the [crown of thorns] of Our Lord God. We were granted an indulgence as it was the eve of the feast of St Francis. From there we went to [the church of] St Dominic because it was the first Sunday of the month, and there took place the procession of the rosary . . .

[After Castiglione del Lago, Montepulciano and Pienza, the company reached Siena on 7 October, where they lodged in the Palace of the Governor.]

On Friday we remained in Siena. In the morning [we heard] mass in the cathedral, and in the afternoon [we went] to [the church of] St Dominic, to see the head of St Catherine, then to the cells and the house of that saint, and from there to [the church of] St Francis. Then back to the usual palace, accompanied by the same three bishops, Monsignor Martelli, the Bishop of Arezzo and that of Montepulciano, who accompanied her for the whole journey, [as well as] the Governor, the Archbishop of Siena, the Bishop of Massa, the Abbot of San Galgano and many other lords, with seven or more carriages and coaches for the gentlewomen who are part of the retinue in the mornings and evenings.

On Saturday morning we went to mass as usual, and then to the convent of the Angels, where we saw the head of San Galgano, a most beautiful relic, and also visited other churches. We also did this in the afternoon. On Sunday 10th we remained in Siena, and the Archbishop said mass for Her Highness. After lunch, in the evening we heard vespers in San Domenico, and then there was a beautiful joust, with the knights breaking three lances each and a rapier. The Grand

Duchess gave the winners three chains with three medals which, it was said, were worth fifty *scudi* or more each.

[Her journey over, Christine was welcomed on her safe return.]

9. How women should behave on pilgrimages and processions, 1613

The Augustinian friar Lucrezio Borsati wrote *I progressi felici di Orsola vergine e martire e della Compagnia sua* which, like many other books written during the previous centuries, uses the story of the pilgrimage of St Ursula to offer women an example of how to behave on pilgrimages. Borsati's tale, of course, does not pretend to be historically accurate, but instead puts forward some of the principles of the Catholic Reformation. In this extract, he describes Ursula and her female companions in Rome, where their visits to churches would gain them indulgences.

Zarri, in Groppi and Scaraffia (eds), (2000), p. 64.

As they wanted to honour God and his female saints, [Ursula and her companions] walked with lowered eyes, moved by fervent desire and warm devotion, full of respect, contrary to the usual habits of girls in those times. They visited the churches where the holy bodies [of saints] were resting, and the venerable bones of male and female holy martyrs of Our Lord Jesus Christ. They would remain there for hours, on their knees, praying with their hands raised. They would give thanks to the Eternal Lord because He had permitted them to see those holy places which they had reached after such a long journey. They would contemplate the cruel torments and the harsh and painful sufferings [the martyrs] had to bear. They could not stop looking at those footprints, those tombs, those sepulchres, kissing those empty marble sarcophagi, embracing the altars containing the holy relics which had been devoutly placed there.

VOTIVE OFFERINGS AND GIFTS

The space around miraculous images was (and in many cases still is) covered with mementoes expressing gratitude from people whose prayers had been answered by the Virgin or by saints. Women's presence is attested at the shrines by their donations and ex-votos. They would leave votive offerings according to their financial means, and receive devout mementoes such as prints, badges, or rosaries. Ex-votos could be made from many different materials, and their iconography could incorporate various references, some of which are obvious, others which are not clear to us today. The following extracts give examples of offerings given by women from ruling families and from the aristocracy, as well as by nuns. They range from silver statues to money given for lamp oil or wax candles. The more ex-votos were visible to the faithful, the greater the power of the image was considered to be.[5]

10. Contessina de' Bardi offers a reliquary to the SS. Annunziata, 1464

The church of the SS. Annunziata in Florence was under Medici protection and patronage. The Medici family could participate in mass and other religious ceremonies from a small chapel next to the tabernacle of the Virgin Annunciate. The space around the tabernacle was crowded with ex-votos and gifts, many of them from members of the Medici family. Contessina de' Bardi (c. 1390–1473) was the wife of Cosimo il Vecchio.[6] Her reliquary is recorded in a register of silver ex-votos offered to the SS. Annunziata.

E. Casalini, *Una icona di famiglia. Nuovi contributi di storia e d'arte sulla SS. Annunziata di Firenze* (Florence, 1998), pp. 84–5.

A silver gilt reliquary in the shape of a pax, with the death of Our Lady, Our Saviour who holds her soul in his arms, the apostles all around, and above God the Father with two small angels. It is made of ivory, with the painted scenes engraved into it. Around it are three red stones, one of which is missing, and some enamelled rosettes, with four rosettes made with pearls, three for each one. There is a silver foliage decoration all around, with two small leaves at the bottom. At the top there is a double rose with silver leaves and three pearls, and two small chains attached to a ring with a small hook, all of this in silver. The Lady Contessina, wife of the late Cosimo de' Medici, offered this on 21 February 1464 [1465]. It weighs 9 ounces and 6 *denari*.

11. Alfonsina Orsini de' Medici commissions an altar-piece from Giovanni Antonio Sogliani

Alfonsina Orsini (1475–1520) was the wife of Piero di Lorenzo de' Medici.[7] In his 'Life of Antonio Sogliani', Vasari describes a votive gift from Alfonsina: an altar-piece with the image of the crucified St Acanthius who was the leader of the 10,000 martyrs. The 'chiesa di Camaldoli' he mentions is the church of S. Salvatore, which belonged to the Camaldolese monks. In 1550 the altarpiece, which is signed and dated 1521, was moved to the church of S. Lorenzo, where it is still located.

Vasari, ed. Milanesi (1906), 5, p. 124.

[Giovanni Antonio Sogliani] painted a panel for the Lady Alfonsina, wife of Piero de' Medici, which was placed as an ex-voto on the altar of the Chapel of the Martyrs in the Camaldolese church in Florence. The panel represented the crucifixion of St Acanthius, with the other martyrs with crosses in their arms. Two of the figures are half-covered with a drapery, while the others are naked, kneeling on the ground with their crosses. There are some small angels in the sky holding palm branches. This painting was made with much care and great skill in the use of colour and in the very expressive heads. It was placed in the said Camaldolese church but, because of the siege of Florence [in 1529], the monastery was taken away from those hermit fathers officiating in the church, and was given to the nuns of San Giovannino, of the order of the Knights of Malta. [The painting] was therefore damaged. It was placed in San Lorenzo by order of Duke Cosimo, in one of the chapels belonging to the Medici family. It is among Sogliani's best works.

12. Pious offerings by women recorded in the inventories at Loreto, 1569–1621

The following extracts list a great variety of luxury artefacts, gifted by women to the Holy House of Loreto, from church vestments made of expensive fabrics, to silver ex-votos and an altar front made of semi-precious stones, a technique called *commesso di pietre dure* for which Florentine artisans were well-known throughout Europe.[8]

F. Grimaldi (ed.), *La historia de la chiesa di Santa Maria di Loreto* (Loreto, 1993), pp. 411–12, 424–5, 448–9.

5 October 1569
First, an altar *paramento* of green and gold brocade, with a silk fringe in different colours, and a frontal decorated with the coat of arms of the late Duchess of Milan, Bianca Maria.

One cope of the same colour as above and gold brocade, with gold friezes and the same coat of arms.

One chasuble of the said brocade, with gold friezes and coat of arms. Also a dalmatic with its girdle, made of the said brocade and with the said coat of arms . . .

One chasuble of white damask with figures, with a frieze in brocade of *pavonazzo* colour, with the coat of arms of the late Lady Bianca.

One dalmatic with a tunicle of the said damask, with amice, alb and girdle with the coat of arms of the said Lady.
18 May 1606
A silver lamp weighing 4 *libbre* and 10 ounces, with the coat of arms of the Lady Margherita Taverna Visconti and of her son Francesco. She left 800 Venetian *lire* to the Holy House so that [the lamp] could be kept burning for nine years.

A silver lamp in the shape of a basin from Lucrezia Bonvisi, who left to the Holy House 200 *scudi* in order to keep it burning in perpetuity in the holy chapel, in a place to be decided.
26 May 1621
A [statue of a] swaddled baby on a silver base, weighing seven *libbre* and four ounces. On the said base there is a cartouche with a coat of arms with a lion on one side and on the other a rose with three lilies above, and the inscription: *ex voto ill.mae dominae Franciscae Isolanae anno MDCXXI.* It was offered as a gift by the said Countess Francesca Isolana from Bologna.

5 June 1621

The Most Serene Lady, Princess [Christine] of Lorraine, Grand Duchess, mother of the Most Serene Grand Duke of Tuscany Cosimo [II] of glorious memory, sent as a gift to the Holy House of Loreto, through the Most Illustrious Marchioness Leonora Consini del Monte Santa Maria:

a front for the altar of the Holy House, made of jasper, amethyst and lapis lazuli. The first frieze acts as altar table and as a cornice. It is made of yellow and green striped Sicilian jasper. Under this cornice there is a frieze of oriental amethyst with some pieces of lapis lazuli, and lower down a small frieze of red and white jasper decorated with yellow jasper from Cyprus. All this is supported by four pilasters in pyramidal form, made of lapis lazuli, with their bases in yellow Cyprus jasper. These four pilasters stand on a frieze of red and white marbled jasper from Sicily. Between the four pilasters are three square panels. In the middle one there is a representation of the Holy House in silver, with the image of the Most Serene Grand Duke in bas-relief, kneeling, dressed in his ducal habit, and around it there is a decoration of silver cherubim and swags. In the other two panels there are, also in silver, the coat of arms of the Most Serene Lady and of the Grand Duke.

THE DEVOTION OF NUNS

The texts in this section are chosen to give the flavour of how nuns used art in communal devotion, and how strong their emotional involvement could be.[9]

13. The *Crucifixion with Scenes from the Passion* by Antonio Campi and the nuns of San Paolo in Milan, 1584

Carlo Borromeo (1538–84), Archbishop of Milan, bequeathed to the nuns of the convent of San Paolo a picture he owned and in front of which he used to pray, a *Crucifixion with Scenes from the Passion*, painted in 1569 by Antonio Campi (Paris, Louvre). The painting was brought to the convent just after his death, and was placed in a chapel in the nuns' part of the church, which in its entirety became a reliquary dedicated to the archbishop.

In the following extract, Paola Antonia Sfondrati writes about this bequest. Her niece Sister Agata Sfondrati, who had collected in the nuns' chapel relics such as Borromeo's shoes, biretta and girdle, describes to the nuns of the convent of Santa Maria in Cremona the emotions of fellow nuns of San Paolo in front of a portrait of Borromeo, and then their joy in receiving his bequest.

B. de Klerck, *I fratelli Campi. Immagini e devozione. Pittura religiosa nel Cinquecento lombardo* (Milan, 2003), pp. 251, 248–9.

i. Paola Antonia Sfondrati, from the 'Historia delle angeliche di San Paolo', c. 1584

Perhaps his [Carlo Borromeo's] most noble bequest was born out of the loving charity he displayed to us more than to many other monasteries, during those dreadful days when he made his will. He left to this congregation, in his memory, one of his dearest and most expensive paintings, where Mount Calvary is represented in a most praiseworthy manner, as the memento of the most bitter Passion of the Lord, His tomb, His Resurrection, all His appearances, and His Ascension. It is said that this was the favourite amongst his paintings, and therefore was in the uppermost oratory in his chamber, where perhaps he uttered his most effective prayers and sighs and flagellated or mortified himself. We now have [this painting], one of the dearest bequests we could ever inherit or wish to possess.

ii. Images and the devotion of the nuns: a letter from Sister Agata Sfondrati, 1584

Agata Sfondrati, of the order of the Angeliche di San Paolo, Milan, to the prioress and the nuns of the convent of Santa Maria in Cremona, 8 December 1584

We entered the school [of the novices], where we keep a portrait of that most illustrious and Reverend Signore [Carlo Borromeo], which was given as a gift to the Most Reverend Mother, the Mistress [of the Novices], two or three months before. When we uncovered that revered image, streams of hot tears poured from our eyes. We were seized by such pain, that for a long time the Mother and the daughters could not speak: it was a view which truly could melt stones. Oh holy virgins, I wish I were able to express the pain in my heart and what I felt when I looked at that holy and noble hand which had given me the bread of life and blessed me so many times, and had dressed me so gladly with this religious habit . . .

A few days later, it pleased God to comfort us when we heard that that most illustrious [Borromeo] of holy memory had bequeathed a painting to us, which, it is said, is the largest and the most expensive he had, and was kept in his secret *camerino*, of which he always carried the key, where he kept his dearest treasures: a true repository of angels. There he had so many times celebrated the Sabbath dedicated to the Lord, offering himself sweetly to Him in a thousand different ways, through sacrifices and the most severe acts of penitence. At this news, all the nuns revived and rejoiced, waiting every day for the precious treasure. Finally on 27 November, after vespers, it was brought [to us]. All of us, grouped in procession and singing the *Miserere* in two choirs, went to receive and take possession of our Father's bequest. We went to the church weeping, remembering how many times we had received our Father in the same way. Walking around all the cloisters, we arrived at the church, and we placed the dear relic in a chapel, where, above an altar, is now this most devout altarpiece which represents most of the Mysteries of the Passion, Resurrection and Ascension of the Lord. It was painted with great skill by Messer Antonio Campi. It is visited with the greatest devotion, and we sing the *Miserere* there, on the third day of each month.

14. Sister Anastasia Martini, on an old painting of scenes from the life of S. Rita da Cascia, c. 1626

During the collection of witness statements leading to the canonisation of Rita of Cascia (Margherita Lotti, 1381–1447) in 1626, Sister Anastasia Martini, *vicaria* and former abbess of the convent of S. Rita, describes an old painting of the saint in the convent, which is now lost. She has no interest in noting artistic qualities in a painting that may have seemed not only worn by

time, as she states, but archaic in style. However, from her perspective the work would have been of great value both as dating
soon after the death of the saintly founder of the convent, and as
validating its traditions. In giving what were seen as the crucial
episodes in her life, it would have moulded the perceptions of the
faithful, many of whom would have left ex-voto images based on
the scenes.

A. Turchini, 'Committenza "popolare" nella devozione a Santa
Rita da Cascia', in M. Tosti (ed.), *Santuari cristiani d'Italia*,
Collection de l'École Française de Rome, 317 (Rome, 2003),
pp. 176–7.

When I entered the convent here of the Blessed Rita [in
1580], I found the old canvas where various deeds of the
Blessed One are depicted, which I describe . . . And it is
remembered not only by myself, since I became a nun; but
also nuns older than me, who are dead, have said that it has
always been said and known amongst other nuns that the
said painting was made soon after the death of the Blessed
One, and that we have placed it many times in this church
on her feast day, but normally we kept it in the oratory where
we say the office, where I have always seen it.

1. First, when the Blessed Rita was in the cradle and five
bees, which owing to the age of the picture cannot be seen or
made out, emerged and entered her mouth, and which watch
her, hovering around the cradle.
2. And then you see the Blessed Rita painted at the entrance
to the convent with a tree behind her, and then the figures of
St John the Baptist, St Augustine, St Nicholas of Tolentino,
with an inscription at their feet: 'When St John the Baptist,
St Augustine and St Nicholas of Tolentino came to the
Blessed Rita in a vision and ordered her to become a nun'.
3. And then you see the Blessed Rita in nun's habit kneeling,
with other nuns standing, and one of them places her hand
on her head, and on the other side portraits of St Augustine
and St Nicholas with an inscription at their feet which says:
'When the Blessed Rita became a nun and took the habit of

St Monica, mother of St Augustine, and was received by the other nuns'.

4. Then you see the Blessed Rita, dressed as a nun with a book before her, kneeling before a Christ with wounded hands and a crown, with a blood-stained thorn in her forehead, with words which can scarcely be read because of age.

5. Then follows the figure of the Blessed One when she is dead, with two people kneeling before her bed, one of whom kisses her hand, and the figures of six standing women who commend themselves to God with praying hands, also with letters below which cannot be read because of their age.

6. Then you also see the Blessed Rita stretched out dead on a bier with hands crossed and an iron grille across, which shows the same place where she is kept today, with lettering below, which also cannot be read because of age.

15. The convent of Santa Margherita, Bologna: devotions in the nuns' church,?1633

From the *Due Libri di diversi Riccordi* of the convent, the account of a procession inside the convent and into the nuns' church to celebrate a new image of the Virgin.

F. Caprara, '"De uno monastero di monache lascivo reformato al ben vivere per el Rosario": Alfonso Lombardi e Parmigianino in S. Margherita', in V. Fortunati (ed.), *Vita artistica nel monastero femminile. Exempla* (Bologna, 2002), p. 166.

13 February [?1633]

I record that on 13 February the holy image of the Queen and Our Virgin Mary of the Rosary was blessed and crowned by the most illustrious Signor Ludovico Malvezzo, who at the time was our vicar, and it was carried in procession all around the convent. Afterwards it was placed on the Altar of the Rosary, in the place which had been prepared for it. The altar was built, decorated and framed in gold by the Most Reverend Lady Maria Placida Barbieri.

Notes

1 See Freedberg (1989), pp. 136–60. Also B. Wisch, 'Key to success: propriety and promotion of miraculous images by Roman confraternities', in E. Thuno and G. Wolf (eds), *The Miraculous Image in the Middle Ages and Renaissance* (Rome, 2004), pp. 161–84.

2 See M. Holmes, 'The elusive origins of the cult of the Annunziata in Florence', in Thuno and Wolf (eds), (2004), pp. 97–121.

3 See: K. J. P. Lowe, 'Secular brides and convent brides: wedding ceremonies in Italy during the Renaissance and Counter-Reformation', in T. Dean and K. J. P. Lowe (eds), *Marriage in Italy 1300–1650* (Cambridge, 1998), pp. 41–65; *Nuns' Chronicles and Convent Culture in Renaissance and Counter-Reformation Italy* (Cambridge, 2003); and also Lowe (2001), for other aspects of life in the *Vergini*.

4 See Rogers and Tinagli (2005), p. 324. On women in confraternities see G. Casagrande, 'Confraternities and lay female *religiosità* in late medieval and Renaissance Umbria', pp. 48–66, and A. Esposito, 'Men and women in Roman confraternities in the fifteenth and sixteenth centuries: roles, functions, expectations', pp. 82–97, both in N. Terpstra (ed.), *The Politics of Ritual Kinship: Confraternities and Social Order in Early Modern Italy* (Cambridge, 1999); E. D. Howe, 'Appropriating space: woman's place in confraternal Life at Santo Spirito in Sassia, Rome', in B. Wisch and D. Cole Ahl (eds), *Confraternities and the Visual Arts in Renaissance Italy* (Cambridge, 2000), pp. 235–58; C. F. Black, *Italian Confraternities in the Sixteenth Century* (Cambridge, 1989).

5 See M. Holmes, 'Ex-votos: materiality, memory, and cult', in M. W. Cole and R. E. Zorach (eds), *The Idol in the Age of Art: Objects, Devotions and the Early Modern World* (Farnham, 2009), pp. 159–81.

6 See F. Mancini, 'Miracoli ed ex voto della SS. Annunziata in Firenze', in L. Sebregondi and R. M. Zaccaria (eds), *Toscana granducale* (Roma, 1996), pp. 180–3.

7 See N. Thomas, 'Alfonsina Orsini de' Medici and the "problem" of a female ruler in early sixteenth-century Florence', *Renaissance Studies*, 14:1 (2000), pp. 70–90, and S. E. Reiss, 'Widow, mother, patron of art: Alfonsina Orsini de' Medici', in Reiss and Wilkins (eds), (2001), pp. 126–57.

8 See chapter 2, text 8.

9 See A. Thomas, *Art and Piety in the Female Religious Communities of Renaissance Italy: Iconography, Space, and the Religious Woman's Perspective* (Cambridge, 2003).

➣ 10 ⬳

PUBLIC DEVOTIONAL PATRONAGE:
PERSONAL AND COLLECTIVE

The suffering of purgatory could be shortened not only by the practices described in the previous chapters, but also by the commissioning of a chapel, an altarpiece or church furnishings, and by providing for Masses for the dead. These would ensure that the deceased would be always be remembered in the prayers of his or her fellow Christians.

A will often specified that a sacred image, or a tabernacle, or a whole funerary chapel with its altarpiece, decoration and appropriate furnishings should be commissioned, and widows would very often be asked to fulfil the wishes of their husbands.[1] Many wills specify that a sum of money should be bequeathed to charitable institutions, while those who belonged to the lower ranks of society would leave whatever money they could for a less expensive offering and memento.

It was the privilege of members of ruling families and of the mercantile and banking elite to be buried in a church, close to saints' relics. A chapel with an altar and its altarpiece, and perhaps a funerary monument as well, with an inscription and coat of arms, was the most impressive way in which the dead could be remembered, and Masses for them would be celebrated there. Patron saints were believed to act as intercessors with the Virgin Mary or Christ, and sometimes they are shown in altarpieces protecting and introducing the donor(s), who may be accompanied by family members.

Not all commissions of religious art for public devotion were dedicated to the dead. This chapter also includes texts which document other kinds of women's patronage, among which are those from women who had dedicated their lives to Christ, or to help others in the name of Christ.

FUNERARY DISPOSITIONS: BEQUESTS FOR THE AFTERLIFE

The voices of women can be heard through extracts from their wills, in which they made provision for specific sums of money to be spent for an altarpiece, or a small tabernacle, or a sumptuous tomb, according to their station in life. In many cases documents are very particular in setting out the wishes of the testatrix, for instance where devotional objects should be placed. As we can see from these examples, some of the wills are very particular about the subject matter of a painting, or even the pose of a statue, while others are not. In some cases we may deduce from the wording of a document that an agreement had been made with a painter, from whom the heirs or the executors later commissioned an altarpiece or a chapel. Bequests of paintings to charitable institutions and requests for a cycle of special masses for the dead were also ways in which the deceased could be remembered.

1. Bequests from ladies of Ferrara
In the first of these extracts the *figura* of the Virgin was almost certainly a painted wood or terracotta sculpture. Many of these figures in fact were dressed and adorned with jewels donated by the faithful. The church of S. Andrea in Ferrara, where the chapel mentioned in this extract was, was destroyed in 1867.

Franceschini (1993), pp. 76, 619.

25 August 1404, Ferrara. Orsola, wife of Filippo da Cavriago.
. . . The said heir must fulfil our commitment to offer a scarlet dress for the statue of the Blessed Virgin Mary which is painted in the church of Sant' Andrea in the Costabili Chapel, and for another scarlet garment for the statue of the son of the Blessed Virgin.
25 May 1463, Crespino. Margherita Guerzi.
. . . Item. It is decreed and ordered that immediately after the death of the said testatrix, a plinth with a capital supporting a small tabernacle with an image of the most Blessed Virgin Mary with her son standing to her right should be built in the village of Villanova Marchesana, on the bank [of the

river] where the waterwheel is, near the house of the Adorni. She wants the son in a graceful posture, and the Virgin Mary to be painted with her right hand on her breast, rather low, turning towards her son standing to her right. She orders that it should be painted in that way and not in another, and wants the said plinth and altar to be suitable for the saying of mass there . . .

2. A chapel frescoed by Piero della Francesca

The frescoes commissioned by the widow Contessina Bartoli (d. 1474) from Piero della Francesca for a chapel in the most important church in Sansepolcro are now lost. Here is an extract from her will and a record of payment for the frescoes.

E. Battisti, *Piero della Francesca*, 2 vols (Milan, 1971), 2, p. 227.

Will of the lady Contessina, widow of the late Lodovico Carsidoni, and daughter of the late Urbano Bartoli from Borgo San Sepolcro.

. . . She asked to be buried in the Badia at Borgo San Sepolcro [now the cathedral of Sansepolcro]. And she left and bequeathed to the sacristy of the said Badia of Borgo fifty florins for the commission and execution of a vestment which is called a cope, made of silk and with the coat of arms of the said testatrix . . .

The said lady Contessina, testatrix, . . . confirmed, approved, ratified and validated the undermentioned bequest made through her son Piersaccone for after her death, as agreed before in the presence of the testatrix, for the paintings and the decoration of a chapel dedicated to the glorious Virgin Mary in the Badia of the said Borgo, fifty florins

12 April 1474. Register of payments to Piero della Francesca Battisti

Master Pietro, son of Benedetto son of Pietro, the painter, is given today 12 April two hundred *lire* from the priors of the Company of Our Lady of the Badia, from the bequest of the lady Contessina, that is the rest of the said bequest for the painting the said Chapel of Our Lady, as it appears in the wills book marked R, fol. 116 *lire* 200 *soldi* 0

3. Andrea del Sarto and an altarpiece for the cathedral of Cortona, 1526

Margherita del Braca Passerini was the mother of Cardinal Silvio Passerini, friend and *datario* of Pope Leo X. In 1526 Margherita became ill, but she regained her health after praying to the Virgin. As thanksgiving, she had a chapel built in the church of Santa Maria dei Servi in Cortona, and commissioned from Andrea del Sarto an altarpiece representing the Assumption of the Virgin, for which she left money in her will. The two kneeling saints in the foreground are linked to Margherita: on the right is St Margaret, the patron of Cortona, who was canonised in 1728, but had been considered a saintly woman since her death. Whether or not a portrait of the donor, the saint conveys her faith and devotion. On the left is St Nicholas, patron saint of Margherita's father and of one of her sons, both called Niccolò. It seems probable that a drawing had been made, which the heirs could consult. The altarpiece (Florence, Galleria Palatina) was put in place in 1528. Here is an extract from Margherita's will.

J. Shearman, *Andrea del Sarto*, 2 vols (Oxford, 1965), p. 400.

28 April 1526
The said testatrix, by the law of bequest, for pious reasons, and for the remission of her sins and the salvation of her soul and of those of her dead [relatives], commanded, wanted and entrusted her heirs to begin and complete an agreement made between her and the Florentine painter Master Andrea [del Sarto], for a panel for the high altar of the church of Santa Maria dei Servi outside the city gate of S. Maria, in the said city [Cortona]. According to the agreement made with Master Andrea over the price of the said panel, one hundred and fifty large gold florins should be spent, and more or less according to the said agreement. She wanted the Assumption of the Most Glorious Virgin Mary to be painted in the same panel, with other figures as may be seen by her heirs . . .

4. An altarpiece in S. Maria Novella, Florence, 1568

The widow Camilla Capponi left instructions in her will of August 1568 for the founding and the decoration of a chapel in the

Dominican church of S. Maria Novella in Florence. The subject of the altarpiece, specified in this text, illustrates the role of the Madonna of the Rosary as intercessor. The commission was given by Camilla's heirs to Giorgio Vasari who, from 1565 to 1572, was working in S. Maria Novella for Cosimo I de' Medici to update the church in line with the recommendations of the Council of Trent. The altarpiece was painted by Vasari's associate Jacopo Zucchi and completed in May 1570. The new altar and altarpiece were placed by Vasari in front of Masaccio's *Trinity* fresco, hiding it completely, but the altarpiece has been moved from its original position, and is now in the Bardi Chapel. The following is an extract from the convent book, giving details of the will.

M. Hall, *Renovation and Counter-Reformation: Vasari and Duke Cosimo in Sta Maria Novella and Sta Croce 1565–1577* (Oxford, 1979), pp. 114–17.

I record that today 25 November 1568, the lady Camilla of good memory, widow of Ser Pietro Arringhetti and daughter of Messer Piero di Recco Capponi, died. In her last will she appointed our Convent of Santa Maria Novella as her universal heir. This was drawn up by Ser Iacopo Nacchi on 4 August 1568 . . .

. . . She asks the convent to build a chapel of dressed stones in one of the bays of the church, to be chosen by the friars, similar to the others which have been built or which will be built, with [an altarpiece representing the Virgin of] the Holy Rosary on panel. She wants a sum of at least 2800 *lire di piccioli* to be spent according to the judgement of the friars and of the convent. This will be done after 18 months, from the time when a sum of 2450 *lire di piccioli* will be credited from her inheritance and her heirs by Benedetto degli Alessandri. In case this is not done, she leaves as her universal heir the Hospital of Santa Maria Nuova, according to her will.

As endowment to the said chapel she leaves a credit at the *Monte* [with the interest] at seven per cent on 266 florins, under the name of the lady Camilla de' Capponi, widow of Paolo Giuntini.

In her will she also endows the said chapel with 70 *lire di piccioli*, which the Company of San Piero Maggiore will pay each year to a student of this convent. This comes from the donation of her Estate of Aiuolo, received some time ago . . .

She leaves this endowment to the convent, requiring them to celebrate a mass for her soul in the said chapel, every morning in perpetuity.

5. Margherita of Austria makes provision for a full-length portrait of herself on her tomb in Piacenza, 1586

Although the last decades of her life had been spent either in the territories of her marital family, the Farnese, in the south of Italy, or in her native Flanders, Margherita wished her tomb to be in Piacenza, where she had spent happy years. The demand that it should be expensive, of bronze, and incorporate a full-length portrait of herself expresses her status as the illegitimate daughter of the Emperor Charles V as well as Duchess of Parma and Piacenza. Margherita died at Ortona a Mare, a small town which she had acquired in 1582. The following is an extract from her will of 3 January 1586. The tomb, which she wished to be finished in three years, was in fact not yet completed in 1621.

Lefèvre (1968), p. 241.

. . . She desires that, when her soul departs from this life to a better one, as she hopes, her body should be buried in the church of S. Sisto in the city of Piacenza, where she wishes and commands that a bronze tomb should be made, with fine workmanship and proportions, raised from the ground, with her effigy at full length, for which not less than 5000 gold *scudi* in gold should be spent. This [tomb] should be completed within three years, and should be placed in front of the Altar of the Holy Sacrament. Wherever she might be at the time of her death, she wishes and commands that her body should be taken to Piacenza, in the church of San Sisto, within a year from the day of her death.

6. Funeral dispositions and prayers for a benefactress of the Zitelle in Venice, 1622

Elisabetta Foppa, from a wealthy Bolognese family, had an altar built in 1610 in the church of the Zitelle in Venice, a charitable institution founded in 1561 to take care of young girls without guardians. Elisabetta gives precise instructions in her will about funerary prayers and masses, and also mentions her gifts to the institution. Her desire to be remembered and to ensure that prayers are said for the salvation of her soul and of her family members is very clear in these extracts from her will.

B. Mazza, 'Committenti e artisti nell'età delle riforme: L'arredo della chiesa di S. Maria della Presentazione', in L. Puppi (ed.), *Le Zitelle: architettura, arte e storia di un'istituzione veneziana* (Venice, 1992), p. 156.

. . . I have first of all to set down the manner of my burial after my beloved Jesus has called me to Him . . . Three masses should be said in the church where my body shall be . . . and two torches should be lit at the Zitelle when my body is taken there, and the girls should sing for me. I want the Lady [Governor of the Zitelle] to give 3 ducats a year to the girls who will sing three masses at my altar each year on the day of burial of our three bodies,[2] and that there will be burning torches at our monument.

I leave to the House of the Zitelle . . . a silver cross with relics . . . which was made before my death for my altar. I want the four bronze candle-holders to be placed on my altar during any solemn festival . . . and the chasubles I have given as a gift and I shall give in the future to be kept in perpetuity and never to be destroyed. I also give to the said House two portraits, of my brother and my sister-in-law, one painted with the Blessed Luigi and the other with St Catherine, which have been placed in the oratory, where every day the girls shall say three *De Profundis* for the souls of the dead of the Foppa family. I declare that I bequeath everything to the House of the Zitelle.

WOMEN COMMISSION FUNERARY CHAPELS AND TOMBS

Artists' contracts, or correspondence with artists, give an account of larger commissions, such as altarpieces or whole chapels. Here we learn about the requirements of the patronesses, who may want their own patron saints, or saints to whom they were especially devoted, to be represented. Specific demands are made about prices, as is the case with Isabella d'Este's commission for a tomb for her friend, the Blessed Osanna Andreasi, or about format and decoration, as we read in the account of Vannozza Cattanei's requirements for her chapel. Some of these documents deal with very practical matters, and are by their nature quite prosaic, but the modern reader should not forget that the requests for certain materials, or discussions about artist's techniques, are always a sign of the patron's desire for something which must be appropriate, and, of course, beautiful, because their commission is a gift to God. Beauty and variety (in the composition, gestures, facial expressions), or the quality of the pigments for a painting, or of the stone for a sculpture or a chapel, the splendour of gold or crystal for a cross or a tabernacle, were always much praised, and should never be ignored by the modern viewer.

7. A chapel for a Dominican tertiary, 1495

Caterina, a Dominican tertiary and a widow from Pesaro, commissions the building and decoration of a funerary chapel dedicated to her patron saint from Almerico di Ventura Fedeli, a painter, architect and ceramist based in Pesaro. The altarpiece is described in detail, and a drawing is provided by the painter.

> P. Berardi, 'Arte e artisti a Pesaro: regesti di documenti di età malatestiana e di età sforzesca', *Pesaro Città e Contà*, 12 (2000), pp. 133–5.

19 December 1495

The virtuous woman Sister Caterina, widow of Geronimo Pietro di Ser Giacomo da Pesaro of the Third Order of the Observants, commissioned and had built in the church of St Dominic in Pesaro a new chapel dedicated to St Catherine of

Siena, who belonged to that order. The said Sister Caterina commissioned the painting and decoration of the said chapel, with columns, friezes and cornices . . . and taking note of this, the venerable father, Friar Mattia di Ponte Corono, Prior of the said convent, and the friars of the order, the venerable Friar Gerolamo Venturini da Pesaro, Syndic and *procuratore* of the said convent . . . made an agreement with Master Almerico, son of the late Master Ventura da Pisa, about the painting of the said chapel . . . Master Almerico solemnly promised the Prior and Syndic to paint and decorate the chapel with an altarpiece on panel to be built at the expense of the said Almerico. In respect of the wood and labour for the altarpiece, all [are to be executed] at the expense of the said Almerico, in respect of the gold and pigments for the said painting of the chapel, the altarpiece, the columns, the friezes and the cornices, decorated and gilded well and adequately with good pigments. The altarpiece should be painted on panel according to a drawing made on paper by the same Almerico, with an image of the glorious Virgin and of the said St Catherine and other figures of saints according to the said drawing, and the said saints should be painted on the said altarpiece according to the Prior . . .

And also to paint the saints and the blessed on the side pilasters of the altarpiece, as he was ordered, that is, four figures in each pilaster at the sides of the altarpiece. And on the predella of the altarpiece he should paint stories from the life of St Catherine. And the panel, pilasters and the other surroundings of the said chapel with everything pertaining to it should be well decorated and painted and coloured with good pigments, according to the reliable opinion of honest men who are knowledgeable about the art of painting, at the expense of the said Almerico, as well as the scaffolding for painting and the gesso to plaster the chapel. And the convent will arrange the plastering of the chapel, and this work for the painting must be done according to the judgement of Almerico. And Almerico promises to begin the painting in the next month of April of the year 1496 and to finish in a year.

8. A famous lady and her burial chapel in S. Maria del Popolo, Rome, 1500

Vannozza Cattanei (1442–1518), mother of Cesare and Lucrezia Borgia, was a woman of considerable means. Apart from substantial financial benefits obtained from Cardinal Roderigo Borgia (later Pope Alexander VI), she owned properties (palaces, houses, shops and inns) in the heart of Rome, and lent money on interest. On 25 February 1500 she obtained from the Augustinian friars of one of the most important churches in Rome, S. Maria del Popolo, the rights to a chapel dedicated to St Lucy next to the main altar, with permission to decorate it with paintings. In 1503 Vannozza, in exchange, left to the friars the palace which Cardinal Borgia had given her many years previously. The contract, drawn up with 'Andrea di Monte Cavallo' and 'Master Giovanni' for a tabernacle and for other work for the chapel, is dated October 1500.

i. The tabernacle

P. Fedele, 'I gioielli di Vannozza ed un'opera del Caradosso', *Archivio della Reale Società Romana di Storia Patria*, 28 (1905), pp. 464–5.

In the name of Our Lord Jesus Christ, amen. All those who shall read this document should be aware that today on 4 October 1500, the lady Vannozza dei Catanei, a Roman citizen, has commissioned a certain work in marble, commonly called a 'tabernacle', from Master Andrea del Monte Cavallo and his associate Master Giovanni di Larigo, stonecutters, to be made similar to the one in the church of San Giacomo degli Spagnoli, to contain the sacred Body of Christ. They have given the drawing of this tabernacle to the lady Vannozza, and have promised to make it [the new tabernacle] in the same way as the other tabernacle, except that, instead of a figure of Christ above the dome there will be a beautiful marble cross, and instead of the two figures of the apostles flanking the dome, there will be two holders for candles. The rest will be worked as from the drawing shown and given to the lady Vannozza, with two small doors. A chalice carved in marble will be on the upper [part] while the lower one will hold the sacrament. On both sides there will be a carved motif or a candle-holder of the right proportions, as a decoration of the tabernacle.

They have also promised to make two beautiful small columns or a balustrade to support the altar table, and to carve the said altar, which the lady Vannozza will pay for, or not, should it not be to her taste.

They will also make a coat of arms in marble, of which they have had a drawing, measuring at least two hands, to be placed above the arch of the chapel in which the tabernacle and the altar will be housed. They have also promised to place the altar and tabernacle, with the coat of arms and the small columns, in her chapel in the church of Santa Maria del Popolo in Rome, and fix them at their expense, but not to the wall which will be built behind the altar. These masters have promised the lady Vannozza to make and put into place these works for forty-three ducats, of which they have received in their own hand ten ducats, at 10 *carlini* per ducat, as a deposit and part payment, since they have agreed that this payment will be made in ducats of *carlini*. The lady Vannozza will pay the rest during the execution of these works, which they have promised to finish by the next month of January without fail. The work will be done in fine, new white marble, appropriately adorned with friezes and other ornaments according to the drawing of the said tabernacle. They have wanted me, Friar Vinicio da Vercelli, friar in Santa Maria del Popolo in Rome, to write this document as a witness, at the presence of Friar Pacifico da Garlasco, Pavia, and of Rinaldo da Pavia, servant of the lady Vannozza, on the day and month stated above.

ii. The inscription

The Carrara marble slab (190x118 cm) with an inscription dedicated to Vannozza Cattanei was probably removed from her chapel in 1658, during the restructuring work commissioned by Pope Alexander VII Chigi. It is now under the porch of the church of S. Marco in Rome.

A. Ferrua, 'Ritrovamento dell'epitaffio di Vannozza Cattaneo [*sic*]', *Archivio della Società Romana di Storia Patria*, 71 (1948), p. 140.

To Vannozza Cattanei, who has been raised to nobility by her children, Cesar of Valence, Juan of Gandia, Jofred of Squillace and Lucrezia of Ferrara. She is distinguished for her probity, noted for her piety, equal in years and wisdom, and gained great merit [for what she did] for the Lateran Hospital. Erected by Geronimo Pico, fiduciary-commissioner and executor of her will. She lived seventy-six years, four months and thirteen days. She died in the year 1518, on 26 November.

9. A tomb for Osanna Andreasi, 1505

Osanna Andreasi (1449–1505), an aristocratic lady from Mantua, was a Dominican tertiary and a much-admired pious woman. She had been a close friend of Isabella d'Este since the latter arrived in Mantua in 1490. Her cult flourished soon after her death, but she was officially proclaimed 'blessed' only in 1694.

When Andreasi died in June 1505, Isabella commissioned a free-standing tomb and funerary monument for her in the church of S. Domenico. However, she did not have much money available. The sculptor Gian Cristoforo Romano, whom Isabella knew well and who was in Milan at the time, was asked to design an elegant but not expensive tomb, with her contribution modestly indicated. The following letters document the progress of the commission. The tomb was built during the same year.

A. Venturi, 'Gian Cristoforo Romano', *Archivio Storico dell'Arte*, 1 (1888), pp. 113–16.

Isabella d'Este, from Mantua, to Gian Cristoforo Romano, in Milan, 12 July 1505

We want to commission a tomb for the body of the Blessed Sister Osanna who died recently, and we want it to be beautiful. It should be placed in a small chapel, the measurements and style of which will be communicated to you by the previous Father Prior of St Dominic here in Mantua, who is coming [to Milan], and has the measurements. Together with him, you will make a drawing of the tomb, which you will then send to me. You will let me know what the price would be, so that we shall send you some money. You could then make the tomb in Milan, where you will be able to find the stones more easily. If you think that you may want to use the jaspers, which we had cut for the door, we shall send them to you. We await your answer.

Gian Cristoforo Romano, from Milan, to Isabella d'Este, 30 July 1505
Most Illustrious and Excellent Mistress,
I have received your letter about the tomb for the Blessed Osanna, and I have spoken with the Prior and have also written to him. I understand that you wish to honour the said blessed woman, but now I need to understand how much Your Ladyship wants to spend on the tomb. As soon as I know, I will make a drawing appropriate to the price. I have been thinking about Your Ladyship's desire to have something dignified while spending as little as possible. I think that it is not possible to make a tomb supported by four columns with their capitals, with a whole sarcophagus where the body can be placed, with its lid, in such a way that everything is well done, and without [adding any] reliefs, for less than one hundred and fifty ducats. The transport will not be expensive, since it is for a church. I therefore would like Your Ladyship to let me know what she wants to do, so that I can organise everything before I leave for Rome – something I have to do in a hurry as I was called by His Holiness the Pope [Julius II]. I do not want to leave, however, before I have assured Your Highness that she will be satisfied. I again recommend myself to you. I am leaving in 2 hours together with Aquila [the physician Sebastiano dell'Aquila] to go to Mortara to see the lady Margherita Cantelma [one of Isabella's friends] who is unwell with a fever. As soon as I see that she is getting better I shall come back to Milan. In the meantime Your Ladyship will let me know everything. About the jaspers, I shall endeavour to use them in such a way that the work will be well done.

Gian Cristoforo Romano to Isabella d'Este, 14 August 1505
Most Illustrious Mistress, I have read what Your Ladyship has written, and I gladly inform you that the four columns for the tomb will be of a type of stone which will be judged

to be of great value, as they are beautiful. In a few days I shall send you a piece [of stone] to show Your Ladyship, together with the drawing. In the meantime I continue to look for other stones, and I shall continue to do so. God willing, it will be finished by the Spring . . .

Gian Cristoforo Romano to Isabella d'Este, 17 September 1505
I am sending you, with [the goldsmith] Paradosso, who is bringing the vase, the drawing of the tomb of the blessed Osanna. It is done so that you can understand both its front and its side, so that you can see it from the front, from the side and also from the other end. The back and the other side will be the same. I have planned it in such a way, that I think it will look very good when finished. And since Your Ladyship has left me free to design it, I have devised something which looks sumptuous and modest, while spending much less than we thought possible: we shall not use the four columns which were one hundred ducats each even if they were half as large as these. Therefore Your Ladyship will see that this is a good thing, and Paradosso will tell you about the agreement between him, me and Marchesino [Stanga, Ludovico il Moro's secretary]. When this work is finished, it will look as if it cost twice as much.
Half of the other stones [I have used] will be of a good black kind, and the other half will be white marble, which will look like Carrara marble, and will be worked so that it shines like silver. Your Ladyship should be reassured about this. I ask Your Ladyship to provide me with the money by the time I have indicated in the letter, so that he [Paradosso] and his workers can finish it by the time the Prior of Rome wants to leave from here and go to Mantua to see the tomb assembled, and place the body of the blessed Osanna inside it with his own hands. And the Father [Padre Gerolamo da Genova] and the Father *Lettore* [Fra Francesco da Ferrara], and all the other fathers who have seen this design, were so pleased with it, that nothing else could have brought them more consolation, and Your Ladyship will gain much in praise and merit.
I have prepared a place for the coat of arms of Your Ladyship, which will be in a modest position, and another

for an inscription on the other side with the name of Your Ladyship. This is done so that the work can be made richer in time: the five candle-holders can eventually be substituted by five figures in the round, in marble or bronze.

I have done this for the faith I have in God and in Your Ladyship, rather than for myself. If I wanted to make another tomb, I would not be able to make it even if I spent 50 ducats more. This is because of the two columns I used, which I found already cut for [Ludovico il] Moro, and got them almost as a present.

Your Ladyship will get a copy of the document, and will find everything there. If there is something Your Ladyship does not like, please let me know, and forgive me: I could not do this better because Paradosso came here. I beg Your Ladyship to let me know if you are satisfied, as I could not be happier. When I am in the presence of His Holiness, I shall introduce myself as a servant of Your Ladyship, trying to bring honour to you in everything.

WOMEN COMMISSION ALTARPIECES

10. A Franciscan tertiary and an altarpiece in Siena Cathedral
G. de Nicola, 'Sassetta between 1423 and 1433', *Burlington Magazine*, 23 (1913), p. 278.

25 March 1430
The Lady Ludovica, a Franciscan tertiary, daughter of the late Francesco di Vanni Bertini from Siena, and wife of the estimable knight the Lord Turino di Matteo, once a member of the Opera of Siena Cathedral, commissions from Master Stefano di Giovanni di Consolo [Sassetta] an altarpiece for the chapel of St Boniface in the cathedral, near the door called 'del Perdono'. He must finish it in one year . . . [The price for the altarpiece was 180 florins.]

11. The Three Magi for the high altar of S. Elena in Castello, Venice, 1525–26
This contract, dated 3 July 1525, for a commission by the widow of a member of the Venetian nobility, stipulates that the paint-

ing, for the high altar of S. Elena in Castello, should be finished by the following Easter. The subject is the Adoration of the Magi, but includes St Helena in a prominent position, adoring the Christ Child. It is now in the Pinacoteca di Brera, Milan.

F. Stefani, 'L'adorazione dei Magi di Palma Vecchio', *Archivio Veneto*, 1 (1871), pp. 167–8.

The painter Master Giacomo Palma [Palma Vecchio], a man of sound judgement, son of the late Ser Antonio, who is present here . . . promises to the lady Orsa, widow of the magnificent lord Simeone Malipiero, also present here and accepting the promise, to paint an altarpiece to be placed on the high altar of the church of the venerable brothers of the order of St Benedict of the Congregation of Monte Oliveto, Santa Elena in Venice. This altarpiece is to be painted with the story of the Three Magi, with everything pertinent and necessary to that story. The said Master Giacomo promises to paint the altarpiece with fine and excellent pigments. The altarpiece must be finished, unless there is a just reason, for the next feast of the Resurrection of Our Lord Jesus Christ, all at his expense, according to what is necessary for the picture. As payment for Master Giacomo, the lady Orsa promises to pay and give to Master Giacomo, here present, who is in agreement, a hundred ducats, at the rate of six *lire* and four *soldi* for each ducat. And the Venerable Friar Luca di Rodrigio, at this time Prior of the monastery of Santa Elena, also present, promises to pay Master Giacomo ten ducats at the same rate as above.

12. The convent of S. Orsola, Mantua, 1604–13
In 1604, after the death of her husband Alfonso II d'Este, Margherita Gonzaga left Ferrara to return to Mantua. She begun to build the convent of S. Orsola, where she went to live together with the ladies of her court. The church of S. Orsola was decorated with other commissions from the Marchioness, among then a number of altarpieces by the court painter Domenico Fetti and by his sister Lucrina, who was a nun in the same convent.

In 1614 Margherita commissioned an altarpiece from Ludovico Carracci, *The Martyrdom of St Ursula*. Here Carracci writes to the Marchioness asking for payment for his as yet unfinished altar-piece, which was finally delivered in 1616. Carracci was paid 250 *scudi*.

G. Perini (ed.), *Gli scritti dei Carracci* (Bologna, 1990), p. 12.

Last year Your Most Serene Highness deigned to honour me, through Father Don Silvio, by commissioning from me a large altarpiece with the Martyrdom of St Ursula. I embraced that work with as much dedication as possible, and made the large canvas at my expense, all in one piece, and the stretcher. I worked on the painting without ever asking for money, even if painters are always assisted with sums paid in advance.

Now I beg Your Most Serene Highness to order that I should be assisted with a sum of money of whatever amount you please, so that I can meet my needs. I will always feel grateful to Your Serene Highness, and I shall finish the painting to perfection. The bearer of this letter, Father Don Francesco Maria, will explain everything. I wish Your Serene Highness every good from God, and I greet you with profound respect.

CONVENTS: NUNS' PATRONAGE

It is quite clear from the texts in this section that, even if they spent their lives within the confines of religious houses, nuns were aware of the work of well-known artists. Abbesses and nuns often belonged to the highest ranks of society, and they relied on their ties of friendship and kinship in order to hear about works of art and to commission new ones. However, they often had to use agents in order to find artists, or to take care of practical matters connected with the commission. The pleasure, pride and devotion they felt for their sacred images, whether ordered by themselves or received as gifts, are evident from many of their letters and from convent documents.[3]

13. Neri di Bicci and a tabernacle for the Host for the convent of Santa Monica, Florence, 1460–61
In his account book Neri di Bicci gives details of many commissions from nuns. Here he notes a commission for a tabernacle

for the small church of Santa Monica, for which the nuns and the Augustinian friars of the nearby church of Santo Spirito act together.

Neri di Bicci, *Le Ricordanze (1453–1475)*, ed. A. Santi (Florence, 1976), p. 162.

Tuesday 31 March 1461
Tabernacle for the Body of Christ
   I record that on that day I delivered to Master Francesco Zoppo, friar in Santo Spirito in Florence, and to the nuns of Santa Monica in Florence, a round tabernacle for the Body of Christ, of about 1 and ⅞ *braccio*, all gilded, painted with 4 or 5 little angels and many other things. It is painted blue with gold stars inside. Everything is well decorated and finished, in wood, gold, blue and everything else needed, all at my expense. For this 8 large florins are due to me. Giovanni, who works for me, took it.
   It has been recorded in Book D fol. 78, 7 large florins.
   Till this 23 April 1461 7 large florins have been given to me in various instalments. Fra Lorenzo, the superior of Santo Spirito, brought them, and they are for the rest of the work.

14. Two nuns in the convent of the Poor Clares of S. Maria di Monteluce, Perugia, commission a tabernacle, together with their family.[4]

In 1476 Iacopa Baldini degli Alfani, mother of two nuns in the convent, Sister Eufrasia and Sister Battista, left 40 florins to be used for a chapel to be built in the sacristy of the convent's church. Two years later, Iacopa gave her daughters 30 florins to commission a chalice or church vestments, also for the sacristy, while her two sons added 350 florins to their mother's donation, and commissioned a tabernacle with the family's coat of arms. After the death of her sister Eufrasia, Battista became Abbess. She then bought a crucifix and a painted curtain for the tabernacle which has been attributed to Francesco di Simone Ferrucci. The following is an extract from the 'Memoriale di Monteluce', the convent chronicle written by Battista degli Alfani.

Battista degli Alfani, *Memoriale di Monteluce cronaca del Mona-stero delle Clarisse di Perugia*, ed. A. Briganti (Perugia, 1983), p. 39.

In the said year, in the month of March, the master who had worked on the tabernacle beautifully carved in marble, made to contain the Sacrament of the Body of Christ, came from Florence to bring the said work. The tabernacle can be seen in the public part of the church. The brothers of Sister Eufrasia and Sister Battista commissioned it with the money that their mother had left to the convent, so that it should be spent on something for the church, according to what her daughters wanted. They, following their devotion, decided that this was what they wanted. They asked their brothers to have it made as they wished and by whom they wished. And they did just that. Since it cost more than what had been left, the said brothers added whatever money was needed.

15. A terracotta *Annunciation* for a Sienese convent, 1521
The Mantellate nuns of the convent of the Paradiso in Siena, unhappy with the results of their commission, order a sculptor to remake a sculpture of the Annunciation for their church. The document shows the use of a male intermediary to deal with legal and financial negotiations with artists. Terracotta statues like this one were often painted or dressed with real clothes.

S. Borghesi and L. Banchi (eds), *Nuovi documenti per la storia dell'arte senese* (Siena, 1898), pp. 424–5.

11 July 1521. It is recorded that the Mantellate nuns of the Paradiso, and Conte Bonsignori on their behalf, some time ago commissioned Master Lorenzo di Mariano, the stone-cutter, to execute a Virgin Annunciate and Angel in terra-cotta. When he had made it, and it was not what they had wanted, he was happy to take it back, agreeing that the said nuns might keep it as a pledge in guarantee of sixty-three *lire*, that is L 63, which the said Master Lorenzo had received for making it. And if it is sold for more than sixty-three *lire*, Master Lorenzo should keep [the difference].

And again they have commissioned him to make two

heads with the arms and the trunk, one-eighth from the waist down, or more as he sees fit, with the arms, made of stucco, that is, a Virgin Annunciate with the face like that which he had made in terracotta, and the head should be a young woman, and the other head should be an angel, like the one he had made. The arms should be made in such a way so that it could be easily dressed. All this [is to be made] at his expense, within two months, for the price of twelve *lire*, that is six *lire* each. And if he gives them to us within one month, he should have eighteen *lire*, that is nine *lire* each. He must make the said heads, trunks and arms solid and not hollow, and in one hand of the Virgin Annunciate he should make a small box, half-open, as would a very good master.

16. A *Lamentation* by Andrea del Sarto for the convent of S. Pietro in Luco, 1524

In 1524, during an outbreak of the plague in Florence, Andrea del Sarto, together with his family and an assistant, Raffaello, had taken refuge in the convent of S. Pietro in Luco in the Mugello, north of Florence. During this period, the Abbess of the convent, Caterina della Casa, commissioned an altarpiece from him for the high altar of the church. The *Lamentation*, with its silent and composed figures intent on contemplating the dead body of Christ and a chalice covered by a paten with the Host, invites the viewer to meditate over Christ's sacrifice and on the mystery of the transubstantiation which takes place during the Mass. Vasari wrote in his 'Life of Andrea del Sarto' that this altarpiece had made the convent famous.[5]

M. Pinelli, '"Di bei Paramenti, di Preziose Argenterie e di molto altro". Appunti per la storia del patrimonio d'arte del Monastero di S. Pietro a Luco', in V. Baldacci (ed.), *'Le Contesse di Luco'. Il monastero Camaldolese femminile di San Pietro a Luco di Mugello: la storia, la fabbrica, l'arte* (Azzano S. Paolo, 2004), p. 123 n. 23.

On 11 October 1524, I, Andrea del Sarto, have received eighty large gold florins for the altarpiece of the high altar and for a lunette with the Visitation, from the Abbess of [the convent of] Luco, the Florentine lady Caterina della Casa, and in faith I have written this in my own hand, on the said day and year.

And I, Raffaello, his assistant, on 6 October 1527 have received from the said Abbess ten gold *scudi* for the execution of the altarpiece by Andrea del Sarto, and in faith I have written this by my own hand.

17. A *Last Supper* for the convent of the Murate, Florence, 1546

In 1546 the Countess of Pitigliano, Faustina Vitelli, a relative of Pope Paul III Farnese, became a professed nun in the convent of the Murate in Florence. On this occasion she donated a *Last Supper* by Giorgio Vasari for the refectory of the convent. The reception of the picture is described by Sister Giustina Niccolini in the following extract from her notes written in 1597.

E. Viviani della Robbia, 'Note e notizie sul Cenacolo del Vasari pel Monastero delle Murate di Fiorenza', in *Studi Vasariani*, Atti del Convegno (Florence, 1952), pp. 222.[6]

In 1546, Sister Faustina, daughter of Vitello Vitelli, for her profession, gave to the Convent the *Last Supper* which today we keep in our refectory, painted by the hand of the excellent painter Master Giorgio [Vasari] from Arezzo, one of the most famous and renowned painters who were in this city [Florence] at that time. This work of his has been considered very beautiful, and as good as any other in Florence, not only by us, but also by all knowledgeable and expert people who have seen it. Everybody thought that it was worth three hundred *scudi*, but we paid only one hundred and thirty four. This seems incredible, as it is such a beautiful work. All the Mothers liked it very much, and they welcomed it gladly, since they had wanted it for a long time because they wished to be reminded, in their refectory, of the Sacramental Supper of Our Lord and his Holy Apostles.

18. The Bergamini Chapel in the church of S. Maurizio (Monastero Maggiore), Milan, 1555

This document records the commission for the decoration of a chapel dedicated to the Resurrection, belonging to the Bergamini family. The agreement with the painters, Giovan Pietro and Aurelio Luini, sons of the more famous Bernardino, was not made by the heirs of Countess Bona Bergamini, but by the Abbess of the convent, Gerolama Brivio. During the 1560s, the Abbess was very active in promoting work in the convent's church.

I. Rossi, *La chiesa di San Maurizio in Milano. Il Monastero Maggiore e le sue due torri* (Milan, 1914), p. 77.

For the bequest from Countess Bergamini:
Agreement between the Abbess Gerolama Brivio and the brothers Giovan Pietro and Aurelio Luini, written by the two brothers, 6 May 1555.

An agreement was made with the Reverend Mother the Abbess . . . to paint the chapel of Countess Bergamini of happy memory in the public part of the church. From the architrave downwards, and outside, there should be two sibyls, and under the vault a dove with its gold rays, made of gold, and the architrave of the vault should also be gilded. On the wall above the altar there should be a Resurrection of Christ, and three thieves [*sic*] at the tomb. On one side, the Magdalen finds Our Lord dressed as a gardener, and on the other side Our Lord dressed as a pilgrim with the two apostles on the way to Emmaus. The pilasters should be decorated with flowers and festoons or other suitable things. The price for this work is . . . [sixty gold *scudi*] for both of us Luini brothers.

19. Paintings by Veronese for the nuns of St Catherine, Venice, 1575

A passage in Ridolfi's 'Vita di Paolo Caliari Veronese Pittore' outlines the artist's religious commissions for nunneries in Venice. The *Mystic Marriage of St Catherine*, described in the first extract, is now in the Accademia, Venice (**figure 11**). In the second extract Ridolfi makes fun of the ignorance of the nuns, who do not understand the 'good principles of art', and instead admire pictures which are full of details.

Carlo Ridolfi, *Le meraviglie dell'arte* [Venice, 1648], ed. D. von Hadeln, 2 vols (Berlin, 1914–24), 1, pp. 328–9.

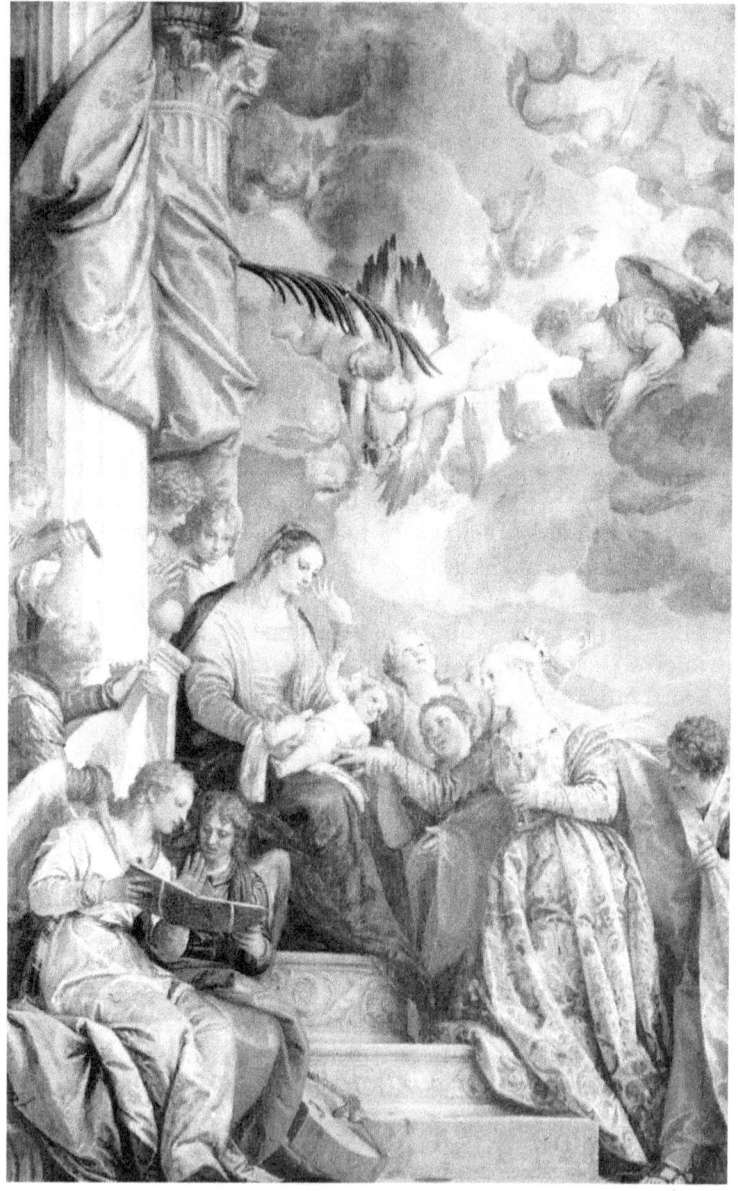

11. Paolo Veronese, *Mystic Marriage of St Catherine*, c. 1565
(Venice, Accademia).

i. In the [convent of] the nuns of St Catherine, on the high altar, he painted that holy princess [St Catherine of Alexandria] . . . swept away in a divine ecstasy, marrying the King of the Universe, who places a ring on her finger as a symbol of their eternal union. Instead of courtiers there are angels dressed with precious garments decorated with gold and embroideries made by a celestial Arachne. Some of them play the most suave music with lutes and lyres, to make the nuptials even happier. There is not a part of that truly wonderful work which is not adorned with beautiful shapes and pleasing colours. The eye, enraptured by such pleasant sights, experiences an example of the celestial beatitude and special delights which Paolo's brush has produced.

ii. He painted for some nuns a medium-sized picture representing Paradise. Here, following the good principles of art, he painted those figures which are further away with less detail and with subdued colours, contrasting with the strength and beauty of the figures which are closer. Since the nuns' eyes could not make out these indistinct figures, nor his customary blue, green and red, and could not distinguish single strands of hair or eyelashes, they were not satisfied. Then a certain Flemish [painter] arrived at the convent with his small pictures, all with gold and pretty colours, with which the nuns fell in love, and so they blamed their misfortune not to have met such a painter for their picture of Paradise. They snatched his pictures from each other's hands, and looked at them as women do, and one would say to another 'You see, sister, how well these eyes are painted, and how beautiful this blond hair is?' Another would praise the coral-like lips, yet another the beauty of the colours, and they would vie with each other in their praises. Therefore the Northerner understood how little they knew, and so he offered to exchange the work of Paolo for one painted by himself, at a price, promising colours taken from the mines of heaven. And the nuns, thinking that this was a good bargain, exchanged their gem for a piece of crystal. And the cunning painter, taking away the [Veronese] painting, despite the artist still being alive, sold it for four hundred *scudi*.

20. Payments for the organ shutters for a Venetian convent, S. Maria della Celestia, 1618

This commission for an important Cistercian convent in Venice, now demolished, was an example of the common Venetian art form of painted organ shutters.

Lanfranchi Strina (ed.), p. 5.

4 November. I receive from the most illustrious lady, Sister Angela Morosini, chamberlain of the convent of the Celestia, as an account for the work on the organ shutters of the said church, that is, a Virgin Annunciate, a St John the Evangelist and a St Alvise, twenty ducats *lire* 65 *soldi* 12

3 December. I receive from Signor Vincenzo dei Busi, on behalf of the most illustrious lady mentioned above, and for the above work, eight *scudi* at the rate of eight *lire* and four *soldi* each, that is *lire* 65 *soldi* 12

9 December. I receive from the said Mother, the lady Sister Angela, 20 ducats *lire* 58 *soldi* 8

21. A marble tabernacle for the convent of S. Verdiana, Florence, 1624

Sister Lucrezia de' Doffi, a nun in the Vallombrosan convent of S. Verdiana in Florence, had commissioned the main altarpiece for the church in 1618 from the Sienese painter Pietro Sorri. She used the income from her own estate for another commission: a tabernacle, now lost, decorated with reliefs with Old Testament stories.

M. Sframeli, 'Tre pittori e un architetto per l'altare maggiore di Santa Verdiana a Firenze', *Paragone Arte*, 45 (1994), p. 176 n. 10.

A tabernacle for the church. I record that during the month of January 1624 the tabernacle was finished and placed on the altar. According to the judgement of Michelangelo Buonarroti [il Giovane], a Florentine gentleman who has expert knowledge of *disegno*, and of other architects and knowledgeable men, it is held to be an object of rare quality both for its *invenzione*, derived from the ancient writings and adapted to the Holy Sacrament, and for its design and workmanship. The director of works was Fabrizio Boschi, the painter and architect, a man of great intellect. It was carved by Master Felice Gamberai, and gilded by Master Francesco Lucherini, all men of remarkable skill in their craft. The price of the whole work was two hundred and sixty-eight ducats in coins, including the ironwork, the stone-cutting and its cover made of striped cloth (*drappo vergato*). This money comes from the income of Sister Lucrezia Doffi, our nun, who, having always felt a generous devotion towards the blessed God and her convent, and having commissioned the whole of the apse chapel out of her own income, wanted to complete her work with the said tabernacle, in honour of the Most Holy Sacrament, and for the help and salvation of her soul.

Notes

1 On the question of memory, and funerary monuments commissioned for men, see A. Butterfield, 'Monument and memory in early Renaissance Florence', in G. Ciappelli and P. L. Rubin (eds), *Art, Memory and Family in Renaissance Florence* (Cambridge, 2000), pp. 135–60; also C. E. King, *Renaissance Women Patrons: Wives and Widows in Italy c. 13300–1550* (Manchester, 1998), chapter 5.

2 Elisabetta Foppa's brother and another member of her family were buried together.

3 See K. J. P. Lowe, 'Nuns and choice: artistic decision-making in Medicean Florence', in E. Marchand and A. Wright (eds), *With or without the Medici: Studies in Tuscan Art and Patronage 1434–1530* (Aldershot, 1998), pp. 129–53.

4 On the Poor Clares of Monteluce, see Wood (1996), pp. 103–12. Battista Alfani also commissioned Raphael's *Coronation*. See Wood (1996), p. 188, with bibliography.

5 Vasari Milanesi (ed). (1906), 5, p. 32.

6 Cited also by P. Barocchi, *Vasari pittore* (Milan, 1964), p. 130.

PART IV

FEMALE ARTISTS, CRAFTSWOMEN AND WRITERS

∗ 11 ∗

FEMALE ARTISTS AND
CRAFTSWOMEN

Research over recent decades has made possible a more accurate
sense of women artists, their contemporary cultural milieux, and
patronage and reception during their lifetime. Little is documented
on women painters living before the sixteenth century, though
they may have existed, but several women painters, sculptors,
engravers and embroiderers began to attract attention from that
time onwards. Their gender might in part have helped their success: their rarity value sometimes attracted the attention of patrons
and collectors.[1] However, it also created fundamental problems for
them in getting a training and making a career. Women were not
allowed to do their apprenticeship in a painter's or sculptor's workshop where they would have studied anatomy and learnt to draw
the human figure – these were crucial for 'history painting', the
artistic genre which had the most prestige. This is why they often
specialised in portraiture, or in the newly fashionable still lifes,
and why the figures of a painter like Plautilla Nelli were criticised.
Female artists often had a father or a brother who was their teacher
and in whose studio they might later work, since they could not
join guilds. Convents were also environments in which girls might
receive training, illuminating manuscripts and probably also painting small-scale devotional pictures. Uccello's daughter Antonia
(1456–91), 'who knew how to draw' according to Vasari, was
taught by her father, who then placed her in a Carmelite convent
presumably so that she could work in a place where her reputation
would be strictly guarded.[2] The need to preserve their reputations
for respectability meant that the continuing support of fathers,
brothers or husbands was very important for women's careers, as
with Artemisia Gentileschi and Lavinia Fontana, or, alternatively,

the protection of a court position, as with Sofonisba Anguissola and Giovanna Garzoni, or the refuge of a convent, as with Lucrina Fetti.

Another group of texts examine the work of craftswomen who sewed, embroidered, and made lace. While most professional dressmakers and embroiderers were in fact men, these crafts had been exercised for centuries by women for their own use or to earn a living, as well as by ladies as an accomplishment. Many aristocratic ladies were well known for their expertise, which was praised as a demonstration of their courtly virtues and achievements. For many women, however, needlework and embroidery were means of earning a living. It seems that some female embroiderers attained a professional status in certain cities, even joining relevant guilds like men. Some succeeded in gaining employment at court, but a much larger number of them worked in workshops which flourished throughout the later sixteenth and seventeenth centuries, as fashion demanded more and more lace to be worn by both men and women. At the end of the sixteenth century in Venice the Dogaressa Morosina Morosini, wife of Doge Marino Grimani, set up a workshop on the island of Burano with one hundred and thirty lacemakers, who worked for the Dogaressa's own wardrobe and for that of important ladies, and also to make special gifts which the Dogaressa sent throughout Europe. She also established a committee to promote lacemaking among the patrician and other women of Venice. Many women reached fame through their craft, and became well known throughout Italy.

THE *VIRTUOSA*: BIOGRAPHIES AND EULOGIES

Renaissance biographies provided information about female artists' lives, but followed certain conventions appropriate to the status and gender of their subjects. When discussing women artists, writers felt a need to stress that they were not threatening or monstrous figures, but possessed virtues proper to women, such as grace, modesty and nobility of behaviour as well as beauty. In addition, they were also gifted with an exceptional skill. They describe good daughters, loyal to their families, and nuns devoutly working for the glory of God.

1. A famous and virtuous lady, 1585

Amongst the glories of the city of Cremona, Campo includes a short biography of Sofonisba Anguissola, highlighting both her skill and fame as a painter and the nobility of her Spanish patrons and the respectability of her life as a married woman. The biographer leaves out the more adventurous aspects of the life of Sofonisba who, after the death of her first husband, left Sicily in 1578 and met her second husband during her journey towards northern Italy, marrying him in Livorno in 1579, against the wills of her brother, of the King of Spain and of Francesco I de' Medici.

Antonio Campo, *Cremona fidelissima città* (Cremona, 1585), p. 50.

. . . Sofonisba, most excellent in painting, has been so successful that her works equal those by any other famous painters. Because of her marvellous skill, she was called to the court of the Catholic King Philip, as court painter to Queen Isabella, who was very fond of Sofonisba both for the excellence of her paintings, and for the many other noble qualities she possesses. The king married her to a noble Sicilian baron and gave her a lifetime annuity of a thousand *scudi*, as well as many gifts. After the death of her husband, she married a gentleman from Genoa, and lives now in that most noble city with much honour and with the greatest reputation because she is not only famous, but is admired by the first ladies of that city for her rare virtues.

2. Lavinia Fontana and the ladies of Bologna

The series of biographies of Bolognese painters, *Felsina Pittrice*, by Carlo Cesare Malvasia [1678] includes Lavinia Fontana (1552–1614). Malvasia describes her in this extract as being feted by her female patrons in Bologna. Lavinia was certainly helped by her father, the successful painter Prospero Fontana, and by the very stimulating cultural milieu in which his family lived. As well as learning to paint, she received an excellent education which certainly served her well in her relationships with her patrons.[3]

Carlo Cesare Malvasia, *Vite dei Pittori Bolognesi*, ed. M. Brascaglie (Bologna, 1971), p. 146.

All ladies in the city competed to have her spend time with them, treating her with much kindness, and demonstrating their affection and respect for her. They considered themselves fortunate to be seen in the street and at gatherings in the company of that talented young woman. They desired nothing more than to be portrayed by her, rewarding her with higher payments than Van Dyck or Justus [Sustermans]. So many favours never made the wise young woman conceited, and the more she was praised, the more she felt humble, so that she was favoured still more and treated with affection.

3. Painting nuns in a Florentine convent

Fra Serafino Razzi wrote about the nun–painters in the convent of St Catherine of Siena in Florence, whose work he knew very well as he was the brother of one of them. Here are extracts on Sister Plautilla Nelli (1523–87) and Sister Maria Razzi. The writer pinpoints a weakness in Nelli's painting which Vasari had previously stressed, arising from her scarce knowledge of anatomy. Nothing is known about her training, but Vasari wrote that she could borrow drawings by Fra Bartolomeo and his workshop from the friars of the nearby convent of San Marco, which she very probably copied.

Fra Serafino Razzi, *Istoria de gli Huomini illustri, così nelle prelature, come nelle Dottrine, del sacro ordine de gli Predicatori* (Lucca, 1596), pp. 369–72.

Sister Plautilla Nelli, a nun in the convent of St Catherine of Siena in Florence, not only lived such a good and chaste life that she shone above all other Sisters in that convent, but has been gifted by our Lord God with a skill superior to ordinary women. In fact, while never being instructed in the skill of painting, she has produced works which have astonished the greatest among the practitioners of this art in her city of Florence. In the church of her convent there are two panels by her hand, and the one representing the Three Magi has been most praised. There are other paintings by her in San Domenico in Perugia and in other places . . . In the cathedral of Florence is a predella with stories from the life of San Zenobius, bishop of the city, and skilfully painted. She has also painted a very great number of miniatures, both in Florence and elsewhere. It must be said that her best works are those which she has copied from others, as can be clearly seen in a picture of the Nativity of Our Lord in the room of their Father Confessor. This has been painted from a picture made by Bronzino for Messer Filippo Salviati. In her paintings the best parts are the faces and features of women, which she was able to see around her. She died as an old woman in 1587, a most devout nun, after being Prioress of her convent many times.

[. . ..]

Sister Maria Angelica Razzi, sister of the writer of this chronicle, who is also in the said convent, works on similar terracotta figures, that is angels, Our Lady and other saints. In the Chapel of the Rosary in Perugia is a figure of Our Lady, seated, with her son asleep on her lap. It has been copied from an image which, till last century, was carried in procession in Florence with much veneration. In the sacristy of the relics in San Marco, in Florence, there is also another figure made by her. In this year 1587 she is [still] alive. May Our Lord bless her.

4. A poem for Fede Galizia, 1609

Fede Galizia (1578–1630) was very probably trained by her father, the miniature painter Nunzio Galizi. She painted portraits, altarpieces, mythological pictures, and a large number of still lifes, a genre which became very popular from the late sixteenth century. This celebratory poem by Cesare Rinaldi (1559–1636) plays on Galizia's powers of observation and her mastery of painting skills. Rinaldi introduces a tension between the act of painting a portrait and that of looking at the male sitter – an interesting observation on 'the female gaze'. The poet also makes a pun about the painter's name 'Fede', 'Faith'.

Rime del Signor Cesare Rinaldi Bolognese (Venice, 1609), p. 228.

Radiant Faith-ful painter,
if sometimes, portraying him,

you gaze at a wild and hopeless lover,
your hand and eyes have different tasks.
One, with learned skill, gives him breath.
They, with beautiful rays burning,
steal his soul and senses,
so that in one moment, alas,
he lives on canvas, while he turns to stone.

5. Lucrina Fetti (fl. c. 1614–51), a nun in Mantua

Domenico Fetti arrived in Mantua as court painter to the Gonzaga in 1614, accompanied by his brothers and sisters.

His sister Giustina entered the convent of S. Orsola, which had been founded in 1599 by the Duchess of Ferrara, Margherita Gonzaga d'Este, and took the name of Sister Lucrina. Giovanni Baglioni was at the Mantua court in 1621–22 and therefore he would have known Lucrina's work. Almost all of her pictures were commissions from Margherita Gonzaga, and were painted for the convent and its church.

> Giovanni Baglioni, *Le vite de' pittori, scultori, architetti ed intagliatori* . . . [Rome, 1642], ed. V. Mariani (Rome, 1935), p. 155.

> Domenico Fetti had a sister, who also was a painter. And the most serene Duke [Ferdinando Gonzaga], who was a great enthusiast for all talents, especially in painting, called not only her, but also her father and the whole family to Mantua, and looked after them all. The young girl became a nun in an excellent convent, where she continued to practice the skill of painting. Working in a good style and with devotion, she not only enriched that convent with various paintings, but also embellished other convents in the noble city of Mantua with her colours.

6. An excellent embroiderer and virtuous woman, 1548

Marietta Talantina was a well-known Venetian embroiderer. In this letter, written for publication, Pietro Aretino praises her womanly virtues as well as her professional skill, and is glad that his daughter Adria, who was living at that time in Marietta's house, could enjoy such an eminent example. Aretino makes the important observation that Talantina designs her own embroideries and lace, and does not just copy them from patterns. She is therefore a true artist.

Aretino, ed. Camesasca (1957–60), 2, pp. 229–30.

To the lady Marietta Talantina, from Venice, May 1548
It would have been enough for Nature, so to leave something for other women, to make you virtuous and good without adding one of those splendours which shine with such light of honesty to enrich a hundred more women, leaving to you such a large part of this gift over which queens would fight. What wonderful works I see issuing from your hands, with the glory of your skill with which you make such church paraments, such wedding collars, such bonnets for brides which increase charm, majesty and love, while heads, bodices and necks of others are adorned with them. The price of silk and gold counts little compared with the value of the embroidery and of your art, because of your knowledge and application which order and arrange the stitches as they should be ordered and arranged . . . Since I love you as a father, I am overcome by the greatest affection and joy when I see that there are masters visiting you who become students when they see the divine works you make. [I see] also a great number of ladies who give you so much work that you cannot cope with more. I know that you never waste any time, so much so that both during winter and summer nights you do not sleep one hour, nor even half. You are troubled neither by children, nor by avarice. In fact, your whole mind is dedicated to the pleasure of your work. You have so much of it. What father could be happier, if Adria, who watches and accompanies you, were like that when she is your age? More than fine and more than praiseworthy is the merit of a young lady who can earn a living for herself and others with this much praised and lovely work of design. Which better dowry could your husband, Messer Martino, receive, than the treasure accumulated from your art? Perhaps games, balls and feasts take you away for one moment from the game you play with your fabrics, silks and veils embroidered and adorned with figures by your needle, your style and

your patterns. Now, for all your virtues, I give to you as a gift my life, the soul of my spirit and of my heart [Aretino's daughter Adria], with which I amuse her and embrace her. Look after her, and give your affection to her as to a daughter. If for nothing else, do it for the fatherly affection I feel for you. She is worthy of your generosity.

7. In praise of the hand and the embroidery of Lucrezia d'Este, Duchess of Urbino

The seduction of colours, fabrics and embroidery, as well as the beauty, skill and imagination of Lucrezia d'Este (1535–98), are celebrated in this sonnet by the poet Torquato Tasso, who spent much time in Ferrara. This is one among a number of poems which Tasso dedicated to Lucrezia, who had returned to Ferrara after her separation from her husband, Francesco Maria II della Rovere.

Torquato Tasso, *Le Rime*, 2 vols (Rome, 1994), 2, pp. 1060–1.

O fair hand, which one happy day,
amongst precious gems and sweet odours,
darted through and pierced together
your silken fabric and our hearts.

When I first gazed at that lap adorned
with fine colour and with varied shapes,
I said, 'What for others brings shame and scandal
is a meadow of scented flowers.'

But then I came to, and in that graceful veil
I recognised the wondrous art
and the fine work of an angelic hand,

equal to that which in the sky
makes fair and well proportioned shapes
with the clear stars during a shady night.

LOOKING FOR PATRONAGE

8. Letters from a proud father

Amilcare Anguissola constantly tried to get patronage for his daughter Sofonisba from one of the northern Italian courts. Many of Sofonisba's self-portraits were painted to promote herself as a painter and an educated gentlewoman.

The first of these two letters was sent to Margherita Paleologa, with a small painting (perhaps a self-portrait) as a gift for a relative. In the second letter Amilcare, writing from Milan to the King of Spain, Philip II, discusses Sofonisba's position as painter to Queen Isabella of Valois. Sofonisba remained at the Spanish court from the end of 1559 till 1573.

R. Sacchi, 'Regesto', in M. Gregori (ed.), *Sofonisba Anguissola e le sue sorelle* (Milan, 1994), pp. 364, 366.

Amilcare Anguissola to Margherita Paleologa, 12 March 1557
Most Illustrious, Excellent and Honoured Lady
I have defended this small picture painted by your servant, my daughter Sofonisba, from the greed of many who have begged me to give it to them. Knowing the reputation of Your Most Excellent Ladyship, however, I have sent it to you, asking you to condescend to give it to Her Ladyship Leonora [the Marchioness Eleonora Gonzaga]. I have willingly promised it to her on behalf of my dearest daughter, while she was in your city enjoying the favour of Your Most Excellent Ladyship.

Together with my whole family I kiss your hands and those of Her Most Illustrious Lady Marchioness. Europa [one of Amilcare's daughter] too regards you with deep respect, and every day prays for your Most Excellent Ladyship . . .

Amilcare Anguissola to Philip II, 6 September 1559
The Duke of Sessa and Count Broccardo have asked me on behalf of Your Majesty to send my first-born daughter to the service of the most serene Queen, your consort. I have immediately acquiesced, as I am your most devout and humble vassal, even if I have felt the greatest pain in my heart, and have caused my family the greatest sadness at the departure of this dearest daughter of ours. She is much loved by us and by all, and held so dear for her virtues and for her high morals. I take comfort, though, when I think that I have given her to the greatest and best King, Catholic

and Christian above all others in the world, and that your house is like a monastery in fame and deeds. I thank the Lord God for giving me the opportunity to serve you in this matter, regretting that, because of my old age and of the task of taking care of my other daughters, I have not been able to come with this daughter of mine to do in person what a good subject should. Now, lest I trouble you further, I conclude [this letter], kissing your feet and your hands, and, together with my family, begging Almighty God to increase your kingdom.

9. Artemisia Gentileschi needs to leave Rome

Orazio Gentileschi wrote this letter to Christine of Lorraine before the end of the trial against the painter Agostino Tassi, whom his daughter Artemisia had accused of rape. Orazio knew that powerful people were secretly working to help Tassi, and that Artemisia's career in Rome would be damaged by the notoriety of the case. After the end of the trial Artemisia married Pietro Antonio Stiattesi, and by 1613 she was working in Florence. In 1616, probably on the recommendation of the Grand Duke, she became a member of the Florentine Accademia del Disegno.

L. Tanfani-Centofanti, *Notizie di artisti tratte da documenti pisani* (Pisa, 1897), pp. 221–4.

Orazio Gentileschi from Rome to Christine of Lorraine, 6 July 1612

Most Serene Lady . . . I find myself with a daughter and three sons. This young girl [whom], God pleasing, I have guided towards becoming a painter, has worked so much during the past three years, that I dare to say there is nobody today who can equal her. She has painted works which the greatest masters in this art cannot equal, as I shall show Your Most Serene Highness at the right time and place.

[. . .]

To repay what I have done for him, he [Agostino Tassi], a scoundrel instigated by a very powerful enemy of mine, tried in every way and through diabolical means to have a look at this daughter of mine. At last, having seen her, he found the way to get into my house. He found the door open, [so] he arrogantly went in and arrived in the *sala*, where my daughter was painting. With blandishments and flattery, he made her fall in love with him, implying that he was the confidant and favourite servant of Their Most Serene Highnesses. Full of vain proposals, he again returned to my house, and forcibly and with menaces he dared to have carnal knowledge of my daughter. Having shut her up in the bedroom, and having attacked her with great violence for six or seven hours, he deflowered her, promising that he would marry her . . . I shall send you an example of my daughter's work as soon as possible, from which you will see her skill and judge how great this outrage is.

10. A letter of recommendation for Giovanna Garzoni

The miniature painter Giovanna Garzoni (1600–70) was well-known for her portraiture and still lifes. In search of patronage, she travelled around Italy, working both for the open market and as court painter. In October 1642 she was in Florence, working for the Medici court, and remained there for over 20 years.

S. Meloni Trkulja and E. Fumagalli, *Nature morte. Giovanna Garzoni* (Paris, 2000), p. 11.

Ferdinando de' Bardi, Medici ambassador in Paris, to the Grand Duke's secretariat in Florence, 25 February 1640
There is, in this city, a certain Signora Garzoni, born in L'Aquila [*sic*, actually Ascoli], an excellent painter of miniatures. She very much wishes to return to Italy, since she cannot get used to French customs. She asked me, through Signor Lumaga [a banker, merchant and art collector] to find out whether His Highness [Ferdinando II de' Medici] would like her to come to Florence. She seems to be willing to accept an honourable position. He showed me some works she had made, which Stefano della Bella [a Florentine artist close to the Medici, at the time living in France] holds in great regard, among which a garland of flowers from life. I answered [Lumaga] that I would write to Your Most Illustrious Lordship about it. As this lady wants to send

you some of her works, I have told him that in one way or another you will be pleased at what she will paint for His Highness, and I think it will be a portrait of the most serene Grand Duchess [Vittoria della Rovere].

SUCCESSES AND FRUSTRATIONS

11. Sofonisba Anguissola at the Spanish court

Sofonisba Anguissola writes to her old painting master Bernardino Campi describing her busy life as court painter to Queen Isabella of Spain. As well as producing a large number of portraits, she was giving painting lessons to the Queen. From the letter it is obvious that not all her tasks at court were a pleasure for Sofonisba, since they took time away from her own work. This letter was first printed in A. Lamo, *Discorso intorno alla scoltura e pittura* (1584).

R. Sacchi, 'Fonti a stampa e letterarie (1550–1625)', in Gregori (ed.) (1994), p. 408.

Sofonisba Anguissola, from Madrid, to Bernardino Campi, 21 October 1551 [*sic*: 1561]
Most magnificent Signor Bernardino,
   Some days ago I received a letter from your esteemed self, which was very dear to me because I received news of your health and your wife's, whom I love as a dearest sister. I shall not be happy till you let her know how much affection I have for her.
   Sir, I have written various letters to you, but have never received a reply. This is the only one I have received, and I had it from Secchi's manservant. I cannot satisfy you as I would like concerning the portrait of the King you request, because I have none, and at the moment I am working on a portrait of the most serene Princess, the sister of our lord the King [Juana, wife of the King of Portugal, Juan Manuel]. [The portrait] is for the Pope, to whom I have sent a portrait of our lady the Queen a few days ago.
   So, my dearest Signor Bernardino, my master, you can see that I am busy painting. Besides, the Queen wants me to

spend a great deal of my time on her own painting, so that she is impatient when I paint, as I cannot be at her disposal. In spite of all this, I shall try my best to fulfil the obligations I have towards you, about this portrait and about any other occasion which may arise. Having said that, I recommend myself to you, and I kiss your hand and that of your most honoured wife for whom I have so much affection, and [I recommend myself] to your mother, Signora Barbara, your sister Signora Francesca, and your father Signor Pietro.

12. Giovanna Garzoni is disillusioned with Naples

Giovanna Garzoni very probably met Cassiano dal Pozzo in Rome, while she was on her way to Naples. Cassiano, a collector at the centre of the artistic life of the time and a friend of many artists, was an important connection between painters and possible patrons. Many of the letters from Garzoni to Cassiano give a very vivid impression of the working conditions of this successful and fashionable painter. Here she relates how, as well as having to contend with courtiers stealing her drawings, she had just lost her most important patron, the Duke of Alcalà, Viceroy of Naples, who had been recalled to Spain for corruption and other various scandals.

Bottari and Ticozzi (eds) (1979–80), 1, pp. 240–2.

Giovanna Garzoni, from Naples, to Cassiano dal Pozzo, in Rome, 19 April 1631
Esteemed sir, you will be wondering why I have not written regularly, as I should have, and why I have not sent you something by my own hand, as I promised you. I am now working on a head of St John the Baptist, which I hope to be able to send you in two weeks' time as a recompense for what I owe you. If I have failed to repay my debt, do not blame me, but the Spaniards. You should believe that, since I have been in the employ of His Excellency [the Duke of Alcalà], I have not wanted to work for anybody else because I serve my masters faithfully. His courtiers, however, have always succeeded in extracting something from me, so much so that I have not had even one hour to make something to satisfy myself. First

of all [I would like to send some works] for the Cardinal, who sent me that money, as you know. Then for Signora Anna [Colonna Barberini], and for you, who have taken so much trouble over me. Here I am again, asking for you to help me.

You should know that the Lord Count of Monterey came here on behalf of the Viceroy, while the Duke of Alcalà is in Spain to account for some good and bad conduct I don't know about. Even if here they say he shall come back, I don't believe it. Now I am here without employment, and therefore I beg you to find me some opportunity for employment in Rome. As to the salary, I leave that to you. My wish is to live and die in Rome. I cannot refrain from reminding you to do rather promptly what I ask, firstly because I need to know whether I'll have to remain here, and secondly because I do not want to come to Rome in the hot season. If I come to Rome, I shall fulfil my promises immediately with as much diligence as possible, both for the cardinal and for Signora Anna, and also for you.

I send you my best wishes for the Holy Festivities, and make humble reverence . . .

Giovanna Garzoni, from Naples, to Cassiano del Pozzo, 12 July 1631
Signor Flaminio Razzante will have told you about my misfortune over your St John. I had finished it with much care, and I had asked the said Signore if he could deliver it to you, when suddenly Herrera, the secretary of the Lord Duke of Alcalà, arrived here with the Lord Marquess di Vico, and they played a true Spanish trick on me. While I was occupied showing them some works I had begun to do for His Excellency, with fine gallantry the Marquess di Vico filched your St John out of my book, and Herrera [took] two other small portraits. I am disgusted for two reasons: the first, and this is the worst, that I have lost the chance of partially repaying my debt to you, for which I am ashamed. The second is that, despite having been warned many times, I have been cheated by a Spaniard.

I have however made another [St John], in a different way, and even if it is not entirely as I would have liked, I hope you will like it, as it is better than the other one. I enclose it with this [letter], and I pray you to accept it gladly as an advance on what I owe you, which is a great deal. Do not consider the quality of the gift, but rather my soul. I aim to paint another more important work for you at a more convenient moment as a sign of my devotion. In the meantime I ask you to remember me to Signora Anna.

13. Artemisia Gentileschi and her patrons
The letter which Artemisia Gentileschi sent from Naples to Ferdinando II de' Medici shows her ability in paying homage to a possible patron, while at the same time flaunting her success by mentioning the King of England, Charles I, the Spanish Viceroy of Naples and the King of Spain, Philip IV, who, amongst others, wanted her works. Artemisia describes the help she has from her brothers, who were acting as her 'secretaries', delivering paintings on her behalf, collecting documents for her, and accompanying her in her journeys. The two paintings sent to Ferdinando II were not acknowledged, leaving Artemisia to worry whether the Grand Duke had been pleased with them.

R. Fuda, 'Un'inedita lettera di Artemisia Gentileschi a Ferdinando II de' Medici', *Rivista d'Arte*, 41, ser. 4, 5 (1989), pp. 167–71.

Artemisia Gentileschi, from Naples, to Ferdinando II de' Medici in Florence, 20 July 1632
Most Serene Highness,
    The arrival of my brother, sent by my father with those paintings for Your Most Serene Lordship, was a lucky chance. Afterwards, following his orders, my brother was to come to Naples to accompany me to His Majesty [the King] of England, who had requested me to enter his service many times before, and had sent my brother. Since I was in Naples in the employment of the Viceroy to finish some works which I had begun for His Catholic Majesty [the King of Spain], I could not satisfy His Majesty of England.
    That King, having been informed from Naples that my works were almost finished, ordered my brother to

accompany me to his service. Before leaving for that country, however, I began to paint these pictures for Your Most Serene Highness, after having worked hard for the Lord Duke of Parma and Modena, and for Cardinal Antonio Barberini.

As Your Most Serene Highness can see from the letters in possession of my brothers, I have left [working for] Your Most Serene Highness as the last achievement of my career, so to be able to paint these works with a quiet and contented mind. I thought that, having served your father the Grand Duke Cosimo [II] and being indebted to him for so many favours and much kindness, I should demonstrate to Your Most Serene Highness the same bond by dedicating these works to you. I am sending them to be placed with reverence at Your Most Serene Highness's feet, to the greatest pleasure of my lord the Viceroy, who has seen them and was pleased that I had painted these works for Your Most Serene Highness. Do not accept my justifications for the weaknesses of my brush, but gratify me with your perceptive and unfailing judgement. Excuse my temerity in wanting to be your servant as my father was, since you honoured him with that most precious letter and gift. I keep them with me, as my father has not been able to receive these honours because my brother, waiting to accompany me there [England], has not yet been in that country.

I am also waiting for a letter of the most serene Duchess of Savoy, who has promised to give it to me so that I can travel to France without any hindrance. She has told my brothers to travel to Turin to obtain the letter and passport.

I respectfully pray Your Most Serene Highness to receive my affection and to count me among your lowest servants.

14. A nun paints for *Madama Reale*, 1643

Orsola Maddalena Caccia (1596–1676) was taught to paint by her father, Guglielmo Caccia. She and her sisters lived in the convent of St Joseph at Moncalvo, in Piedmont, which Guglielmo had funded. She was one of the favourite painters of *Madama Reale*, Christine of Bourbon, daughter of Henri IV and Maria de' Medici, who was at that time Regent of the Duchy of Savoy. Here Sister Orsola write to her patroness about her commission for two religious works.

'L'arte negli stati sabaudi ai tempi di Carlo Emanuele I, di Vittorio Amedeo I, e della reggenza di Cristina di Francia, dai manoscritti del Conte Alessandro Baudi di Vesne', *Atti della Società Piemontese di Archeologia e Belle Arti*, 14 (1932), p. 144.

26 March 1643

Your Royal Highness, on the last 2 February I received a letter from Your Royal Highness, in which you let me know of your affection and of your commission for two paintings, one representing the Nativity of Our Lord, and the other St John the Baptist . . . As I have now begun to work on your commission, I would like to ask you to let me know whether the painting of St John the Baptist should represent the birth of that saint, or something else. I have already begun the painting of the Nativity of Our Lord Jesus Christ, and I am enclosing some strings which are the measurements of that picture. You will agree that both pictures should have the same measurements, so that the figures in each painting should be of the same proportions in order to look right.

I pray that God will grant me good health so I can fulfil my desire to serve Your Royal Highness. I also beg you to take pity on this sisterhood of ours and condescend to give me some money so I can provide for the needs of this community, and to supply me with some pigments which I need to finish these paintings in the way which can do justice to the merits of Your Royal Highness. I confirm my intent to serve you with the little talent that Our Lord will grant me. . .

Sister Orsola, Mother Abbess

MONEY MATTERS: CONTRACTS AND PAYMENTS

15. Contract for *The Stoning of St Stephen* for S. Paolo fuori le Mura, Rome

In 1603 Lavinia Fontana, her husband Gian Paolo Zappi and their children left Bologna for Rome, where Zappi had important connections. For the signing of the contract of this commission for an altarpiece for one of the seven most important churches in Rome, Lavinia was represented by her husband, who acted as her agent.

The painting was lost in the fire which destroyed S. Paolo fuori le Mura in 1823.

R. Galli, *Lavinia Fontana pittrice* (Imola, 1940), pp. 118–22.

In the name of Our Lord Jesus Christ, amen. In the year one thousand six hundred and three from the birth of Our Lord, on 19 February, in the Palace and in the presence of the Most Illustrious and Reverend Lord, my lord the Cardinal of Ascoli, and for the one side the Reverend Friar Lord Angelo da Genova, Abbot of San Paolo outside [the Walls], near Rome, and for the other Signor Gio. Paolo Zappi from Imola, painter, who is present here, the husband of Signora Lavinia Fontana from Bologna, painter, who is not present here, agree to the following.

The Very Reverend Father Abbot agrees that Signora Lavinia should paint the altarpiece for the altar near that of the Assumption of the Blessed Virgin, in the church of San Paolo outside the Walls, near Rome, with the story of the first martyr, St Stephen, for the same price as all other altarpieces painted for the same church of San Paolo, according to the following terms and conditions.

Firstly, if Signora Lavinia paints the said altarpiece to a standard comparable to the others in the church, according to the opinion of experts in painting, the said Very Reverend Father Abbot promises [to give her] the same payment as for any of the others in the said church.

Secondly, if Signora Lavinia's altarpiece surpasses [the others] in beauty and excellence, she will agree to accept the judgement of the Most Illustrious and Reverend Lord the Cardinal of Ascoli and of the Very Reverend Father Abbot, as to the difference in beauty and excellence. On the other hand, should the altarpiece of Signora Lavinia, who is not here present, be not equal but inferior to the other altar-pieces in this church, she will agree to a proportional decrease in her payment.

Furthermore Signora Lavinia promises to deliver the finished work next year, 1604, at the end of March, more or less, according to the decision of the Most Illustrious Cardinal of

Ascoli, and of the Father Abbot. The Very Reverend Father Abbot promises to provide the stretcher, the canvas, the ultramarine, the [paint for the] undercoat and the varnish, as was done for Master Giovanni del Borgo, painter of the altarpiece of St Benedict in the said church of San Paolo.

Furthermore, the Very Reverend Father Abbot promises to give the said materials and the payment for the said altarpiece in the same way and manner as was done with the other painters. Should Signora Lavinia pass away having received part of the payment, Signor Gio. Paolo here present promises, on behalf of himself and his heirs, to return all that Signora Lavinia received, that is money, pigments and other materials to be used for the making of the altarpiece.

And so that the Very Reverend Father Abbot can know what the said altarpiece might be like, he requests Signora Lavinia to show him the drawing of the said altarpiece. The Very Reverend Father Abbot may then change the drawing according to his liking. First and foremost, the drawing will be judged by the Most Illustrious Lord Cardinal of Ascoli.

I, Don Leone, Rector of Monte Cavallo, have written and signed this with my own hand, on this day 19 February 1603, in the presence of the Most Illustrious Lord Cardinal of Ascoli, and the Very Reverend Father Abbot, according to his wish.

I, Don Leone, witness the above.

I, Gio. Paolo Zappi, accept and promise this, on my behalf and on behalf of my wife Signora Lavinia, in my own hand.

16. The salary of Giovanna Garzoni

In 1632 Giovanna Garzoni accepted a post as court painter to Christine of Bourbon, Duchess of Savoy. It was probably Cassiano dal Pozzo, a native of Turin, who had recommended her. Garzoni remained in Turin till the death of the Duke of Savoy in 1637.

G. Casale, *Giovanna Garzoni 'insigne miniatrice' 1600–1670* (Milan and Rome, 1991), p. 8.

From the Duke of Savoy to the Treasurer General, 10 January 1633

Since we wish to establish a suitable arrangement for Giovanna Garzoni from Ascoli, miniature painter to my wife Madama Reale . . . we request you to pay to the said Giovanna Garzoni the yearly sum of a thousand Italian gold *scudi* at the rate of three *lire* each, [to be paid] on each quarter, as we have stipulated for her salary.

PRACTICAL MATTERS

17. Working space for Lavinia Fontana
Leaving Bologna, Lavinia Fontana arrived in Rome, where she is first documented in April 1604, as a guest in the palace of Cardinal Alessandro d'Este. This note deals with the problems of space which painters working on a large altarpiece could have, if they did not have a workshop of their own.

M. T. Cantaro, *Lavinia Fontana bolognese 'pittora singolare' 1552–1614* (Milan and Rome, 1989), p. 313.

Virginio Roberti, agent of Cardinal d'Este in Rome, 24 April 1604
Signora Lavinia, the Bolognese painter who lives in the palace belonging to Your Most Illustrious Lordship, is painting a picture for the church of San Paolo in Rome. She wishes to paint it with all possible care, but since her rooms have such a low ceiling that the picture does not fit, she would like to be able to work for the next two months in a large and spacious room, one which nobody currently uses, until she finishes it. Because this lady deserves much for her skill, as well as for the picture she is painting, I have promised her to help her in this matter, [asking] Your Most Illustrious Lordship to grant her this favour, and therefore I beg Your Most Illustrious Lordship to give her permission, and I shall count it amongst all the favours received [from you].

18. The painter Giustina Fetti enters the convent of S. Orsola
When Domenico Fetti arrived in Mantua with his brothers and sisters, his sister Giustina gave Margherita Gonzaga as a gift a

number of relics she had brought from Rome, among which were relics of St Lucrina. A donation from Duke Ferdinando Gonzaga provided the dowry which allowed Giustina to enter the prestigious convent of S. Orsola, where she appropriately took the name of Sister Lucrina. Giustina produced works for many of the spaces within the convent, including both parts of the church, and Margherita Gonzaga's own private apartment.

C. A. Gladen, 'Suor Lucrina Fetti, pittrice in una corte mantovana seicentesca', in G. Pomata and G. Zarri (eds), *I monasteri femminili come centri di cultura fra Rinascimento e Barocco* (Rome, 2005), p. 129.

By ducal warrant, 3 December 1614
. . . Given and paid one hundred and fifty *scudi* at the rate of one *lira* each to the Lady Giustina Fetti, sister of Signor Domenico Fetti, painter to His Highness, who has entered as a nun the convent of the Ursulines, built by the Most Serene Lady of Ferrara. These one hundred and fifty *scudi* are a free gift from His Highness, for such a purpose.

19. Arrangements for Giovanna Garzoni, 1632
Christine of Bourbon writes to the Savoyard ambassador in Rome asking him to make arrangements for Giovanna Garzoni's journey to Turin, where she was going to be employed as her court painter.

'L'arte negli stati Sabaudi ...' *Atti della società piemontese di archeologia e belle arti*, 14 (1932), p. 799.

Christine of Bourbon, in Turin, to Ludovico d'Agliè, 28 April 1632
As we very much wish to have the miniature painter Giovanna Garzoni here at our service as soon as possible, we recommend you to help her by authorising everything she needs to arrive here quickly and safely. For this purpose we are sending you a passport for her, so that she can use it . . . We are also sending you a letter of credit for a hundred *doppi* for her travelling expenses.

NEEDLEWORK: NUNS, WORKERS AND LADIES

Skills in needlework and weaving were seen as particularly suited to women: after all, the goddess Minerva was the protector of these crafts. Many girls would have learned how to sew and embroider from childhood, at home or in convents, and would have continued to improve their skills throughout their lives. In most religious institutions throughout Italy, either convents or *conservatori* for young girls often belonging to aristocratic families, needlework – sewing, embroidery and lacemaking – was practised during the whole of our period.

Nuns of all orders were expert needlewomen, sewing and embroidering church vestments and paraments. They also worked on commission, sewing fine linen and accessories for men's and women's clothing. The nuns of the Augustinian convent of S. Monica in Florence, for example, used to embroider chemises with gold thread for Eleonora di Toledo. For nuns, needlework and embroidery were important means of making money for their convents, though stricter enforcement of *clausura* during the Catholic Reformation often made this more difficult.

20. The nuns of S. Verdiana embroider a bishop's mitre and special vestments

During the second half of the fifteenth century, the convent of S. Verdiana and its related church of S. Ambrogio in Florence were under the protection and patronage of the Medici. The nuns in S. Verdiana, as skilled needlewomen, embroidered church vestments, and also reused precious fabrics given to them. These two extracts are from the convent's account books. The nuns mentioned in the first extract came from families of the Florentine elite. The second extract mentions a gift of white damask from Maria Ginevra Alessandri, a patron of the convent together with her husband Giovanni di Cosimo de' Medici.[4]

M. Sframeli, "'Ricamato da mano angelica": un'attribuzione settecentesca per l'*Incoronazione della Vergine* di Paolo Schiavo', *Arte Cristiana*, 83 (1995), pp. 323–4.

. . . A beautiful mitre, made of crimson cloth, embroidered with gold and pearls, and raised gold motifs everywhere. In the middle is a gold frieze in a pattern of squares, and above it are roundels with precious stones and enamels. This mitre is embroidered by Sister Angela degli Arrighi, both in the parts decorated with pearls and on the frieze. As we were in a hurry, the work was done in S. Giorgio [another convent of Augustinian nuns]. One of the bands on the gloves was embroidered by Sister Caterina de' Guasconi, and the other by Sister Nicolosa degli Amadori. Sister Girolama de' Vecchietti embroidered the bands of the mitre. We did all the designs and the work on the mitre, and all the nuns and lay sisters, for their devotion, have contributed to the expenses for the mitre *lire* 107.

We have received from the wife of Giovanni di Cosimo de' Medici two parts of her gown of white damask, out of which we made an altar-cloth for the high altar, for the feast day of S. Verdiana. We embroidered it with gold, crimson and green silk, according to the patterns of the fabric. Sister Angela embroidered it.

21. The nuns of the Convento del Paradiso, Pian di Ripoli, buy a cartoon, silk and gold to embroider an altar frontal

The nuns and the friars of the Brigittine convent of the Paradiso at Pian di Ripoli were well known for their embroidered altar frontals, friezes and church vestments. These records from the convent's account book outline the nuns' expenses for their work on an altar frontal commissioned by Fra Niccolò da Milano for the high altar of the Dominican church of S. Maria Novella in Florence. The painter Paolo di Stefano [Paolo Schiavo] designed a cartoon with fifteen stories from the life of the Virgin, which the nuns bought from him. The fabric for the frontal was provided by the patron, but the nuns dealt directly with a silk merchant and the workshop of a gold-beater [*battiloro*] for their materials: silk threads; copper leaf; and gold leaf and yellow silk, which the nuns themselves made into gold thread.

M. C. Improta and A. Padoa Rizzo, 'Paolo Schiavo fornitore di disegni per ricami', *Rivista d'Arte*, 41, ser. 4, 5 (1989), pp. 55–6.

14 October 1466

To Paolo Schiavo, painter, up till 26 May, nine *lire* and ten small *soldi* for the drawing [cartoon] of an altar frontal for the church of S. Maria Novella in Florence, about eight *braccia* [about 480 cm] long, with fifteen stories [from the life] of Our Lady.

[another hand] I received the said money in two instalments, given by the Abbess. Amounting to *Lire* 9 s 10 d_

To Fruisino Calderini, silk merchant, up till 3 June, ten *lire a*nd eight *soldi*. They are for the silk weft in various colours, brought in two consignments for the embroidery the nuns are making, and for one ounce and two *denari* of yellow, twisted silk for the spun gold for the said embroideries. Leonardo di Pietro Saragli [Serragli?] took the said money. They are for any other deal he still has with the nuns, in the green book marked B, fol. 509 [another hand] *Lire* 10 s 8 d_

Today 14 October

To Giovanni di Paolo Federighi and his partners, *battilori*, till 13 June, eight large florins, Fra Salvi took from Sister Margheritina. They are for eight ounces of gold leaf, to be spun for the altar frontal for S. Maria Novella. And he sold us the said gold leaf for five *lire* and five *soldi* an ounce. In total he gets forty-two *lire*. The said florins were rated at five *lire* and nine *soldi* each *Lire* 43 s 4 d_

[. . .]

To the said Giovanni and partners, on the said day, five *lire* and sixteen *soldi*, two small *denari*, which are for three ounces of yellow silk for the spun gold, which we bought from said Giovanni. Fra Salvi took the said money in various instalments from Sister Margheritina, in the green book marked B, fol. 509 [another hand] *Lire* 5 s 16 d_ [*sic*]

Two ounces of copper leaf [*orpello*] bought for the embroidery, one *lira* [. . .]

To Giovanni di Paolo Federighi and partners, *battilori*, on the said day four *lire* and sixteen *soldi*. They are for some silk and gold which we got from him for the altar frontal for

S. Maria Novella. Fra Salvi took it. [Recorded] in the green
book marked B, fol. 509 *Lire* 4 s 16 d_

NEEDLEWORK FOR MONEY

22. A seamstress and embroiderer of church vestments
The *Opera* of Florence Cathedral employs Lucrezia as embroiderer
and seamstress for the cathedral. She was the wife of Luca di Ser
Cristoforo da Montevarchi, who was in charge of providing the
Opera with building materials.

> P. Meli and S. Tognetti, *Il principe e il mercante nella Toscana
> del Quattrocento. Il magnifico Signore di Piombino Jacopo III
> Appiani e le aziende Maschiani di Pisa* (Florence, 2006), p.
> 155, n. 45.

11 August 1496
. . . To repair, or to make and sew anew . . . each and all
paraments and vestments in silk, linen and wool in the
time which pleases you, for the convenience of those in the
church or its sacristy.

23. From the Statutes of the Milanese Embroiderers' Guild
In Milan, the number of lay female embroiderers was higher than
in all other places in Italy.
The Statutes of the Embroiderers' Guild of 19 December 1583,
which deals with both male and female workers, includes regulations for women embroiderers and for their apprentices in order
to protect this important category of workers, setting down the
reciprocal obligations.

> M. T. Binaghi Olivari, 'I ricamatori milanesi', in P. Venturoli
> (ed.), *I tessili nell'età di Carlo Bascapè vescovo di Novara
> (1593–1615)* (Novara, 1994), pp. 119–21.

Chapter 30. If any [embroidery] mistress has already any
work to be embroidered at home, nobody else is permitted to
send her more work.
If any embroidery mistress has sent any embroidery for

another woman to work on, no other master who has other work to do is permitted to send it to be embroidered by the latter mistress.

In the same way this same mistress is not permitted to accept any embroidery, nor do any embroidery for another master, until she has finished all the embroidery for the first master, under penalty of ten gold *scudi*. This fine will be paid both by the said mistress and the second master.

The said mistress is however allowed to take in work from other masters, if the first master does not have sufficient work for her.

Chapter 31. All the mistresses and women must be registered with the Badia, and similarly they have to register with the Badia all young girls they take on to learn the art of embroidery.

All the mistresses and women who now work on embroideries, and will do so in the future, must be enrolled at the Badia in the Register of Mistresses, unless they are in a religious order.

When they register they have to pay twenty *soldi* each, to be retained by the said Guild. Furthermore, all the young girls who make an agreement with a mistress and who begin to learn to embroider, must put down in writing the agreement made in the Guild, and the time stipulated. They must also pay ten *soldi* each. Those who do not will be fined one gold *scudo*, to be enforced by the Guild.

Chapter 32. Those who have made an agreement with masters or mistresses will not be able to leave.

Those who have made an agreement with embroidery masters or mistresses are not allowed for any reason to break the agreement and go to work elsewhere before the stipulated time.

Chapter 39. No one can claim to be a master falsely.

It is established that from this moment onward no one who belongs to this Guild can be a master without having demonstrated that he has become a master, or worker or apprentice, according to the Register Books of the Guild, and that he has observed these regulations, having been enrolled as above.

At the death of a Master, his wife is allowed to work as an embroiderer during the time she wears a widow's weeds but not after that.

Notes

1 F. H. Jacobs, *Defining the Renaissance 'Virtuosa': Women Artists and the Language of Art History and Criticism* (Cambridge, 1997); J. Dabbs, *Life Stories of Women Artists, 1550–1800: an Anthology* (Farnham, 2009); P. Tinagli, *Women in Italian Renaissance Art* (Manchester, 1997), pp. 17–76.
2 Vasari, ed. Milanesi (1906), 2, p. 217.
3 See C. P. Murphy, 'Lavinia Fontana and female life cycle experience in late sixteenth-century Bologna', in G. A. Johnson and S. F. Matthews Grieco (eds), *Picturing Women in Renaissance and Baroque Italy* (Cambridge, 1997), pp. 111–38.
4 See N. R. Thomas, *The Medici Women: Gender and Power in Renaissance Florence* (Aldershot, 2003), p. 86.

WOMEN WRITING ON ART AND ARTEFACTS

The previous chapters have included many texts written by women, some to do with patronage or other relationships with artists, some describing the decorative elements at ceremonies such as courtly weddings and triumphal entries. However, though often vivid and sometimes intended for diffusion within a social circle, they do not really form part of a considered literary oeuvre, as do the examples in this chapter. The intention here will be to show how, as part of their serious literary expression, women authors used architecture and artefacts, at times describing actual examples, at times inventing novel ones, at others exploring the issues involved in their creation or reception.

The examples mostly come from the mid-sixteenth century and later, in this reflecting the rise of the published female writer.[1] They need to be considered in the light not only of the authors' differing experiences of the art and artefacts of their day, but of the conventions of both literary, and art-critical cultures. The longer, more descriptive passages connect with the admiration for skill in *ekphrasis* – vivid word-painting – that was part of the legacy of antiquity picked up by Renaissance humanists and writers.[2] Some well-regarded examples in both antique and modern literature had taken artefacts as their subjects – the shield of Achilles in Homer, the palace of the sun in Ovid, the objects and buildings in Sannazaro's *Arcadia* or in the *Hypnerotomachia Poliphili*. Other literary genres rooted in antiquity, but further developed in the Renaissance, were the humanist letter, the occasional verse and the poem on a painted or sculpted portrait.[3] All these were adopted by women writers and used for their different literary purposes. These authors had become aware of the development of a richer and more differentiated art-critical vocabulary during the fifteenth century by those concerned with the visual arts, and words associated with this such as *devoto* (used of devotional images), *disegno* or *ingegno* sometimes passed into the language of women writing on artefacts.[4] Women from social elites who wrote poetry and literary letters, like Veronica Gambara, and were in contact with figures such as Bembo or Aretino who were at the forefront of aesthetic debates, were well aware of the developing art discourse. By the mid-sixteenth century, we arrive at the time of further growth and diffusion of art criticism, in informal discussions between figures with whom women writers, notably Laura Battiferri, would have associated, or in the printed dialogues which might purport to be based on meetings where women participated, most famously Vittoria Colonna in Francisco de Holanda's *Dialogues*. These printed works made contemporary debates on topics such as the nature and value of art and its specific genres, or the achievement of the moderns versus the ancients, available to later women writers in general.

BUILDINGS, THEIR CONTENTS AND GARDENS

The texts in this section all come from within much longer works, each with their particular themes, to which these *ekphraseis* may contribute. They also register to differing degrees the taste of the author or the culture within which they moved.

1. Lucrezia Tornabuoni (c. 1425–82) describes the palace of Ahasuerus, c. 1470–75

In this religious narrative poem, the opulence of the loggia in the palace of the Assyrian king Ahasuerus in part reinforces the power and splendour of his figure, and thus the triumph of the Jewish heroine, Esther, who later becomes his wife. The elements in the decoration – multicoloured marble, vaulted ceilings embellished with stars, *millefleurs* tapestries and other hangings – conform to the taste of the late fifteenth-century Florentine patriciate, as do the vessels of precious materials. These would have been displayed on occasions such as the marriage of Lucrezia's daughter Nannina de' Medici with Bernardo Rucellai in 1466.

Lucrezia Tornabuoni de' Medici, *La storia di. . . Ester*, in *I poemetti sacri di Lucrezia Tornabuoni*, ed. F. Pezzarossa (Florence, 1978), pp. 73–5, Lucrezia Tornabuoni de' Medici, *Sacred Narratives*, ed. and trans. J. Tylus (Chicago, 2000), pp. 170–2.

> This worthy lord had in the city,
>> for his recreation, a garden,
>> or, rather, a gracious and lovely orchard,
> and to reach it the direct route
>> was through a loggia
>> all of precious stones and fine workmanship.
> It was made by many skilled masters –
>> columns of shining alabaster supported it,
>> each decorated and well delineated;
> half were of shining porphyry,
>> and the others of serpentine, so embellished
>> that they seemed of emerald.
> The walls surrounding it
>> were of precious stones so finely wrought
>> that twilight seemed like day there.
> Its pavement was, in truth,
>> so shining with its jasper
>> that it was most imposing to behold.
> The vaulting of the loggia
>> was of a polished, brilliant sapphire,
>> stupefying the mind to think on it,
> seemingly work not human but divine.
>> On this vault were stars
>> in enamelled gold: against the ultramarine
> their rays and flames sparkled
>> dazzling the eye to look on them:
>> may I repeat how beautiful they were.
> Now, continuing with my account,
>> I must describe the decoration that remains
>> as far as I am capable.
> And though there remains much to report
>> on the great awnings (*apparato*) in the garden
>> which lent it a dignified covering:
> hangings of silks, of fine silver and gold

of many types and various colours:
this white and green, the others alexandrine [a purplish
colour].
They were embroidered with roses and flowers
so finely, with great mastery
that never were such worthy labours seen;
the white and pink roses
so well set out against the green background
that a description would almost seem a lie;
no one of them yielding to nature,
nor the other flowers in this work:
violets, fleur-de-lis and green foliage.
The ropes supporting them
were in part spun gold, in part of silk.
Proceeding, I will not delay:
within the palace, my memory recalls
chambers and halls like what I describe,
all of similar quality.
But to recount fully the beauty
of the dwelling of the King and its decoration
I would need a strong intelligence,
so my skills are almost exhausted
and I must now turn my mind
to recount what was for sustenance.
Of ivory were the trestles on which lay
the platform (*palco*) and headpiece wrought in ebony,
which seemed a graceful piece indeed.
So well embellished were the golden beds
with pearls and gems, one was stunned
to gaze at such fine handiwork.
And to lend ornament to the meal, the King
ordered vessels for drinking and eating,
since the noble banquet required it,
all of precious and costly stones:
diamonds and emeralds of worth
with other fine stones of high price;
this to do his barons honour
and present a similar appearance
to demonstrate his magnanimous spirit.

And not resting from morn to night,
  he made decoration so splendid
  a description would seem incredible.

2. Veronica Franco (1546–91) on the setting of the villa at Fumane, 1575

The long description of the della Torre villa at Fumane outside Verona, which the writer had visited and which still exists, completes her 1575 poem cycle, the *Terze rime*. Much space is given to the gardens and scenery surrounding the villa which make its harmonies complete. Though the building, like Tornabuoni's, is opulent, its stylistic features reflect a later Renaissance taste, with the classical architectural elements and perspectives, real or painted, found in contemporary Veneto villas. Franco's self-conscious musings on memory, the balance between nature and art, and the mimetic qualities of the visual arts, connect the passage with the art-theoretical discussions of the later Renaissance.[5]

Veronica Franco, *Terze rime*, 25, lines 19–21, 34–9, 127–41, in Franco, ed. Jones and Rosenthal (1998), pp. 252–55, 258–61.

Ever before my eyes I have the wonderful dwelling,
  in which, though far in body, in my mind
  I dwell, without it leaving me . . .
    In this [state of mind], I straight away take up my pen;
  and to satisfy my feeling, depict this place
  as truly as I can make it.
    Though I know I am daunted by this lofty task,
  drawn on by my own yearning,
  artlessly I draw and paint what I know . . .
    Art yields not the prize to nature
  in the artistry of the garden, adorned
  with cultivated trees, their foliage ever green;
    above which rises, slightly elevated
  the architecture of a fine palace,
  such as the Sun's, once written of by poets,[6]
    well worth a treasure beyond value
  for the building itself, and for its decoration,
  unequalled both in richness and in beauty.

The exquisite marbles and shining porphyry,
cornices, arches, columns, reliefs and friezes,
figures, perspectives, gilding and silver
　these are of a nature and a price
unequalled in quality by the palaces
of ancient emperors and kings.

3. Lucrezia Marinella (1571–1653), on the palace of Diocletian and the chamber of the nymph Armilla, 1605

Marinella's long pastoral romance, *Arcadia felice*, like its famous predecessor, Sannazaro's *Arcadia*, incorporates many passages describing buildings or artefacts. The opulent villa of the Emperor Diocletian in Arcadia is the most sustained of these. Its rich materials and its fertile garden resemble the previous examples, but more personal to Marinella is the emphasis on elements of scientific interest, such as the botanical information in the garden section or, here, the planning of the building to take account of lighting and wind direction. This was emphasised in the construction of Veneto villas from the mid-sixteenth century onwards, notably those of Palladio, whose cross-shaped hall in the Villa Barbaro at Maser was perhaps known to Marinella directly or indirectly.

Lucrezia Marinella, *Arcadia felice* [Venice, 1605], ed. F. Lavocat (Florence, 1998), pp. 39, 156–7.

The abode of Diocletian was situated on a large plain, as if amidst a theatre surrounded by gentle hills, and showed itself as excellent and marvellous through its precious marble, fine pictures and wonderful structure. In this dwelling there was a grand salon made in the form of a cross terminating in four ample doors, one of which formed a gracious entrance for the first rays of young Aurora, the other on the opposite side allowed one to admire the weary Apollo, clad in purple splendour, sinking into the bosom of the Ocean. One of the other two endured the formidable force of the stormy Aquilone, and the other bore with little pleasure the onerous breezes of the rainy Austro. There were in this abode exquisite chambers, whose pavements were purer than fine coral: the beautiful cornices were gilded and worked with various enamels; one saw painted walls, in which art vied with the workings of nature its subtlety . . .

[Later in the work, the Emperor Diocletian and company are taken by the nymph Armilla to a magnificent chamber containing a tomb. Here the author displays much greater visual sensitivity than before, seeming to show awareness of the Veneto-Byzantine mosaic tradition of tesserae, often of precious material, glinting in a dusky light.]

Full of marvel at the words of the beautiful nymph, they followed in her footsteps, and, together proceeding through one of the doors cut into the rock, they turned right onto a large passageway, until they reached a fine chamber. This was lit by no ray of Apollo, even though it shone radiantly; perhaps the realm of the Sun, or the chamber of Aurora would have resembled it if they had reached them. Only a large brazier, crowned with its live flames, stood in their midst, which emitted so much radiance from the light with which Nature in her beauty had endowed it, that each minute one could see things as clearly as if Phoebus were showing them with his flaming torch. The upper part of this sacred cell was painted with finer azure than was ever seen, even when the night sky is calm and clear of any cloud, and in its serene expanse twinkled stars of polished gold. The walls were of dark red corals, pearls, rubies, green emeralds and other precious stones, all worked delicately, even divinely, in mosaic. On one side a rich bed was to be seen, carved in the same manner, with upright columns, luminous white like a snowy mountain, with a shining gold frieze, amongst which were seen the cerulean sapphire sparkling with its heavenly light, and the hard diamond twinkling amidst the other stones, yet the precious stones had little value compared with the artifice which had placed them with industrious diligence. This bed was covered with a spread of gold and vermilion silk. The pavement was gleaming and white, and amidst its shining pallor rubies, crystals and topazes were placed with such subtle art as to astonish even the sense of wonder; these superb gems were struck by the light emanating from the glowing brazier, redoubling their lively brilliance.

ANCIENT HISTORY AND MYTHOLOGY

4. Veronica Franco on 'Loves of the Gods' textiles, 1575

The opulence of the architecture at Fumane was equalled by the villa's contents. For Franco, the *cortigiana onesta*, the hangings in the bedroom, whether embroideries or tapestries, demonstrate the power of erotic love and the mimetic skill of the artist. The episodes are taken from Jove's transformations in Ovid's *Metamorphoses*, extremely well-known and popular in Renaissance art.

> Veronica Franco, *Terze rime*, 25, 142–83, in Franco, ed. Jones and Rosenthal (1998), pp. 260–3.

But the comforts and materials inside
are so luxurious as to make the other delights
seem poor compared with them.
    In the chambers, splendid with golden hangings,
on the paving, shining with gems,
white beds stand on gilded feet.
    Above each one are suspended all around
hangings of varied silk and purple cloth-of-gold,
which touch and embrace the framework of the beds;
    each one is covered and decorated
with embroidered cloth or other rich appliqué work
so that no embellishment is lacking.
    On all sides of the curtains and coverlets
in different designs and different techniques
varied and painstaking artifice is shown.
    Here are shown gods descending from heavens
transformed into different shapes,
seized with love for nymphs;
    faces flushed with passion,
restlessly they pursue their desire
where the hot fire drives them.
    Here Io is seen, changed into a cow,
and a guard closes his hundred eyes,
at the sound of the god who would kill him.[7]
    Elsewhere Danae rejoices,
in the place where she was shut and imprisoned;

to see Jove rain down to her bosom in a shower of gold.[8]
    In another part, Jove, changed into a bull,
bears Europa away; elsewhere as an eagle, he grasps
Ganymede, and carries him to the heavenly choir.[9]
    Again, Licaon's daughter, made a bear,
while her son, in ignorance, tries to kill her,
is raised to the sky, still bear-like.
    Not only has she become a heavenly bear
marked out by stars as such a form,
but her son represents another celestial bear.[10]
    How powerful is our human ingenuity,
which makes feigned things seem real
through the power of colour and *disegno*!
    With silk and gold and differently dyed wools
in the fabrics that adorn these rooms
through imitation, reality itself is vanquished.

5. Marinella on rural scenes painted in Diocletian's palace, 1605

Scenes set in landscapes were popular as decoration for villas or palaces around 1600, although the particular subjects chosen by Marinella were mostly uncommon in the real-life painting of her day. The stories, many taken from Plutarch's *Lives*, allowed her to indulge the moralising bent of her later writings, and, with their messages of restraint and renunciation, connected with the overarching theme of the work, an emperor's rejection of power and luxury in favour of a simpler life.

Marinella, ed. Lavocat (1998), pp. 39–41.

The skilled hand of the inventive painter had on one side brought alive with spirited colour Marcus Curius Dentatus, who when he had vanquished the Samnites, the Sabines, the Lucanians, and chased King Pyrrhus out of Italy, went to enjoy the sweetness of quiet solitude in rustic places: he seemed to cut down the over-fertile branches of fecund vines with a sharp blade. Not far off the great Scipio Africanus could be detected, who conquered Sifaces, dominated Africa, subjugated Spain, conquered Hannibal and, even more importantly, himself, and then retired to the villa of Linternus. The figure of one formerly fired up by the flames of battle was shown taking pleasure in seeing trees planted with his own hands, and occupying himself with the cultivation of flowers and fruit. On another the aged Laertes was seen, dressed in rough cloth and happy in his condition, but thinking of his lost son Ulysses, turning and tilling the too hard soil with his sharp hoe, so that it produced good and abundant fruit. Not far away from him was shown the good painter Gaius Fabricius, who despised the gold and silver offered him by the Samnites, and lived amongst the poverty and neglect of the countryside: in front of him several sheep, followed by small lambs, seemed to move in step, and with them the citizens of the woods, dressed in rough cloth as befits them, with twisted sticks in hand to guide them . . . Then King Alcinous was seen amidst his garden, harvesting ripe seeds from dry flower-heads and gathering together many roses and jasmine flowers so that the fair Nausicaa might bedeck her golden locks and snowy bosom with them. Behind them one made out the mournful Saturn, who after fleeing the wrath of Jove and the King of Greece lived contentedly in Latium: with his bent plough he breaks up the hard ground, which he would then sow with his fertile seed. All these figures were depicted with such a skilful hand, that if you had trusted your senses, you would have believed that to give the magnanimous Emperor some company, Nature had returned to bring back to life these glorious heroes, who show greatness amidst their wretchedness.

ALLEGORIES

6. Chiara Matraini 'paints' Vice, 1595

Admiration for skill in devising ingenious allegories or emblems was widespread among the educated in the sixteenth century. Both authors in this section invent visual allegories which make their didactic concerns vivid, in this showing an *ingegno* akin to that which the good painter should display. The later work of the Lucchese poet Chiara Matraini (1515–1604) was much concerned with moral and religious themes.

C. Matraini, *Rime e lettere*, ed. G. Rabitti (Bologna, 1989), pp. 142–3.

To Messer Ginasio Ugoberti
She shows in what form she would paint Vice.

Many days have passed, most honoured Messer Ginasio, since you asked me in one of your letters in what form I thought Vice should be depicted. I have never given you a reply until now, as I was considering how, with my low and feeble intellect, I could imagine a brutish, bizarre or bestial shape that would adequately demonstrate the cruel nature of such a vile, horrible and damnable monster. At last I decided – more to obey you than, as I think, to satisfy you – I would give my opinion, which is as follows. Firstly, I would draw on top of a great globe for the earth a semi-goat, that is, from the middle downwards a goat and from the middle upwards a small man, or dwarf, with his face turned towards his shoulders, to signify how Vice is a lack or defect of human nature, and that a man who follows it turns away from his rational nature and like a goat goes wandering amidst earthly and impermanent things to satiate his dishonest and bestial appetites. In addition, I also think that the dwarf should have a great quantity of snakes instead of hair, to warn everyone that the man who is vicious has always malign and deadly thoughts in his head. I would also give him two bats' wings on his shoulders, to convey that the vicious man, like this nasty creature, flees from the light of the sun of truth, towards the darkness of ignorance and sin. Then above the shoulder of this strange and horrible monster I should like a maiden to be seated, beautiful in all her features apart from the ears, which I would show as donkey-like, and her eyes as blind, to show how the soul was created by God as beautiful in all its parts, but in letting itself be transported where Vice guides it, it becomes blind in reason and intellect, and makes itself ignorant through the ears of the heart, which does not hear or hearken to divine counsel, nor holy guidance. I would also depict the maiden tied with an iron chain which the malevolent and monstrous Vice holds with right hand, and an unsheathed knife with the left, to show to everyone that when she is led to the end of this precipitous path, she will finally be killed by him. Lastly, the semi-goat should have a scorpion's tail, since like the scorpion he goes about with open claws, a gesture of embrace, and with the tail poisons and strikes down. Similarly, in the beginning Vice seems pleasingly alluring, but in the end poisons and kills the soul which follows it.

7. An allegorical fountain in the garden of Moderata Fonte's Leonora, 1592

Moderata Fonte (1555–92) introduces as one of the settings for her dialogue in defence of women an imaginary garden with an elaborate fountain. This clearly connects both with the author's actual family name (Pozzo, or well) and her pseudonym, and allows her to devise emblems of personal significance. These obviously relate to the different ideals for women that the characters debate, arguing for chastity and the attractions of an untrammelled solitary life.

Fonte, ed. Chemello (1988), pp. 219–23; ed. Cox (1997), pp. 50–5.

So, having seen that the sun was already hidden behind some small clouds, they[11] all agreed to go down into the beautiful garden, wanting to enjoy themselves a little, and so, taking each other's hands, they made their way gaily . . . When they entered it, it would have been impossible to express in words how utterly lovely and delightful they found it. All laid out there were little trees of an intense green cut in different shapes: some in pyramids, others in the form of mushrooms, melons or other things, with espaliered ones around and mingled with well-trimmed laurels, chestnuts, box trees and pomegranates, not differing in height by so much as a leaf. There were the finest orange trees and cedars with flowers and fruit with a scent so pleasing that they delighted the heart no less than the sight of whoever smelt them. I shall refrain from enumerating the quantity and variety of lovely vases sculpted with cedars and delicate flowers in different varieties and tiny myrtles, and the softest lawns which formed triangles, ovals, squares and other shapes of graceful artifice. There were pergolas of jasmine, labyrinths of evergreen ivy and groups of boxes cut into figures to make any expert marvel. Of the fruit I will not speak, for they were of every kind, according to their season, and in great quantity, and the useful plants, placed among the ornamental ones at tasteful intervals, made such a lovely vista, that the women could not remain still.

And so, wandering from place to place, they came to a beautiful fountain built in the middle of the garden with more rare and painstaking workmanship than could be expressed. On each facade and at the side of the fountain was a standing figure of a beautiful woman, with hair interlaced, from whose breasts cascaded artfully, as if from a double fountain, abundant clear, fresh and sweet water. Each one of these women had a garland of laurel on her head and in her left hand carried an olive branch and in her right, various emblems. However, one of them held a gleaming white ermine above her shoulder, keeping it away from her breast so as not to drench it, and the scroll she carried with her left bore this verse:

'Death rather than stain to my body.'

The other held in her right hand a phoenix, which lives unique in the world, and in her left it was written:

'I live alone for all time, I die and am reborn.'

The third carried a Sun and her scroll said:

'Alone, I illuminate myself and all around.'

The fourth supported a lantern whose light revealed a tiny butterfly burning to death, and the scroll bore this sentence:

'Victim of a vision of beauty, I myself am burnt.'

The fifth had a peach as device, with a peach leaf and a verse which said;

'All too different is the message of the heart from that of the tongue.'

But the sixth carried a crocodile and the caption went:

'I first kill man, and then, when he is dead, mourn him.'

Each of these figures also had a letter written on their foreheads, and the first had an A, the second a T, the third an S, the fourth an H, the fifth and I, the sixth an M.[12] And the ensemble was so precisely and divinely wrought that it seemed more living and natural than feigned and artificial.

When they had finished [eating], Cornelia asked Leonora if she knew the meaning of figures and, if so, whether she would kindly explain the significance of the mottoes and devices.

'Yes, gladly', answered Leonora. 'You know that this house, like this garden, was owned by an aunt of mine, as you know from having heard of her. I know that none of you ever met her, since she lived many years in Padua, where she recently died. As a girl she never wanted to marry, and so, living on the good income my grandfather left her, she had this garden created (with no expense spared, since it was her greatest delight) as beautiful as you see. She also had this lovely fountain made, with the figures all according to her plan, which in conformity with her opinion was opposed to the male sex. For the first figure placed here is Chastity, which she so much loved, and the *impresa* and the motto are quite clear to see. The next is Solitude and the emblem is the phoenix, meaning that she liked to live alone, and that she lived for herself, and died and was reborn only through the fame of her good works. The third is Freedom and the device is the Sun, which, free and illuminated only by itself, spreads its light to the entire universe, meaning that my aunt, free and alone, came to radiate many praiseworthy and valued qualities and also shared the treasures of her virtues with every good soul who knew her. Under the command and rule of a husband, she probably would not have done this. The fourth is Naivety and the device is a butterfly who is burned by the light, meaning that wretched women who are married place too much belief in the insincere sweet-talk and false flattery of men, who seem outwardly so well disposed and charming in mien, so that the women, thinking that they would always be as good as they seemed at first, let themselves be trapped in the net and fall into the fire that burns and consumes them to their death. The fifth is Falsehood and the device is the peach, which resembles a heart with its leaves in the shape of a tongue, with the motto which relates to the deceit and falsehood of men, whose words convey love and fidelity towards us women, but in their hearts are the reverse. The sixth is Cruelty and the device of the Crocodile signifies that man bites and kills the woman entangled with him, and then, bestially, feigns sympathy.'

ON PORTRAITS

8. Girolama Corsi Ramos on her portrait by Carpaccio, 1494–96

During the Renaissance many sonnets were written on portraits, sometimes derived from Petrarch's pair on Simone Martini's images of his beloved Laura, others connecting more closely with Greek and Latin sources.[13] This example by Girolama Corsi (c. 1460–1507), of Florentine origins but settled in Venice from 1494, on her own portrait by Carpaccio, now lost, plays with the common themes of the masterful artist competing with nature, and the portrait that almost seems to speak.

> Vărzaru, 'Tre fonti letterarie riguardanti l'opera di Vittore Carpaccio', *Revue Roumaine d'Histoire de l'Art*, 15 (1978), pp. 117–20.

That which his intellect wished to display,
in here portraying my very figure,
he placed in the work with all skill and care
to make my tongue ready to speak.
But heaven did not wish to allow this,
saying a mortal man robs and usurps
powers owned by Nature herself,
in making a wooden panel seem like a living figure.
If you had seen me, you would not be able
to say which is I, though sometimes the true one,
Seems, falsely, to be another silent one, [saying:]
'Victor made me, as you see,
worthy of fame and a higher renown
as he is a good and true master of such art'.

9. Gaspara Stampa imagines a portrait of her lover, before 1554

The Paduan poet (1523/24–54), who is known to have associated with intellectuals well-informed on artistic matters, here shows herself aware of a much-debated topic of her time, namely whether the visual arts, and portraiture in particular, were capable of presenting inward qualities of character as well as outward appearances.[14] In this sequence of four sonnets, Stampa challenges the artist to portray both of these: the supreme physical beauty of her lover, and the different psychological aspects he might display to his different associates. Other imaginary portraits might present her own fluctuating sentiments, resulting from his distance or proximity.

Gaspara Stampa, *Rime* (1554), LV–LVIII, ed. M. Bellonci and R. Ceriello (Milan, 1976), pp. 114–17.

You who in marble, pigment, bronze or wax,
imitate and conquer Nature,
forming one or another figure
with little likeness to its true form,
    come all of you, a gracious band
to form the loveliest creature
the Prime Mover ever shaped
since making with his own hands the first creation.
    Portray my count, and make sure
to portray what is within and what without,
so that this work may lack nothing.
    Only give him a double heart
as you see that he truly has
his and my own, which Love has given him.

Then, on the other side, portray me,
as you see I actually am:
alive, lacking soul or heart in my bosom,
through a miracle of Love a rare and novel art;
    like a ship that drifts without rigging,
lacking rudder, lacking any kind of sail,
ever gazing at the blessed light
of its sunset, everywhere sinking.
    And take care that this my likeness
on the left side is wretched and miserable,
on the right happy and triumphant:
    my happy side means this,

that now I find my lord before me,
the other, my fear he'll soon be with another woman.

What good would it do, lord, vainly to strive
to portray and sculpt you in marble or on paper,
whether by others famed in art
or by glorious Buonarroti or Titian,
    if I have sculpted what is open and clear
in my head and bosom piece by piece,
so that the image never departs from thence
whether you're near or else drawing away?
    But perhaps you wish to be portrayed
with the loyal, gracious countenance
you show in every deed, in every action;
    though, weary, daring scarcely to say it,
I bear your imprint, which I feel in practice,
somewhat fickle and disdainful.

10. Veronica Franco is edified by portraits of clerics and saints at Fumane, 1575

The theme of portraiture as conveying inner qualities is pursued in a different way by Veronica Franco, in her lines on images of distinguished clerics and holy men in the Villa della Torre. The passage comes just after her appreciation of fabrics decorated with erotic fables, and may be intended to balance this with a claim for the moral instructiveness of other types of art. This interest in the moral potential of art occurs throughout Renaissance art theory, but was restated with a particular emphasis during the mid-to-late sixteenth century under the influence of religious reform.

Franco, *Terze rime*, 25, 199–222, in Franco ed. Jones and Rosenthal (1998), pp. 262–5.

There every pope is portrayed
more living than in nature,
made on canvas with paint and shading;
and as such majesty requires.
Such holy images are situated

separate from the others, in a superior place.
Similarly, in a style befitting them,
there are also the portraits of those
who support a blessed entrance to heaven;
as many cardinals as ever existed in the world
are there, in the company of popes and bishops,
and many other churchmen like them.
So that this heavenly residence
may resemble paradise, it contains
the faces of people so saintly and pious.
From the many examples of men shown there
one can come to a perfect understanding
of what is fitting for the priesthood:
though dead, these men can still teach the living -
indeed, they live in such a way in heaven
that their names will always be famous on earth.
And though some I cannot recognise or name,
I know that they were pure in spirit
and that they defeated the Devil's power.
Thus portrayed, their brows inspire us
to admire them reverently, and awaken in us
thoughts of the most lofty things:
they make the man who holds the sceptre
of this gracious house[15] hope, by following them,
to rise to heaven by the steps they have taken.

11. Isabetta Coreglia, on her portrait by Pietro Paolini

The Lucchese poet Isabetta Coreglia (c. 1605–60), who enjoyed some success during her lifetime, wrote a series of unpublished poems on different works by the painter Pietro Paolini (1603–81). They may have been composed over the 1630s, 40s or 50s, as there seems to have been a longstanding family connection with the artist. Carlo Paolini had requested that his brother make a portrait of Isabetta, resulting in her poems addressed to each man: Pietro's is given here.

E. Struhal, 'Pittura e poesia a Lucca nel Seicento: il caso di Pietro Paolini', in *Lucca città d'arte e i suoi archivi*, ed. M. Seidel and R. Silva (Venice, 2001), no. 11, fol. 46, p. 402.

Pietro, your hand, made
to rival Nature,
and present the Idea of Beauty
should not be made to paint
the confused horrors of my face
since you would then compose your colours in vain.
You know well that the Sun
lends the brush light and gilds the world,
chases Night away and makes Dawn surge.
I am the Night, and you the living Sun: repelled by me
you'll make dark light, and your brush
shape not me, but a face of beauty.

RELIGIOUS IMAGES

Many women authors writing on religious images, even those
conversant with matters artistic, concentrate on the devotional subject-matter, rather than the way in which it was pic-
tured. However, the following examples to varying degrees pay
attention to the artistic skill and visual qualities shown in the
paintings.

12. Veronica Gambara on a *Magdalen* by Correggio, August 1528

The poet Veronica Gambara (1485–1550) corresponded with
several people who were well informed on matters relating to
art and was herself a patron of the arts. In this carefully crafted
letter informing Isabella d'Este of a talented local artist, Correggio,
whom Isabella would eventually use in her *studiolo*, Gambara is
able both to describe concisely what the painting depicts, and to
commend the beauty and eloquence of the figure, which in producing the desired devotional response demonstrate the artist's
mastery.

A. Luzio and R. Renier, *La coltura e le relazioni letterarie di
Isabella d'Este Gonzaga*, ed. S. Albonica (Turin, 2005), p. 159.

I should fail in my duty to Your Excellency if at the same
time I did not tell you of the masterpiece of painting which

our Antonio Allegri [Correggio] had just completed, as I know so well how your Excellency delights in such things, as one so well-informed. The picture represents the Magdalen in the desert in a dark cavern, where she has fled to make penitence. She kneels on the right, lifting clasped hands to heaven to beg pardon for her sins. Her beautiful attitude, and the noble and intense sorrow expressed on her most lovely face, are marvellous, so that everyone who has seen the picture is filled with wonder. In this work the painter has expressed all that is most sublime in the art of which he is so great a master.

13. Vittoria Colonna, on St Luke's painting of the Virgin Mary, c. 1540

This sonnet came from a collection of her verse which Colonna (c. 1490–1547) presented to Michelangelo around 1540 in Rome. Whereas elsewhere (chapter 7, text 16.i) she showed admiration for Michelangelo's delicacy and polish, here she seems to argue that the unsophisticated means of the evangelist icon painter do not impede him from expressing some of the spiritual qualities of the Virgin.

Vittoria Colonna, *Sonnets for Michelangelo*, ed. and trans. A. Brundin (Chicago, 2005), no. 45, pp. 90–93.

While Luke was made worthy to depict the Virgin,
Since he had an inward conception of God's mysteries,
He used all his ingenuity
Truly to shape the appearance of divine beauty,
But the immense idea so overwhelmed his breast,
That like an overflowing vase of water
Which could take no more, the lofty conception
Emerged little by little, flawed and imperfect.
He captured in part the sweetly grave expression,
But failed to make her lifelike, perhaps despising
The strong highlights and fierce shadows used in art.
It suffices that his humble methods and gentle act
Direct one to God, ascend, move, and in beholding it
all dark mists disperse from the heart.

14. Laura Battiferri, on a painting of St Helena (before c. 1564)
Laura Battiferri (1523–89), though closely connected with artistic circles through her sculptor-husband Bartolommeo Ammannati and his friends, here does not discuss the visual qualities of the work by an unknown author, and it is not clear whether the painting shows or only implies the act of discovery. It is the subject, Helena's ardent faith, that is intended to engage and inspire the viewer.

> Laura Battiferri, ed. and trans. V. Kirkham, in *Laura Battiferra and her Literary Circle* (Chicago, 2006), 23 [92], pp. 244–5.

On the panel painting of the Discovery of the Cross

> She leaves the famous banks of the Tiber
> forgetful of every royal task,
> a woman fired with ardent, lofty yearning
> to see the unknown waves of the Jordan;
>   to find what a wicked Jew conceals,
> sanctified wood where God eternal,
> made mortal man, to save man died,
> bitterly tortured, harshly, deeply wounded,
>   and to adore Him in a form so gracious
> and so pious, most marvellously expressed
> by the hand and intellect of the good painter.
>   Fortunate HELENA, how much praise
> and thanks we owe your pious devotion
> for such a gift now granted to us all.

15. Isabetta Coreglia on Pietro Paolini's *Penitent Magdalen*, c. 1623
One of three verses written by Coreglia on Paolini's painting of a converted Magdalene at the feet of Christ, this poem has the lachrymose sensuality typical of much 'Counter-Reformation' writing on penitential themes.

> Struhal (2001), no. 5, fol. 42v, p. 401.

> Pietro, this mourner
> this lovely penitent,
> eloquent in her silence

speaks, that she has spirit and life,
and, turned to her Sovereign Lord,
seems a lovely living sky, raining tears.

She mingles tears and sighs,
and sighs with broken kisses,
kisses of her torments.
Truthful messengers,
may you be called to a higher, finer life,
and expire on this canvas from sweetness alone.

Prostrate at the holy feet,
milk blends with vermilion,
profiting from her sighs,
they have become creators;
and the locks, which flow in golden tresses
place a rich treasure before immortal Jove.

ON THE HANDIWORK OF WOMEN

16. Chiara Matraini to Florida Amaranti, on lace collars and cuffs made for Amaranti's husband, 1595

In this letter published with two accompanying sonnets in 1595, Matraini praises the delicate handiwork of her friend, dignified by evoking the legend of Arachne and Minerva, rivals in weaving, and seen as binding the married couple together. In the second sonnet, a new twist is given to a trope familiar in Renaissance poetry, of the lover envying an article of clothing which touches his beloved's body.

Matraini, ed. Rabitti (1989), pp. 175–7.

Here, my dear Madonna Florida, are the two sonnets I have composed in your name, as you asked me, on the delicate needlework that you have prepared for your most beloved and honoured consort. If they are not as fine and ornate as would befit your merits, you must excuse the weakness of my feeble intellect, and exempt a spirit ever ready to make you something that might be beneficial and agreeable to you.

May these linen pieces round his lovely neck
be the yoke of my sweet and gentle love,
which, like an adamantine key,
ever binds that constant faith, with which I adorn him.
    May it never give him shame or scorn -
a burden for one less worthy – and not constrain
the dashing hand, which also clothes, alas,
the soul, which dwells within it.
    May the strands that composed the noble canvas
which displayed the supreme skill of Arachne,
be strong laces for the hand which will tie me.
    And may the graceful needlework never constrict him,
nor the arms which Love hides and conceals from me,
all that we humans can find sweet and dear.

No rubies, sapphires, pearls nor gold
were ever valued at whatever price
around a rich and regal cloak or frieze
as much as you, my noble handiwork, will be,
    being owned by the dearest and most worthy Treasure
that Nature ever formed, divine, distinguished,
with a spirited, fine and lofty soul,
for ever so much loved and honoured by me.
    O happy ones, who in so fond a fashion,
clasping the neck and both the arms,
with how secure a peace will you enjoy him!
    But I, for my part, never can enjoy his sight,
nor ever hear that he delights
in loving me, as I love him.

ON THE WORK OF ARTISTS AND THE ARTS

17. Laura Battiferri on the death of Michelangelo, 1564

As part of the elaborate ceremonies staged in Florence for
the funeral of Michelangelo in 1564, literary figures placed on
his catafalque in S. Croce poems, which were later printed by
Jacopo Giunti. Two were by Battiferri, a member of the Academy
which had organised the proceedings, and were perhaps the
most conspicuous sixteenth-century examples of a female

author writing on art. Part of the second poem, a *canzone*, is
given here.

Laura Battiferri, in Jacopo Giunti, *Esequie del divino
Michelangelo Buonarroti* (Florence, 1564), ed. and trans.
R. and M. Wittkower (London, 1964), pp. 126–9; ed. Kirkham
(2006), pp. 286–9.

How many charming flowers have you gathered
in your ample lap, O Flora,
but gentle Flora, drop them now
and fill your lovely bosom
only with bitter laments, unleashing
broken cries and tearful wailing,
since your loss
(and you know how great it is)
far exceeds all others, since he
who spares no one,
with his sharp darts has struck
him, who with his wondrous art,
rivalled on earth the Art of Nature.
. . .
Alas cruel arrow, that strives today
to end our happy state.
Today, through your savage blow,
deprived of all ornament is the world,
which he once made lofty and joyful
with his celestial mastery,
and with foreshortenings and outlines and light and shade
embracing marble and hollowing out the shadows.
Such sweet breath he gave
both to lovely paint and to stone
whilst this divine Angel dwelt on earth,
that whoever saw his creations
was filled with amazement, almost
transformed to stone at the fine work.
O destiny high and rare,
O forms unique and novel,
in which you showed clearly and distinctly

the truth as feigned,
and feigned, the truth, so others knew not
where the real object could be found,
since in you are seen both spirit, flesh, and bones.

18. Moderata Fonte's female characters discuss the visual arts, 1600

Many of the passages in this chapter have shown women writers as well versed in standard subjects recurring in discussions on art during the Renaissance: the artist in competition with Nature, the extent to which the artist could portray inward states, the relative nobility of painting and sculpture. In her *Merito delle donne*, Fonte shows each of her seven female speakers contributing to such a discussion. Neither topics nor opinions are original – although the author manages to include remarks on a woman painter (Marietta Tintoretto) and on the falsehood of men – but the passage testifies to the diffusion of art-critical culture amongst civic women by 1600.

Fonte, ed. Chemello (1988), pp. 159–61; ed. Cox (1997), pp. 225–7.

'I think the poet has much in common with the painter', said Lucrezia, 'since just as the latter in his manner paints and varies lines and colours, with forms, spaces, shadows, lines, indents and protuberances, so the pen of the skilful poet gives substance with different words to the fine designs which he has imagined and conceived in his mind'.

'Excellently spoken', said Corinna, 'the comparison is so apt that no one could fault it'.

'Oh, I wouldn't say that', said Cornelia, 'since the sight of a fine portrait, taken from life by any excellent painter, where you vividly sense all the substance, lines, expression and actions of the figure, so that it seems to breathe, speak and possess senses and movement, is, I believe, much more valuable, and a superior work to ten lines on the same subject, even ones of the highest quality'.

'You are completely wrong', said Corinna, 'since painting is a dead body and poetry a disembodied soul; therefore just as the soul is more noble than the body, so a composition in words is nobler than one in pigments'.

'So painting would be the body of poetry, and poetry the soul of painting', said Cornelia.

'Absolutely', said Corinna, 'but let's leave this subject. Still, painting has the great merit of preserving the living image of a person after their death, for the memory of posterity.'

'Quite', said the Queen, 'but the painter must be excellent enough to do justice to the art form'.

'Who is there in our day', said Cornelia, 'worthy to be named a distinguished and famous painter?'

'I have heard people say', said Lucrezia, 'that Signor Jacopo Tintoretto and one of his daughters are amazingly able.'

'Signor Paolo Veronese performs miracles in that art, as I've seen with my own eyes', said the Queen.

'Well, I admit painting is a wonderful art', said Elena, 'but I think that sculpture also has many merits, and perhaps is finer than painting as it has the third dimension, which is extremely important as representing the character and shape of an image more fully than does painting, which, though it might convey relief with shading, still lacks the force and immediacy of sculpture'.

'You don't understand', said Corinna, 'why painting in all its methods is much superior, is numbered among the Liberal Arts and is more powerful than is sculpture. Even if sculpture does have the relief that you mention, painting is not without it, as even you admit: relief not as touched but as seen. Moreover, painting possesses a nobler expressiveness and perfection because of its lively colours.'

'In ancient times', replied Elena, 'those wise Romans would perpetuate their images and memory more through sculpture than through painting, as witnessed by so many ruined remains throughout the city of Rome'.

'Perhaps', Corinna added, 'they thought that something worked in stone would be more durable than a canvas or panel. Still, they did not reject painting.'

'Oh', said Leonora, 'if one could only find a painter or sculptor good enough to be able to portray from life the inherent nature of men, so that all the secrets of their hearts could clearly be discerned, so that their false exteriors could no longer deceive us in our naivety. Because even if some of us, as Lucrezia says, do understand their wickedness and yet continue to love them and endure being made fools by them, there are still many others who would not put up with so much evil and abuse, their deceit and tall tales.'

Notes

1 Overviews of Italian female writers are in R. Russell (ed.), *Italian Women Writers: A Bibliographical Sourcebook* (Westport, CT, 1994), L. A. Stortoni and M. Prentice Lillie (eds), *Women Poets of the Italian Renaissance* (New York, 1997), and especially V. Cox, *Women's Writing in Italy 1400–1650* (Baltimore, 2008).

2 On *ekphrasis* as it affected Renaissance writing about art, see M. Baxandall, *Giotto and the Orators: Humanist Observers of Painting in Italy and the Discovery of Pictorial Composition* (Oxford, 1971), and N. E. Land, *The Viewer as Poet: The Renaissance Response to Art* (University Park, PA, 1994), with bibliographies.

3 The humanist letters of Laura Cereta contain two notable examples of *ekphrasis*, on embroideries she had made, not included here as having been written in Latin. See Laura Cereta, *Collected Letters of a Renaissance Feminist*, ed. D. Robin (Chicago, 1997), pp. 25–6, 31–4.

4 See M. Rogers, 'Becoming articulate: Women writing on the visual arts in Renaissance Italy', *Acta ad Archaeologiam et Artium Historiam Pertinentia*, 23, new series 8 (2009), pp. 250–72.

5 See M. Rogers, 'Courtesan and connoisseur: Veronica Franco on the Villa della Torre at Fumane', in T. Frangenburg (ed.), *Poetry on Art. Renaissance to Romanticism* (Donington, 2003), pp. 114–34.

6 In Ovid, *Metamorphoses* II, 1–7.

7 The god Mercury, disguised as a shepherd, caused the hundred-eyed Argus to sleep, before slaying him; *Metamorphoses* I, 671–720.

8 *Metamorphoses* IV, 610–11.

9 *Metamorphoses* II, 847–75; X, 155–61.

10 Callisto; see *Metamorphoses* II, 417–95; later reference is to the Great and Little Bear constellations into which the characters were transformed.

11 The seven women friends participating in the dialogue.

12 The meaning of the letters is unknown.

13 See J. Shearman, *Only Connect . . . Art and the Spectator in the Italian Renaissance* (Princeton, 1992), pp. 108–48, though focusing on the theme of the apparent engagement of the painted image with the spectator.

14 For bibliography on Stampa, see F. Bassanese, *Gaspara Stampa* (Boston, 1983).

15 Marcantonio della Torre, the clerical owner of the villa.

≈ ≈

BIBLIOGRAPHY

PRIMARY SOURCES

Adorni, B., 'Il ruolo di Margherita d'Austria nella costruzione del Palazzo Farnese a Piacenza', in S. Mantini (ed.), *Margherita d'Austria: costruzioni politiche e diplomazia tra corte Farnesiana e monarchia spagnola* (Rome, 2003), pp. 107–25.

Ahrendt, M. S., 'The Cultural Legacy and Patronal Stewardship of Margherita Paleologa (1510–1566), Duchess of Mantua and Marchesa of Monferrat' (PhD dissertation, Washington University, St Louis, 2002).

Alberti, Leon Battista, *L'Architettura*, ed P. Portoghesi, trans. G. Orlandi, 2 vols (Milan, 1966).

Alfani, Battista degli, *Memoriale di Monteluce cronaca del Monastero delle Clarisse di Perugia*, ed. A. Briganti (Perugia, 1983).

Allori, Alessandro, *I Ricordi*, ed I. B. Supino (Florence, 1908).

Altieri, Marco Antonio, *'Li Nuptiali'*, ed. E. Narducci (Rome, 1873).

Antonino, *Opera a ben vivere*, ed. C. Angelini (Milan, 1926).

Archivio di Stato di Firenze, Guardaroba 85.

— Magistrato dei Pupilli 183.

— Mediceo del Principato (MdP), vol. 1176.

Aretino, Pietro, *Lettere sull'arte*, ed. E. Camesasca. 4 vols (Milan, 1957–60).

Armenini, Gian Battista, *De'veri precetti della pittura* [1587], ed. M. Gorreri (Turin, 1988).

'L'arte negli stati sabaudi ai tempi di Carlo Emanuele I, di Vittorio Amedeo I, e della reggenza di Cristina di Francia, dai manoscritti del Conte Alessandro Baudi di Vesne', *Atti della Società Piemontese di Archeologia e Belle Arti*, 14 (1932).

Baglioni, Giovanni, *Le vite de' pittori, scultori, architetti ed intagliatori . . .* [Rome, 1642], ed. V. Mariani (Rome, 1935).

Barocchi, P. and G. Gaeta Bertelà (eds), *Collezionismo mediceo e storia artistica. II. Il cardinale Carlo, Maria Maddalena, Don Lorenzo, Ferdinando II, Vittoria della Rovere, 1621–1666*, 3 vols (Florence, 2005).

Barzaghi, A., *Donne o cortigiane?* (Verona, 1980).

Battisti, E., *Piero della Francesca*, 2 vols (Milan, 1971).

Belgrano, L. T., *Della vita privata dei genovesi* (Genoa, 1875).

Bellinazzi, A. and F. Martelli, 'Il palazzo di Pinti dagli Scala ad Alessandro de' Medici e ai della Gherardesca', in A. Bellinazzi (ed.), *La casa del cancelliere. Documenti e studi sul palazzo di Bartolomeo Scala a Firenze* (Florence, 1998), pp. 137–68.

Bembo, Pietro, *Lettere*, ed. E. Travi, 4 vols (Bologna, 1987–93).

Berardi, P., 'Arte e artisti a Pesaro: regesti di documenti di età malatestiana e di età sforzesca', *Pesaro Città e Contà*, 12 (2000).

Bernardino da Siena, *Prediche volgari sul Campo di Siena. 1427*, ed. C. Delcorno, 2 vols (Milan, 1989).

Bertolotti, A., 'Le arti minori alla corte di Mantova', *Archivio Storico Lombardo*, ser. 2, vol. 5, anno 15 (1888), pp. 419–590.

— *Le arti minori alla corte di Mantova nei secoli XV, XVI, XVII* (Milan, 1889).

Bertoni, G. and E. P. Vicini, *Il castello di Ferrara ai tempi di Niccolò III. Inventario della suppellettile del castello (1436)* (Bologna, 1906).

Bicci, Neri di, *Le Ricordanze (1453–1475)*, ed. A. Santi (Florence, 1976).

Binaghi Olivari, M. T., 'I ricamatori milanesi', in P. Venturoli (ed.), *I tessili nell'età di Carlo Bascapè vescovo di Novara (1593–1615)* (Novara, 1994), pp. 97–123.

Bini, D., 'Isabella d'Este e la cultura del cibo', in D. Bini (ed.), *Isabella d'Este la primadonna del Rinascimento* (Modena and Mantua, 2001), pp. 225–38.

Borghesi, S. and L. Banchi, *Nuovi documenti per la storia dell'arte senese* (Siena, 1898).

Bottari, G. and S. Ticozzi (eds), *Raccolta di lettere sulla pittura, scultura e architettura*, 8 vols (Milan, 1822–25, repr. Bologna, 1979–80).

Braghirolli, W., *Lettere inedite di artisti del secolo XV cavate dall'archivio Gonzaga* (Mantua, 1878).

Brandmüller, W., 'Paola Gonzaga e il giubileo di Martino V', in A. Groppi and L. Scaraffia (eds), *Le donne ai tempi del giubileo. 'Con singolar modestia e insolita devozione'* (Milan, 2000), pp. 73–80.

Brown, C. M., 'Little known and unpublished documents concerning Andrea Mantegna, Bernardino Parentino, Pietro Lombardo, Leonardo da Vinci and Filippo Benintendi' (Part One), *L'Arte*, 6 (1969), pp. 140–64.

— *Isabella d'Este and Lorenzo da Pavia: Documents for the History of Art and Culture in Renaissance Mantua* (Geneva, 1982).

— '"Al suo amenissimo Palazzo di Porto": Biagio Rossetti and Isabella d'Este', *Atti e Memorie. Accademia Nazionale Virgiliana di Scienze, Lettere ed Arti*, new ser., 58 (1990), pp. 33–56.

— *'Per dare qualche splendore a la gloriosa città di Mantua'. Documents for the Antiquarian Collection of Isabella d'Este* (Rome, 2002).

— 'Ricordi dell'archivio', in G. Delmarcel and C. M. Brown (eds), *Gli arazzi dei Gonzaga nel Rinascimento* (Milan, 2010), pp. 223–63.

Bury, M., 'Bernardo Vecchietti, patron of Giambologna', in *I Tatti Studies. Essays in the Renaissance*, 1 (1985), pp. 13–56.

Cadogan, J. K., *Domenico Ghirlandaio. Artist and Artisan* (New Haven and London, 2000).

Caffi, M., 'Il Castello di Pavia', *Archivio Storico Lombardo*, ser. 1, vol. 3, anno 3 (1876), pp. 543–59.

Calmo, Andrea, *Delle lettere di M. Andrea Calmo* (Venice, 1572).

Calvi, G., 'Abito, genere, cittadinanza nella Toscana moderna, secoli XVI–XVII', *Quaderni Storici*, 110 (2002), pp. 478–503.

Campo, Antonio, *Cremona fidelissima città* (Cremona, 1585).

Campori, G., *Lettere artistiche inedite* (Modena, 1866).

— 'L'arazzeria estense', *Atti e Memorie delle Regie Deputazioni di Storia Patria per le Provincie Modenesi e Parmensi*, 1:8 (1876); repr. as facsimile monograph (Sala Bolognese, 1980).

— *I pittori degli Estensi nel secolo XV* (Modena, 1886).

Cantaro, M. T., *Lavinia Fontana bolognese 'pittora singolare' 1552–1614* (Milan and Rome, 1989).

Caprara, F., '"De uno monastero di monache lascivo reformato al ben vivere per el Rosario": Alfonso Lombardi e Parmigianino in S. Margherita', in V. Fortunati (ed.), *Vita artistica nel monastero femminile. Exempla* (Bologna, 2002), pp. 146–67.

Carnesecchi, C., *Cosimo I e la sua legge suntuaria del 1546* (Florence, 1902).

Caroli, F., *Fede Galizia* (Turin, 1989).

Cartwright, J., *Beatrice d'Este Duchess of Milan 1475–1497. A Study in the Renaissance* (London and New York, 1926).

Casale, G., *Giovanna Garzoni 'insigne miniatrice' 1600–1670* (Milan and Rome, 1991).

Casalini, E., *Una icona di famiglia. Nuovi contributi di storia e d'arte sulla SS. Annunziata di Firenze* (Florence, 1998).

Casanova, E., 'La donna senese del Quattrocento nella vita privata', *Bollettino Senese di Storia Patria*, 8:1 (1901), p. 95.

Casola, Pietro, *Viaggio a Gerusalemme*, ed. A. Paoletti (Alessandria, 2001).

Cavalier Reale, Il, *La felicissima entrata della serenissima regina di Spagna, Donna Margherita d'Austria, nella città di Ferrara il 13. Novembre MDXCVIII* (Ferrara, 1598).

Cellini, Benvenuto, *La Vita*, ed. G. Davico Bonino (Turin, 1973).

Chong, A., D. Pegazzano and D. Zikos, *Ritratto di un banchiere del Rinascimento. Bindo Altoviti tra Raffaello e Cellini* (Milan, 2004).

Colonna, Vittoria, *Sonnets for Michelangelo*, ed. and trans. A. Brundin. (Chicago, 2005).

Comacchio, L., *Storia di Asolo*, 16 vols (Asolo, 1980).

Conti, E., E. Guidotti and R. Lunari (eds), *La civiltà fiorentina del Quattrocento* (Florence, 1993).

Corsani, C., 'Le trasformazioni architettoniche del complesso della Quiete', in C. De Benedictis (ed.), *Villa La Quiete. Il patrimonio artistico del conservatorio delle Montalve* (Florence, 1997), pp. 1–30.

Corsini Sforza, L., 'La collezione di Caterina Nobili Sforza contessa di Santafiora', *L'Arte*, 1 (1898), pp. 273–8.

Crowe, J. A. and G. B. Cavalcaselle, *Titian: His Life and Times*, 2 vols (London, 1877).

Cruciani, F., *Teatro nel Rinascimento a Roma 1450–1550* (Rome, 1983).

Datini, Francesco, *Le lettere alla moglie Margherita (1385–1410)*, ed. E. Cecchi (Prato, 1990).

Del Grosso, M. A., *Donna nel Cinquecento tra letteratura e realtà* (Salerno, 1989).

Delucca, O., *Artisti a Rimini fra Gotico e Rinascimento. Rassegna di fonti archivistiche* (Rimini, 1997).

Di Macco, M. 'Arredo di palazzo e collezionismo di corte. La quadreria', in M. Di Macco and G. Romano (eds), *Diana trionfatrice. Arte di corte nel Piemonte nel Seicento* (Turin, 1989), pp. 96–8.

Di Majo, I., 'Vittoria Colonna, il Castello di Ischia e la cultura delle corti', in P. Ragionieri (ed.), *Vittoria Colonna e Michelangelo* (Florence, 2005), pp. 19–32.

Dina, A., 'Isabella d'Aragona duchessa di Milano e di Bari', *Archivio Storico Lombardo*, ser. 5, vol. 8, anno 48 (1921), pp. 269–457.

Dio, Giovanni di, *Decor puellarum: zoe honore de le donzelle: la quale da regola forma e modo al stato de le honeste donzelle* (Venice, 1471).

Dominici, Giovanni, *Lettere spirituali*, ed. M. T. Casella and G. Pozzi (Freiburg, 1969).

— *Life and Death in a Venetian Convent*, ed. and trans. D. Bornstein (Chicago, 2000).

Eiche, S. 'Prologue to the Villa Imperiale frescoes', *Notizie di Palazzo Albani*, 20 (1991), pp. 99–119.

Fedele, P., 'I gioielli di Vannozza ed un'opera del Caradosso', *Archivio della Reale Società Romana di Storia Patria*, 28 (1905), pp. 452–71.

Ferino-Pagden, S., *Vittoria Colonna. Dichterin und Muse Michelangelos* (exhibition catalogue, Vienna, 1997).

Ferrarini, G., *Memoriale estense (1476–1489)*, ed. P. Griguolo (Rovigo, 2006).

Ferrua, A., 'Ritrovamento dell'epitaffio di Vannozza Cattaneo [sic]', *Archivio della Società Romana di Storia Patria*, 71 (1948), pp. 139–41.

Fonte, Moderata, *Il Merito delle donne*, ed. A. Chemello (Mirano and Venice, 1988).

— *The Worth of Women*, ed. and trans. V. Cox (Chicago, 1997).

Forti Grazzini, N., *L'arazzo ferrarese* (Milan, 1982).

Franceschini, A., *Artisti a Ferrara in età umanistica e rinasci-*

mentale. *Testimonianze archivistiche. Parte I dal 1341 al 1471* (Ferrara and Rome, 1993).

— *Artisti a Ferrara in età umanistica e rinascimentale. Testimonianze archivistiche, Parte II, Tomo I, dal 1472 al 1492* (Ferrara and Rome, 1995).

Franco, Veronica, *Lettere dall'unica edizione del MDLXXX con proemio e nota iconografica*, ed. B. Croce (Naples, 1949).

— *Poems and Selected Letters*, ed. A. R. Jones and M. E. Rosenthal (Chicago, 1998).

Frati, L., *La vita privata di Bologna dal secolo XIII al XVII* (Bologna, 1900).

Fuda, R., 'Un'inedita lettera di Artemisia Gentileschi a Ferdinando II de' Medici', *Rivista d'Arte*, XLI, ser. 4, 5 (1989), pp. 167–71.

Gaglione, M., 'Quattro documenti per la storia di S. Chiara in Napoli', *Archivio Storico per le Province Napoletane*, 121 (2003), pp. 399–431.

Galli, R., *Lavinia Fontana pittrice* (Imola, 1940).

Gandini, L. A., *Isabella, Beatrice e Alfonso d'Este infanti. Documenti inediti del secolo XV* (Modena, 1896).

Gaye, G., *Carteggio inedito d'artisti dei secoli XIV, XV, XVI*, 3 vols (Florence, 1839–40).

Geisenheimer, H., 'Spigolature poccettiane', *Arte e Storia*, 28:3 (1909), pp. 70–80.

Gigli, Giacinto, *Diario di Roma*, ed. M. Barberito, 2 vols (Rome, 1994).

Giunti, Jacopo, *Esequie del divino Michelangelo Buonarroti* (Florence, 1564), ed. and trans. R. and M. Watchtower (London, 1964).

Gladen, C. A., 'Suor Lucrina Fetti, pittrice in una corte mantovana seicentesa', in G. Pomata and G. Zarri (eds), *I monasteri femminili come centri di cultura fra Rinascimento e Barocco* (Rome, 2005), p. 129.

Goldenberg Stoppato, L., 'La Cappella delle Reliquie in Palazzo Pitti', in M. Gregori (ed.), *Fasto di Corte. La decorazione murale nelle residenze dei Medici e dei Lorena*, 2 vols (Florence, 2005), 1, pp. 137–43.

Golzio, V., *Raffaello nei documenti, nelle testimonianze dei contemporanei e nella letteratura del suo secolo* (Città del Vaticano, 1936, repr. Farnborough, 1971).

Gregori, M. (ed.), *Fasto di Corte. La decorazione murale nelle residenze dei Medici e dei Lorena*, 2 vols (Florence, 2005).

Grimaldi, F., 'Pellegrini e pellegrinaggi a Loreto nei secoli XIV–XVIII', *Bollettino Storico della Città di Foligno*, supplement 2 (2001), pp. 428–31.

Grimaldi, F. (ed.), *La historia de la chiesa di Santa Maria di Loreto* (Loreto, 1993).

Gronau, G., *Documenti artistici urbinati* (Florence, 1936).

Groppi, A. and L. Scaraffia (eds), *'Con singolar modestia e insolita devozione'. Le donne ai tempi del giubileo* (Milan, 2000).

Hall, M., *Renovation and Counter-Reformation: Vasari and Duke Cosimo in Sta Maria Novella and Sta Croce 1565–1577* (Oxford, 1979).

Hartt, F., *Giulio Romano*, 2 vols (New Haven, 1958; 2nd edn, New York, 1981).

Hickson, S., 'Diplomazia e pellicce nella Mantova del Rinascimento: Margherita Paleologo e uno *zibellino* per Maria d' Aragona', *Civiltà Mantovana*, 129 (spring 2010), pp. 92–106.

Holanda, Francisco de, *Dialogues with Michelangelo* [c. 1540–48], ed. D. Hemsoll, trans. C. B. Holroyd (London, 2006).

Improta, M. C. and A. Padoa Rizzo, 'Paola Schiavo fornitore di disegni per ricami', *Rivista d'Arte*, 41, ser. 4, 5 (1989), pp. 25–56.

Iotti, R., 'Phenice unica, virtuosa e pia. La corrispondenza culturale di Isabella', in D. Bini (ed.), *Isabella d'Este la primadonna del Rinascimento* (Modena and Mantua, 2001), pp. 167–83.

Kirkham, V. (ed. and trans.), *Laura Battiferra and her Literary Circle* (Chicago, 2006).

Klerck, B. de, *I fratelli Campi. Immagini e devozione. Pittura religiosa nel Cinquecento lombardo* (Milan, 2003).

Kristeller, P., *Andrea Mantegna* (Berlin and Leipzig, 1902).

Lazzarinti, I. (ed.), *Carteggio degli oratori mantovani alla corte sforzesca (1450–1500)*, 15 vols (Rome, 1999–2003).

Lecchini Giovannoni, S., *Alessandro Allori* (Turin, 1991).

Lefèvre, R., 'Il testamento di Margherita d'Austria, duchessa di Parma e Piacenza', *Palatino* (1968), pp. 240–50.

L'Occaso, S., *Fonti archivistiche per le arti a Mantova tra Medioevo e Rinascimento (1382–1459)* (Mantua, 2005).

— 'Margherita Gonzaga d'Este: pitture tra Mantova e Ferrara

intorno al 1600', *Atti e Memorie. Accademia Nazionale Virgiliana di Scienze, Lettere ed Arti*, new ser., 73 (2005), pp. 81–126.

Lodovisi, A., and Trent, G. (eds), *I Vignola: Giacomo e Giacinto Barozzi* (Vignola, 2004).

Lotto, Lorenzo, *Il 'Libro di spese diverse'*, ed. P. Zampetti (Venice, 1969).

Luzio, A., 'Nuovi documenti su Leonardo da Vinci', *Archivio Storico dell'Arte*, 1 (1888), pp. 45–6.

— *La galleria dei Gonzaga venduta all'Inghilterra nel 1627–28* (Milan, 1913).

Luzio, A. and R. Renier, 'Della relazioni di Isabella d'Este Gonzaga con Ludovico e Beatrice Sforza', *Archivio Storico Lombardo*, ser. 2, vol. 7, anno 17 (1890), pp. 346–99.

— *Mantova e Urbino. Isabella d'Este ed Elisabetta Gonzaga nelle relazioni famigliari e nelle vicende politiche* (Turin and Rome, 1893).

— 'La coltura e le relazioni letterarie di Isabella d'Este Gonzaga', *Giornale Storico della Letteratura Italiana*, 34 (1899), pp. 1–97.

— *La coltura e le relazioni letterarie di Isabella d'Este Gonzaga*, ed. S. Albonico (Turin, 2005).

Macinghi Strozzi, Alessandra, *Tempo di affetti e di mercanti. Lettere ai figli esuli* (Milan, 1987).

Malacarne, G., 'Il segno di Isabella: stemmi, motti, imprese', in D. Bini (ed.), *Isabella d'Este la primadonna del Rinascimento* (Modena and Mantua, 2001), pp. 185–201.

Malaguzzi Valeri, F., *La corte di Ludovico il Moro*, 4 vols (Milan, 1913–23).

Malvasia, Carlo Cesare, *Vite dei Pittori Bolognesi*, ed. M. Brascaglie (Bologna, 1971).

Marinella, Lucrezia, *Arcadia felice* [Venice, 1605], ed. F. Lavocat (Florence, 1998).

— *Nobiltà et l'eccellenza delle donne, co' difetti et mancamenti de gli uomini* (Venice, 1621).

Marinis, T. de (ed.), *Le nozze di Costanzo Sforza e Camilla d'Aragona celebrate a Pesaro nel maggio 1475* (Florence, 1946).

Matraini, Chiara, *Lettere* (Venice, 1597).

— *Rime e lettere*, ed. G. Rabitti (Bologna, 1989).

Mazza, B., 'Committenti e artisti nell'età delle riforme: L'arredo della chiesa di S. Maria della Presentazione', in L. Puppi (ed.), *Le Zitelle: architettura, arte e storia di un'istituzione veneziana* (Venice, 1992), pp. 129–61.

Mazzi, C., *La casa di Maestro Bartalo di Tura* (Siena, 1900).

Medici, Caterina de, *Lettres*, ed. H. de la Ferrière-Percy *et al.*, 11 vols (Paris, 1880–1943).

Meli, P., and S. Tognetti, *Il principe e il mercante nella Toscana del Quattrocento. Il magnifico Signore di Piombino Jacopo III Appiani e le aziende Maschiani di Pisa* (Florence, 2006).

Meloni Trkulja, S. and E. Fumagali, *Nature morte. Giovanna Garzoni* (Paris, 2000).

Merkel, C., *I beni della famiglia di Puccio Pucci: inventario del secolo XV illustrato* (n.p., n.d.).

Milanesi, G., *Nuovi documenti per la storia dell'arte toscana dal XII al XV secolo* (Florence, 1901).

Molmenti, P., *Storia di Venezia nella vita privata*, 3 vols (Bergamo, 1905–8).

Morselli, A., *Il corredo nuziale di Caterina Pico (1474)* (Modena, 1956), pp. 97–102.

Morsolin, B., 'Maddalena Campiglia poetessa vicentina del secolo XVI', *Atti dell'Accademia Olimpica di Vicenza*, 17 (1882), pp. 66–74.

Muraro, M., *Il libro secondo di Francesco e Jacopo dal Ponte* (Bassano, 1992).

Negro, E. and N. Roio (eds), *Francesco Francia e la sua scuola* (Modena, 1998).

Nelson, J. (ed.), *Suor Plautilla Nelli (1523–1588) the First Woman Painter of Florence* (Florence, 2000).

Nicola, G. de, 'Sassetta between 1423 and 1433', *Burlington Magazine*, 23 (1913), pp. 207–15, 276–83, 332–6.

Niccoli, O., *Storie di ogni giorno in una città del Seicento* (Rome and Bari, 2002).

Novi Chavarria, E., *Sacro, pubblico e privato. Donne nei secoli XV–XVIII* (Naples, 2009).

Palvarini Gobio Casali, M., *La ceramica a Mantova* (Ferrara, 1987).

Pardi, G. (ed.), 'Diario ferrarese dall'anno 1409 sino al 1502 di autori incerti', in Rerum italicarum scriptores, vol. 24, p. 17 (Bologna, 1928–37).

Pazzi, Maria Maddalena de', *I quaranta giorni*, ed. M. Rolfo (Palermo, 1996).

Pedrazzoli, A., 'La Marchesa Isabella d'Este Gonzaga a diporto sul Lago di Garda colla sua corte', *Archivio Storico Lombardo*, ser. 2, vol. 7, anno 17 (1890), pp. 866–78.

Perini, G. (ed.), *Gli scritti dei Carracci* (Bologna, 1990).

Piccinelli, R., *Le collezioni Gonzaga. Il carteggio tra Firenze e Mantova* (Milan, 2000).

Piccolomini, Alessandro, *Della institutione di tutta la vita de l'homo nato nobile e in città libera* [1542] (Venice, 1545).

— *La Raffaella, ovvero Dialogo della bella creanza delle donne* [Venice, 1539], ed. G. Alfano (Rome, 2001).

Pinelli, M.,'"Di bei Paramenti, di Prezione Argenterie e di molto altro". Appunti per la storia del patrimonio d'arte del Monastero di S. Pietro a Luco', in V. Baldacci (ed.), *'Le Contesse di Luco'. Il monastero Camaldolese femminile di San Pietro a Luco di Mugello: la storia, la fabbrica, l'arte* (Azzano S. Paolo, 2004), pp. 120–34.

Pizzorusso, C., 'La Quiete. Giovanni da San Giovanni e Alessandro Adimari', *Artista*, 1 (1989), pp. 86–97.

Politecchi, M. L. (ed.), *Il palazzo di Federico da Montefeltro* (Urbino, 1985).

Portilioli, A., 'La nascità di Massimiliano Sforza', *Archivio Storico Lombardo*, ser. 1, vol. 9 (1882), pp. 325–34.

Ragionieri, P. (ed.), *Vittoria Colonna e Michelangelo* (Florence, 2005).

Raphael, *Raffaello: gli scritti*, ed. E. Camesasca (Milan, 1993).

Razzi, Fra Serafino, *Istoria de gli Huomini illustri, così nelle prelature, come nelle Dottrine, del sacro ordine de gli Predicatori* (Lucca, 1596).

Ridolfi, Carlo, *Le meraviglie dell'arte* [Venice, 1648], ed. D. von Hadeln, 2 vols (Berlin, 1914–24).

Rinaldi, Cesare, *Rime del Signor Cesare Rinaldi Bolognese* (Venice, 1609).

— *Sophonisba Anguissola e le sue sorelle* (exhibition catalogue, Cremona 1994, Vienna 1995, Washington 1995).

Rossi, I., *La chiesa di San Maurizio in Milano. Il Monastero Maggiore e le sue due torri* (Milan, 1914).

Rucellai, Giovanni, *Giovanni Rucellai ed il suo Zibaldone, 'Il Zibaldone Quaresimale'*, ed. A. Perosa (London, 1960).

Sacchi, R., 'Fonti a stampa e letterarie (1550–1625)', in *Sofonisba Anguissola e le sue sorelle* (Cremona 1994, Vienna 1995, Washington 1995), pp. 403–11.

— 'Regesto', in *Sofonisba Anguissola e le sue sorelle* (Cremona 1994, Vienna 1995, Washington 1995), pp. 361–402.

Sansovino, Francesco, *Venetia città nobilissima et singolare* [Venice, 1581], reprint (Bergamo, 2002).

Sanuto, Marino, *I diarii (MCCCCXCVI–MDXXXIII)*, 58 vols (Bologna, 1969–70).

Schiaparelli, A., *La casa fiorentina e i suoi arredi nei secoli XIV e XV* [1908], 2 vols (Florence, 1983).

Sevesi, P., 'Il monastero delle Clarisse di S. Apollinare, Milano', *Archivium Franciscanum historicum*, 18 (1925), pp. 525–58; 19 (1926), pp. 76–99.

Sframeli, M.,'Tre pittori e un architetto per l'altare maggiore di Santa Verdiana a Firenze', *Paragone arte*, 45 (1994), pp. 171–7.

— '"Ricamato da mano angelica": un'attribuzione settecentesca per l'*Incoronazione della Vergine* di Paolo Schiavo', *Arte Cristiana*.

Shearman, J., *Andrea del Sarto*, 2 vols (Oxford, 1965).

— *Raphael in Early Modern Sources 1483–1602*, 2 vols (New Haven and London, 2003).

Signori, F. (ed.), *La famiglia di Jacopo nei documenti d'archivio* (Bassano, 1992).

Sorelli, F., *La santità imitabile: 'Leggenda di Maria da Venezia' di Tommaso da Siena* (Venice, 1984).

Spallanzani, M., 'Un "fornimento" di maioliche di Montelupo per Clarice Strozzi de' Medici', *Faenza*, 70 (1984), pp. 381–7.

Speroni, Sperone, *Contra le Cortigiane* (?1575), in *Opere di M. Sperone Speroni degli Alvarotti*, 5 vols (Venice, 1740).

Stampa, Gaspara, *Rime* (1554), ed. M. Bellonci and R. Ceriello (Milan, 1976).

Stefani, F., 'L'adorazione dei Magi di Palma Vecchio', *Archivio Veneto*, 1 (1871), pp. 166–8.

Struhal, E., 'Pittura e poesia a Lucca nel Seicento: il caso di Pietro Paolini', in *Lucca città d'arte e i suoi archivi*, ed. M. Seidel and R. Silva (Venice, 2001), pp. 389–404.

Tanfani-Centofani, L., *Notizie di artisti tratte da documenti pisani* (Pisa, 1897).

Tasso, Torquato, *Le Rime*, 2 vols (Rome, 1994).

Tinelli, Tiberio, *Libretto dei conti del pittore Tiberio Tinelli (1618–1633)*, ed. B. Lanfranchi Strina (Venice, 2000).

Titian, *Tiziano: le lettere*, ed. C. Grandini (Belluno, 1977).

Tornabuoni de' Medici, Lucrezia, *I poemetti sacri*, ed. F. Pezzarossa (Florence, 1978).

— *Sacred Narratives*, ed. and trans. J. Tylus (Chicago, 2000).

Trissino, Giangiorgio, *I ritratti di M. Giovan Giorgio Trissino* (Rome, 1524).

Tuohy, T., *Herculean Ferrara: Ercole d'Este (1471–1505) and the Invention of a Ducal Capital* (Cambridge, 1996).

Turchini, A., 'Committenza "popolare" nella devozione a Santa Rita da Cascia', in M. Tosti (ed.), *Santuari cristiani d'Italia*, Collection de l'École Française de Rome, 317 (Rome, 2003), pp. 171–94.

Urlichs, L., 'Beiträge zur Geschichte der Kunstbestrebungen und Sammlungen Kaisers Rudolph II', *Zeitschrift für Bildende Kunst*, 5 (1870), pp. 45–53.

Vărzaru, S., 'Tre fonti letterarieri riguardanti l'opera di Vittore Carpaccio', *Revue Roumaine d'Histoire de l'Art*, 15 (1978), pp. 117–20.

Vasari, Giorgio, *Le Vite* [Florence, 1568], ed. G. Milanesi, 8 vols (Florence, 1906).

— *Il libro delle Ricordanze di Giorgio Vasari*, ed. A. Del Vita (Arezzo, 1938).

Vecellio, Cesare, *De gli Habiti Antichi et Moderni. . .*[1598], *La moda nel Rinascimento*, ed. M. F. Rosenthal and A. R. Jones (London, 2008).

Venturelli, P., 'L'abito delle dame di Milano tra il 1539 e il 1599. Ornamento e colore', in A. G. Cavagna and G. Butazzi (eds), *Le trame della moda* (Rome, 1995), pp. 333–73.

Venturi, A., 'Relazioni artistiche tra le corti di Milano e Ferrara nel secolo XV', *Archivio Storico Lombardo*, ser. 2, vol. 2, anno 12 (1885), pp. 225–80.

— 'Il Cupido di Michelangelo', *Archivio Storico dell' Arte*, 1 (1888), pp. 1–13.

— 'Gian Cristoforo Romano', *Archivio Storico dell'Arte*, 1 (1888), pp. 107–18.

— 'Quadri in una cappella estense del 1586', *Archivio Storico dell'Arte*, 1 (1888), pp. 425–6.

— 'Nuovi documenti', *Archivio Storico dell'Arte*, 7 (1894), pp. 52–4.
— 'Pittori della corte ducale a Ferrara nella prima decade del secolo XVI', *Archivio Storico dell'Arte*, 7 (1894), pp. 54–7.
Verdon, T. C., 'The Art of Guido Mazzoni' (PhD dissertation, Yale University, 1975),
Viviani della Robbia, E., *La figlia di Galileo* (Florence, 1942).
— 'Note e notizie sul Cenacolo del Vasari pel Monastero delle Murate di Fiorenza', in *Studi Vasariani, Atti del Convegno* (Florence, 1952), pp. 221–4.
Waldman, L. A., *Baccio Bandinelli and Art at the Medici Court* (Philadelphia, 2004).
Winspeare, F., *Isabella Orsini e la corte medicea del suo tempo* (Florence, 1961).
Zaffanella, C., 'Isabella d'Este e la moda del suo tempo', in D. Bini (ed.), *Isabella d'Este la primadonna del Rinascimento* (Modena and Mantua, 2001), pp. 209–23.
Zarri, G., 'Sante pellegrine: Orsola e le compagne', in A. Groppi and L. Scaraffia (eds), *'Con singolar modestia e insolita devozione'. Le donne ai tempi del giubileo* (Milan, 2000), pp. 49–72.

SELECTED SECONDARY SOURCES

Ajmar-Wollheim, M. and F. Dennis (eds), *At Home in Renaissance Italy* (London, 2006).
Ajmar-Wollheim, M., F. Dennis and A. Matchette (eds), *Approaching the Renaissance Interior: Sources, Methodologies, Debates* (Oxford, 2007).
Bayer, A. (ed.), *Art and Love in Renaissance Italy* (New Haven and London, 2008).
Bornstein, D. and Rusconi, R. (eds), *Women and Religion in Medieval and Renaissance Italy* (Chicago and London, 1996).
Brown, D. A. (ed.), *Virtue and Beauty: Leonardo's Ginevra de' Benci and Renaissance Portraits of Women*, exhibition catalogue, National Gallery of Art, Washington DC (Washington, 2001).
Bury, M., *The Print in Italy 1550–1620* (London, 2001).
Campbell, C., *Love and Marriage in Renaissance Florence: The Courtauld Wedding Chests* (London, 2009).
Cavallo, S. and S. Evangelisti (eds), *Domestic Institutional Interiors in Early Modern Europe* (Farnham, 2009).

Ciapelli, G. and P. Rubin (eds), *Art, memory and family in Renaissance Florence* (Cambridge, 2000).

Dabbs, J., *Life Stories of Women Artists, 1550–1800: An Anthology* (Farnham, 2009).

Fantoni, M., L. C. Matthew and S. F. Matthews Grieco (eds), *The Art Market in Italy: 15th–17th Centuries* (Modena, 2003).

Fortini Brown, P., *Private Lives in Renaissance Venice: Art, Architecture and the Family* (New Haven and London, 2004).

Freedberg, D., *The Power of Images: Studies in the History and Theory of Response* (Chicago and London, 1989).

Frick, C. C., *Dressing Renaissance Florence: Families, Fortunes and Fine Clothing* (Baltimore, 2002).

Gilbert, C. E., 'What did the Renaissance patron buy?', *Renaissance Quarterly*, 51:2 (1998), pp. 392–450.

Goldthwaite, R. A., 'The Florentine palace as domestic architecture', *American Historical Review*, 77 (1972), pp. 977–1012.

— *Wealth and the Demand for Art in Italy, 1300–1600* (Baltimore, 1993).

Herald, J., *Renaissance Dress in Italy 1400–1500* (London, 1981).

Hills, H., *Invisible City: The Architecture of Devotion in Seventeenth-Century Neapolitan Convents* (Oxford, 2004).

— *Gender and Devotion in Early Modern Italy* (Basingstoke, 2005).

— (ed.), *Architecture and the Politics of Gender in Early Modern Europe* (Aldershot, 2003).

Hughes, D. O., 'Sumptuary laws and social relations in Renaissance Italy', in P. Findlen (ed.), *The Italian Renaissance: The Essential Readings* (Malden, MA), pp. 124–50.

Italian Women Artists from Renaissance to Baroque, exhibition catalogue, National Museeum of Women in the Arts, Washington DC (Milan, 2007).

Jacobs, F. H., *Defining the Renaissance Virtuosa* (Cambridge, 1997).

Johnson, G. A. and S. Matthews Grieco (eds), *Picturing Women in Renaissance and Baroque Italy* (Cambridge, 1997).

Kasl, R., 'Holy households: art and devotion in Renaissance Venice', in R. Kasl (ed.), *Giovanni Bellini and the Art of Devotion* (Indianapolis, 2004), pp. 59–89.

King, C. E., *Renaissance Women Patrons: Wives and Widows in Italy c. 1300–1550* (Manchester, 1998).

Klapisch-Zuber, C., *Women, Family and Ritual in Renaissance Italy*, trans. L. G. Cochrane (Chicago and London, 1985).

Kovesi Killerby, K., *Sumptuary Laws in Italy 1200–1500* (Oxford, 2001).

Ladis, A. and S. E. Zurow, *Visions of Holiness: Art and Devotion in Renaissance Italy* (Athens, GA, 2001).

Laver, M., *Virgins of Venice* (London, 2006).

Lawrence, C. (ed.), *Women and Art in Early Modern Europe: Patrons, Collectors and Connoisseurs* (University Park, PA, 1996).

Lindow, J., *The Renaissance Palace in Florence: Magnificence and Splendour in Fifteenth-Century Italy* (Aldershot, 2007).

Lowe, K. J. P., 'Elections of abbesses and notions of identity in fifteenth- and sixteenth-century Italy, with special reference to Venice', *Renaissance Quarterly*, 54:2 (2001), pp. 389–429.

— *Nuns' Chronicles and Convent Culture in Renaissance and Counter-Reformation Italy* (Cambridge, 2003).

Lydecker, J. K., 'The Domestic Setting of the Arts in Renaissance Florence' (PhD dissertation, Johns Hopkins University, 1987).

McIver, K. A., *Women, Art and Architecture in Northern Italy, 1520–1580: Negotiating Power* (Aldershot, 2006).

— 'Women of power: what women say as builders of secular architecture in early modern Italy', *Acta ad Archaelogiam et Artium Historiam Pertinentia*, 22:8 (2009), pp. 171–92.

Monnas, L., *Merchants, Princes and Painters: Silk Fabrics in Italian and Northern Paintings 1300–1500* (New Haven and London, 2008).

Morse, M. A., 'Creating sacred spaces: the religious visual culture of the Renaissance Venetian *casa*', *Renaissance Studies*, 21:2 (2007), pp. 151–84.

Murphy, C., 'Lavinia Fontana and Le Dame della Città: understanding female artistic patronage in late sixteenth-century Bologna', *Renaissance Studies*, 10:2 (1996), pp. 190–208.

Musacchio, J. M., *The Art and Ritual of Childbirth in Renaissance Italy* (New Haven and London, 1999).

— *Art, Marriage and the Family in the Florentine Renaissance Palace* (New Haven, 2008).

O'Malley, M. and E. Welch (eds), *The Material Renaissance* (Manchester, 2007).

Orsi Landini, R. and B. Niccoli (eds), *Moda a Firenze 1540–1580: lo stile di Eleonora di Toledo e la sua influenza* (Florence, 2005).

Panizza, L. (ed.), *Women in Italian Renaissance Culture and Society* (Oxford, 2000).

Reiss, S. E. and D. G. Wilkins (eds), *Beyond Isabella: Secular Women Patrons of Art in Renaissance Italy* (Kirksville, MO, 2001).

Richardson, C. (ed.), *Clothing Culture, 1350–1650* (Aldershot, 2004).

Rogers, M. and P. Tinagli, *Women in Italy, 1350–1650: Ideals and Realities. A Sourcebook* (Manchester, 2005).

Schmidt, V. M., *Painted Piety: Panel Paintings for Personal Devotion in Tuscany, 1250–1400* (Florence, 2005).

Smith, A., 'Gender, ownership and domestic space: inventories and family archives in Renaissance Verona', *Renaissance Studies*, 12:3 (1998), pp. 375–91.

— 'Material goods and female identity in Renaissance palaces', in P. Lanaro, P. Marini and G. M. Varanini (eds), *Edilizia privata nella Verona rinascimentale* (Milan, 2000), pp. 134–53.

Strocchia, S. T., *Nuns and Nunneries in Renaissance Florence* (Baltimore, 2009).

Syson, L. and P. Thornton, *Objects of Virtue: Art in Renaissance Italy* (London, 2001).

Thomas, A., *Art and Piety in the Female Religious Communities of Renaissance Italy: Iconography, Space, and the Religious Woman's Perspective* (Cambridge, 2003).

Thornton, P., *Italian Renaissance Interiors 1400–1600* (London, 1991).

Tinagli, P., *Women in Italian Renaissance Art* (Manchester, 1997).

Tomas, N. R., *The Medici Women: Gender and Power in Renaissance Florence* (Aldershot, 2003).

Trexler, R., 'Florentine religious experience. The sacred image', *Studies in the Renaissance*, 19 (1972), pp. 7–41.

Valone, C., 'Roman matrons as patrons: various views of the cloister wall', in C. Monson (ed.), *The Crannied Wall: Women, Religion and the Arts in Early Modern Europe* (Ann Arbor, 1992), pp. 49–72.

— 'Women on the Quirinal hill: patronage in Rome 1560–1630', *Art Bulletin*, 76 (1994), pp. 129–46.

— 'Architecture as a Public Voice for Women in sixteenth-century Rome', *Renaissance Studies*, 15:3 (2001), pp. 301–27.

Welch, E., 'Public magnificence and private display: Pontano's "De Splendore"', *Journal of Design History*, 15 (2002), pp. 211–28.

Welch, E., *Shopping in the Renaissance: Consumer Cultures in Italy 1400–1600* (New Haven and London, 2005).

— 'Art on the edge: hair and hands in Renaissance Italy', *Renaissance Studies*, 23:3 (2009), pp. 241–68.

Wisch, B. and D. Cole Ahl (eds), *Confraternities and the Visual Arts in Renaissance Italy* (Cambridge, 2000).

Wood, J. M., *Women, Art and Spirituality: The Poor Clares of Early Modern Italy* (Cambridge, 1996).

Woods-Marsden, J., *Renaissance Self-Portraiture* (New Haven and London, 1998).

INDEX

Index